SQL

A Beginner's Guide

Second Edition

SQL
A Beginner's Guide

Second Edition

Robert Sheldon

McGraw-Hill/Osborne

New York   Chicago   San Francisco
Lisbon   London   Madrid   Mexico City
Milan   New Delhi   San Juan
Seoul   Singapore   Sydney   Toronto

The McGraw·Hill Companies

McGraw-Hill/Osborne
2100 Powell Street, 10th Floor
Emeryville, California 94608
U.S.A.

To arrange bulk purchase discounts for sales promotions, premiums, or fund-raisers, please contact **McGraw-Hill**/Osborne at the above address. For information on translations or book distributors outside the U.S.A., please see the International Contact Information page immediately following the index of this book.

SQL: A Beginner's Guide, Second Edition

1234567890 FGR FGR 019876543

ISBN 0-07-222885-7

Publisher   Brandon A. Nordin
Vice President & Associate Publisher   Scott Rogers
Acquisitions Editor   Lisa McClain
Senior Project Editor   LeeAnn Pickrell
Acquisitions Coordinator   Athena Honore
Technical Editor   Greg Guntle
Copy Editor   Margaret Berson
Proofreader   Marion Selig
Indexer   James Minkin
Computer Designers   Carie Abrew, Tara A. Davis
Illustrators   Kathleen Fay Edwards, Melinda Moore Lytle, Michael Mueller, Lyssa Wald
Series Design   Jean Butterfield
Series Cover Design   Sarah F. Hinks

This book was composed with Corel VENTURA™ Publisher.

About the Author

Robert Sheldon has worked as a consultant and technical writer for a number of years. As a consultant, he has managed the development and maintenance of web-based and client-server applications and the databases that supported those applications. In addition, he has designed and implemented various Access and SQL Server databases and has used SQL to build databases, create and modify database objects, query and modify data, and troubleshoot system- and data-related problems. Robert has also written or cowritten eight books on various network and server technologies, one of which received a Certificate of Merit from the Puget Sound Chapter of the Society for Technical Communication. In addition, two of the books that Robert has written focus exclusively on SQL Server design and implementation. Robert has also written and edited a variety of other documentation related to SQL databases and other computer technologies. In addition, his writing includes material outside the computer industry—everything from news articles to ad copy to legal documentation—and he has received two awards from the Colorado Press Association.

Contents at a Glance

Contents

Acknowledgments

A s with any publication, too many people were involved in the development of *SQL: A Beginner's Guide, Second Edition* to be able to name them all, but I would at least like to acknowledge the editors and staff at McGraw-Hill/Osborne whom I had the pleasure of working with directly. My special thanks go to Lisa McClain, the acquisitions editor; Athena Honore, the acquisitions coordinator; and LeeAnn Pickrell, the project editor. Together the three of them kept this project moving forward smoothly and professionally and provided me with an immeasurable degree of help along the way. Along with these three, I want to acknowledge Margaret Berson, the copy editor, and all the other editors, proofreaders, indexers, designers, illustrators, and other participants whose names I never learned. In addition, I want to acknowledge Greg Guntle, the technical editor, for his attention to detail, his grasp of the subject matter, and his invaluable input into the book's content. I also want to thank my agent, Danielle Jatlow at Waterside Productions, Inc., for making this project happen and for her continual support in all my efforts. Finally, I want to thank my friend, mentor, and sometimes co-author Ethan Wilansky for his encouragement, support, and answers to my endless questions throughout the course of this project and other projects that I have tackled throughout the years.

Introduction

Relational databases have become a common mainstay for systems that provide data storage for various types of applications. Programming languages such as C or COBOL or scripting languages such as VBScript or JavaScript must often access a data source in order to retrieve or modify data through the application. Many of these data sources are managed by a relational database management system (RDBMS) that relies on the Structured Query Language (SQL) to create and alter database objects, add data to and retrieve data from the database, and modify data that has been added to that database.

SQL is the most widely implemented language for relational databases. SQL not only allows you to manage data within the database, but also manage the database itself. By using SQL statements, you can access an SQL database directly by using an interactive client application or through an application programming language or scripting language. Regardless of which method you use to access a data source, you should have a foundation in how to write SQL statements that allows you to access relational data. *SQL: A Beginner's Guide, Second Edition* provides you with such a foundation. It describes the types of statements that SQL supports and explains how they're used to manage databases and their data. By working through the modules in this book, you'll build a strong foundation in basic SQL and gain a comprehensive understanding of how to use SQL to access data in your relational database.

Who Should Read This Book

SQL: A Beginner's Guide is recommended for anyone trying to build a foundation in SQL programming. The book is designed specifically for those who are new or relatively new to SQL; however, those of you who need a refresher in SQL will also find this book beneficial. Whether you're an experienced programmer, have had some web development experience, are a database administrator, or are new to programming and databases, *SQL: A Beginner's Guide* provides a strong foundation that will be useful to any of you wishing to learn more about SQL. In fact, any of the following individuals will find this book helpful when trying to understand and use SQL:

- The novice new to database design and SQL programming

- The analyst or manager who wants to better understand how to implement and access SQL databases

- The database administrator who wants to learn more about programming

- The technical support professional or testing engineer who must perform ad hoc queries against an SQL data source

- The web developer writing applications that must access SQL databases

- The third-generation language (3GL) programmer embedding SQL within an application's source code

- Any other individual who wants to learn how to write SQL code that can be used to create and access databases within an RDBMS

Whichever category you might fit into, an important point to remember is that the book is geared toward anyone wanting to learn standard SQL, not a product-specific version of the language. The advantage of this is that you can take the skills learned in this book and apply them to real-world situations, without being limited to product standards. You will, of course, still need to be aware of how the product you work in implements SQL, but with the foundation provided by the book, you'll be able to move from one RDBMS to the next and still have a basic understanding of how SQL is used. As a result, this book is a useful tool to anyone new to SQL-based databases, regardless of the product used. SQL programmers need only adapt their knowledge to the specific RDBMS.

What Content the Book Covers

SQL: A Beginner's Guide is divided into three parts. Part I introduces you to the basic concepts of SQL and explains how to create objects within your database. Part II provides you with a foundation in how to retrieve data from a database and modify the data that's stored in the database. Part III provides you with information about advanced data access techniques that allow you to expand on what you learned in Part I and Part II. In addition to the three parts, *SQL: A Beginner's Guide* contains appendixes that include reference material for the information presented in the three parts.

Description of the Book's Content

The following outline describes the contents of the book and shows how the book is broken down into task-focused modules.

Part I: SQL Databases

Part I introduces you to SQL and the SQL environment and explains how to create database objects within that environment. You'll also learn how to use constraints in your table definitions to enforce data integrity.

Module 1: Introduction to Relational Databases and SQL   This module introduces you to relational databases and the relational model, which forms the basis for SQL. You'll also be provided with a general overview of SQL and how it relates to RDBMSs.

Module 2: Working with the SQL Environment   This module describes the components that make up the SQL environment. You'll also be introduced to the objects that make up a schema, and you'll learn how to create a schema within your SQL environment. You'll also be introduced to the concept of creating a database object in an SQL implementation that supports the creation of database objects.

Module 3: Creating and Altering Tables   In this module, you'll learn how to create SQL tables, specify column data types, create user-defined types, and specify column default values. You'll also learn how to alter a table definition and delete that definition from your database.

Module 4: Enforcing Data Integrity   This module explains how integrity constraints are used to enforce data integrity in your SQL tables. The module includes information on table-related constraints, assertions, and domain constraints. You will learn how to create NOT NULL, UNIQUE, PRIMARY KEY, FOREIGN KEY, and CHECK constraints.

Module 5: Creating SQL Views   In this module, you'll learn how to add views to your SQL database. You'll also learn how to create updateable views and how to drop views from the database.

Module 6: Managing Database Security   In this module, you'll be introduced to the SQL security model and learn how authorization identifiers are defined within the context of a session. You'll then learn how to create and delete roles, grant and revoke privileges, and grant and revoke roles.

Part II: Data Access and Modification

Part II explains how to access and modify data in an SQL database. You'll also learn how to use predicates, functions, and value expressions to manage that data. In addition, Part II describes how to join tables together and use subqueries to access data in multiple tables.

Module 7: Querying SQL Data   This module describes the basic components of the SELECT statement and how the statement is used to retrieve data from an SQL database. You'll learn how to define each clause that makes up the SELECT statement and how those clauses are processed when querying a database.

Module 8: Modifying SQL Data   In this module, you'll learn how to modify data in an SQL database. Specifically, you'll learn how to insert data, update data, and delete data. The module reviews each component of the SQL statements that allow you to perform these data modifications.

Module 9: Using Predicates   In this module, you'll learn how to use predicates to compare SQL data, return null values, return similar values, reference additional sources of data, and quantify comparison predicates. The module describes the various types of predicates and shows you how they're used to retrieve specific data from an SQL database.

Module 10: Working with Functions and Value Expressions   This module explains how to use various types of functions and value expressions in your SQL statements. You'll learn how to use set functions, value functions, value expressions, and special values in various clauses within an SQL statement.

Module 11: Accessing Multiple Tables   This module describes how to join tables in order to retrieve data from those tables. You will learn how to perform basic join operations, join tables with shared column names, use the condition join, and perform union operations.

Module 12: Using Subqueries to Access and Modify Data   In this module, you'll learn how to create subqueries that return multiple rows and that return only one value. You'll also learn how to use correlated subqueries and nested subqueries. In addition, you'll learn how to use subqueries to modify data.

Part III: Advanced Data Access

Part III introduces you to advanced data-access techniques such as SQL-invoked routines, triggers, and cursors. You'll also learn how to manage transactions and how to access SQL data from your host program.

Module 13: Creating SQL-Invoked Routines
This module describes SQL-invoked procedures and functions and how you can create them in your SQL database. You'll learn how to define input parameters, add local variables to your routine, work with control statements, and use output parameters.

Module 14: Creating SQL Triggers
This module introduces you to SQL triggers and explains how to create insert, update, and delete triggers in your SQL database. You'll learn how triggers are automatically invoked and what types of actions they can take.

Module 15: Using SQL Cursors
In this module, you'll learn how SQL cursors are used to retrieve one row of data at a time from a result set. The module explains how to declare a cursor, open and close a cursor, and retrieve data from a cursor. You'll also learn how to use positioned UPDATE and DELETE statements after you fetch a row through a cursor.

Module 16: Managing SQL Transactions
In this module, you'll learn how transactions are used to ensure the integrity of your SQL data. The module describes how to set transaction properties, start a transaction, set constraint deferrability, create savepoints in a transaction, and terminate a transaction.

Module 17: Accessing SQL Data from Your Host Program
This module describes the four methods supported by the SQL standard for accessing an SQL database. You'll learn how to invoke SQL directly from a client application, embed SQL statements in a program, create SQL client modules, and use an SQL call-level interface to access data.

Part IV: Appendixes

The appendixes include reference material for the information presented in the first three parts.

Appendix A: Answers to Mastery Checks
This appendix provides the answers to the Mastery Check questions listed at the end of each module.

Appendix B: SQL:1999 Keywords
This appendix lists the reserved and nonreserved keywords as they are used in SQL statements and defined in the SQL:1999 standard.

Appendix C: SQL Code Used in the Book's Projects   This appendix contains a copy of the SQL statements that are used in the projects throughout the modules. The appendix also provides the code specific to creating the Inventory database and populating that database with data. (The Inventory database is created and used in most of the projects in the book.)

Module Content

As you can see in the outline, *SQL: A Beginner's Guide* is organized into modules. Each module focuses on a set of related tasks. The module contains the background information you need to understand the various concepts related to those tasks, explains how to create the necessary SQL statements to perform the tasks, and provides examples of how those statements are created. In addition, each module contains additional elements to help you better understand the information covered in that module:

- **Progress Check**   Each module contains two or more sets of questions that are interspersed within the content of the module. The questions are meant to help you understand key points presented in a particular section. The answers to these questions are provided at the bottom of the page where the questions appear.

- **Ask the Expert**   Each module contains one or two Ask the Expert sections that provide information on questions that might arise about the information presented in the module.

- **Mastery Check**   Each module ends with a Mastery Check, which is a set of questions that tests you on the information and skills you learned in that module. The answers to the Mastery Check are included in Appendix A.

SQL: A Beginner's Guide is organized into a logical structure that corresponds to the process of creating an SQL database. Each module builds on previous modules so that you're continuously applying the skills that you learned earlier to the information you're being taught in the current module. By the end of the book, you'll have created a database, created tables within that database, enforced data integrity on the tables, queried and modified data within the database, and implemented advanced data access techniques.

Because of the book's organization, it is recommended that you work through the modules in the order that they're presented. If you already have experience with SQL databases, you might want to use the book more as a reference and simply skip to the module that provides the information that you're looking for. However, most readers should start at the beginning and work their way through each module.

In addition to the module elements already mentioned (Progress Check, Ask the Expert, and Mastery Check), each module includes examples of SQL syntax and actual statements. Each module also includes one or more projects that allow you to apply the information that you learned in the module.

SQL Syntax

The syntax of an SQL statement refers to the structure used for that statement, as outlined in SQL:1999. Most modules will include the syntax for one or more statements so that you have an understanding of the basic elements contained in those statements. For example, the following syntax represents the information you need when you define a CREATE TABLE statement:

```
<table definition> ::=
CREATE [ { GLOBAL | LOCAL } TEMPORARY ] TABLE <table name>
( <table element> [ { , <table element> } . . . ] )
[ ON COMMIT { PRESERVE | DELETE } ROWS ]
```

NOTE

Do not be concerned about the meaning of the SQL code at this time. This example is meant only to show you how SQL statements are represented in this book.

As you can see, a statement's syntax can contain many elements. Notice that most of the words used within the statement are shown in uppercase. The uppercase words are SQL keywords that are used to formulate the SQL statement. (For a complete list of SQL:1999 keywords, see Appendix B.) Although SQL does not require that keywords be written in uppercase, I use that convention in this book so that you can easily identify the keywords within a statement. In addition to the keywords, the syntax for an SQL statement includes a number of other elements that help define how a particular statement should be created:

- **Square brackets**   The square brackets indicate that the syntax enclosed in those brackets is optional. For example, the ON COMMIT clause in the CREATE TABLE statement is optional.

- **Angle brackets**   The angle brackets enclose information that represents a placeholder. When a statement is actually created, the placeholder is replaced by the appropriate SQL elements or identifiers. For example, you should replace the <table name> placeholder with a name for the table when you define a CREATE TABLE statement.

- **Curly brackets**   The curly brackets are used to group elements together. The brackets tell you that you should first decide how to handle the contents within the brackets and then determine how they fit into the statement. For example, the PRESERVE | DELETE set of keywords is enclosed by curly brackets. You must first choose PRESERVE or DELETE and then deal with the entire line of code. As a result, your clause can read ON COMMIT PRESERVE ROWS, or it can read ON COMMIT DELETE ROWS.

- **Vertical bars**   The vertical bar can be read as "or," which means that you should use the PRESERVE option or the DELETE option.

- **Three periods** The three periods indicate that you can repeat the clause as often as necessary. For example, you can include as many table elements (represented by <table element>) as necessary.

- **Colons/equal sign** The ::= symbol (two consecutive colons plus an equal sign) indicates that the placeholder to the left of the symbol is defined by the syntax following the symbol. In the syntax example, the <table definition> placeholder equals the syntax that makes up a CREATE TABLE statement.

By referring to the syntax, you should be able to construct an SQL statement that creates database objects or modifies SQL data as necessary. However, in order to better demonstrate how the syntax is applied, each module also contains examples of actual SQL statements.

Examples of SQL Statements

Each module provides examples of how SQL statements are implemented when accessing an SQL database. For example, you might see an SQL statement similar to the following:

```
CREATE TABLE CDInventory
( CompactDiscID INT, CDTitle VARCHAR (60), LabelID INT ) ;
```

Notice that the statement is written in special type to show that it is SQL code. Also notice that keywords are all uppercase. (You don't need to be concerned about any other details at this point.)

The examples used in the book are pure SQL, meaning that they're based on the SQL:1999 standard. You'll find, however, that in some cases your SQL implementation does not support an SQL statement in exactly the same way as it is defined in the standard. For this reason, you might also need to refer to the documentation for a particular product to be sure that your SQL statement conforms to that product's standards. Sometimes it might be only a slight variation, but there might be times when the product statement is substantially different from the SQL statement.

The examples in each module are based on a database related to an inventory of compact discs. However, the examples are not necessarily consistent in terms of the names used for database objects and how those objects are defined. For example, two different modules might contain examples that reference a table named CDInventory. However, you cannot assume that the tables used in the different examples are made up of the same columns or contain the same content. Because each example focuses on a unique aspect of SQL, the tables used in examples are defined in a way specific to the needs of that example, as you'll see as you get into the modules. However, this is not the case for projects, which use a consistent database structure throughout the book.

Module Projects

Each module contains one or two projects that allow you to apply the information that you learned in the module. A project is broken down into steps that walk you through the process of completing a particular task. Many of the projects include related files that you can download from our Web site at http://www.osborne.com. The files usually include the SQL statements used within the projects. In addition, the SQL statements are also included in Appendix C.

The projects are based on the Inventory database. You'll create the database, create the tables and other objects in the database, add data to those tables, and then manipulate that data. Because the projects build on one another, it is best that you complete them in the order that they're presented in the book. This is especially true for the modules in Part I, in which you create the database objects, and Module 7, in which you insert data into the tables. However, if you do plan to skip around, you can refer to Appendix C, which provides the code necessary to create the database objects and populate the tables with data.

To complete most of the projects in this book, you'll need to have access to an RDBMS that allows you to enter and execute SQL statements interactively. If you're accessing an RDBMS over a network, check with the database administrator to make sure that you're logging in with the credentials necessary to create a database and schema. You might need special permissions to create these objects. Also verify whether there are any parameters you should include when creating the database (for example, log file size), restrictions on the name you can use, or restrictions of any other kind. Be sure to check the product's documentation before working with any database product.

Part I

SQL Databases

Module 1

Introduction to Relational Databases and SQL

3

In 1999, the American National Standards Institute (ANSI) and the International Organization for Standardization (ISO) published their long-awaited SQL standard, which was dubbed "SQL:1999" (also known as SQL3). The SQL:1999 standard, like its predecessor SQL-92, is based on the relational data model, which defines how data can be stored and manipulated within a relational database. Relational database management systems (RDBMSs) such as Oracle or SQL Server use the SQL standard as a foundation for their products, providing database environments that support both SQL and the relational data model.

CRITICAL SKILL
1.1 Understand Relational Databases

Structured Query Language (SQL) supports the creation and maintenance of the relational database and the management of data within that database. However, before I go into a discussion about relational databases, I want to explain what I mean by the term *database*. The term itself has been used to refer to anything from a collection of names and addresses to a complex system of data retrieval and storage that relies on user interfaces and a network of client computers and servers. There are as many definitions for the word database as there are books about them. Despite the lack of an absolute meaning, most sources agree that a database, at the very least, is a collection of data organized in a structured format that is defined by *metadata* that describes that structure. You can think of metadata as data about the data being stored; it defines how the data is stored within the database.

Over the years, a number of database models have been implemented to store and manage data. Several of the more common models include the following:

● **Hierarchical**   This model has a parent-child structure that is similar to an inverted tree, which is what forms the hierarchy. A parent table can have many child tables, but a child table can have only one parent table. Although the model has been highly implemented, it is often considered unsuitable for many applications because of its inflexible structure and lack of support for complex relationships. Still, many implementations have introduced functionality that works around these limitations.

● **Network**   This model addresses some of the limitations of the hierarchical model. It still uses an inverted tree structure, but tables are organized into a set structure that relates pairs of tables into owners and members. Any one table can participate in any set with other tables in the database, which supports more complex queries than are possible in the hierarchical model. Still, the network model has its limitations. You have to be very familiar with the database to work through the set structures, and it's difficult to change the structure without affecting applications that interact with the database.

● **Relational**   This model addresses many of the limitations of both the hierarchical and network models. In a hierarchical or network database, the application relies on a defined implementation of that database, which is then hard-coded into the application. If you add a new attribute to the database, you must modify the application, even if it doesn't use the attribute. However, a relational database is independent of the application; you can modify the structure without impacting the application. In addition, the structure of the relational database is based on the relation, or table, which provides the ability to define complex relationships between these relations. Each relation can be thought of as an entity in its own right, without the cumbersome limitations of a hierarchical or owner/member model that restricts how relationships can be defined between tables. In the following section, "The Relational Model," I'll discuss the model in more detail.

Hierarchical and network databases are found in legacy systems and are still used in many organizations. However, the relational model has replaced many of these systems and is the model most extensively implemented by modern database products, and it is the relational model that provides the foundation for SQL.

The Relational Model

If you've ever had the opportunity to look at a book about relational databases, you have quite possibly seen the name of Dr. E. F. Codd referred to in the context of the relational model. In 1970 Codd published his seminal paper, "A Relational Model of Data for Large Shared Data Banks," in the journal *Communications of the ACM,* Volume 13, Number 6 (June 1970). Codd defines a relational data structure that protects data and allows that data to be manipulated in a way that is predictable and resistant to error. The relational model, which is rooted primarily in the mathematical principles of set theory and predicate logic, supports easy data retrieval, enforces data accuracy and consistency, and provides a database structure independent of the applications accessing the stored data.

At the core of the relational model is the relation. A *relation* is a set of columns and rows collected in a table-like structure that represents a single entity made up of related data. Each relation comprises one or more attributes (columns). An *attribute* groups similar types of data together. For example, in Figure 1-1 the CDName attribute contains the titles of compact discs (CDs), while artist names and copyright dates are listed in separate attributes.

As you can see in Figure 1-1, each attribute has an associated domain. A *domain* defines the type of data that can be stored in a particular attribute; however, a domain is not the same thing as a data type. A *data type,* which is discussed in more detail in Module 3, is a specific kind of constraint associated with a column, whereas a domain, as it is used in the relational model, has a much broader meaning and describes exactly what data can be included in an attribute associated with that domain. For example, the Copyright attribute is associated with the Year domain. The domain can be defined so that the attribute includes only data whose values and format are limited to years, as opposed to days or months. The domain might also limit the data to a specific range of years. A data type, on the other hand, restricts the format of the data, but not the values, unless those values somehow violate the format.

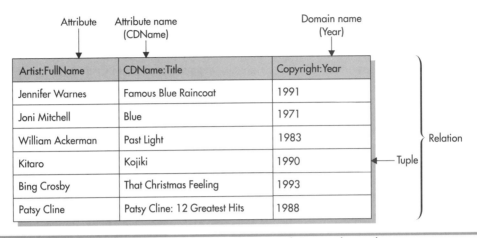

Figure 1-1 Relation made up of the Artist, CDName, and Copyright attributes

Data is stored in a relation in tuples (rows). A *tuple* is a set of data whose values make up an instance of each attribute defined for that relation. Each tuple represents a record of related data. (In fact, the set of data is sometimes referred to as a *record*.) For example, in Figure 1-1 the second tuple from the top contains the Joni Mitchell value for the Artist attribute, the Blue value for the CDName attribute, and the 1971 value for the Copyright attribute. Together these three values form a tuple.

NOTE

The terms relation, attribute, and tuple are used primarily when referring to the relational model. SQL uses the terms table, column, and row to describe these items. Because the relational model is based on mathematical principles and SQL is concerned more with the physical implementation of the model, the meanings for the model's terms and the SQL language's terms are slightly different, but the underlying principles are the same. The SQL terms are discussed in more detail in Module 2.

The relational model is, of course, more complex than the attributes and tuples that make up a relation. Two very important considerations in the design and implementation of any relational database are the normalization of data and the associations of relations among the various types of data.

Normalizing Data

Central to the principles of the relational model is the concept of *normalization*, the process of organizing a database into a structure that preserves the integrity of the stored data and minimizes redundant data. A normalized database is one that conforms to the rules of the relational model. These rules, referred to as *normal forms*, provide specific guidelines on how data should be organized in order to prevent inconsistencies in and loss of data as the database is being used.

When the original relational model was presented, it included three normal forms. Although additional normal forms have been added since then, the first three still cover most situations when normalizing data, and since my intent here is primarily to introduce you to the process of normalization, I'll discuss only those three forms.

First Normal Form   The first normal form provides the foundation for the second and third forms. The first form includes the following guidelines:

- Each attribute of a tuple must contain only one value.

- Each tuple in a relation must contain the same number of values.

- Each tuple in a relation must be different.

As you can see in Figure 1-2, the second tuple and the last tuple violate the first normal form. In the second tuple, the CDName attribute and the Copyright attribute each contain two values. In the last tuple, the Artist attribute contains three values.

If you were to normalize the data, you would create additional tables that allow you to separate the data so that each attribute contains only one value, each tuple contains the same number of values, and each tuple is different, as shown in Figure 1-3. The data now conforms to the first normal form.

Artist	CDName	Copyright
Jennifer Warnes	Famous Blue Raincoat	1991
Joni Mitchell	Blue; Court and Spark	1971; 1974
William Ackerman	Past Light	1983
Kitaro	Kojiki	1990
Bing Crosby	That Christmas Feeling	1993
Patsy Cline	Patsy Cline: 12 Greatest Hits	1988
Jose Carreras; Placido Domingo; Luciano Pavarotti	Carreras Domingo Pavarotti in Concert	1990

Figure 1-2 Relation that violates the first normal form

ArtistID	ArtistName
10001	Jennifer Warnes
10002	Joni Mitchell
10003	William Ackerman
10004	Kitaro
10005	Bing Crosby
10006	Patsy Cline
10007	Jose Carreras
10008	Placido Domingo
10009	Luciano Pavarotti

ArtistID	CDID
10001	99301
10002	99302
10002	99303
10003	99304
10004	99305
10005	99306
10006	99307
10007	99308
10008	99308
10009	99308

CDID	CDName	Copyright
99301	Famous Blue Raincoat	1991
99302	Blue	1971
99303	Court and Spark	1974
99304	Past Light	1983
99305	Kojiki	1990
99306	That Christmas Feeling	1993
99307	Patsy Cline: 12 Greatest Hits	1988
99308	Carreras Domingo Pavarotti in Concert	1990

Figure 1-3 Relations that conform to the first normal form

Notice that there are duplicate values in the second relation; the ArtistID value of 10002 is repeated and the CDID value of 99308 is repeated. However, when the two attribute values are taken together, the tuple as a whole forms a unique combination, which means that, despite the duplications, each tuple in the relation is different.

Second Normal Form   The second normal form states that a relation must be in first normal form and that all attributes in the relation are dependent on the entire candidate key. A *candidate key* is a set of one or more attributes that uniquely identify each tuple. For example, in the relation shown in Figure 1-4, you might decide to designate the Artist and CDName attributes as a candidate key. Together, these values uniquely identify each tuple. However, the Copyright attribute is dependent only on the CDName attribute, and not on the Artist attribute. Even though the relation conforms to the first normal form, it violates the second normal form. Again, the solution might be to separate the data into different relations, as you saw in Figure 1-3.

Third Normal Form   The third normal form, like the second normal form, is dependent on the relation's candidate key. To adhere to the guidelines of the third normal form, a relation must be in second normal form and nonkey attributes must be independent of each other and dependent on the key. For example, the candidate key in the relation shown in Figure 1-5 is the ArtistID attribute. The ArtistName and Agency attributes are both dependent on the key and are independent of each other. However, the AgencyState attribute is dependent on the Agency attribute and not on the key. Therefore it violates the conditions of the third normal form. This attribute would be better suited in a relation that includes data about agencies.

Candidate key ⟵───────────────────────⟶

Artist	CDName	Copyright
Jennifer Warnes	Famous Blue Raincoat	1991
Joni Mitchell	Blue	1971
Joni Mitchell	Court and Spark	1974
William Ackerman	Past Light	1983
Kitaro	Kojiki	1990
Bing Crosby	That Christmas Feeling	1993
Patsy Cline	Patsy Cline: 12 Greatest Hits	1988

Figure 1-4 Relation with two attributes forming the candidate key

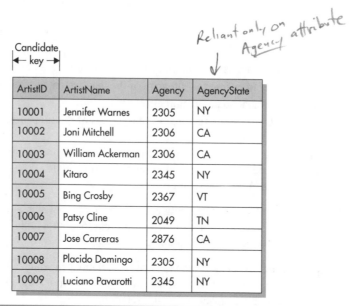

Candidate ⟵ key ⟶

Reliant only on Agency attribute ↓

ArtistID	ArtistName	Agency	AgencyState
10001	Jennifer Warnes	2305	NY
10002	Joni Mitchell	2306	CA
10003	William Ackerman	2306	CA
10004	Kitaro	2345	NY
10005	Bing Crosby	2367	VT
10006	Patsy Cline	2049	TN
10007	Jose Carreras	2876	CA
10008	Placido Domingo	2305	NY
10009	Luciano Pavarotti	2345	NY

Figure 1-5 Relation with an attribute that violates the third normal form

NOTE

In the theoretical world of relational design, the goal is to store data according to the rules of normalization. However, in the real world of database implementation, it is a common practice to *denormalize* data, which means to deliberately violate the rules of normalization, particularly the second and third normal forms. Denormalization is used primarily to improve performance or reduce complexity in cases where an overnormalized structure complicates implementation. Still, the goal of normalization is to ensure data integrity, and denormalization should be performed with great care.

Progress Check

1. What are the main components of a relation?

2. Which guidelines should you adhere to when normalizing data according to the first normal form?

Relationships

So far, my focus in this module has been on the relation and how to normalize data. However, an important component of any relational database is how those relations are associated with each other. These associations, or *relationships,* link relations together in ways that are meaningful to each other, helping to ensure the integrity of the data so that an action taken in one relation does not negatively impact data in another relation.

A relational database supports three primary types of relationships:

- **One-to-one**   A relationship between two relations in which a tuple in the first relation is related to only one tuple in the second relation, and a tuple in the second relation is related to only one tuple in the first relation.

- **One-to-many**   A relationship between two relations in which a tuple in the first relation is related to one or more tuples in the second relation, but a tuple in the second relation is related to only one tuple in the first relation.

- **Many-to-many**   A relationship between two relations in which a tuple in the first relation is related to one or more tuples in the second relation, and a tuple in the second relation is related to one or more tuples in the first relation.

---

1. The main components of a relation are the attributes (columns), their domains, and the tuples (rows).

2. According to the first normal form, each attribute of a tuple must contain only one value, each tuple in a relation must contain the same number of values, and each tuple in a relation must be different.

The best way to illustrate these relationships is to look at a data model of several relations (shown in Figure 1-6). I've named the relations to make referencing them easier. As you can see, all three types of relationships are represented:

- A one-to-one relationship exists between the ArtistAgencies relation and the ArtistNames relation. For each artist listed in the first relation, there can be only one artist listed in the second relation, and vice versa.

- A one-to-many relationship exists between the ArtistNames relation and the ArtistCDs relation. For each artist in the first relation, one or more tuples for that artist can be listed in the second relation. In other words, each artist could have made one or more CDs. However, for each artist listed in the second relation, there can be only one related tuple for that artist in the first relation.

- A one-to-many relationship exists between the ArtistCDs relation and the CompactDiscs relation. For each CD, there can be one or more artists; however, the CD can be listed only once in the CompactDiscs relation.

- A many-to-many relationship exists between the ArtistNames relation and the CompactDiscs relation. For every artist, there can be one or more CDs, and for every CD, there can be one or more artist.

NOTE

A many-to-many relationship is physically implemented by adding a third relation between the first and second relation to create two one-to-many relationships. In Figure 1-6, the ArtistCDs relation was added between the ArtistNames relation and the CompactDiscs relation.

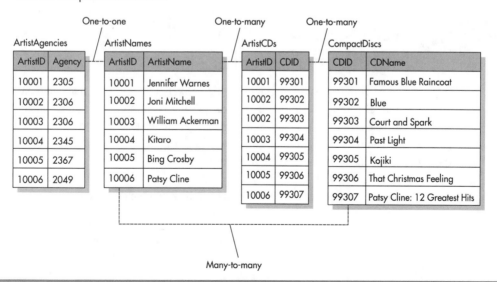

Figure 1-6 Types of relationships between relations

Ask the Expert

Q: You mention that relationships between relations help to ensure data integrity. How do relationships make that possible?

A: Suppose your data model includes a relation (named ArtistNames) that lists all the artists who have recorded CDs in your inventory. Your model also includes a relation (named ArtistCDs) that matches artist IDs with compact disc IDs. If a relationship exists between the two relations, tuples in one relation will always correspond to tuples in the other relation. As a result, you could prevent certain actions that could compromise data. For example, you would not be able to add an artist ID to the ArtistCDs relation if that ID wasn't listed in the ArtistNames relation.

Q: What do you mean by the term *data model?*

A: By data model, I'm referring to a type of diagram that represents the structure of a database. The model identifies the relations, attributes, keys, domains, and relationships within that database. Some database designers will create a logical model and physical model. The logical model is based more on relational theory and applies the appropriate principles of normalization to the data. The physical model, on the other hand, is concerned with the actual implementation, as the data will be stored in an RDBMS. Based on the logical design, the physical design brings the data structure down to the real world of implementation.

Project 1-1 Normalizing Data and Identifying Relationships

```
Prj01-1a.jpg
Prj01-1b.jpg
```

As a beginning SQL programmer, it's unlikely that you'll be responsible for normalizing—or denormalizing—data. Still, it's important that you understand these concepts, just as it's important that you understand the sorts of relationships that can exist between relations. Normalization and relationships, like the relations themselves, help to provide the foundation on which SQL is built. As a result, this project focuses on the process of normalizing data and identifying the relationships between relations. To complete the project, you need only a paper and pencil on which to sketch the data model.

Step by Step

1. Review the relation in the following illustration:

CDID	CDName	Category
99301	Famous Blue Raincoat	Folk, Pop
99302	Blue	Folk, Pop
99304	Past Light	New Age
99305	Kojiki	New Age, Classical
99306	That Christmas Feeling	Christmas, Classics
99307	Patsy Cline: 12 Greatest Hits	Country, Pop, Classics

Identify any elements that do not conform to the three normal forms. You will find that the Category attribute contains more than one value for each tuple, which violates the first normal form.

2. Normalize the data according to the normal forms. Sketch out a data model that includes the appropriate relations, attributes, and tuples. Your model will include three tables, one for the list of CDs, one for the list of music categories (for example, Pop), and one that associates the CDs with the appropriate categories of music. View the Prj01-1a.jpg file online for an example of what your data model might look like.

3. On the illustration you drew, identify the relationships between the relations. Remember that each CD can be associated with one or more categories, and each category can be associated with one or more CDs. View the Prj01-1b.jpg file online to view the relationships between relations.

Project Summary

Data models are usually more specific than the illustrations shown in this project. Relationships and keys are clearly marked with symbols that conform to a particular type of data modeling system, and relationships show only the attributes, but not the tuples. However, for the purposes of this module, it is enough that you have a basic understanding of normalization and the relationships between relations. The project is meant only as a way for you to better understand these concepts and how they apply to the relational model.

1.2 Learn about SQL

Now that you have a fundamental understanding of the relational model, it's time to introduce you to SQL and its basic characteristics. As you might recall from the "Understand Relational Databases" section earlier in this module, SQL is based on the relational model, although it is not an exact implementation. While the relational model provides the theoretical underpinnings of the relational database, it is SQL, the language, that supports the physical implementation of that database.

SQL, a nearly universally implemented relational language, is different from other languages such as C, COBOL, and Java, which are procedural. A procedural language defines *how* an application's operations should be performed and the order in which they are performed. A nonprocedural language, on the other hand, is concerned more with the results of an operation; the underlying software environment determines how the operations will be processed. This is not to say that SQL supports no procedural functionality. For example, stored procedures, added to many RDBMS products a number of years ago, are part of the SQL:1999 standard and provide procedural-like capabilities. (Stored procedures are discussed in Module 13.)

However, SQL still lacks many of the basic programming capabilities of most other computer languages. For this reason, SQL is often referred to as a data *sublanguage* because it is most often used in association with application programming languages such as C and Java, languages that are not designed for manipulating data stored in a database. As a result, SQL is used in conjunction with the application language to provide an efficient means of accessing that data, which is why SQL is considered a sublanguage.

The SQL Evolution

In the early 1970s, after the relational data model had been published, IBM began to develop a language and a database system that could be used to implement that model. When it was first defined, the language was referred to as Structured English Query Language (SEQUEL), and when it was later revised, the name was changed to SQL. As word got out that IBM was developing a relational database system based on SQL, other companies began to develop their own SQL-based products. In fact, Relational Software, Inc., now the Oracle Corporation, released their database system before IBM got their product to the market. As more vendors released their products, SQL began to emerge as the standard relational database language.

In 1986 ANSI released the first published standard for the language (SQL-86). The standard was updated in 1989 and again in 1992. SQL-92 represented a major revision of the language, expanding on and improving features of the earlier versions. Seven years later, in 1999, the latest version of the SQL standard, SQL:1999, was released, representing yet another large step forward in bringing SQL up to date with the real-world implementations of database systems and the needs of those who use those systems.

Since the release of the SQL:1999 standard, RDBMS vendors have been working to implement the new standard into their products. However, it should be noted that in some cases, the standard is merely catching up with functionality already implemented in the database systems. For example, stored procedures and triggers are new to the SQL standard but have been implemented in RDBMSs for many years. SQL:1999 is merely standardizing the language used to implement functionality that already exists.

NOTE

Although I discuss stored procedures in Module 13 and triggers in Module 14, I thought I'd give you a quick definition of each. A *stored procedure* is a set of SQL statements that are stored as an object in the database on the server but can be invoked by a client simply by calling the procedure. A *trigger* is similar to a stored procedure in that it is a set of SQL statements stored as an object in the database on the server. However, rather than being invoked from a client, a trigger is invoked automatically when some predefined event occurs, such as inserting or updating data.

Object Relational Model

The SQL:1999 standard does more than build on and expand SQL-92. As I have discussed, SQL is based on the relational model. This is true for SQL-92 as well as SQL:1999. However, unlike SQL-92, which is founded on a purely relational model, SQL:1999 extends that model to include object-oriented constructs into the language. These constructs are based on the concepts inherent to *object-oriented programming*, a programming methodology that defines self-contained collections (objects) of data structures and routines. In object-oriented languages such as Java and C++, the objects interact with one another in ways that allow the language to address complex problems that were not easily resolved in traditional languages.

With the advent of object-oriented programming—along with advances in hardware and software technologies and the growing complexities of applications—it became increasingly apparent that a purely relational language was inadequate to meet the demands of the real world. Of specific concern was the fact that SQL could not support complex and user-defined data types or the extensibility required for more complicated applications.

Fueled by the competitive nature of the industry, RDBMS vendors took it upon themselves to augment their products and incorporate object-oriented functionality into their systems. The SQL:1999 standard follows suit and extends the relational model with object-oriented capabilities, such as methods, encapsulation, and complex user-defined data types, making SQL an *object-relational* database language.

Conformance to SQL:1999

Once SQL was standardized, it followed that the standard would also define what it took for an implementation of SQL (an RDBMS product) to be considered in conformance to that standard. For example, the SQL-92 standard provided three levels of conformance: Entry, Intermediate, and Full. Most popular RDBMSs reached only Entry level conformance. Because of this, SQL:1999 takes a different approach to setting conformance standards. For a product to be in conformance with SQL:1999, it must support the Core SQL level of conformance. Core SQL in the SQL:1999 standard basically consists of all the Entry level compliance requirements of SQL-92, some of the Intermediate and Full levels, and a few features new to SQL:1999.

In addition to the Core SQL level of conformance, vendors can claim conformance to one of the nine *packages* of features that are part of the SQL language. Each package describes a standard for a set of related functionality as implemented through SQL. For example, the eighth package (PKG008) provides details on active database features, which are related to basic trigger capabilities.

TIP

You can view information about these packages or any other information about the SQL:1999 standard by purchasing a copy of the appropriate standard document published by ANSI and ISO. The standard is divided into five documents. The first document (ANSI/ISO/IEC 9075-1-1999) includes an overview of all five parts. You can purchase these documents online at the ANSI Electronic Standards Store (http://webstore.ansi.org/) or the NCITS Standards Store (http://www.cssinfo.com/ncits.html).

Types of SQL Statements

Although SQL is considered a sublanguage because of its nonprocedural nature, it is nonetheless a complete language in that it allows you to create and maintain database objects, secure those objects, and manipulate the data within the objects. One common method used to categorize SQL statements is to divide them according to the functions they perform. Based on this method, SQL can be separated into three types of statements:

- **Data Definition Language (DDL)**   DDL statements are used to create, modify, or delete database objects such as tables, views, schemas, domains, triggers, and stored procedures. The SQL keywords most often associated with DDL statements are CREATE, ALTER, and DROP. For example, you would use the CREATE TABLE statement to create a table, the ALTER TABLE statement to modify the table's properties, and the DROP TABLE statement to delete the table definition from the database.

- **Data Control Language (DCL)**   DCL statements allow you to control who has access to specific objects in your database. With the DCL statements, you can grant or restrict access by using the GRANT or REVOKE statements, the two primary DCL commands. The DCL statements also allow you to control the type of access each user has to database objects. For example, you can determine which users can view a specific set of data and which users can manipulate that data.

- **Data Manipulation Language (DML)**   DML statements are used to view, add, modify, or delete data stored in your database objects. The primary keywords associated with DML statements are SELECT, INSERT, UPDATE, and DELETE, all of which represent the types of statements you'll probably be using the most. For example, you can use a SELECT statement to retrieve data from a table and an INSERT statement to add data to a table.

Most SQL statements that you'll be working with fall neatly into one of these categories, and I'll be discussing a number of these statements throughout the remainder of the book.

NOTE

There are a number of ways you can classify statements in addition to how they're classified in the preceding list. For example, you can classify them according to how they're executed or whether or not they can be embedded in a standard programming language. The SQL:1999 standard provides seven broad categories based on function. However, I use the preceding method because it is commonly used in SQL-related documentation and because it is a simple way to provide a good overview of the functionality inherent in SQL.

Types of Execution

In addition to defining how the language can be used, the SQL:1999 standard provides details on how SQL statements can be executed. These methods of execution, known as *binding styles,* not only affect the nature of the execution, but also determine which statements, at a minimum, must be supported by a particular binding style. The standard defines four methods of execution:

- **Direct invocation**   By using this method, you can communicate directly from a front-end application, such as SQL*Plus Worksheet in Oracle or Query Analyzer in SQL Server, to the database on the SQL server. (These can be on the same computer.) You simply enter your query into the application window and execute your SQL statement. The results of your query are returned to you almost immediately, or as immediately as processor power and database constraints permit. This is a quick way to check data, verify connections, and view database objects. However, the SQL standard's guidelines about direct invocation are fairly minimal, so the methods used and SQL statements supported can vary widely from product to product.

- **Embedded SQL** In this method, SQL statements are encoded (embedded) directly in the host programming language. For example, you can embed SQL statements within C application code. Before the code is compiled, a preprocessor analyzes the SQL statements and splits them out from the C code. The SQL code is converted to a form the RDBMS can understand, and the remaining C code is compiled as it would be normally.

- **Module binding** This method allows you to create blocks of SQL statements (modules) that are separate from the host programming language. Once the module is created, it is combined into an application with a linker. A module contains, among other things, procedures, and it is the procedures that contain the actual SQL statements.

- **Call-level interface (CLI)** A CLI allows you to invoke SQL statements through an interface by passing SQL statements as argument values to subroutines. The statements are not precompiled as they are in embedded SQL and module binding. Instead, they are executed directly by the RDBMS.

Direct invocation, although not the most common method used, is the one I'll be using primarily for the examples and projects in this book because it supports the submission of *ad hoc* queries to the database and generates immediate results. However, embedded SQL is currently the method most commonly used for executing data. I discuss this method, as well as module binding and CLI, in greater detail in Module 17.

Progress Check

1. How does SQL differ from other computer languages such as Java, C, and COBOL?

2. What are the three basic types of SQL statements?

3. What four methods can be used to execute SQL statements?

---

1. Java, C, and COBOL are procedural languages, but SQL is a nonprocedural sublanguage that is often used in association with application programming languages.

2. The three basic types of SQL statements are DDL, DCL, and DML statements.

3. SQL statements can be executed by using direct invocation, embedding, module binding, and CLI.

Ask the Expert

Q: You state that, for an RDBMS to be in conformance with the SQL:1999 standard, it must comply with Core SQL. Are there any additional requirements that a product must adhere to?

A: Yes. In addition to Core SQL, an RDBMS must support either embedded SQL or module binding. Most products support only embedded SQL, with some supporting both. The SQL standard does not require RDBMS products to support direct invocation or CLI, although most do.

Q: What are the seven categories used by the SQL:1999 standard to classify SQL statements?

A: The SQL standard classifies statements into the following categories: schema, data, transaction, control, connection, session, and diagnostics. Keep in mind that these classifications are merely a tool that you can use to better understand the scope of the language and its underlying concepts. Ultimately, it is the SQL statements themselves—and what they can do—that is important.

CRITICAL SKILL
1.3 Use a Relational Database Management System

Throughout this module, when discussing the relational model and SQL, I've often mentioned RDBMSs and how they use the SQL standard as the foundation for their products. A *relational database management system* is a program or set of programs that store, manage, retrieve, modify, and manipulate data in one or more relational databases. IBM's DB2 and the shareware product MySQL are both examples of RDBMSs. These products, like other RDBMSs, allow you to interact with the data stored in their systems. Although an RDBMS is not required to be based on SQL, most products on the market are SQL-based and strive to conform to the SQL standard. At a minimum, these products claim Entry level conformance with the SQL-92 standard and are now working toward Core SQL conformance with SQL:1999.

In addition to complying with SQL standards, most RDBMSs support other features, such as additional SQL statements, product-based administrative tools, and graphical user interface (GUI) applications that allow you to query and manipulate data, manage database objects, and administer the system and its structure. The types of functionality implemented and the methods used to deliver that functionality can vary widely from product to product. As databases grow larger, become more complicated, and are distributed over greater areas, the RDBMS products used to manage those databases become more complex and robust, meeting the demands of the market as well as implementing new, more sophisticated technologies.

SQL Standard Versus Product Implementations

At the core of any SQL-based RDBMS is, of course, SQL itself. However, the language used is not pure SQL. Each product extends the language in order to implement vendor-defined features and enhanced SQL-based functionality. Consequently, every vendor supports a slightly different variation of SQL, meaning that the language used in each product is implementation-specific. For example, SQL Server uses Transact-SQL and Oracle uses PL/SQL, while other products use their own version of the language. As a result, the SQL statements that I provide in the book might be slightly different in the product implementation that you're using.

Throughout the book, I will be using pure SQL in most of the examples and projects. However, I realize that, as a beginning SQL programmer, your primary interest is in implementing SQL in the real world. For that reason, I will at times use SQL Server (with Transact-SQL) or Oracle (with PL/SQL) to demonstrate or clarify a particular concept that can't be fully explained by pure SQL alone.

One of the advantages to using a product like Oracle or SQL Server is that they both support direct invocation through a front-end GUI application. SQL Server uses the Query Analyzer interface, shown in Figure 1-7. The GUI interface makes it possible for you to create *ad hoc* SQL queries and view their results, allowing you to apply what you're learning in the book to an actual SQL environment. Oracle's solution for a front-end GUI is the SQL*Plus Worksheet interface, shown in Figure 1-8.

My use of these two products by no means implies that I'm endorsing either of them over any other commercial products (such as Sybase or Informix) or shareware products (such as MySQL or PostgreSQL), and indeed you're encouraged to use whatever RDBMS you have

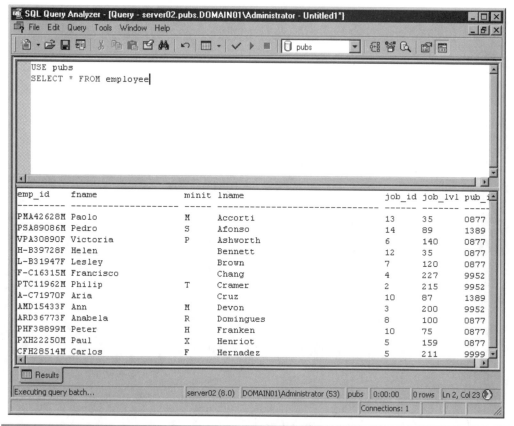

Figure 1-7 Using Query Analyzer in SQL Server 2000

available, assuming it supports most of the functionality that I'll be discussing in this book. However, I'm choosing SQL Server and Oracle because I want to be able to demonstrate how SQL is implemented in the real world and how SQL might differ from an implementation-specific version of the language, and these two products supply me with the vehicles to do this. Keep in mind that, in order for you to gain a full understanding of SQL and be able to use it in various RDBMS products, you will need to understand both standard SQL and the language as it is implemented in the products you'll be using.

```
SQL*Plus Worksheet                                                    _ □ ×
    File  Edit  Worksheet  Help                                  ORACLE
    SELECT * FROM scott.emp




    EMPNO ENAME      JOB          MGR HIREDATE      SAL      COMM    DEPTNO
    ----- ---------- ---------- ----- --------- -------- -------- ----------
     7369 SMITH      CLERK       7902 17-DEC-80      800                 20
     7499 ALLEN      SALESMAN    7698 20-FEB-81     1600      300        30
     7521 WARD       SALESMAN    7698 22-FEB-81     1250      500        30
     7566 JONES      MANAGER     7839 02-APR-81     2975                 20
     7654 MARTIN     SALESMAN    7698 28-SEP-81     1250     1400        30
     7698 BLAKE      MANAGER     7839 01-MAY-81     2850                 30
     7782 CLARK      MANAGER     7839 09-JUN-81     2450                 10
     7788 SCOTT      ANALYST     7566 19-APR-87     3000                 20
     7839 KING       PRESIDENT        17-NOV-81     5000                 10
     7844 TURNER     SALESMAN    7698 08-SEP-81     1500        0        30
     7876 ADAMS      CLERK       7788 23-MAY-87     1100                 20
     7900 JAMES      CLERK       7698 03-DEC-81      950                 30
     7902 FORD       ANALYST     7566 03-DEC-81     3000                 20
     7934 MILLER     CLERK       7782 23-JAN-82     1300                 10

    14 rows selected.
```

Figure 1-8 Using SQL*Plus Worksheet in Oracle9i

Project 1-2 Connecting to a Database

Although this book focuses primarily on pure SQL, in order to try out the examples and do most of the projects, you'll need access to an RDBMS in order to execute SQL statements. As a result, one of the first things you should do is to make sure you're able to access an SQL environment. This project will help you do that; however, unlike most other projects in the book, this one will require more effort on your part to go to resources outside the book to set yourself up with an RDBMS that allows you to invoke SQL statements directly. To that end, this project tries to get you started, but you must use your own initiative to ensure that you have an environment in which you're comfortable working.

Step by Step

1. Identify the RDBMS you plan to use for the projects in this book. Perhaps there is a system you're already familiar with or one that's available to you in your work environment. If you don't have anything available at work and you're not ready to purchase a product, check online to see what might be available. Some RDBMS vendors allow you to download a free trial copy of the software. For example, you can download Oracle9i at http://otn.oracle.com/, or you can download SQL Server at http://www.microsoft.com/sql/evaluation/trial/default.asp. (You might need a high-speed Internet connection if the files are too large. This is certainly the case for the Oracle files.)

   One other product you might consider is Ocelot. You can download their RDBMS for free from http://www.ocelot.ca/index.htm. It's quick to download, simple to install, and their GUI front-end application—Ocelot SQL Demo—is easy to use and connects to the SQL-environment as soon as you open it. According to the Ocelot web site, their product supports a full implementation of SQL-92, and they have already implemented many SQL:1999 features. In addition, the language used in Ocelot is pure SQL and is not implementation-specific.

   Before you decide on a system, spend the time necessary to research the product to make sure it supports direct invocation, preferably though a GUI application, and can run in your computer environment. Also check to see how much of the SQL:1999 standard it supports and review any licensing agreements to make sure you're in compliance. If a system is available through your work, be sure to talk to database and network administrators to determine what server you should use, how and whether you should download a copy, and how to make your connection to the SQL server. You'll often need an account to connect to the RDBMS, so if this is the case, find out what username and password you should use.

2. Once you've established which RDBMS you'll be using, install it on your computer. If you'll be connecting to a system over the network, you'll need to install only the client tools on your local computer.

3. Open the client GUI that allows you to directly invoke SQL statements. When you open the GUI, you might be prompted for a username and password. When and if you're prompted varies depending on the product you're using, whether you're connecting over the network, whether the RDBMS is set up as a stand-alone system, and other variables specific to the product. In addition, a product such as SQL Server offers security integrated with the operating system, so you may be prompted for a server name only.

4. Execute a SELECT statement in the application input window. I realize that we haven't covered SELECT statements yet, but the basic syntax is relatively easy:

```
SELECT * FROM <table>
```

(continued)

The *<table>* placeholder should be replaced with the name of a table in an existing database.

The purpose of this exercise is simply to verify that you have connectivity with the data stored in your RDBMS. Most systems include sample data, and it is that data that you're trying to connect to. Check product documentation or check with the database administrator to verify whether a database exists that you can access.

If you're working in Oracle, you can execute the following statement:

```
SELECT * FROM scott.emp;
```

To execute the statement, type it in the input window of SQL*Plus Worksheet and then press F5.

If you're working in SQL Server, you can execute the following statement:

```
USE pubs
SELECT * FROM employee
```

To execute the statement, type it in the input window of Query Analyzer and then press F5.

If you're working in Ocelot, you can execute the following statement:

```
SELECT * FROM ocelot.emps;
```

To execute the statement, type it in the input window of Ocelot SQL Demo and then press ENTER.

Once you execute the statement, the results of your query appear in the output window. At this point, don't concern yourself with the meaning of each word in the SQL statement or with the query results. Your only concern is to make sure everything is working. If you can't execute the statement, check with your database administrator or the product documentation.

5. Close the GUI application without saving your query.

Project Summary

As I said at the beginning of the project, this project is different from most of the other ones in the book because you are, for the most part, on your own to establish connectivity with your RDBMS. Again, this is because SQL is a language standard, independent of RDBMS implementations, and vendor-specific issues are, for the most part, beyond the scope of this book. In addition, the methods used to connect to a database, the tools available to make those connections, and the way in which an RDBMS is set up vary from product to product, environment to environment, and even operating system to operating system. However, the time you take now to research which product you'll use and to make sure you can connect to data in an existing database will prove invaluable to you in your ability to apply the information discussed in the rest of the book.

Module 1 Mastery Check

1. What is a database?

2. Which of the following objects make up a relation?

   A. Data types

   B. Tuples

   C. Attributes

   D. Forms

3. A(n) _____ is a set of data whose values make up an instance of each attribute defined for that relation.

4. What are the differences between the first normal form and the second normal form?

5. A relation is in third normal form if it is in second normal form and if it complies with the other guidelines of that form. What are those guidelines?

6. What are the three primary types of relationships supported by a relational database?

7. In your data model, you have two relations associated with each other by a many-to-many relationship. How will this relationship be physically implemented in a relational database?

8. How does SQL differ from programming languages such as C, COBOL, and Java?

9. What factors have contributed to the SQL:1999 standard incorporating object-oriented capabilities?

10. Which level of conformance must an RDBMS support in order to comply with SQL:1999?

    A. Entry

    B. Core

    C. Full

    D. Intermediate

11. What are the differences between a DDL statement and a DML statement?

12. What method of executing SQL statements would you use if you want to communicate directly with an SQL database from a front-end application?

13. What four methods does the SQL:1999 standard support for the execution of SQL statements?

14. What is a relational database management system?

15. What is an example of an RDBMS?

Module 2

Working with the SQL Environment

I n Module 1, I discuss relational theory, SQL, and relational database management systems (RDBMSs). In this module, I want to take this discussion one step further and introduce you to the SQL environment, as it is defined in the SQL:1999 standard. The SQL environment provides the structure in which SQL is implemented. Within this structure, you can use SQL statements to define database objects and store data in those objects. However, before you start writing SQL statements, you should have a basic understanding of the foundations on which the SQL environment is built so you can apply this information throughout the rest of the book. In fact, you might find it helpful to refer back to this module often to help gain a conceptual understanding of the SQL environment and how it relates to the SQL elements you'll learn about in subsequent modules.

Understand the SQL Environment

The *SQL environment* is, quite simply, the sum of all parts that make up that environment. Each distinct part, or component, works in conjunction with other components to support SQL operations such as creating and modifying objects, storing and querying data, or modifying and deleting that data. Taken together, these components form a model on which an RDBMS can be based. This does not imply, however, that RDBMS vendors adhere strictly to this model; what components they implement and how they implement them are left, for the most part, to the discretion of those vendors. Even so, I want to provide you with an overview of the way in which the SQL environment is defined, in terms of its distinct components, as they are described in the SQL:1999 standard.

The SQL environment is made up of six types of components, as shown in Figure 2-1. The SQL client and SQL servers are part of the SQL implementation and are therefore subtypes of that component.

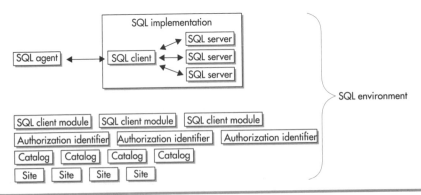

Figure 2-1 The components of the SQL environment

Notice that there is only one SQL agent and one SQL implementation, but there are multiple components for other types, such as catalogs and sites. According to SQL:1999, there must be exactly one SQL agent and SQL implementation and zero or more SQL client modules, authorization identifiers, and catalogs. The standard does not specify how many sites are supported, but implies multiple sites.

Each type of component performs a specific function within the SQL environment. Table 2-1 describes the six types.

Component Type	Description
SQL agent	Any structure that causes SQL statements to be executed. The SQL agent is bound to the SQL client within the SQL implementation.
SQL implementation	A processor that executes SQL statements according to the requirements of the SQL agent. The SQL implementation includes one SQL client and one or more SQL servers. The SQL client establishes SQL connections with the SQL servers and maintains data related to interactions with the SQL agent and the SQL servers. An SQL server manages the SQL session that takes place over the SQL connection and executes SQL statements received from the SQL client.
SQL client module	A collection of SQL statements that are written separately from your programming application language but that can be called from within that language. SQL client modules reside within the SQL environment and are processed by the SQL implementation, unlike embedded SQL, which is written within the application programming language and precompiled before the programming language is compiled. SQL client modules are discussed in more detail in Module 17.
Authorization identifier	An identifier that represents a user or role that is granted specific access privileges to objects and data within the SQL environment. A user is an individual security account that can represent an individual, an application, or a system service. A *role* is a set of predefined privileges that can be assigned to a user or to another role. I discuss authorization identifiers, users, and roles in Module 6.
Catalog	A group of schemas collected together in a defined namespace. Each catalog contains the Information Schema, which includes descriptors of a number of schema objects. The catalog itself provides a hierarchical structure for organizing data within the schemas. (A *schema* is basically a container for objects such as tables, views, and domains, all of which I'll be discussing in greater detail in the next section, "Understand SQL Catalogs.")
Site	A site is a placeholder for a value or set of values associated with a specified data type. Sites are made up of SQL data, most of which comes from the base tables. You can think of each value as an object that can be assigned a data type; the site is the place that holds that object. If this all seems confusing to you, it is. The SQL:1999 standard is not very clear about what it means by sites. The concept of sites is new to SQL:1999, and no doubt it will be clarified in subsequent releases of the standard. For now, it's enough that you know that a site represents one type of component in the SQL environment.

Table 2-1 The Component Types Supported in an SQL Environment

For the most part, you need to have only a basic understanding of the components that make up an SQL environment (in terms of beginning SQL programming). However, one of these components—the catalog—plays a more critical role than the others, with regard to what you'll be learning in this book. As a result, I will be going into this topic in more detail and explaining how it relates to the management of data and the objects that hold that data.

Understand SQL Catalogs

In the previous section, "Understand the SQL Environment," I state that an SQL environment is the sum of all parts that make up that environment. You can use the same logic to describe a *catalog,* in that a catalog is a collection of schemas and these schemas, taken together, define a namespace within the SQL environment.

NOTE

A *namespace* is a naming structure that identifies related components in a specified environment. A namespace is often depicted in an inverted tree configuration to represent the hierarchical relationship of objects. For example, suppose your namespace includes two objects: object1 and object2. If the namespace is called name1, the full object names will be name1.object1 and name1.object2 (or some such naming configuration), thus indicating that they share the same namespace.

Another way to look at a catalog is as a hierarchical structure with the catalog as the parent object and the schemas as the child objects, as shown in Figure 2-2. At the top of the hierarchy is the SQL environment, which can contain zero or more catalogs (although an environment with zero catalogs wouldn't do you much good because the catalog is where you'll find the data definitions and SQL data). The schemas are located at the third tier, beneath the catalog, and the schema objects are at the fourth tier.

You can compare the relationships between the objects in a catalog to the relationships between files and directories in your computer's operating system. The catalog is represented by a directory off the root; the schemas, by subdirectories; and the schema objects, by files within the subdirectories.

Like the hierarchical structure of a file system, the structure of a catalog is *logical* in nature; that is, a file system is presented in a hierarchical form (like that of Windows Explorer), but that doesn't mean that the files are actually stored hierarchically on your hard disk. In the same sense, the catalog hierarchy is merely a representation of the relationships between objects in your SQL environment. It doesn't imply any physical containment or organization. How these objects are actually implemented, with regard to the catalog structure, and which ones are implemented are left to the discretion of the RDBMS vendor. In fact, the SQL:1999 standard doesn't define language for the creation or deletion of catalogs; this too is left up to the vendors, and few systems even support catalogs.

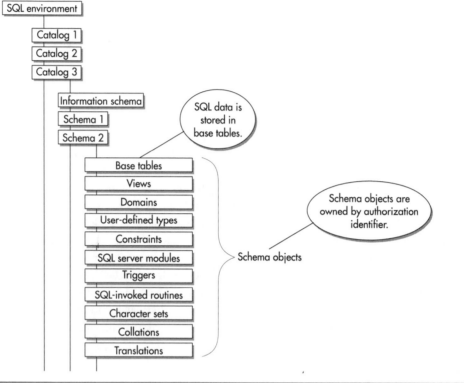

Figure 2-2 The components of a catalog

Schemas

Each catalog contains one or more schemas. A *schema* is a set of related objects that are collected under a common namespace. The schema acts as a container for those objects, which in turn store the SQL data or perform other data-related functions. Each schema, the objects contained in the schema, and the SQL data within those objects are owned by the authorization identifier associated with that schema.

Unlike catalogs, schemas are widely implemented in RDBMS products. However, as with catalogs, SQL leaves most of the implementation details up to the vendor, although the standard does provide language for the creation and deletion of schemas. For creating a schema, the CREATE SCHEMA statement is used, and for deleting a schema, the DROP SCHEMA statement is used. Creating and deleting schemas are discussed in more detail in the "Create a Schema" section.

The treatment of schemas in an RDBMS can vary widely from the standard, and therefore, it's important that you read the product documentation carefully if you want to create a schema in your SQL environment. For example, Oracle9i allows you to create schemas but you cannot delete (drop) them. In addition, if you use the PL/SQL statement CREATE SCHEMA, the system doesn't actually create a schema. (The system creates a schema automatically when a user is created.) Instead, the PL/SQL statement merely allows you to create objects in your schema and grant privileges on those objects all within one transaction.

Information Schema

Each catalog contains a special schema named INFORMATION_SCHEMA. This schema contains definitions for a number of schema objects, mostly views. A *view* is a virtual table that allows you to view data collected from actual tables. By using these views, you can display the definitions of objects in that catalog as though it were SQL data. You cannot change any of the data—if you did you would be changing the object definitions themselves—but you can display information simply by querying the appropriate view.

As with most SQL features, how the Information Schema is implemented and what functionality is supported varies from product to product, although these implementations are usually fairly straightforward. For example, SQL Server 2000 includes a view in the Information Schema named INFORMATION_SCHEMA.COLUMNS. If you query this view, the results will include a list that contains information about every column accessible to the current user within the current database. The results include such information as the column name, the data type assigned to that column, and the owner (authorization identifier) who owns that column.

Schema Objects

At the bottom tier of the catalog hierarchy sit the schema objects. The *schema objects* are a set of related components that are contained within a schema. This is the level where the SQL data is stored and, consequently, the level that concerns SQL programmers the most. By using SQL, you'll be able to define SQL objects, modify those definitions, and store and manipulate SQL data within the objects. In fact, most of what you'll be doing in this book from here on in has a direct impact on or is directly connected with the schema objects.

The SQL:1999 standard defines 11 types of schema objects. These objects, described in Table 2-2, provide the foundation for the SQL environment and the structure for the way in which

Schema Object	Description
Base table	The basic unit of data management in the SQL environment. A table is made up of columns and rows and is analogous to a relation (with its attributes and tuples) in relational theory. Each column is associated with a data type and holds values that are somehow related to each other. For example, a table about customers would contain columns that contain data about those customers, such as their names and addresses. (See Module 3.)

Table 2-2 The Types of Objects That Can Be Defined in Each Schema

Schema Object	Description
View	A virtual table that is created when the view is invoked (by calling its name). The table doesn't actually exist, only the SQL statement that defines the table. When that statement is invoked, the view pulls data from base tables and displays the results as if you're viewing the results of a base table query. (See Module 5.)
Domain	A user-defined object that can be specified in place of a data type when defining a column (a process part of creating or altering a table definition). A domain is based on an SQL data type but can include a default value and a constraint, which further limits the values that can be stored in a particular column. (See Module 4.)
User-defined type (UDT)	A user-defined object that can be specified in place of a data type when defining a column. SQL supports two types of UDTs: distinct and structured. Distinct types are based on SQL data types and their defined values. Structured types are made up of attribute values, each of which is based on an SQL data type. (See Module 3.)
Constraint	A restriction defined on a table, column, or domain that limits the type of data that can be inserted into the applicable object. For example, you can create a constraint on a column that restricts the values that can be inserted into that column to a specific range of numbers. (See Module 4.)
SQL server module	A module that contains SQL-invoked routines. A module is an object that contains SQL statements, routines, or procedures. An SQL-invoked routine is a function or procedure that can be invoked from SQL. Both functions and procedures are types of SQL statements that can pass parameters (values passed to a statement when you invoke that statement). A *function* can receive input parameters and return a value based on the expression included in the function statement. A *procedure* can pass input and output parameters. (See Module 13.)
Trigger	An object associated with a base table that defines an action to be taken when an event occurs related to that table. The trigger can specify that data be inserted into, deleted from, or updated in a base table. For example, a row deleted from one table might cause data to be deleted from another table. (See Module 14.)
SQL-invoked routine	A function or procedure that can be invoked from SQL. An SQL-invoked routine can be a schema object or be embedded in a module, which is also a schema object. (See Module 13.)
Character set	A collection of character attributes that define how characters are represented. A character set has three attributes: the repertoire, form-of-use, and default collation. The repertoire determines which characters can be expressed (for example, A, B, C, and so on); the form-of-use determines how the characters are represented as strings to hardware and software (for example, one byte per character, two bytes per character); and the default collation determines how those strings compare with one another.
Collation	A set of rules that control how character strings compare with one another within a particular repertoire. This information can then be used to order the characters (for example, A comes before B, B comes before C). A default collation is defined for each character set.
Translation	An operation that maps characters from one character set to characters in another set. Translations can include such operations as translating characters from upper- to lowercase or from one alphabet into another.

Table 2-2 The Types of Objects That Can Be Defined in Each Schema *(continued)*

Ask the Expert

Q: You describe a domain as a user-defined object that is based on a data type but can include a default value and a constraint. How does this type of domain differ from a domain as you describe it in the relational model?

A: In many ways the two are the same, and for all practical purposes, you can think of an SQL domain as a counterpart to a domain in the relational model. There is one subtle difference, however; a domain in the relational model is merely a description of the data that can be included in an entity (column) associated with that particular domain. An SQL domain, on the other hand, restricts the data that can be inserted into the column. An SQL domain does this through the use of constraints, which are validation rules that are part of the system of data integrity. The main idea to keep in mind is that a domain in the relational model is a logical concept, whereas an SQL domain is a physical one.

Q: When you talk about schema objects, you mention base tables. Does SQL support any other types of tables?

A: The SQL:1999 standard supports three types of tables: base tables, derived tables, and viewed tables. The base table is a type of table whose data is actually stored somewhere. In other words, SQL data is stored in a base table. If you query one or more of those tables, a set of data, specific to the query, is returned in a table format. The returned table (the result of your query) is known as a *derived table*. A *viewed table* is another name for a view, which is a virtual table whose definition is stored but whose data is derived from base tables at the time the view is called.

data is stored within that environment. I'll be discussing most of these objects in greater detail later in the book; as a result, I've included references, where appropriate, to the applicable modules.

As I said, I'll be discussing most of the items in the table in greater detail later in the book. However, the last three items, which are all related to character sets, are covered only briefly. The character sets, collations, and translations supported by RDBMSs can vary from product to product, so too can the implementation of these features. Throughout this book, the examples and projects I'll be giving you all rely on whatever the default character set is for the product that you're using. If you want to change that character set, either at the default level or the table level, you should first carefully review the product documentation to find out what is supported and how those features are implemented.

Then What Is a Database?

As you might have noticed, nowhere in the structure of the SQL environment or a catalog is there mention of a database. The reason for this is that nowhere in the SQL:1999 standard is the term database defined. In fact the only mention of a database, in terms of how it might fit into the structure of the SQL environment, is that you can consider the sites to be the database, although this is offered more as a suggestion than an absolute definition or as a key to understanding how databases fit into the environment. In fact, the standard uses the word primarily to refer to SQL as a database language but never actually defines a database.

This approach might be fine for the standard, but in the real world, it can be difficult for an RDBMS to create an SQL environment without creating some sort of component that users can point to and say, "Yes, there is the database." And indeed, most products allow you to create, alter, and delete objects that are called databases. For example, in SQL Server 2000 and in Oracle9i, you can use their management consoles (SQL Server Enterprise Manager and Oracle Enterprise Manager Console) to view the database objects. Each console provides an overview of their data environments in a directory-like structure that includes a Databases node. In both cases, the Databases node contains a list of available databases. Figure 2-3 shows how SQL Server Enterprise Manager organizes its data environment.

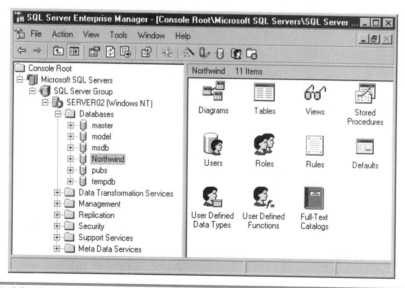

Figure 2-3 SQL Server Enterprise Manager with the Databases node expanded

NOTE

If you're using the Ocelot RDBMS, you cannot create a database. Ocelot sticks to a strict SQL format, with catalogs, schemas, and schema objects. Be sure to read the Ocelot documentation for an overview of how this structure is represented.

In Module 1, I state that a database is a collection of data organized in a structured format that is defined by the metadata that describes that structure. In both SQL Server and Oracle you can see how this definition applies. Both systems (and any true RDBMS you're working with) collect the data in a structured format and define that data by the use of schemas, which contain the metadata. This definition can also be applied to the SQL standard and its construction of the SQL environment and catalogs. SQL data is stored in an organized format within base tables. These base tables are contained within a schema, which defines those tables, thereby defining the data. So even though the SQL:1999 standard doesn't actually define the term database, it nonetheless supports the concept of a database, as do the RDBMS products that implement SQL.

Progress Check

1. What are the six types of components that make up an SQL environment?

2. How is a domain related to a catalog, within the hierarchy of the SQL environment?

3. What are the differences between a base table and a view?

---

1. The SQL agent, the SQL implementation, SQL client modules, authorization identifiers, catalogs, and sites.

2. A domain is a schema object, which is a child object of the schema. The schema is a child object of a catalog.

3. A base table is the basic unit of data management in the SQL environment. A table is made up of columns and rows and is analogous to a relation (with its attributes and tuples) in relational theory. A view is a virtual table that is created when the view is invoked (by calling its name). The table doesn't actually exist, only the SQL statement that is defined when the view is created. When that statement is invoked, the view pulls data from base tables and displays the results as if you're viewing the results of a base table query.

CRITICAL SKILL

2.3 Name Objects in an SQL Environment

Up to this point in the book, I have provided you with a lot of conceptual and background information. The reason for this is that I wanted you have a basic foundation in SQL before you actually start writing SQL statements. I believe that, with this information, you will be better able to grasp the logic behind the SQL code that you create and the reason for creating it, but I have no doubt that you're more than ready to start writing those statements.

However, before I actually start getting into the meat of SQL, there's one more topic that I need to cover briefly—object identifiers. An *identifier* is a name given to an SQL object. The name can be up to (but not including) 128 characters and must follow defined conventions. An identifier can be assigned to any object that you can create with SQL statements, such as domains, tables, columns, views, or schemas. The SQL:1999 standard defines two types of identifiers: regular identifiers and delimited identifiers.

Regular identifiers are fairly restrictive and must follow specific conventions:

- The names are not case-sensitive. For example, ArtistNames is the same as ARTISTNAMES and artistnames.

- Only letters, digits, and underscores are allowed. For example, you can create identifiers such as First_Name, 1stName, or FIRST_NAME.

- No SQL reserved keywords can be used.

NOTE

A *keyword* is a word that is part of the SQL lexicon. There are two types of SQL keywords: reserved and nonreserved. As the name suggests, the reserved keywords cannot be used for any purpose other than as they are intended to be used within an SQL statement. The nonreserved words have no such restriction. For a complete list of the SQL keywords, see Appendix B.

SQL is insensitive to case, with regard to regular identifiers. All names are changed to uppercase by SQL when they are stored, which is why 1stName and 1STNAME are read as identical values.

Delimited identifiers are not as restrictive as regular identifiers, but they still must follow specific conventions:

- The identifier must be enclosed in a set of double quotation marks, such as the "ArtistNames" identifier.

- The quotation marks are not stored in the database, but all other characters are stored as they appear in the SQL statement.

- The names are case-sensitive. For example, "ArtistNames" *is not* the same as "artistnames" or ARTISTNAMES, but "ARTISTNAMES" *is* the same as ARTISTNAMES and ArtistNames (because regular identifiers are converted to uppercase).

- Most characters are allowed, including spaces.

- SQL reserved keywords can be used.

When you're deciding on how to name your SQL objects, there are a number of systems that you can follow. The first choice you'll have to make is whether you want to use regular or delimited identifiers. You'll also want to decide on other issues, such as case and the use of underscores. For example, you could name a table CompactDiscTitles, compact_disc_titles, COMPACT_DISC_TITLES, "Compact Disc Titles", or some other form of that name. The important part to remember is that you should pick a system and stick with it throughout the coding for a particular database.

NOTE

For the examples and projects in this book, I use regular identifiers with mixed case (for example, CompactDiscTitles).

Qualified Names

All schema object identifiers are qualified by the logical way in which they fit into the hierarchical structure of the SQL environment. A fully qualified name includes the name of the catalog, the name of the schema, and the name of the schema object, each separated by a period. For example, suppose you have a table named CDArtists. The table is in the CompactDiscs schema, which is in the Music catalog. The fully qualified name for that table would be Music.CompactDiscs.CDArtists.

The way in which these naming conventions play out in various RDBMS products depends on how that product has implemented the structure of the SQL environment. For example, a fully qualified name in SQL Server is based on the server name, database name, owner name, and object name. In this case, a table named Artists might have a fully qualified name of Server01.MusicDB.dbo.Artists, where Server01 is the name of the server, MusicDB is the name of the database, and dbo (which refers to database owner) is the name of the object owner. To determine how fully qualified names are handled for a particular RDBMS, check the product documentation.

Progress Check

1. Which type of identifier allows you to use a reserved keyword?

2. You are working in a schema named Music, which is in a catalog named Media. What is the fully qualified name for the CompactDiscs table?

CRITICAL SKILL

Create a Schema

Now that you have a fundamental understanding of how to use identifiers to name SQL objects, you're ready to start writing SQL statements. I'll begin with the CREATE SCHEMA statement because schemas are at the top of the SQL hierarchy, in terms of which objects the SQL:1999 standard allows you to create. (Remember, SQL doesn't provide any sort of CREATE CATALOG or CREATE DATABASE statement. It's left up to the RDBMS vendors to determine how and whether to implement these objects.) In the next section, "Create a Database," I will slip out of SQL mode and discuss database creation because most RDBMS products support the creation of database objects, and you'll probably find that you'll want to create a database in order to try out the examples and projects in this book.

The place to start with any type of SQL statement is the syntax that defines that statements. The following syntax shows the basic components of the CREATE SCHEMA statement:

```
CREATE SCHEMA <name clause>
[ <character set or path> ]
[ <schema elements> ]
```

NOTE

The angle brackets contain information that serves as a placeholder for a value or clause related to that information. For example, <name clause> is a placeholder for keywords and values related to naming the schema. The square brackets, on the other hand, mean that the clause is optional. You do not have to specify a character set, path, or schema element.

Let's look at the syntax for the CREATE SCHEMA statement piece by piece. The SQL keywords CREATE SCHEMA alert the SQL implementation to the type of statement being executed. This is followed by the <name clause> placeholder, which can include a name for

1. A delimited identifier
2. Media.Music.CompactDiscs

the schema, an authorization identifier (preceded by the AUTHORIZATION keyword), or both. As a result, the name clause can take any one of the following forms:

- <schema name>

- AUTHORIZATION <authorization identifier>

- <schema name> AUTHORIZATION <authorization identifier>

The <authorization identifier> value specifies who owns the schema and its objects. If none is specified, the value defaults to the current user. If no <schema name> value is specified, a name is created that's based on the authorization identifier.

The next clause, <character set or path>, allows you to set a default character set, a default path, or both. The name of the character set is preceded by the DEFAULT CHARACTER SET keywords and specifies a default character set for the new schema. The path specifies an order for searching for SQL-invoked routines (procedures and functions) that are created as part of the CREATE SCHEMA statement. (SQL-invoked routines are discussed in Module 13.)

The <schema elements> clause is made up of various types of other SQL statements that you can include in the CREATE SCHEMA statement. For the most part, this clause allows you to create schema objects such as tables, views, domains, and triggers. The advantage to this is that objects are added right to the schema when you create it, all in one step.

Now that you've seen the syntax for a CREATE SCHEMA statement, let's look at an example. The following code creates a schema named Inventory. The statement also specifies an authorization identifier name Mngr and a character set named Latin1.

```
CREATE SCHEMA Inventory AUTHORIZATION Mngr
DEFAULT CHARACTER SET Latin1
CREATE TABLE Artists
( ArtistID INTEGER, ArtistName CHARACTER (20) ) ;
```

Notice that the code sample includes a CREATE TABLE statement. This is one of the elements that can be specified as part of the <schema elements> clause. You can include as many statements as you want. This particular statement creates a table named Artists that contains the ArtistID column and the ArtistName column. (I discuss the CREATE TABLE statement in great detail in Module 3.)

In addition to defining a CREATE SCHEMA statement, SQL:1999 also defines a DROP SCHEMA statement, as shown in the following syntax:

```
DROP SCHEMA <schema name>
CASCADE | RESTRICT
```

The first line is fairly straightforward; the named schema will be removed from the system. The second line has two options: CASCADE and RESTRICT.

NOTE

The vertical bar (|) symbol can be read as "or," which means that you should use the CASCADE option *or* the RESTRICT option.

If the CASCADE option is specified, all schema objects and SQL data within those objects are deleted from the system. If the RESTRICT option is used, the schema is deleted only if no schema objects exist. This method is used as a safeguard against deleting any objects that you do not want deleted. It's meant as a way to make you verify that the objects you're deleting are what you want to delete before you actually delete the schema.

Now let's look at an example of the DROP SCHEMA statement. The following code removes the Inventory schema:

```
DROP SCHEMA Inventory CASCADE ;
```

Notice that the CASCADE option is used, which means that all schema objects and SQL data will be removed.

Progress Check

1. What does the <authorization identifier> value specify in a CREATE SCHEMA statement?

2. What type of information can be included in the <name clause> of a CREATE SCHEMA statement?

---

1. The <authorization identifier> value specifies who owns the schema and its objects.

2. The <name clause> can include a name for the schema, an authorization identifier (preceded by the AUTHORIZATION keyword), or both.

CRITICAL SKILL
2.5 # Create a Database

Despite the fact that the SQL standard does not define what a database is, let alone provide a statement to create any sort of database object, there is a good possibility that you'll be working with an RDBMS that not only supports the creation of a database object, but uses that object as the foundation for its hierarchical structure in the management of data objects. Consequently, you might find that, in order to work through the examples and projects in this book, you want to create a test database so you have an environment in which you can create, alter, or delete data objects or data as necessary, without risking the loss of data definitions or data from an actual database. (Ideally, you'll be working with an RDBMS that is a clean installation, without any existing databases, except preinstalled system and sample databases.)

If you've already worked with an RDBMS, you might be familiar with how database objects are organized within that system. For example, if you take a look again at Figure 2-3, you can see that SQL Server organizes the server's databases into a logical structure beneath the Databases node. Each database node (for example, Northwind) contains child nodes that represent the different types of objects associated with that particular database. As you can see, the Northwind database currently lists 11 types of objects: Diagrams, Tables, Views, Stored Procedures, Users, Roles, Rules, Defaults, User-Defined Data Types, User-Defined Functions, and Full-Text Catalogs. For a definition of how SQL Server defines each of these objects, you should view the product documentation, which you should do for any RDBMS.

Most products that support database objects also support language to create those objects. For example, Oracle, MySQL, and SQL Server all include the CREATE DATABASE statement in their SQL-based languages. (Ocelot does not.) However, which parameters can be defined when building that statement, what permissions you need in order to execute that statement, and how a system implements the database object vary from product to product, but most products use the same basic syntax to create a database object:

```
CREATE DATABASE <database name>
<additional parameters>
```

Before creating a database in any system, make sure to first read the product documentation, and if appropriate, consult with a database administrator to be sure that it is safe for you to add a database object to the SQL environment. Once you create the database, you can create schemas, tables, views, and other objects within that database, and from there, populate the tables with the necessary data.

Project 2-1 Creating a Database and a Schema

In Module 1, Project 1-2, you established access to an RDBMS. In that project, you used a front-end application that allowed you to directly invoke SQL statements. You will be using that application for this project (and the rest of the projects in the book) to create a database and a schema, or whichever of these functions your system supports. Once you create the database, you should work within the context of that database for future examples and projects. If your system supports schema creation but not database creation, you should work within the context of that schema for the other projects.

Step by Step

1. Open the client application that allows you to directly invoke SQL statements. If applicable, check with the database administrator to make sure that you're logging in with the credentials necessary to create a database and schema. You might need special permissions to create these objects. Also verify whether there are any parameters you should include when creating the database (for example, log file size), restrictions on the name you can use, or restrictions of any other kind. Be sure to check the product documentation before going any further.

2. Create a database named Inventory (if your RDBMS supports this functionality). Depending on the product you're using, you'll be executing a statement that's similar to the following:

```
CREATE DATABASE Inventory ;
```

   If you're required to include any additional parameters in the statement, they would most likely be included in the lines following the CREATE DATABASE clause. Once you execute the statement, you should receive some sort of message telling you that the statement has been executed successfully.

3. Connect to the new database. The method for doing that will vary from product to product. In Oracle, you can connect to a database by clicking Change Database Connection in SQL*Plus Worksheet and then entering the appropriate logon information. In SQL Server, it's simply a matter of selecting the appropriate database from the list of databases in the Query Analyzer toolbar, or you can execute the following statement:

```
USE Inventory
```

4. Create a schema named CDInventory (if your RDBMS supports this functionality). Create the schema under your current authorization identifier. Do not include any schema elements at this time. In most cases, you will be executing a statement that looks similar to the following:

```
CREATE SCHEMA CDInventory ;
```

(continued)

Project Summary

Projects of this sort can be complicated because they're so dependent on how RDBMS products have implemented various features. As a result, you must rely heavily on product documentation (which you should be using anyway) and, if applicable, database administrators. However, now that you've gotten through this project and have created the necessary database or schema environment, you should be ready to move on to the examples and projects in the rest of the book. Because you've laid the necessary foundation, you're now ready to create, alter, and drop data objects and insert, modify, and delete the data stored in those objects.

✔ Module 2 Mastery Check

1. What are the differences between an SQL agent and an SQL implementation?

2. Which component of an SQL environment represents a user or role that is granted specific access privileges to objects and data?

   A. Catalog

   B. Authorization identifier

   C. SQL client module

   D. SQL agent

3. A(n) _____ is a collection of schemas that form a namespace within the SQL environment.

4. What is a schema?

5. Which statement do you use to add a schema to an SQL environment?

   A. ADD SCHEMA

   B. INSERT SCHEMA

   C. CREATE SCHEMA

6. What is the name of the schema that contains definitions for schema objects in a catalog?

7. What are the 11 types of schema objects that can be contained in a schema?

8. What is a view?

9. Which schema objects provide the basic unit of data management in the SQL environment?

    A. Views

    B. Domains

    C. Base tables

    D. Character sets

10. How does the SQL:1999 standard define a database?

11. An _____ is a name given to an SQL object.

12. How is a regular identifier distinguished from a delimited identifier in an SQL statement?

13. Which type of identifier permits spaces to be used as part of the name of an object?

14. Your SQL environment includes a catalog named Inventory. In that catalog is a schema named CompactDiscs, and in that schema is a table named Artists. What is the qualified name of that table?

15. What three forms can the <name clause> component of a CREATE SCHEMA statement take?

16. What are the differences between the CASCADE option and the RESTRICT option in a DROP SCHEMA statement?

Module 3

Creating and Altering Tables

In an SQL environment, tables are the basic unit of data management. Most SQL programming you do is related either directly or indirectly to those tables. As a result, before you can insert data into your database or modify that data, the appropriate tables must have been created or you must create them. The SQL:1999 standard provides three statements that allow you to define, change, and delete table definitions from an SQL environment. You can use the CREATE TABLE statement to add a table, the ALTER TABLE statement to modify that definition, or the DROP TABLE statement to delete the table and its data from your database. Of these three statements, the CREATE TABLE statement has the most complex syntax. Not only is this because of the various types of tables supported by SQL, but because a table definition can include many elements. However, despite these complexities, table creation is a fairly straightforward process, once you understand the basic syntax.

CRITICAL SKILL

3.1 Create SQL Tables

As you might recall from Module 2, SQL supports three types of tables: base tables, derived tables, and viewed tables. Most base tables are schema objects that hold SQL data. Derived tables are the results you see when you request (query) data from the database. Viewed tables are another name for views, which I discuss in Module 5. You can think of a viewed table as a type of named derived table, with a view definition stored in the schema.

In this module, you'll be working with base tables. In fact, most of what you'll be working with directly throughout this book (as well as your programming career) are base tables; however, not all base tables are the same. Some are persistent (permanent) and some are temporary. Some are schema objects and some are contained in modules. All module base tables are also temporary tables. SQL supports four types of base tables:

- **Persistent base tables**   A named schema object defined by a table definition in a CREATE TABLE statement. Persistent base tables hold the SQL data that is stored in your database. This is the most common type of base table and is often what is being referred to when talking about base tables or tables. A persistent base table always exists as long as the table definition exists, and can be called from within any SQL session.

- **Global temporary tables**   A named schema object defined by a table definition in a CREATE GLOBAL TEMPORARY TABLE statement. Although the table definition is a part of the schema, the actual table exists only when referenced within the context of an SQL session. When the session ends, the table no longer exists. The table created in one session cannot be accessed from another SQL session. The contents are distinct within each SQL session.

- **Created local temporary tables**   A named schema object defined by a table definition in a CREATE LOCAL TEMPORARY TABLE statement. Like a global temporary table, the created local temporary table can be referenced only within the context of an SQL session and cannot be accessed from another SQL session. However, a global temporary table can be accessed from anywhere within the associated SQL session, whereas a created local temporary table can be accessed only within the associated module. The contents are distinct within that module.

- **Declared local temporary tables**   A table declared as part of a procedure in a module. The table definition is not contained in the schema and does not exist until that procedure is executed. Like other temporary tables, the declared local temporary table can be referenced only within the context of the SQL session.

NOTE

An *SQL session* refers to the connection between a user and an SQL agent. During this connection, a sequence of consecutive SQL statements are invoked by this user and then executed. A *module* is an object that contains SQL statements, routines, or procedures. Modules are discussed in Module 13 and Module 17.

Progress Check

1. What three types of tables does SQL support?

2. What four types of base tables does SQL support?

3. Which base tables are created as schema objects?

As you can see, you can use a form of the CREATE TABLE statement to create all base table types except declared local temporary tables. Throughout the rest of the module, I will primarily be discussing persistent base tables, although I'll be touching on the subject of temporary tables in subsequent modules. In the meantime, let's take a look at the syntax in a CREATE TABLE statement:

```
CREATE [ { GLOBAL | LOCAL } TEMPORARY ] TABLE <table name>
( <table element> [ { , <table element> } . . . ] )
[ ON COMMIT { PRESERVE | DELETE } ROWS ]
```

1. Base tables, derived tables, and viewed tables (views)

2. Persistent base tables, global temporary tables, created local temporary tables, and declared local temporary tables

3. Persistent base tables, global temporary tables, and created local temporary tables

NOTE

The curly brackets are used to group elements together. For example, in the first line of syntax, the GLOBAL | LOCAL keywords are grouped together. The brackets tell you that you should first decide how to handle the contents within the brackets and then determine how they fit into the clause. In the first line, you should use either GLOBAL or LOCAL along with TEMPORARY. However, the entire clause is optional. The three periods (in the second line) tell you that you can repeat the clause as often as necessary. In this case, you could add as many <table element> clauses as your definition requires.

The syntax I've shown here provides only the basics of the CREATE TABLE statement, which is actually far more complex. (The syntax and its explanations take up about 38 pages of the SQL:1999 standard.) Even so, the syntax provided here is enough of a foundation for you to create the majority of tables that you're likely to be using.

In the first line of the syntax, you designate whether the table is temporary and you provide a name for the table, so you have three options:

- CREATE TABLE <table name>

- CREATE GLOBAL TEMPORARY TABLE <table name>

- CREATE LOCAL TEMPORARY TABLE <table name>

Depending on the RDBMS in which you're working, you might have to qualify the table name by including a schema name, authorization identifier, or database name (for example, Inventory.Artists).

The second line of the syntax allows you to specify the parts that make up the table, such as columns. (I'll return to that in a moment.) The third line of the syntax applies only if you're creating a temporary table. The clause allows you to specify whether or not the table should be emptied when a COMMIT statement is executed. A COMMIT statement is used in a transaction to commit changes to the database. I discuss transactions in Module 16.

You can think of the <table element> clauses as the meat of a CREATE TABLE statement. It is here that you define columns, constraints, and other elements specific to the table you're creating. You can define one or more <table element> clauses. If you define more than one, you must separate them with commas. Of the elements that you can create, we'll be focusing primarily on columns (in this module) and constraints (in Module 4). Let's take a closer look at the syntax that is used to define a column:

```
<column name> { <data type> | <domain> }
[ <default clause> ] [ <column constraint> ] [ COLLATE <collation name> ]
```

In the first line of the syntax, you must provide a column name and declare a data type or user-defined domain. I discuss data types in the "Specify Column Data Types" section later in this module, and I discuss domains in Module 4.

In the second line of the syntax, you have the option to provide a default value (see the "Specify Column Default Values" section), column constraints (see Module 4), or a collation (see Module 2).

At its most basic, a CREATE TABLE statement might look something like the following statement:

```
CREATE TABLE Artists
( ArtistID INTEGER, ArtistName CHARACTER (60) ) ;
```

In this statement, I'm creating a table named Artists, a column named ArtistID, and a column named ArtistName. The ArtistID column is associated with the INTEGER data type, and the ArtistName column is associated with the CHARACTER data type. Notice that the two column definitions are separated by a comma. If you execute the CREATE TABLE statement, your table will look similar to the table shown in Figure 3-1.

NOTE

The rows of data would not be in a table until you have actually added that data. The rows are shown here merely to give you an idea of the type of table that this statement would create.

Before I go any further with my discussion about creating a table, let's take a closer look at data types, which play an integral role in any column definition.

ArtistID: INTEGER	ArtistName: CHARACTER (60)
10001	Jennifer Warnes
10002	Joni Mitchell
10003	William Ackerman
10004	Kitaro
10005	Bing Crosby
10006	Patsy Cline
10007	Jose Carreras
10008	Placido Domingo
10009	Luciano Pavarotti

Figure 3-1 The ArtistID and ArtistName columns of the Artists table

Ask the Expert

Q: When you discussed the various types of tables that SQL supports, you talked briefly about temporary tables. What do you use temporary tables for?

A: Temporary tables provide you with a way to store temporary results within the context of your session. You might find that you need a place to store this data in order to take a certain course of action. You can explicitly create a persistent base table, store data in that table, and then drop the table when you're finished, but the temporary table allows you to do the same without having to explicitly destroy the table each time you use it. In other words, the temporary table is a useful tool when you need to store data for only a specific period of time. For example, suppose you have an application that allows you to generate a quarterly report based on your inventory at the end of the reporting period. The application might need to gather the data into a meaningful collection to generate the report; however, once the report is generated, the application no longer needs to store that data, so the table can be deleted. One of the advantages of using a temporary table is that, because it is unique to a session, the table cannot interact with other users or sessions. As a result, the RDBMS doesn't have to take special steps to lock the transaction to prevent other users from accessing the data within the temporary tables, which can result in better performance.

CRITICAL SKILL
3.2 Specify Column Data Types

Whenever you define a column in a CREATE TABLE statement, you must, at the very least, provide a name for the column and an associated data type or domain. The data type or domain (discussed in Module 4) restricts the value that can be entered into that column. For example, some data types limit a column's value to numbers, while other data types allow any character to be entered. SQL supports three types of data types:

- **Predefined**   Predefined data types are the most common. Each predefined data type is a named element (using an SQL keyword) that limits values to the restrictions defined by that database. SQL includes five types of predefined data types: string, numeric, datetime, interval, and Boolean.

- **Constructed**   Constructed data types, which are new to SQL:1999, are also a named element but tend to be more complex than predefined data types because they can hold multiple values. Constructed types allow you to *construct* more complicated structures than more traditional data types. A thorough discussion of these types is beyond the scope of this book, but I wanted to mention them so you know that they exist.

- **User-Defined**   User-defined data types are based on predefined types or attribute definitions and are added as schema objects to the SQL environment. SQL supports two types of user-defined data types: distinct and structured. The distinct type is based on a predefined data type, and the structured type is based on attribute definitions. I discuss user-defined types in the "Create User-Defined Types" section later in this module.

Although all implementations of SQL support data types, which data types are supported varies from product to product. However, as a beginning SQL programmer, you'll find that most implementations support the basic (more traditional) data types, which are the ones I will be using in the examples and projects throughout the book. These more traditional data types, sometimes known as primitive types, are all part of the SQL predefined data types, which I describe in the following sections. Don't try to memorize each of these types, but start becoming familiar with the differences between them. You'll find that, as you start using specific data types, you'll become more comfortable with them. In the meantime, refer back to the following sections as often as necessary whenever you're working with table definitions or SQL data.

String Data Types

The string data types are made up of types that permit values based on character sets or on data bits. The values permitted by string types can be fixed in length or varying, depending on the specific type. SQL defines four types of string data types:

- **Character strings**   Permitted values must be drawn from a specific character set, either the default set or a set defined at the time that the column is being defined. Character string data types include CHARACTER, CHARACTER VARYING, and CHARACTER LARGE OBJECT.

- **National character strings**   Permitted values are similar to character strings except that the character set associated with these data types is defined by the implementation. As a result, when a national character string data type is specified, the values associated with that data type must be based on the character set specified by the relational database management system (RDBMS) for the national character strings. The national character string data types include NATIONAL CHARACTER, NATIONAL CHARACTER VARYING, and NATIONAL CHARACTER LARGE OBJECT.

- **Bit strings**   Permitted values are based on data bits (binary digits), rather than character sets or collations, which means that these data types allow only values of 0 or 1. SQL supports two types of bit string data types: BIT and BIT VARYING.

- **Binary strings**   Permitted values are similar to bit strings, except that they are based on bytes (referred to as *octets* in SQL:1999), rather than on bits. As a result, no character sets or collations are associated with them. (A byte is equal to eight bits, which is why the SQL standard uses the term octet.) SQL supports only one binary string data type: BINARY LARGE OBJECT.

Now that you have an overview of the types of string data types, let's take a closer look at each one. Table 3-1 describes each of these data types and provides an example of a column definition that uses the specific type.

Data Type	Description/Example
CHARACTER	Specifies the exact number of characters (which must be from a character set) that will be stored for each value. For example, if you define the number of characters as 10, but the value contains only six characters, the remaining four characters will be spaces. The data type can also be referred to as CHAR. Example: `FullName CHAR (60),`
CHARACTER VARYING	Specifies the greatest number of characters (which must be from a character set) that can be included in a value. The number of characters stored is exactly the same number as the value entered, so no spaces are added to the value. The data type can also be referred to as CHAR VARYING or VARCHAR. Example: `FullName VARCHAR (60),`
CHARACTER LARGE OBJECT	Stores large groups of characters, up to the specified amount. The number of characters stored is exactly the same number as the value entered, so no spaces are added to the value. The data type can also be referred to as CLOB. Example: `ArtistBio CLOB (200K),`
NATIONAL CHARACTER	Operates just like the CHARACTER data type, except that it's based on an implementation-defined character set. The data type can also be referred to as NATIONAL CHAR and NCHAR. Example: `FullName NCHAR (60),`
NATIONAL CHARACTER VARYING	Operates just like the CHARACTER VARYING data type, except that it's based on an implementation-defined character set. The data type can also be referred to as NATIONAL CHAR VARYING or NCHAR VARYING. Example: `FullName NCHAR VARYING (60),`
NATIONAL CHARACTER LARGE OBJECT	Operates just like the CHARACTER LARGE OBJECT data type, except that it's based on an implementation-defined character set. The data type can also be referred to as NCHAR LARGE OBJECT or NCLOB. Example: `ArtistBio NCLOB (200K),`

Table 3-1 String Data Types with Example Column Definitions

Data Type	Description/Example
BIT	Specifies the exact number of bits that can be stored for each character. For example, if you define the number of bits as 2 but the value contains only 1 bit, the remaining bit will be a space. If the number of bits is not specified, 1 bit is stored. Example: `InStock BIT,`
BIT VARYING	Specifies the greatest number of bits that can be included in a value. The number of bits stored is exactly the same number as the value entered, so no spaces are added to the value. Example: `InStock BIT VARYING (2),`
BINARY LARGE OBJECT	Stores large groups of bytes, up to the specified amount. The number of bytes stored is exactly the same number as the value entered, so no spaces are added to the value. The data type can also be referred to as BLOB. Example: `ArtistPic BLOB (1M),`

Table 3-1 String Data Types with Example Column Definitions *(continued)*

Numeric Data Types

As you probably guessed by the name, the values specified by the numeric data types are numbers. All numeric data types have a precision and some have a scale. The *precision* refers to the number of digits (within a specific numeric value) that can be stored. The *scale* refers to the number of digits in the fractional part of that value (the digits to the right of the decimal point). For example, the number 435.27 has a precision of 5 and a scale of 2. A scale cannot be a negative number or be larger than the precision. A scale of 0 indicates that the number is an integer and contains no fractional component. SQL defines two types of numeric data types:

● **Exact numerics**   Permitted values have a precision and scale, which, for some numeric data types, are defined by the implementation. Exact numeric data types include NUMERIC, DECIMAL, INTEGER, and SMALLINT.

● **Approximate numerics**   Permitted values have a precision but no scale. As a result the decimal point can float. A *floating-point* number is one that contains a decimal point, but the decimal point can be located at any place within that number, which is why an approximate numeric is said to have no scale. Approximate numeric data types include REAL, DOUBLE PRECISION, and FLOAT.

Table 3-2 describes each of the numeric data types and provides an example of a column definition that uses the specific type.

Data Type	Description/Example
NUMERIC	Specifies the precision and the scale of a numeric value. You can specify the precision only and use the implementation-defined (default) scope, or you can specify the precision and scope. If you specify neither the precision nor the scope, the implementation will provide both values. Example: `ArtistRate NUMERIC (5,2),`
DECIMAL	Specifies values similar to those of the NUMERIC data type. However, if the implementation-defined precision is higher than the specified precision, values with the higher precision will be accepted, but the scale will always be what you specify. Example: `ArtistRoyalty DECIMAL (5,2),`
INTEGER	Specifies a value with an implementation-defined precision and a 0 scope, meaning that only integers are accepted and you do not specify any parameters with this data type. The data type can also be referred to as INT. Example: `ArtistID INT,`
SMALLINT	Specifies a value similar to an INTEGER data type. However, the precision defined by the implementation must be smaller than the INTEGER precision. Example: `ArtistID SMALLINT,`
FLOAT	Specifies the precision of a numeric value, but not the scope. This data type is useful if you think you'll be migrating your system from one hardware platform to another. Example: `ArtistRoyalty FLOAT (6),`
REAL	Specifies a value with an implementation-defined precision, but without a scope. The precision must be smaller than the precision defined for a DOUBLE PRECISION data type. Example: `ArtistRoyalty REAL,`
DOUBLE PRECISION	Specifies a value with an implementation-defined precision, but without a scope. The precision must be greater than the precision defined for the REAL data type. The implication is that the value of the precision should be double that of the REAL data type, but each implementation defines *double* differently. Example: `ArtistRoyalty DOUBLE PRECISION,`

Table 3-2 Numeric Data Types with Example Column Definitions

Datetime Data Types

As the name implies, datetime data types are concerned with tracking dates and times. SQL defines three datetime types—DATE, TIME, and TIMESTAMP—and variations on these types. These variations are related to Universal Coordinated Time (UCT), which used to be called Greenwich Mean Time (GMT), and the various time zones. Table 3-3 describes each of the datetime data types and provides an example of a column definition that uses the specific type.

Data Type	Description/Example
DATE	Specifies the year, month, and day value of a date. The year is four digits and supports the values 0001 through 9999; the month is two digits and supports the values 01 through 12; and the day is two digits and supports the values 01 through 31. Example: `DateHired DATE,`
TIME	Specifies the hour, minute, and second values of a time. The hour is two digits and supports the values 00 through 23; the minute is two digits and supports the values 00 through 59; and the second is at least two digits and supports values 00 through 61.999. The data type includes no fractional digits unless you specify them. For example, TIME (3) would give you three fractional digits. The data type can also be referred to as TIME WITHOUT TIME ZONE. Example: `SongTime TIME (2),`
TIME WITH TIME ZONE	Specifies the same information as the TIME data type except that the value also includes information specific to UTC and time zones. The values added to the data type range from −11:59 to +12:00. Example: `EventTime TIME WITH TIME ZONE (2)`
TIMESTAMP	Combines the values of TIME and DATE. The only difference is that with the TIME data type, the default number of fractional digits is 0, but with the TIMESTAMP data type, the default number is 6. You can specify a different number of fractional digits by including a parameter, such as TIMESTAMP (4). The data type can also be referred to as TIMESTAMP WITHOUT TIME ZONE. Example: `PurchaseDate TIMESTAMP (3),`
TIMESTAMP WITH TIME ZONE	Specifies the same information as the TIMESTAMP data type except that the value also includes information specific to UTC and time zones. The values added to the data type range from −11:59 to +12:00. Example: `PurchaseDate TIMESTAMP WITH TIME ZONE (2),`

Table 3-3 Datetime Data Types with Example Column Definitions

Interval Data Type

The interval data type is closely related to the datetime data types. The value of an interval data type represents the difference between two datetime values. SQL supports two types of intervals:

- **Year-month intervals**   The interval data type specifies intervals between years, months, or both. You can use only the YEAR and MONTH fields in a year-month interval.

- **Day-time intervals**   The interval data type specifies intervals between any of the following values: days, hours, minutes, or seconds. You can use only the DAY, HOUR, MINUTE, and SECOND fields in a day-time interval.

You cannot mix one type of interval with the other. For example, you cannot define an interval data type that uses the YEAR field and the HOUR field.

The interval data type uses the keyword INTERVAL followed by an <interval qualifier> clause. The clause is a complex series of rules that describe how the INTERVAL data type can be defined to express intervals involving years, months, days, hours, minutes, or seconds. In addition, the leading field (the first word) in the clause can be defined with a precision (p). The precision is the number of digits that will be used in the leading field. If a precision isn't specified, the default is 2. For year-month intervals, you can specify one of the following interval data types:

- INTERVAL YEAR
- INTERVAL YEAR (p)
- INTERVAL MONTH
- INTERVAL MONTH (p)
- INTERVAL YEAR TO MONTH
- INTERVAL YEAR (p) TO MONTH

There are many more options for day-time intervals because you have more fields to choose from. For example, you can specify any of the following interval types using the DAY field as a leading field or stand-alone field:

- INTERVAL DAY
- INTERVAL DAY (p)
- INTERVAL DAY TO HOUR
- INTERVAL DAY (p) TO HOUR
- INTERVAL DAY TO MINUTE
- INTERVAL DAY (p) TO MINUTE
- INTERVAL DAY TO SECOND
- INTERVAL DAY (p) TO SECOND
- INTERVAL DAY TO SECOND (x)
- INTERVAL DAY (p) TO SECOND (x)

When the SECOND field is the trailing field (the last word), you can specify an additional precision (*x*), which defines the number of digits after the decimal point. As you can see from these examples, there are many more day-time interval data types that can be defined. Keep in mind, however, that the leading field must always be greater than the trailing field. For example, the YEAR field is greater than MONTH, and HOUR is greater than MINUTE.

If you were going to use an interval data type in a column definition, it might look something like the following:

```
DateRange INTERVAL YEAR (4) TO MONTH,
```

In this example, a value in this field will include four digits for the year, a hyphen, and then two digits for the month, for example, 1999-08. If a precision were not specified for the year, the year range could include only two digits (00 through 99).

In addition to the complexity of the rules that govern the use of the INTERVAL data type, few implementations support it, making it unlikely that you will be using it anytime soon. For that reason, I won't be spending any more time on this data type and will not be using it in any other examples or projects in the book.

Boolean Data Type

The Boolean data type (unlike the interval data types) is very straightforward and easy to apply. The data type supports a true/false construct that permits only three values: true, false, or unknown. A null value evaluates to unknown. (In SQL, a *null* value is used to signify that a value is undefined or not known. I discuss null values in Module 4.)

The values in the Boolean data type can be used in SQL queries and expressions for comparison purposes. (I discuss comparisons in Module 9.) Boolean comparisons follow specific logic:

● True is greater than false.

● A comparison involving a null value or unknown value will return an unknown result.

● A value of unknown can be assigned to a column only if it supports null values.

To use the Boolean data type, you must use the BOOLEAN keyword with no parameters, as shown in the following example:

```
ArtistHasAgent BOOLEAN,
```

The ArtistHasAgent column will accept only the values of true, false, and unknown.

Ask the Expert

Q: How do the predefined data types in SQL compare to the data types you find in other programming languages?

A: For the most part, it is unlikely that data types from two different languages will be the same. A set of data types in one language can vary in structure and semantics from a set of data types in another language. These differences, sometimes called *impedance mismatch,* can lead to the loss of information when an application draws data from an SQL database. In fact, it's often a good idea to know which language will be used for applications as the database is being designed. In some cases, the database design can affect which application language you can use to manipulate data in an SQL database. However, SQL includes a data conversion expression named CAST. The CAST expression allows you to convert data from one data type to another data type, allowing the host language to access values that it wouldn't have been able to handle in its original form. The CAST expression is discussed in more detail in Module 10.

Q: Can SQL data types be assigned to objects other than columns?

A: Every SQL data value, or literal, belongs to a data type. For example, data types can be assigned to the parameters of externally invoked procedures. Externally invoked procedures are procedures that are contained within an SQL client module. A procedure is an SQL statement (or series of statements) that can be called from another element in the code, which in the case of externally invoked procedures is external code. A parameter, which is the literal that belongs to a data type, is a value that is passed to the procedure and used as the procedure is processed. The parameter acts as a placeholder for that value. SQL client modules are discussed in Module 17.

NOTE

The Boolean data type is based on a specific type of computer logic known as Boolean, which evaluates conditions of true or false in a given operation or expression. Many programming languages support Boolean logic through the use of logical operators such as AND, OR, and NOT, for example, "ItemA IS NOT FALSE" or "ItemA AND ItemB OR ItemC IS TRUE." In SQL, Boolean logic is implemented through the use of comparison operators to compare values within various data types. I discuss these operators in Module 9.

Using SQL Data Types

Now that you've taken a look at the various predefined data types, let's look at a CREATE TABLE statement that defines a table with columns that use different data types. In the following example, the statement is creating a table named Artists that includes four columns:

```
CREATE TABLE Artists
( ArtistID INT,
ArtistFullName VARCHAR (60),
ArtistDOB DATE,
PosterInStock BOOLEAN ) ;
```

As you can see, the ArtistID column is a numeric data type, the ArtistFullName column a string data type, the ArtistDOB column is a datetime data type, and the PosterInStock is a Boolean data type. Figure 3-2 illustrates what this table might look like.

Progress Check

1. What are the five types of predefined data types?

2. What are the differences between character string data types and bit string data types?

3. What does the precision of a numeric data type refer to?

---

1. String, numeric, datetime, interval, and Boolean

2. Character strings permit values that are drawn from a specific character set, either the default set or a set defined at the time that the column is being defined. Bit strings permit values that are based on data bits (binary digits), rather than character sets or collations, which means that these data types allow only values of 0 or 1.

3. The precision refers to the number of digits (within a specific numeric value) that can be stored.

ArtistID: INT	ArtistFullName: VARCHAR (60)	ArtistDOB: DATE	PosterInStock: BOOLEAN
10001	Jennifer Warnes	1947-03-03	False
10002	Joni Mitchell	1943-11-07	Unknown
10005	Bing Crosby	1904-05-02	True
10006	Patsy Cline	1932-09-08	True
10008	Placido Domingo	1941-01-21	False
10009	Luciano Pavarotti	1935-10-12	Unknown

Figure 3-2 The Artists table defined with different data types

CRITICAL SKILL
3.3 Create User-Defined Types

In Module 1, I mention that the SQL:1999 standard has incorporated some of the principles of object-oriented programming (OOP) into its language. One example of this is the user-defined type, sometimes referred to as the user-defined data type. The user-defined type is a type of data type (stored as a schema object) that is in part defined by the programmer and in part based on one or more data types. SQL supports two types of user-defined types:

- **Structured types**   These types are made up of one or more attributes that are each based on another data type, including predefined types, constructed types, and other structured types. In addition to being associated with a data type, each attribute can include a default clause and can specify a collation. A structured type can include methods in its definition. A *method* is a type of function that's associated with a user-defined type. A *function* is a named operation that performs predefined tasks that you can't normally perform by using SQL statements alone. It is a type of routine that takes input parameters and returns values based on those parameters.

- **Distinct types**   These types are simply based on predefined data types and whatever parameters are defined for that data type, if parameters are required or desired.

SQL provides a CREATE TYPE statement for defining user-defined types. However, the language used for creating a user-defined type can vary from product to product. In addition, the features that are supported in a user-defined type also vary widely. For example,

SQL Server 2000 does not support a CREATE TYPE statement. Instead you use a built-in system stored procedure and supply the necessary parameters to create the type, and the type you're creating is basically a distinct type.

Despite the differences with and limitations of product implementations, I want to at least provide you with an example of how the CREATE TYPE statement is used to create a distinct type. In the following statement, I create a user-defined type that is based on the NUMERIC data type:

```
CREATE TYPE Salary AS NUMERIC (8,2)
FINAL ;
```

Once you've created the type, you can use it in a column definition as you would a predefined data type:

```
CREATE TABLE Employees
( EmployeeID INTEGER, EmployeeSalary SALARY ) ;
```

Any values you add to the EmployeeSalary column would have to conform to the specifications of the NUMERIC data type, which has a precision of 8 and a scale of 2. As a result, a value could be anything from 0 to 999999.99. The nice part about this is that you can then use the SALARY user-defined type in any other tables that require similar values.

CRITICAL SKILL
3.4 Specify Column Default Values

Another valuable feature that SQL supports is the ability to specify a default value for a column when you're using the CREATE TABLE statement to create a table. The syntax for a simple column definition with a default value looks like this:

<column name> <data type> DEFAULT <default value>

The <column name> and <data type> placeholders, which you should now be familiar with, are followed by the DEFAULT keyword. After the DEFAULT keyword, you must specify a value for the <default value> placeholder. This value can be a literal, which is an SQL data value (such as *To be determined*); a datetime value function, which is a function that allows you to perform operations related to dates and times (discussed in Module 10); or a session-related user function, which is a function that returns user-related information (discussed in Module 10).

Whichever type of value you use for the <default value> placeholder, it must conform to the data requirements of the data type specified in the column definition. For example, if you define a column with an INT data type or a CHAR (4) data type, you cannot specify a default value of *Unknown*. In the first case, INT requires a numeric value, and in the second case, CHAR (4) requires that the value contain no more than four characters.

In the following example, I use the CREATE TABLE statement to define a table named Artists, which contains three columns:

```
CREATE TABLE Artists
( ArtistID INT,
ArtistName VARCHAR (60),
PlaceOfBirth VARCHAR (60) DEFAULT 'Unknown' ) ;
```

Notice that the PlaceOfBirth column includes the default value Unknown. The value is acceptable because it conforms to the data requirements of the VARCHAR (60) data type. Also notice that the default value is enclosed in single quotes. You must use single quotes for character string values. Figure 3-3 illustrates what this table might look like if it were populated with rows of data.

If you were to insert any new rows into this table and you didn't know the artist's place of birth, the system would automatically insert a value of Unknown.

Progress Check

1. What are the differences between a structured user-defined type and a distinct user-defined type?

2. You are creating an SQL table named CDLabels that includes one column named CompanyName. The column requires a VARCHAR (60) data type and a default value of *Independent.* How should you write the SQL statement?

---

1. Structured types are made up of one or more attributes that can each be based on another data type, including predefined types, constructed types, and other structured types. Distinct types are based on predefined data types and whatever parameters are defined for that data type, if parameters are required or desired.

2. You should use the following statement:

```
CREATE TABLE CDLabels
( CompanyName VARCHAR (60) DEFAULT 'Independent' ) ;
```

ArtistID: INT	ArtistFullName: VARCHAR (60)	PlaceOfBirth: VARCHAR (60)
10001	Jennifer Warnes	Unknown
10002	Joni Mitchell	Fort MacLeod, Alberta, Canada
10005	Bing Crosby	Tacoma, Washington, United States
10006	Patsy Cline	Winchester, Virginia, United States
10008	Placido Domingo	Madrid, Spain
10009	Luciano Pavarotti	Unknown

Figure 3-3 A default value of Unknown for the PlaceOfBirth column

Project 3-1 Creating SQL Tables

Prj03.txt   You've probably noticed that I've been using CD-related data for the examples I've
shown you so far. We will be carrying this theme throughout the book as we begin
to build a database that tracks the CD inventory of a small business. In this project, you will
create three tables that are related to the Inventory database, which you created in Module 2,
Project 2-1. Before you begin, take a look at a simple data model (Figure 3-4) that shows the
three tables you'll be creating. Each table is represented by a rectangle, with the name of the
table above the rectangle and the name of the columns, along with their data types, listed
within the rectangle.

   We will be using the data model throughout the book—as it evolves into a more complex
structure—to define the objects in our database. You can also download the Prj03.txt file,
which contains the SQL statements used in this project.

Step by Step

1. Open the client application for your RDBMS and connect to the Inventory database.
   You will be creating all objects within that database. (If your RDBMS doesn't support
   the creation of a database and instead you created the CDInventory schema, you should
   create all your objects within that schema.)

Figure 3-4 Simple data model of the Inventory database

Project
3-1

Creating SQL Tables

(continued)

2. The first table that you will create is the CompactDiscs table. Notice that it includes three columns, two of which have an INT data type and one that has a VARCHAR (60) data type. This table will hold data about the compact discs in your inventory. The CompactDiscID column will contain numbers that uniquely identify each CD. The CDTitle column will contain the actual names of the CDs. The LabelID column will contain numbers that identify the companies that published the CDs. Enter the following SQL statement into your client application's input window:

```
CREATE TABLE CompactDiscs
( CompactDiscID INT, CDTitle VARCHAR (60), LabelID INT ) ;
```

3. Verify that you have entered the correct information and execute the statement. You should receive a message confirming that the statement has been successfully executed.

4. The next table that you will create is the CDLabels table. The table includes the LabelID column, which uniquely identifies each company that publishes the CDs, and the CompanyName column, which lists the actual names of the companies. Enter and execute the following code:

```
CREATE TABLE CDLabels
( LabelID INT, CompanyName VARCHAR (60) ) ;
```

5. The final table that you will create is the MusicTypes table. The table includes the TypeID column, which uniquely identifies each category of music, and the TypeName column, which lists the actual names of the categories of music (for example, Blues or Jazz). Enter and execute the following code:

```
CREATE TABLE MusicTypes
( TypeID INT, TypeName VARCHAR (20) ) ;
```

6. Close the client application.

Project Summary

Your database should now contain three new tables. These tables will serve as a foundation for other projects in the book. As you progress through these projects, you will modify these tables, create additional tables, insert data into the tables, and then query and manipulate that data. By the time you've completed all the projects, you'll have created and populated a small database that stores data about an inventory of compact discs.

CRITICAL SKILL
3.5 Alter SQL Tables

Taking what you've learned about creating tables, you can use the ALTER TABLE statement to modify the definitions of base tables stored in your database (as schema objects). At its most basic, the syntax for the ALTER TABLE statement looks like this:

```
ALTER TABLE <table name>
  ADD [COLUMN] <column definition>
| ALTER [COLUMN] <column name>
    { SET DEFAULT <default value> | DROP DEFAULT }
| DROP [COLUMN] <column name> { CASCADE | RESTRICT }
```

The statement allows you to take three different actions: adding columns, altering columns, or dropping columns.

NOTE

The ALTER TABLE statement also allows you to add or drop table constraints. A table constraint is a rule that restricts what data can be entered into the table. The table constraint is part of the table definition, but is not part of any specific column definitions. Constraints are discussed in detail in Module 4.

The <column definition> placeholder in the ADD [COLUMN] clause is similar to the column definition section of the CREATE TABLE statement. You provide a column name and a data type or domain. You also have the option of adding a default clause, a column constraint, or a collation. For example, you can use the following statement to alter the Artists table so that it includes a DateOfBirth column:

```
ALTER TABLE Artists
ADD COLUMN ArtistDOB DATE ;
```

Unlike the ADD [COLUMN] clause, the ALTER [COLUMN] clause is limited to two actions: setting a default or deleting the default. For example, suppose your Artists table includes a PlaceOfBirth column, but no default has been defined for that column. You can add a default by using the following statement:

```
ALTER TABLE Artists
ALTER COLUMN PlaceOfBirth SET DEFAULT 'Unknown' ;
```

You can also drop the default by using the following statement:

```
ALTER TABLE Artists
ALTER COLUMN PlaceOfBirth DROP DEFAULT ;
```

The final clause in the syntax—DROP [COLUMN]—provides two options for deleting a column and its data from a table: the CASCADE keyword and the RESTRICT keyword. You might remember these keywords from the discussion about the DROP SCHEMA statement in Module 2. If the CASCADE option is specified, the column and the data within the column are deleted regardless of whether other objects reference the column. Any views, constraints, routines, or triggers that reference the column are also dropped. If the RESTRICT option is used, the column is deleted only if no views, constraints, routines, or triggers reference the column. For example, the following statement deletes the PlaceOfBirth column and the data stored in the column, regardless of dependencies:

```
ALTER TABLE Artists
DROP COLUMN PlaceOfBirth CASCADE ;
```

In general, the ALTER TABLE statement is a handy one to know because invariably, table definitions are going to change, and so too are the types of data stored in those tables. However, this statement, like most SQL statements, can vary widely from implementation to implementation, in terms of how the specifics of the statement are applied. As always, be sure to check your product documentation.

CRITICAL SKILL

3.6 Delete SQL Tables

As you might imagine, the process of deleting a table and its stored data is very straightforward. The following syntax shows you how easy this process is:

DROP TABLE <table name>{ CASCADE | RESTRICT }

The only real decision you need to make when deleting the table is whether to choose the CASCADE option or the RESTRICT option. As in previous syntax examples, the two options determine whether you should delete the table and its data if the table is being referenced by other objects. If CASCADE is used, the table and its data are deleted, along with any views, constraints, routines, or triggers that reference the table. If RESTRICT is used, the table is deleted only if no such dependencies exist. For example, the following statement deletes the Artists table and the data stored in the column, regardless of dependencies:

```
DROP TABLE Artists CASCADE ;
```

Ask the Expert

Q: What if you want to delete the data in a table, but not the table definition itself?

A: Rather than using the DROP TABLE statement, you would use the DELETE statement. The DELETE statement deletes all rows from a table or deletes only specific rows, as defined within the statement. This is not the same as the DROP TABLE statement, which removes the table definition and the data. I discuss the DELETE statement in more detail in Module 8.

Q: You state that, when a default value is defined for a column, the value is automatically inserted into the column when you add a row to the table but don't specify a value for that particular column. What happens if your column definition doesn't include a default and you try to insert that row?

A: The action that is taken depends on whether null values are permitted within the column. A null value means that the value is not known. This is not the same as a zero, blank, or default. If a null value is present, then the data is not available. By default, all columns permit null values, although you can override the default (discussed in Module 4). If you try to insert a row without specifying a specific value, a null value will be inserted into that column if the column permits null values. If the column does not permit null values, you will not be able to insert a row without defining that specific value.

Q: I've often heard the term *indexes* discussed in relation to creating SQL tables. How do you create indexes?

A: Oddly enough, the SQL:1999 standard does not support the creation and maintenance of indexes, nor does it define what an index is or mention them in any way. For those of you not familiar with them, an *index* is a set of pointers (in a subsidiary table) that correspond to rows in a table. Indexes speed up queries and improve performance, making data access much more efficient. As a result, nearly every RDBMS supports some form of indexing, and indeed they are an important part of that product. However, the method used to implement indexing varies greatly, so each product provides its own system to set up and maintain their indexes. For example, the CREATE INDEX statement is available in some products; however, the syntax for the statement can vary. As always, be sure to review the product documentation.

Project 3-2 Altering and Deleting SQL Tables

Prj03.txt   Throughout the lifecycle of nearly any database, the likelihood that business requirements will change and the database will have to be altered is almost a foregone conclusion. As a result, you will no doubt run into situations in which table definitions have to be modified or they have to be deleted. In this project, you will create a table, drop that table, re-create it, and then change it by deleting a column. By the time you are finished, you will have added one more table to the Inventory database and will be making use of that table in later projects. You can download the Prj03.txt file, which contains the SQL statements used in this project.

Step by Step

1. Open the client application for your RDBMS and connect to the Inventory database (or CDInventory schema).

2. You will create a table named CompactDiscTypes. The table will include the CompactDiscID column and the TypeID column. Both columns will be assigned an INT data type. Enter and execute the following code:

```
CREATE TABLE CompactDiscTypes
( CompactDiscID INT, TypeID INT ) ;
```

3. You will now delete the table from the database. Enter and execute the following code:

```
DROP TABLE CompactDiscTypes CASCADE ;
```

4. You will now re-create the table you created in step 2, only this time you'll include a third column named CDTitle with a data type of VARCHAR (60). Enter and execute the following code:

```
CREATE TABLE CompactDiscTypes
( CompactDiscID INT, CDTitle VARCHAR (60), TypeID INT ) ;
```

5. Your next step will be to delete the CDTitle column. Enter and execute the following code:

```
ALTER TABLE CompactDiscTypes
DROP COLUMN CDTitle CASCADE ;
```

6. The CompactDiscTypes table should now contain only the CompactDiscID column and the TypeID column. Close the client application.

Project Summary

The Inventory database should now contain four tables: CompactDiscs, CDLabels, MusicTypes, and CompactDiscTypes. The CompactDiscTypes table, which you just created, contains two columns, CompactDiscID and TypeID, both of which are defined with the INT data type. In subsequent projects, you will continue to build on this database by adding new tables and modifying existing ones.

Module 3 Mastery Check

1. Which kinds of base tables can you create by using a CREATE TABLE statement?

   A. Persistent base tables

   B. Global temporary base tables

   C. Created local temporary tables

   D. Declared local temporary tables

2. What is the primary difference between a global temporary table and a created local temporary table?

3. You're creating a table named Agents. The table includes the AgentID column, which has an INT data type, and the AgentName column, which has a CHAR (60) data type. What SQL statement should you use?

4. What are the three types of data types that SQL supports?

5. What are the four types of string data types?

6. A(n) _____ data type permits values that are based on data bits, rather than character sets or collations. This type of data type allows only values of 0 and 1.

7. What are the precision and the scale of the number 5293.472?

8. What are the differences between exact numeric data types and approximate numeric data types?

9. Which data types are exact numeric data types?

   A. DOUBLE PRECISION

   B. DECIMAL

   C. REAL

   D. SMALLINT

10. A(n) _____ data type specifies the year, month, and day values of a date.

11. What are the two types of interval data types that SQL supports?

12. Which data type should you use to support a true/false construct that can be used for comparing values?

13. You are creating a distinct user-defined type named City. The user type is based on the CHAR (40) data type. Which SQL statement should you use?

14. You're creating a table named Customers. The table includes the CustomerName column and the CustomerCity column. Both columns have a VARCHAR (60) data type. The CustomerCity column also has a default value of *Seattle*. Which SQL statement should you use?

15. Which SQL statement should you use to delete a column from an existing table?

16. Which SQL statement should you use to delete a table definition and all its SQL data from a database?

17. Your database includes a table named OperaSingers. You want to add a column named Nationality to the table. The column should have a VARCHAR (40) data type. What SQL statement should you use?

18. You want to delete the table definition for the OperaSingers table from your database. You also want to delete all the data and any dependencies on the table. What SQL statement should you use?

Module 4

Enforcing Data Integrity

An SQL database must do more than just store data. It must ensure that the data it does store is correct. If data is inaccurate or inconsistent, the integrity of that data may have been compromised, bringing into question the reliability of the database itself. In order to ensure the integrity of the data, SQL provides a number of *integrity constraints,* rules that are applied to base tables that constrain the values that can be placed into those tables. You can apply constraints to individual columns, to individual tables, or to multiple tables. In this module, I discuss each type of constraint and explain how you can apply them to your SQL database.

4.1 Understand Integrity Constraints

SQL integrity constraints, which are usually referred to simply as constraints, can be divided into three categories:

- **Table-related constraints**   A type of constraint that is defined within a table definition. The constraint can be defined as part of the column definition or as an element in the table definition. Constraints defined at the table level can apply to one or more columns.

- **Assertions**   A type of constraint that is defined within an assertion definition (separate from the table definition). An assertion can be related to one or more tables.

- **Domain constraints**   A type of constraint that is defined within a domain definition (separate from the table definition). A domain constraint is associated with any column that is defined within the specific domain.

Of these three categories of constraints, table-related constraints are the most common and include the greatest number of constraint options. Table-related constraints can be divided into two subcategories: table constraints and column constraints. The constraints in both these subcategories are defined in the table definition. A column constraint is included with the column definition, and a table constraint is included as a table element, similar to the way columns are defined as table elements. (Module 3 discusses table elements and column definitions.) Both column constraints and table constraints support a number of different types of constraints. This is not the case for assertions and domain constraints, which are limited to only one type of constraint. Figure 4-1 provides an overview of the types of constraints that can be created.

At the top of the illustration, you can see the three categories of constraints. Beneath the Table-Related Constraints category are the Column Constraints subcategory and the Table Constraints subcategory, each of which contains specific types of constraints. For example, table constraints can include unique (UNIQUE constraints and PRIMARY KEY constraints),

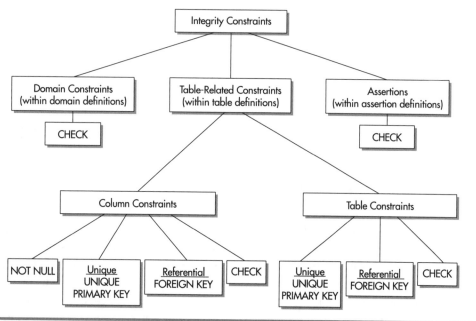

Figure 4-1 Types of SQL integrity constraints

referential (FOREIGN KEY constraints), and CHECK constraints, while column constraints can include the NOT NULL constraint as well as unique, referential, and CHECK constraints. However, domains and assertions support only CHECK constraints.

NOTE

In some places, the SQL:1999 standard uses the term *table constraint* to refer to both types of table-related constraints. I use the term *table-related* to avoid confusion.

As Figure 4-1 shows, there are five different types of constraints: NOT NULL, UNIQUE, PRIMARY KEY, FOREIGN KEY, and CHECK. In SQL, UNIQUE constraints and PRIMARY KEY constraints are both considered unique constraints, and FOREIGN KEY constraints are considered referential constraints. The rest of the module is devoted to explaining what each of these constraints mean and how to apply them.

Progress Check

1. What are the three categories of integrity constraints?

2. What are the differences between a column constraint and a table constraint?

3. What types of constraints can you include in a column definition?

CRITICAL SKILL
4.2 # Use NOT NULL Constraints

In Module 3, I told you that *null* signifies that a value is undefined or not known. This is not the same as a zero, a blank, or a default value. Instead, it indicates that a data value is absent. You can think of a null value as being a flag. (A *flag* is a character, number, or bit that indicates a certain fact about a column. The flag serves as a marker that designates a particular condition or existence of something.) In the case of null, if no value is provided for a column, the flag is set, indicating that the value is unknown, or null. Every column has a *nullability* characteristic that indicates whether the column will accept null values. By default, all columns accept null values. However, you can override the default nullability characteristic by using a NOT NULL constraint, which indicates that the column will *not* accept null values.

NOTE

Some RDBMSs allow you to change the default nullability of any new column you create. In addition, some systems support a NULL constraint, which you can use to designate that a column will accept null values.

The NOT NULL constraint can be used as a column constraint only. It is not supported for table constraints, assertions, or domain constraints. Implementing a NOT NULL constraint is a very straightforward process. Simply use the following syntax when creating a column definition:

<column name> { <data type> | <domain> } NOT NULL

---

1. Table-related constraints (sometimes referred to simply as table constraints), assertions, and domain constraints

2. Both types of constraints are defined in the table definition. A column constraint is included with the column definition, and a table constraint is included as a table element, similar to the way columns are defined as table elements.

3. NOT NULL, UNIQUE, PRIMARY KEY, FOREIGN KEY, and CHECK

ArtistID: INT	ArtistFullName: VARCHAR (60)	PlaceOfBirth VARCHAR (60)
10001	Jennifer Warnes	NULL
10002	Joni Mitchell	Fort MacLeod, Alberta, Canada
10005	Bing Crosby	Tacoma, Washington, United States
10006	Patsy Cline	Winchester, Virginia, United States
10008	Placido Domingo	Madrid, Spain
10009	Luciano Pavarotti	NULL

Figure 4-2 Null values appearing in the PlaceOfBirth column of the CompactDiscArtists table

For example, suppose you want to create a table named CompactDiscArtists that requires three columns: ArtistID, ArtistFullName, and PlaceOfBirth. You want to make sure that any new rows that are added to the table include a value for the ArtistID column and a value for the ArtistFullName column. To do this, you add a NOT NULL constraint to both column definitions, as shown in the following SQL statement:

```
CREATE TABLE CompactDiscArtists
( ArtistID INT NOT NULL,
ArtistFullName VARCHAR (60) NOT NULL,
PlaceOfBirth VARCHAR (60) ) ;
```

Notice that the PlaceOfBirth column does not include a NOT NULL constraint. As a result, if a value isn't supplied for this column (when a row is inserted), a null value will be inserted. (The null flag will be set.) Figure 4-2 shows what the table might look like if rows were inserted that contained no value for the PlaceOfBirth column.

As you can see, the ArtistID and ArtistFullName columns do not—and cannot—contain null values. The PlaceOfBirth column, on the other hand, contains two null values.

CRITICAL SKILL
4.3 Add UNIQUE Constraints

If you refer back to Figure 4-1, you'll see that both column constraints and table constraints support unique constraints. You'll also see that that there are two types of unique constraints: UNIQUE and PRIMARY KEY. In this section, I focus on the UNIQUE constraint. The PRIMARY KEY constraint is discussed in the "Add PRIMARY KEY Constraints" section later in this module.

The UNIQUE constraint allows you to require that a column or set of columns contains unique values only. For example, take a look at Figure 4-3, which shows the CDInventory table. The table contains three columns: Artist, CDName, and Copyright.

You might decide that you want the values in the CDName column to be unique so that no two CD names can be alike. If you applied a UNIQUE constraint to the column, you would not be able to insert a row that contained a CDName value that already existed in the table. Now suppose that you realize that making the CDName values unique is not a good idea because it is possible for more than one CD to share the same name. You decide to take another approach and use a UNIQUE constraint on the Artist and CDName columns. That way, no Artist/CDName pair can be repeated. You can repeat an Artist value or a CDName value, but you cannot repeat a value pair. For example, the table already contains a row with an ArtistID value of Joni Mitchell and a CDName value of Blue. If a UNIQUE constraint had been applied to these two columns, you could not add another row that contained *both* of these values.

Now that you have a basic understanding of how UNIQUE constraints are applied, let's take a look at the syntax that you use to create them. Remember, I said that you can create a UNIQUE constraint that is either a column constraint or a table constraint. To create a column constraint, add it as part of the column definition, as shown in the following syntax:

<column name> { <data type> | <domain> } UNIQUE

If you want to add a unique constraint as a table constraint, you must add it as a table element in the table definition, as shown in the following syntax:

[CONSTRAINT <constraint name>]
UNIQUE (<column name> [{, <column name> } . . .])

Artist: VARCHAR (40)	CDName: VARCHAR (60)	Copyright: INT
Jennifer Warnes	Famous Blue Raincoat	1991
Joni Mitchell	Blue	1971
William Ackerman	Past Light	1983
Kitaro	Kojiki	1990
Bing Crosby	That Christmas Feeling	1993
Patsy Cline	Patsy Cline: 12 Greatest Hits	1988

Figure 4-3 The CDInventory table with the Artist, CDName, and Copyright columns

As you can see, applying a UNIQUE constraint as a column constraint is a little simpler than applying it as a table constraint. However, if you apply the constraint at the column level, you can apply it to only one column. Regardless of whether you use column constraints or table constraints, you can define as many UNIQUE constraints as necessary in a single table definition.

Now let's return to the table in Figure 4-3 and use it to create code examples for applying UNIQUE constraints. In the first example, I apply a UNIQUE constraint to the CDName column:

```
CREATE TABLE CDInventory
( Artist VARCHAR (40), CDName VARCHAR (60) UNIQUE, Copyright INT ) ;
```

I can also apply UNIQUE constraints to other columns, but that would not have the same effect as combining two columns into one table constraint, as shown in the following example:

```
CREATE TABLE CDInventory
( Artist VARCHAR (40), CDName VARCHAR (60), Copyright INT,
CONSTRAINT un_ArtistCD UNIQUE ( Artist, CDName ) ) ;
```

The Artist column and CDName column must now contain unique value pairs in order for a row to be added to the CDInventory table.

Until now, I have told you that a UNIQUE constraint prevents duplicate values from being entered into a column or columns defined with that constraint. However, there is one exception to this—the null value. A UNIQUE constraint permits multiple null values in a column. As with other columns, null values are permitted by default. You can, however, override the default by using the NOT NULL constraint in conjunction with the UNIQUE constraint. For example, you can add NOT NULL to the CDName column definition:

```
CREATE TABLE CDInventory
( Artist VARCHAR (40), CDName VARCHAR (60) NOT NULL UNIQUE, Copyright INT ) ;
```

You can also add NOT NULL to a column definition that's referenced by a table constraint:

```
CREATE TABLE CDInventory
( Artist VARCHAR (40), CDName VARCHAR (60) NOT NULL, Copyright INT,
CONSTRAINT un_ArtistCD UNIQUE (CDName) ) ;
```

In each case, both the NOT NULL constraint and the UNIQUE constraint are applied to the CDName column, which means the CDName values must be unique and no null values are allowed.

Progress Check

1. What type of constraint should you use if you want to prevent null values from being inserted into a column?

2. What are the two types of unique constraints?

3. You're defining a UNIQUE constraint named CDArtistUnique on the ArtistName column and the CDName column. What SQL code should you use for the constraint definition?

CRITICAL SKILL
4.4 # Add PRIMARY KEY Constraints

As I mentioned in the "Add UNIQUE Constraints" section, a PRIMARY KEY constraint, like the UNIQUE constraint, is a type of SQL unique constraint. Both types of constraints permit only unique values in the specified columns, both types can be applied to one or more columns, and both types can be defined as either column constraints or table constraints. However, PRIMARY KEY constraints have two restrictions that apply only to them:

- A column that is defined with a PRIMARY KEY constraint cannot contain null values. Even if you do not specify NOT NULL in the column definition, the column still must contain a data value.

- Only one PRIMARY KEY constraint can be defined for each column.

The reason for these restrictions is the role that a primary key plays in a table. As you might recall from Module 1, each row in a table must be unique. This means that at least one column or a combination of columns must contain unique values. These columns are known as a candidate key. A *candidate key* is a set of one or more columns that uniquely identify each row. For example, in Figure 4-4, the candidate key in the CDArtists table is the ArtistID column. Each value in the column must be unique. That way, even if the ArtistName values and Agency values are duplicated, the row is still unique because the ArtistID value is always unique.

A candidate key can be defined with a UNIQUE constraint or a PRIMARY KEY constraint. However, each table should include a primary key even if no UNIQUE constraints are defined.

---

1. NOT NULL
2. UNIQUE and PRIMARY KEY
3. You should use the following code:

```
CONSTRAINT CDArtistUnique UNIQUE ( ArtistName, CDName )
```

Candidate Key

ArtistID: INT	ArtistName: VARCHAR (60)	Agency: INT
10001	Jennifer Warnes	2305
10002	Joni Mitchell	2306
10003	William Ackerman	2306
10004	Kitaro	2345
10005	Bing Crosby	2367
10006	Patsy Cline	2049
10007	Jose Carreras	2876
10008	Placido Domingo	2305
10009	Luciano Pavarotti	2345

Figure 4-4 The candidate key in the CDArtists table

Because a primary key cannot accept null values, it acts as the definitive measure by which a row's uniqueness can be ensured. Primary keys are also useful when one table references another through the use of foreign keys. (See the "Add FOREIGN KEY Constraints" section later in this module.) To define the primary key, you must use the PRIMARY KEY constraint to specify which column or columns will serve as the table's primary key. The process of defining a PRIMARY KEY constraint is very similar to that of defining a UNIQUE constraint. If you want to add a PRIMARY KEY constraint to a column definition, use the following syntax:

```
<column name> { <data type> | <domain> } PRIMARY KEY
```

If you want to add a PRIMARY KEY constraint as a table constraint, you must add it as a table element in the table definition, as shown in the following syntax:

```
[ CONSTRAINT <constraint name> ]
PRIMARY KEY ( <column name> [ {, <column name> } ... ] )
```

As with the UNIQUE constraint, you can use a column constraint to define a primary key if you're including only one column in the definition. For example, if you were to define a PRIMARY KEY constraint for the table shown in Figure 4-4, you would use the following SQL statement:

```
CREATE TABLE CDArtists
( ArtistID INT PRIMARY KEY, ArtistName VARCHAR (60), Agency INT ) ;
```

If you want to apply the constraint to multiple columns—or you simply want to keep it as a separate definition—then you must use a table constraint:

```
CREATE TABLE CDArtists
( ArtistID INT, ArtistName VARCHAR (60), Agency INT,
CONSTRAINT pk_ArtistID PRIMARY KEY ( ArtistID, ArtistName ) ) ;
```

This method creates a primary key on the ArtistID column and the ArtistName column, so no two value pairs can be the same, although duplicates can exist within the individual column.

You might find that you want to define both PRIMARY KEY and UNIQUE constraints on a table. To do so, you simply define the constraints as you normally would. For example, the following SQL statement defines a PRIMARY KEY constraint on the ArtistID column and a UNIQUE constraint on the ArtistName column:

```
CREATE TABLE CDArtists
( ArtistID INT PRIMARY KEY, ArtistName VARCHAR (60), Agency INT,
CONSTRAINT un_ArtistName UNIQUE (ArtistName) ) ;
```

You would achieve the same results with the following code:

```
CREATE TABLE CDArtists
( ArtistID INT, ArtistName VARCHAR (60) UNIQUE, Agency INT,
CONSTRAINT pk_ArtistID PRIMARY KEY (ArtistID) ) ;
```

NOTE

I used a UNIQUE constraint in these SQL statements only as a way to demonstrate how the constraint can be used in a table with a primary key. Most likely, you would not want to use a UNIQUE constraint for the ArtistName column because it is possible for two artists to share the same name. (For example, two different blues artists, both of whom lived in the earlier part of the last century, went by the name of Sonny Boy Williamson.)

Ask the Expert

Q: Can the columns in a table belong to both a UNIQUE constraint and a PRIMARY KEY constraint?

A: Yes, as long as they're not the exact same columns. For example, suppose you have a table that includes three columns: ArtistID, ArtistName, and PlaceOfBirth. You can define a PRIMARY KEY constraint that includes the ArtistID and ArtistName columns, which would ensure unique value pairs in those two columns, but values within the individual columns could still be duplicated. However, you can then define a UNIQUE constraint that includes only the ArtistName column to ensure that those values are unique as well. (This probably isn't the best design, but it illustrates my point.) You can also create a UNIQUE constraint that includes the ArtistName and PlaceOfBirth columns to ensure unique value pairs in those two columns. However, the only thing you can't do is create a UNIQUE constraint that includes the ArtistID and ArtistName columns because they're already included in the PRIMARY KEY constraint.

Q: You state that a column that is included in a PRIMARY KEY constraint will not accept null values. What happens if that column is configured with a NOT NULL constraint as well?

A: Nothing different happens. The table is still created in the same way. A column definition that includes PRIMARY KEY is saying the same thing as a column definition that includes NOT NULL PRIMARY KEY. In fact, prior to SQL-92, the NOT NULL keywords were required on all columns included in a PRIMARY KEY constraint. The same was true for UNIQUE constraints. It wasn't until SQL-92 that null values were permitted in a UNIQUE constraint, which clearly set them apart from PRIMARY KEY constraints.

CRITICAL SKILL

4.5 Add FOREIGN KEY Constraints

Up to this point, the types of constraints that I've discussed have had to do primarily with ensuring the integrity of data within a table. The NOT NULL constraint prevents the use of null values within a column, and the UNIQUE and PRIMARY KEY constraints ensure the uniqueness of values within a column or set of columns. However, the FOREIGN KEY constraint is different in that it is concerned with how data in one table relates to data in another table, which is why it is known as a *referential constraint*—it references another table.

You might recall from Module 1 that tables in a relational database are linked together in a meaningful way in order to ensure the integrity of the data. This association between tables forms a relationship that provides *referential integrity* between tables. Referential integrity prevents the manipulation of data in one table from adversely affecting data in another table. Let's take a look at an example that illustrates this point. Figure 4-5 shows two tables (CDTitles and CDPublishers) that are each defined with a primary key. The CDTitleID column in the CDTitles table is configured with a PRIMARY KEY constraint, as is the PublisherID column in the CDPublishers table. Both these columns are shaded in the illustration.

Notice that the CDTitles table contains a column named PublisherID. This column includes values from the PublisherID column of the CDPublishers table. In fact, the PublisherID values in the CDTitles table should include only values that come from the PublisherID column in the CDPublishers table. You should not be able to insert a row into CDTitles if the PublisherID value is not listed in the CDPublishers table. At the same time, if you alter or delete a PublisherID value in the CDPublishers table, you should be able to predict the outcome of your action if those same values exist in the CDTitles table. These results can be achieved by using a FOREIGN KEY constraint. A FOREIGN KEY constraint enforces referential integrity between two tables by ensuring that no action is taken on either table that affects the data protected by the constraint.

In the tables shown in Figure 4-5, the FOREIGN KEY constraint must be configured on the PublisherID column of the CDTitles table. The FOREIGN KEY constraint restricts the values in that column to the values of a candidate key (usually the primary key) in the related table. Only valid data values are permitted in the FOREIGN KEY column or columns.

CDTitles

CDTitleID: INT	CDTitle: VARCHAR (60)	PublisherID: INT
11001	Famous Blue Raincoat	5422
11002	Blue	5402
11003	Past Light	5412
11004	Kojiki	5409
11005	That Christmas Feeling	5403
11006	Patsy Cline: 12 Greatest Hits	5403

CDPublishers

PublisherID: INT	CompanyName: VARCHAR (60)
5403	MCA Records
5402	Reprise Records
5409	Geffen
5412	Windham Hill Records
5422	Private Music

Figure 4-5 The relationship between the CDTitles table and the CDPublishers table

NOTE

The table that contains the foreign key is the *referencing table*. The table that is being referenced by the foreign key is the *referenced table*. Likewise, the column or columns that make up the foreign key in the referencing table are referred to as the *referencing columns*. The columns being referenced by the foreign key are the *referenced columns*.

When creating a FOREIGN KEY constraint, you must follow several guidelines:

- The referenced columns must be a candidate key in the referenced table. The primary key is most commonly used for the referenced columns.

- A FOREIGN KEY constraint can be created as a table constraint or column constraint. If you create the foreign key as a column constraint, you can include only one column. If you create the foreign key as a table constraint, you can include one or more columns.

- The foreign key in the referencing table must include the same number of columns that are being referenced, and the referencing columns must each be configured with the same data types as their referenced counterparts. However, the referencing columns do not have to have the same name as the referenced columns.

- If you don't specify the referenced columns when you define a FOREIGN KEY constraint, then the columns defined in the primary key of the referenced table are used as the referenced columns.

These guidelines will become clearer as I explain how to implement a foreign key. First, let's take a look at the basic syntax used to create that constraint. If you want to add a FOREIGN KEY constraint as a column constraint, you must add the constraint to a column definition, as shown in the following syntax:

```
<column name> { <data type> | <domain> } [ NOT NULL ]
REFERENCES <referenced table> [ ( <referenced columns> ) ]
[ MATCH { FULL | PARTIAL | SIMPLE } ]
[ <referential triggered action> ]
```

If you want to add a PRIMARY KEY constraint as a table constraint, you must add it as a table element in the table definition, as shown in the following syntax:

```
[ CONSTRAINT <constraint name> ]
FOREIGN KEY ( <referencing column > [ {, <referencing column> } . . . ] )
REFERENCES <referenced table> [ ( <referenced columns> ) ]
[ MATCH { FULL | PARTIAL | SIMPLE } ]
[ <referential triggered action> ]
```

As you can see, a FOREIGN KEY constraint is a bit more complicated than the constraint syntax you've looked at so far. However, creating a basic FOREIGN KEY constraint is a relatively straightforward process. Let's take a look at one first, and then we'll go on to the more complex language elements.

In the following example, I use a CREATE TABLE statement to create the CDTitles table (shown in Figure 4-5) and define a column constraint:

```
CREATE TABLE CDTitles
( CDTitleID INT, CDTitle VARCHAR (60),
PublisherID INT REFERENCES CDPublishers ) ;
```

This statement defines a FOREIGN KEY constraint on the PublisherID column. Notice that, in order to add a column constraint, all you had to do was add the REFERENCES keyword and the name of the referenced table. Also notice that the foreign key contains the same number of columns as the primary key in the referenced table, and the referenced and referencing columns are the same data type. Remember, if you're not referencing the primary key in the referenced table, then you must also include the name of the column or columns, for example, REFERENCES CDPublishers (PublisherID).

NOTE

Before you can create a foreign key on a table, the referenced table must already exist and a UNIQUE or PRIMARY KEY constraint must be defined for that table.

In the next example, I create a foreign key that is a table constraint. Unlike the previous example, I include the name of the referenced column in this constraint definition, even though it isn't necessary:

```
CREATE TABLE CDTitles
( CDTitleID INT, CDTitle VARCHAR (60), PublisherID INT,
CONSTRAINT fk_PublisherID FOREIGN KEY (PublisherID)
REFERENCES CDPublishers (PublisherID) ) ;
```

The last two lines of code are the constraint definition. The name of the constraint, fk_PublisherID, follows the CONSTRAINT keyword. After that, the FOREIGN KEY keywords indicate the type of constraint, which is followed by the referencing column name, PublisherID. This is the name of the column that the constraint is being placed on. If there were more than one column name, they would be separated by commas. The name of the referencing column is then followed by the REFERENCES keyword, which is followed by the name of the referenced table, CDPublishers. The name of the referenced column follows the name of the referenced table.

That's all there is to it. Once the constraint is defined, you would not be able to insert values into the PublisherID column of the CDTitles table unless those values appeared in the primary key of the CDPublishers table. You should note, however, that the values in the foreign key do not have to be unique, as they must be in the CDPublishers primary key. Values in the foreign key can be repeated any number of times, unless the column is limited by a unique constraint.

Before I move on to discussing the other elements of the FOREIGN KEY syntax, let's take a quick look at a foreign key that includes multiple columns. In Figure 4-6, there are two tables: PerformingArtists and ArtistsMusicTypes.

The primary key on the PerformingArtists table is defined on the ArtistFullName and ArtistDOB columns. The following SQL statement creates the ArtistsMusicTypes table, which includes a foreign key made up of the ArtistName and DOB columns:

```
CREATE TABLE ArtistsMusicTypes
( ArtistName VARCHAR (60), DOB DATE, TypeID INT,
CONSTRAINT fk_CDArtists FOREIGN KEY ( ArtistName, DOB )
REFERENCES PerformingArtists (ArtistFullName, ArtistDOB) ) ;
```

PerformingArtists

ArtistFullName: VARCHAR (60)	ArtistDOB: DATE	PlaceOfBirth: VARCHAR (60)	PosterInStock: BOOLEAN
Jennifer Warnes	1947-03-03	Unknown	False
Joni Mitchell	1943-11-07	Fort MacLeod, Alberta, Canada	Unknown
Bing Crosby	1904-05-02	Tacoma, Washington, U.S.A.	True
Patsy Cline	1932-09-08	Winchester, VIrginia, U.S.A.	True
Placido Domingo	1941-01-21	Madrid, Spain	False
Luciano Pavarotti	1935-10-12	Unknown	Unknown

ArtistsMusicTypes

ArtistName: VARCHAR (60)	DOB: DATE	TypeID: INT
Jennifer Warnes	1947-03-03	10
Jennifer Warnes	1947-03-03	06
Joni Mitchell	1943-11-07	10
Joni Mitchell	1943-11-07	05
Joni Mitchell	1943-11-07	12
Bing Crosby	1904-05-02	05
Bing Crosby	1904-05-02	13
Patsy Cline	1932-09-08	02
Patsy Cline	1932-09-08	10
Placido Domingo	1941-01-21	19
Luciano Pavarotti	1935-10-12	19

Figure 4-6 A foreign key made up of multiple columns

Ask the Expert

Q: In Figure 4-6 and in the preceding examples, you created a FOREIGN KEY constraint on the ArtistName and DOB columns in the ArtistsMusicTypes table. What would the primary key be for this table?

A: Remember that a primary key must uniquely identify each row in a table. However, because value pairs in the ArtistName and DOB columns can be repeated (which means that they can be repeated in the individual columns as well), those two columns cannot be used by themselves as a primary key for this table. On the other hand, the TypeID column can have repeating values as well, so that column cannot be used by itself. In addition, you probably wouldn't want to combine the TypeID column with one of the other two columns because it is conceivable that you would have repeating rows (for example, two artists with the same name performing the same types of music, such as the two blues musicians named Sonny Boy Williamson, or two artists with the same date of birth performing the same type of music). As a result, your best solution is to roll all three columns into the primary key. Together, the three columns would uniquely identify each row because it is highly unlikely that anyone would share the same name, date of birth, and type of music (although anything is possible, which is why, ultimately, unique identifiers are the best way to go).

In this statement, there are two referencing columns (ArtistName and DOB) and two referenced columns (ArtistFullName, ArtistDOB). The ArtistName column has the same data type as the ArtistFullName column, and the DOB column has the same data type as the ArtistDOB column. As you can see, the referencing columns do not have to have the same name as their referenced counterparts.

The MATCH Clause

Now that you have an understanding of how to define a basic FOREIGN KEY constraint, let's look at another line of the FOREIGN KEY syntax:

[MATCH { FULL | PARTIAL | SIMPLE }]

You can tell from the brackets that this is an optional clause. The purpose of it is to allow you to decide how to treat null values in the foreign key columns, with regard to permitting values to be inserted into the referencing columns. If the columns do not permit null values, then the MATCH clause does not apply. You have three options that you can use in the MATCH clause:

- If MATCH FULL is specified, all referencing columns must have a null value or none of these columns can have a null value.

- If MATCH PARTIAL is specified, one or more referencing columns can have null values as long as the remaining referencing columns have values that equal their corresponding referenced columns.

- If MATCH SIMPLE is specified and one or more referencing columns have null values, then the remaining referencing columns can have values that are not contained in the corresponding referenced columns. The SIMPLE option is implied if the MATCH clause is not included in the FOREIGN KEY constraint definition.

The best way to illustrate each of these MATCH options is through examples of valid and invalid data that can be inserted in the referencing columns. Going back to our example shown in Figure 4-6, you can see that the foreign key in the ArtistsMusicTypes table is made up of two referencing columns: ArtistName and DOB. Table 4-1 provides examples for data that can and cannot be inserted into the foreign key columns. The examples are based on data in the primary key columns of the PerformingArtists table.

NOTE

You probably wouldn't want to permit null values in your referencing columns in the ArtistsMusicTypes table, particular for the ArtistName column. And if either of these columns were used in the primary key, you would not be able to permit null values. However, in order to demonstrate how the MATCH options work, let's assume that null values are permitted.

MATCH Option	Valid Data Examples	Invalid Data Examples
FULL	Joni Mitchell, 1943-11-07 NULL, NULL	NULL, 1943-11-07 Joni Mitchell, NULL Joni Mitchell, 1802-08-03
PARTIAL	Patsy Cline, 1932-09-08 NULL, 1932-09-08 Patsy Cline, NULL NULL, NULL	NULL, 1802-08-03 Henryk Górecki, NULL Patsy Cline, 1947-03-03
SIMPLE	Bing Crosby, 1904-05-02 NULL, 1904-05-02 Bing Crosby, NULL NULL, 1802-08-03 Henryk Górecki, NULL NULL, NULL	Bing Crosby, 1802-08-03 Bing Crosby, 1947-03-03 Henryk Górecki, 1947-03-03

Table 4-1 Valid and Invalid Examples of the MATCH Options

If you decide to use the MATCH clause, you simply add it to the end of your FOREIGN KEY constraint definition, as shown in the following SQL statement:

```
CREATE TABLE ArtistsMusicTypes
( ArtistName VARCHAR (60), DOB DATE, TypeID INT,
CONSTRAINT fk_CDArtists FOREIGN KEY ( ArtistName, DOB )
REFERENCES PerformingArtists MATCH FULL ) ;
```

To insert data into the referencing columns (ArtistName and DOB), both values have to be null or they must be a valid data pair from the referenced columns in the PerformingArtists table.

The <referential triggered action> Clause

The final clause in the FOREIGN KEY constraint syntax is the optional <referential triggered action> clause. The clause allows you to define what types of actions should be taken when attempting to update or delete data from the referenced columns—if that attempt would cause a violation of the data in the referencing columns. For example, suppose you try to delete data from a table's primary key. If that primary key is referenced by a foreign key and if the data to be deleted is stored in the foreign key, then deleting the data from the primary key would cause a violation in the data in the foreign key. Data in referencing columns must always be included in the referenced columns.

The point to remember about the <referential triggered action> clause is that you are including in the definition of the referencing table (through the foreign key) an action that should be taken as a result of something being done to the referenced table. This can be clarified by taking a look at the syntax for the <referential triggered action> clause:

ON UPDATE <referential action> [ON DELETE <referential action>]
| ON DELETE <referential action> [ON UPDATE <referential action>]
<referential action> ::=
CASCADE | SET NULL | SET DEFAULT | RESTRICT | NO ACTION

NOTE

The ::= symbol (two consecutive colons plus an equal sign) is used in the SQL:1999 standard to separate a placeholder in the angle brackets from its definition. In the preceding syntax, the <referential action> placeholder is defined. The placeholder is used in the code preceding the definition. You would then take the definition (the five keywords) and use them in place of the <referential action> placeholder as it is used in the ON UPDATE and ON DELETE clauses.

As you can see from the syntax, you can define an ON UPDATE clause, an ON DELETE clause, or both, and you can define them in any order. For each of these clauses you can choose one of five referential actions:

- If CASCADE is used and data is updated or deleted in the referenced columns, the data in the referencing columns is updated or deleted.

- If SET NULL is used and data is updated or deleted in the referenced columns, the values in the corresponding referencing columns are set to null. Null values have to be supported in the referencing columns for this option to work.

- If SET DEFAULT is used and data is updated or deleted in the referenced columns, the values in the corresponding referencing columns are set to their default values. Default values must be assigned to the referencing columns for this option to work.

- If RESTRICT is used and you try to update or delete data in your referenced columns that would cause a foreign key violation, you are prevented from performing that action. Data in the referencing columns can never violate the FOREIGN KEY constraint, not even temporarily.

- If NO ACTION is used and you try to update or delete data in your referenced columns that would cause a foreign key violation, you are prevented from performing that action. However, data violations can occur temporarily under certain conditions during the execution of an SQL statement, but the data in the foreign key is never violated in its final state (at the end of that execution). The NO ACTION option is the default used for both updates and deletes, if no referential triggered action is specified.

If you decide to use the <referential triggered action> clause, you simply add it to the end of your FOREIGN KEY constraint definition, as shown in the following SQL statement:

```
CREATE TABLE ArtistsMusicTypes
( ArtistName VARCHAR (60), DOB DATE, TypeID INT,
CONSTRAINT fk_CDArtists FOREIGN KEY ( ArtistName, DOB )
REFERENCES PerformingArtists ON UPDATE CASCADE ON DELETE CASCADE ) ;
```

If you update data in or delete data from the referenced columns in PerformingArtists, those changes will be made to the referencing columns in the ArtistsMusicTypes table.

Progress Check

1. What two restrictions are placed on PRIMARY KEY constraints that are not placed on UNIQUE constraints?

2. How does a referential constraint differ from a unique constraint?

3. How do the referencing columns in a FOREIGN KEY constraint compare to the referenced columns in a candidate key?

4. What three options can you use in a MATCH clause?

Project 4-1   Adding NOT NULL, Unique, and Referential Constraints

```
Prj04.txt
```

In Module 3, Project 3-1 and Project 3-2, you created several tables that you added to the Inventory database (or the CDInventory schema). In this project, you will add a number of constraints to the tables and create new tables that are also defined with constraints. However, rather than use the ALTER TABLE statement to modify the tables that you already created, you will be re-creating those tables. The advantage to this is that you'll be able to see the complete table definition, as it relates to the updated data model, shown in Figure 4-7.

The data model incorporates a few more elements than you have seen before. It identifies tables, columns within those tables, data types for those columns, constraints, and relationships between tables. You should already be familiar with how tables, columns, and data types are represented, so let's take a look at constraints and relationships:

- The columns included in the primary key are in the top section of the table, and the other columns lie in the bottom section. For example, in the CompactDiscs

---

1. A column that is defined with a PRIMARY KEY constraint cannot contain null values, and only one PRIMARY KEY constraint can be defined for each column.

2. A unique constraint ensures the uniqueness of values within a column or set of columns. A referential constraint is concerned with how data in one table relates to data in another table. The association between tables forms a relationship that provides referential integrity between tables, thus preventing the manipulation of data in one table from adversely affecting data in another table.

3. The foreign key in the referencing table must include the same number of columns that are being referenced, and the referencing columns must each be configured with the same data types as their referenced counterparts.

4. FULL, PARTIAL, and SIMPLE

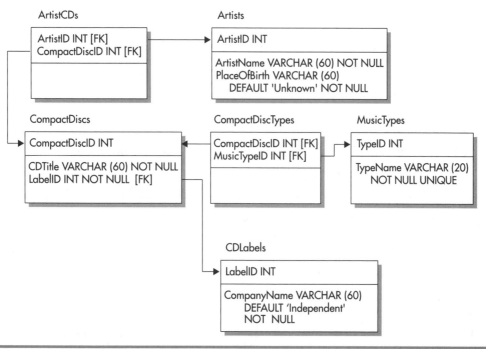

Figure 4-7 Data model for the Inventory database

4

Enforcing Data Integrity

Project
4-1

Adding NOT NULL, Unique, and Referential Constraints

table, the CompactDiscID column is the primary key. In some cases, as in the CompactDiscTypes table, all columns are included in the primary key.

- Each foreign key is represented by an [FK].

- Defaults, UNIQUE constraints, and NOT NULL constraints are identified with the column.

- Relationships, as defined by foreign keys, are represented by lines that connect the foreign key in one table to the candidate key in another table.

You'll find the data model useful not only for this project, but for other projects in the book, all of which will continue to build upon or use the Inventory database. You can also download the Prj04.txt file, which contains the SQL statements used in this project.

(continued)

NOTE

Data models come in many varieties. The model I use here is specific to the needs of the book. You'll find in the real world that the models will differ from what you see here. For example, relationships between tables might be represented differently, and column definition information might not be quite as extensive.

Step by Step

1. Open the client application for your RDBMS and connect to the Inventory database.

2. You first need to drop the four tables (CompactDiscs, CompactDiscTypes, MusicTypes, and CDLabels) that you already created. Enter and execute the following SQL statements:

```
DROP TABLE CompactDiscs CASCADE ;
DROP TABLE CompactDiscTypes CASCADE ;
DROP TABLE MusicTypes CASCADE ;
DROP TABLE CDLabels CASCADE ;
```

NOTE

If you created either the Artists table or the ArtistCDs table when trying out examples or experimenting with CREATE TABLE statements, be sure to drop those as well.

Now you can begin to re-create these tables and create new ones. You should create the tables in the order outlined in this project because the tables referenced in foreign keys will have to exist—with primary keys created—before you can create the foreign keys. Be sure to refer to the data model in Figure 4-7 for details about each table that you create.

3. The first table that you're going to create is the MusicTypes table. It contains two columns: TypeID and TypeName. You'll configure the TypeID column as the primary key, and you'll configure a UNIQUE constraint and NOT NULL constraint on the TypeName column. Enter and execute the following SQL statement:

```
CREATE TABLE MusicTypes
( TypeID INT, TypeName VARCHAR (20) NOT NULL,
CONSTRAINT un_TypeName UNIQUE (TypeName),
CONSTRAINT pk_MusicTypes PRIMARY KEY (TypeID) ) ;
```

4. The next table that you'll create is the CDLabels table. The table includes the LabelID column, which will be defined as the primary key, and the CompanyName column, which will be defined with a default and the NOT NULL constraint. Enter and execute the following SQL statement:

```
CREATE TABLE CDLabels
( LabelID INT, CompanyName VARCHAR (60) DEFAULT 'Independent' NOT NULL,
CONSTRAINT pk_CDLabels PRIMARY KEY (LabelID) ) ;
```

5. Now that you've created the CDLabels table, you can create the CompactDiscs table. The CompactDiscs table contains a foreign key that references the CDLabels table. This is why you created CDLabels first. Enter and execute the following SQL statement:

```
CREATE TABLE CompactDiscs
( CompactDiscID INT, CDTitle VARCHAR (60) NOT NULL, LabelID INT NOT NULL,
CONSTRAINT pk_CompactDiscs PRIMARY KEY (CompactDiscID),
CONSTRAINT fk_LabelID FOREIGN KEY (LabelID) REFERENCES CDLabels ) ;
```

6. The next table, CompactDiscTypes, includes two foreign keys, along with its primary key. The foreign keys reference the CompactDiscs table and the MusicTypes table, both of which you've created. Enter and execute the following SQL statement:

```
CREATE TABLE CompactDiscTypes
( CompactDiscID INT, MusicTypeID INT,
CONSTRAINT pk_CompactDiscTypes PRIMARY KEY ( CompactDiscID, MusicTypeID ),
CONSTRAINT fk_CompactDiscID_01 FOREIGN KEY (CompactDiscID)
   REFERENCES CompactDiscs,
CONSTRAINT fk_MusicTypeID FOREIGN KEY (MusicTypeID)
   REFERENCES MusicTypes ) ;
```

7. Now you can create the Artists table. Enter and execute the following SQL statement:

```
CREATE TABLE Artists
( ArtistID INT, ArtistName VARCHAR (60) NOT NULL,
PlaceOfBirth VARCHAR (60) DEFAULT 'Unknown' NOT NULL,
CONSTRAINT pk_Artists PRIMARY KEY (ArtistID) ) ;
```

8. The last table you'll create (at least for now) is the ArtistCDs table. Enter and execute the following SQL statement:

```
CREATE TABLE ArtistCDs
( ArtistID INT, CompactDiscID INT,
CONSTRAINT pk_ArtistCDs PRIMARY KEY ( ArtistID, CompactDiscID ),
CONSTRAINT fk_ArtistID FOREIGN KEY (ArtistID) REFERENCES Artists,
CONSTRAINT fk_CompactDiscID_02 FOREIGN KEY (CompactDiscID)
   REFERENCES CompactDiscs ) ;
```

9. Close the client application.

Project Summary

Your database now has six tables, each one configured with the necessary defaults and constraints. In this project, we followed a specific order for creating the tables in order to more easily implement the foreign keys. However, you could have created the tables in any order, without

(continued)

4

Enforcing Data Integrity

Project
4-1

Adding NOT NULL, Unique, and Referential Constraints

their foreign keys—unless the referenced table was already created—and then added in the foreign keys later, but this would have added extra steps. In fact, had you wanted to, you could have altered the tables that had existed prior to this project (rather than dropping them and then re-creating them), as long as you created primary keys on the referenced tables before creating foreign keys on the referencing tables. Regardless of the approach that you take, the end result should be that your database now has the necessary tables to begin moving on to other components of SQL.

CRITICAL SKILL
4.6 # Define CHECK Constraints

Earlier in the module, in the "Understand Integrity Constraints" section, I discussed the various constraint categories and the types of constraints they support. (Refer back to Figure 4-1 for an overview of these categories.) One type of constraint—the CHECK constraint—can be defined as table constraints, column constraints, domain constraints, or within assertions. A CHECK constraint allows you to specify what values can be included in a column. For instance, you can define a range of values (for example, between 10 and 100), a list of values (for example, blues, jazz, pop, country), or a number of other conditions that restrict exactly what values are permitted in a column.

CHECK constraints are the most flexible of all the constraints and are often the most complicated. Despite this, the basic syntax used for a CHECK constraint is relatively simple. To create a column constraint, use the following syntax in a column definition:

<column name> { <data type> | <domain> } CHECK (<search condition>)

To create a table constraint, use the following syntax in a table definition:

[CONSTRAINT <constraint name>] CHECK (<search condition>)

I'll be discussing domain constraints and assertions later in this section.

As you can see by the syntax, a CHECK constraint is relatively straightforward. However, the values used for the <search condition> clause can be very extensive and, consequently, quite complex. The best way for you to learn about the clause is by looking at examples. However, most <search condition> components are based on the use of predicates in order to create the search condition. A *predicate* is an expression that operates on values. For example, a predicate can be used to compare values (for instance, Column1 > 10). The greater-than symbol (>) is a comparison predicate, sometimes referred to as a *comparison operator*. In this case, the predicate verifies that any value inserted into Column1 is greater than 10.

Many <search condition> components also rely on the use of subqueries. A *subquery* is an expression that is used as a component within another expression. Subqueries are used when an expression must access or calculate multiple layers of data, such as having to search a second table to provide data for the first table.

Both predicates and subqueries are complicated enough subjects to be beyond the scope of a discussion about CHECK constraints, and indeed each subject is treated separately in its own module. (See Module 9 for information about predicates and Module 12 for information about subqueries.) Despite the fact that both topics are discussed later in the book, I want to provide you with at least a few examples of CHECK constraints to give you a feel of how they're implemented in an SQL environment.

The first example we'll look at is a CHECK constraint that defines the minimum and maximum values that can be inserted into a column. The following table definition in this example creates three columns and one CHECK constraint (as a table constraint) that restricts the values of one of the columns to a range of numbers between 0 and 30:

```
CREATE TABLE CDTitles
( CompactDiscID INT, CDTitle VARCHAR (60) NOT NULL, InStock INT NOT NULL,
CONSTRAINT ck_InStock CHECK ( InStock > 0 AND InStock < 30 ) ) ;
```

If you were to try to enter a value into the InStock column other than 1 through 29, you would receive an error. You can achieve the same results by defining a column constraint:

```
CREATE TABLE CDTitles
( CompactDiscID INT, CDTitle VARCHAR (60) NOT NULL,
InStock INT NOT NULL CHECK ( InStock > 0 AND InStock < 30 ) ) ;
```

Let's take a closer look at the <search condition> clause in these statements, which in this case is "(InStock > 0 AND InStock < 30)." The clause first tells us that any value entered into the InStock column must be greater than 0 (InStock > 0). The AND keyword tells us that the conditions defined on either side of AND must be applied. Finally, the clause tells us that the value must be less than 30 (InStock < 30). Because the AND keyword is used, the value must be greater than 0 *and* less than 30.

Another way that a CHECK constraint can be used is to explicitly list the values that can be entered into the column. This is a handy option if you have a limited number of values and they're not likely to change (or will change infrequently). The following SQL statement creates a table that includes a CHECK constraint that defines in which decade the music belongs:

```
CREATE TABLE CDTitles
( CompactDiscID INT, CDTitle VARCHAR (60) NOT NULL, Era CHAR (5),
CONSTRAINT ck_Era CHECK ( Era IN
    ( '1940s', '1950s', '1960s', '1970s', '1980s', '1990s', '2000s' ) ) ) ;
```

The value entered into the Era column must be one of the seven decades represented by the search condition. If you tried to enter a value other than a null value or one of these seven, you would receive an error. Notice that the IN operator is used to designate that the Era column values must be one of the set of values enclosed by parentheses after IN.

If the number of parentheses starts to get confusing to you, you can separate your code into lines that follow the embedding of those parentheses. For example, the preceding statement can be written as follows:

```
CREATE TABLE CDTitles
(
    CompactDiscID INT, CDTitle VARCHAR (60) NOT NULL, Era CHAR (5),
    CONSTRAINT ck_Era CHECK
    (
      Era IN
      (
          '1940s', '1950s', '1960s', '1970s', '1980s', '1990s', '2000s'
      )
    )
) ;
```

Each set of parentheses and its content is indented to a level that corresponds to the level of embedding for that particular clause, just like an outline. Using this method tells you exactly which clauses are enclosed in which set of parentheses, and the statement is executed just the same as if you hadn't separated out the lines. The downside is that it takes up a lot of room (which is why I don't use this method in this book), although it might be a helpful tool for you for those statements that are a little more complicated than others.

Now let's look at one other example of a CHECK constraint. This example is similar to the first one we looked at, only this one is concerned with values between certain numbers:

```
CREATE TABLE CDTitles
( CompactDiscID INT, CDTitle VARCHAR (60) NOT NULL, InStock INT NOT NULL,
CONSTRAINT ck_InStock CHECK
    ( ( InStock BETWEEN 0 AND 30 ) OR ( InStock BETWEEN 49 AND 60 ) ) ) ;
```

In this statement, you use the BETWEEN operator to specify a range. Because you are creating two different ranges, you enclose each range specification in parentheses: "(InStock BETWEEN 0 AND 30)" and "(InStock BETWEEN 49 AND 60)." These two range specifications are then connected by an OR keyword, which indicates that either one *or* the other condition must be met. As a result, any value entered into the InStock column must be from 1 through 29 or from 50 through 59.

As I said earlier, you will learn more about search conditions in Module 9. At that time, you'll see just how flexible the CHECK constraint is. And when used with subqueries (see Module 12), they provide a powerful tool for explicitly defining what values are permitted in a particular column.

Defining Assertions

An assertion is merely a type of CHECK constraint that can be applied to multiple tables. For this reason an assertion must be created separately from a table definition. To create an assertion, use the following syntax:

CREATE ASSERTION <constraint name> CHECK <search conditions>

Creating an assertion is very similar to creating a table CHECK constraint. After the CHECK keyword, you must provide the necessary search conditions. Now let's take a look at an example. Suppose the CDTitles table includes a column for the number of compact discs in stock. You want the total for that table to always be less than the maximum inventory you want to carry. In the following example, I create an assertion that totals the values in the InStock column and verifies that the total is less than 5000:

```
CREATE ASSERTION as_AvgInStock CHECK
    ( ( SELECT SUM (InStock) FROM CDTitles ) < 5000 );
```

In this statement, I am using a subquery, "(SELECT SUM (InStock) FROM CDTitles)," and comparing it to 5000. The subquery begins with the SELECT keyword, which is used to query data from a table. The SUM function adds the values in the InStock column, and the FROM keyword specifies which table the column is in. The results of this subquery are then compared (using the less than comparison operator) to 5000. If you try to add a value to the InStock column that would cause the total to exceed 5000, you would receive an error.

Creating Domains and Domain Constraints

The last type of CHECK constraint is the kind that you insert into a domain definition. For the most part, the constraint definition is similar to what you've seen before, except that you do not tie the constraint to a specific column or table. In fact, domain constraints use the VALUE keyword when referring to the value within a column defined with that particular domain. Let's look at the syntax for creating a domain:

```
CREATE DOMAIN <domain name> [ AS ] <data type>
[ DEFAULT <default value> ]
[ CONSTRAINT <constraint name> ] CHECK ( <search condition> )
```

You should already be familiar with most of the elements in this syntax. I discuss data types and default clauses in Module 3, and the constraint definition is similar to what you've seen so far in this module.

In the following example, I create a domain that's based on the INT data type and that requires all values to be between 0 and 30:

```
CREATE DOMAIN StockAmount AS INT
CONSTRAINT ck_StockAmount CHECK (VALUE BETWEEN 0 AND 30 );
```

The only really new item here (other than the CREATE DOMAIN clause) is the keyword VALUE, which, as I said, refers to the value of the column defined with the StockAmount domain. As a result, if you try to insert a value (into one of those columns) that is not between 0 and 30, you will receive an error.

Progress Check

1. What kinds of constraints can include CHECK constraints?

2. You're creating a CHECK constraint that includes the following search condition: "(InStock BETWEEN 0 AND 30)." What does this mean?

3. What keyword is used within a domain constraint to refer to the value within a column?

---

1. Table constraints, column constraints, domain constraints, and assertions
2. Values inserted into the InStock column must be within the range of 0 and 30.
3. VALUE

Project 4-2　Adding a CHECK Constraint

`Prj04.txt`　　In this project, which is relatively short, you will be using the ALTER TABLE statement to modify the CompactDiscs table. You will be adding a column to the table and then defining a CHECK constraint for that column that restricts the values that can be entered into the column. The additional column and constraint will have no impact on other tables in the Inventory database or on the relationship between tables. You can download the Prj04.txt file, which contains the SQL statements used in this project.

Step by Step

1. Open the client application for your RDBMS and connect to the Inventory database.

2. You're going to modify the CompactDiscs table by adding the InStock column. Enter and execute the following SQL statement:

```
ALTER TABLE CompactDiscs
ADD COLUMN InStock INT NOT NULL ;
```

3. Now that the column exists, you can add a CHECK constraint to the table definition. You could have entered the constraint as a column constraint, but adding it separately as a table constraint allows you to do each step separately so you can see the results of your actions. The CHECK constraint limits the values that can be entered into the InStock column. Each value must be greater than 0, but less than 50. Enter and execute the following SQL statement:

```
ALTER TABLE CompactDiscs
ADD CONSTRAINT ck_InStock CHECK ( InStock > 0 AND InStock < 50 ) ;
```

4. Close the client application.

Project Summary

The new column, InStock, tracks the number of each compact disc listed in the CompactDiscs table. The ck_InStock constraint restricts the number per row to an amount between 0 and 50. Now that the table has been updated, you cannot add any values that would violate the constraint.

Module 4 Mastery Check

1. What is the difference between a table constraint and an assertion?

2. What does a null value signify?

3. Which of the following types of constraints support NOT NULL constraints?

    A. Table constraints

    B. Column constraints

    C. Domain constraints

    D. Assertions

4. You are creating a table that includes a column that allows null values but whose non-null values should be unique. Which type of constraint should you use?

5. You're creating a table that includes the TypeName column. The column is defined with the CHAR (10) data type and requires a UNIQUE constraint, which you'll define as a column constraint. What SQL code should you use for the column definition?

6. What two restrictions apply to PRIMARY KEY constraints but not to UNIQUE constraints?

7. You're creating a PRIMARY KEY constraint named pk_ArtistMusicTypes on the ArtistMusicTypes table. The primary key includes the ArtistName and ArtistDOB columns. What SQL code should you use for a table constraint?

8. How does a referential constraint differ from a unique constraint?

9. A(n) _____ constraint enforces referential integrity between two tables by ensuring that no action is taken to either table that affects the data protected by the constraint.

10. You're creating a table that includes a column named BusinessTypeID, with a data type of INT. The column will be defined with a FOREIGN KEY constraint that references the primary key in a table named BusinessTypes. The foreign key will be added as a column constraint. What SQL code should you use for the column definition?

11. What three options can you use in the MATCH clause of a FOREIGN KEY constraint?

12. What are the two types of referential triggered actions that can be defined in a FOREIGN KEY constraint?

13. You're creating a FOREIGN KEY constraint and want the values in the referencing column to be updated if values in the referenced column are updated. Which <referential triggered action> clause should you use?

    A. ON UPDATE RESTRICT

    B. ON UPDATE NO ACTION

    C. ON UPDATE CASCADE

    D. ON UPDATE SET DEFAULT

14. What syntax should you use for a CHECK constraint that you're defining as a table constraint?

15. What types of constraints can you define within an assertion?

16. You're creating a CHECK constraint on the NumberInStock column. You want to limit the values that can be entered into the column to the range of 11 through 29. What should you use for the <search condition> clause of the constraint?

Module 5

Creating SQL Views

As you learned in Module 3, persistent base tables store the SQL data in your database. However, these tables are not always in a form useful to you if you want to look at only specific data from one table or data from multiple tables. For this reason, the SQL:1999 standard supports the use of viewed tables, or views. A *view* is a virtual table whose definition exists as a schema object. Unlike persistent base tables, there is no data stored in the view. In fact, the table does not actually exist, only the definition that defines the viewed table. It is this definition that allows you to call specific information from one or more tables, based on the query statements in that definition. Once you create a view, you simply invoke it by calling its name in a query as you would a base table. The data is then presented as though you were looking at a base table.

CRITICAL SKILL
5.1 # Add Views to the Database

Before I go too deeply into the specifics of views, I want to review quickly some of what I discuss in Module 2 and Module 3. A view, as you might recall, is one of three types of tables supported by SQL, along with base tables and derived tables. Most base tables are schema objects and come in four types: persistent base tables, global temporary tables, created local temporary tables, and declared local temporary tables. Of these four types, it is the persistent base tables that hold the actual SQL data. Derived tables, on the other hand, are merely the results you see when you query data from the database. For example, if you request data from the CompactDiscs table, the results of your request are displayed in a table-like format, which is known as the derived table.

In some ways, a view is a cross between a persistent base table and a derived table. It is like a persistent base table in that the view definition is stored as a schema object and has a unique name within that schema that can be invoked as you would a base table. However, a view is like a derived table in that no data is stored in association with the view. Both derived tables and views are types of virtual tables. The data is called from one or more base tables when you invoke the view. In fact, you can think of a view as merely a named derived table, with the view definition stored in the schema. The data results that you see when you call a view are not stored anywhere but are derived from existing base tables.

Views can be useful tools when accessing different types of data. One of the main advantages of using views is that you can define complex queries and store them within the view definition. That way, rather than having to re-create those queries every time you need them, you can instead invoke the view. In addition, views can be a handy way to present information to users without providing them with more information than they need or information that they should not see. For example, you might want users in your organization to have access to certain employee records, but you might not want information such as social security numbers or pay rates available to those users, so you can create a view that provides only the information that they should see. Views can also be used to synthesize complex structures and present information in a way that is easier for some users to understand, which in effect hides the underlying structure of the database from the users.

Now that you have an overview of what views are, let's take a look at a few examples that illustrate how data is extracted from base tables into the type of derived table that is presented by a view definition. The first example we'll look at, shown in Figure 5-1, is based on the CompactDiscInventory table, which includes six columns. Suppose you want to be able to view only the CDTitle, Copyright, and InStock columns. You could create a view that extracts these three columns from the table and displays them as if the data existed in its own table, as

CompactDiscInventory

CompactDiskID: INT	CDTitle: VARCHAR (60)	Copyright: INT	LabelID: INT	DiskID: INT	InStock: INT
99301	Famous Blue Raincoat	1991	5422	1299	6
99302	Blue	1971	5402	1232	26
99303	Court and Spark	1974	5270	1287	18
99304	Past Light	1983	5412	1292	2
99305	Kojiki	1990	5409	1255	5
99306	That Christmas Feeling	1993	5403	1216	3
99307	Patsy Cline: 12 Greatest Hits	1988	5403	1210	25
99308	Carreras Domingo Pavarotti in Concert	1990	5312	1276	22
99310	Henryk Górecki: Symphony No. 3	1992	5270	1266	8

CompactDisksInStock

CompactDisc	Copyright	InStock
Famous Blue Raincoat	1991	6
Blue	1971	26
Court and Spark	1974	18
Past Light	1983	2
Kojiki	1990	5
That Christmas Feeling	1993	3
Patsy Cline: 12 Greatest Hits	1988	25
Carreras Domingo Pavarotti in Concert	1990	22
Henryk Górecki: Symphony No. 3	1992	8

Figure 5-1 The CompactDiscsInStock view, based on the CompactDiscInventory table

shown in Figure 5-1. The CompactDiscsInStock view contains a query that defines exactly what data should be returned by the view.

You might have noticed that the column names in the view are different from the column names of the CompactDiscInventory table, even though the data within the columns is the same. This is because you can assign names to view columns that are different from the originating table, or you can assign the same names. If you don't assign any names, the view columns inherit the names from the originating table. The same is true of data types. The view columns inherit their data types from their respective table columns. For example, the CompactDisc column in the CompactDiscsInStock view inherits the VARCHAR (60) data type from the CDTitle column of the CompactDiscInventory table. You don't specify the VARCHAR (60) data type anywhere within the view definition.

As you can see, a view allows you to define which columns are returned when you invoke the view. The definition for the CompactDiscsInStock view specifies three columns; however, it could have specified any columns from the CompactDiscInventory table. In addition to columns, a view definition can specify which rows are returned. For example, Figure 5-2 shows the CDsInStock1990s view. Notice that it contains the same columns as the CompactDiscsInStock view (shown in Figure 5-1), but there are fewer rows. In this case, the view definition not only specifies the three columns from the CompactDiscInventory table, but also specifies that only rows whose values in the Copyright column fall between 1989 and 2000 are returned.

In the previous two examples, we have looked at views that derive data from only one table; however, you can create views based on multiple tables. This is particularly useful if you want to display related information that spans more than one table. Let's take a look Figure 5-3, which includes the CDInventory table and the Labels table. The CDInventory table

CDsInStock1990s

CompactDisc	Copyright	InStock
Famous Blue Raincoat	1991	6
Kojiki	1990	5
That Christmas Feeling	1993	3
Carreras Domingo Pavarotti in Concert	1990	22
Henryk Górecki: Symphony No. 3	1992	8

Figure 5-2 The CDsInStock1990s view, based on the CompactDiscInventory table

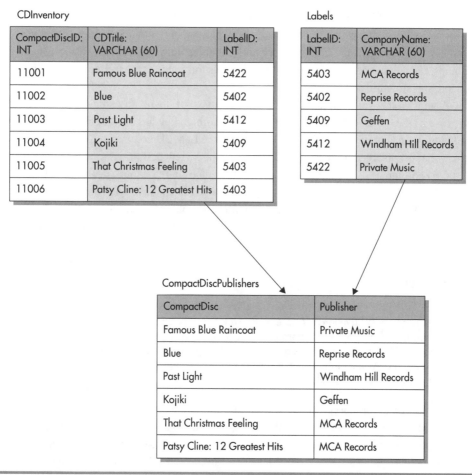

Figure 5-3 The CompactDiscPublishers view, based on the Labels and CDInventory tables

contains a list of CDs in your inventory, and the Labels table contains a list of companies that publish CDs.

Suppose you have users who want to be able to see the names of the CD and the publisher, but who are not interested in the CompactDiscID or LabelID values. And they certainly aren't interested in having to look in two different locations to compare LabelID values in order to match up CDs with company names. One solution is to create a view that matches up this information for them, while at the same time displaying only the information that is useful to them. In the case of the CDInventory and Labels table, you can create a view (named CompactDiscPublishers in Figure 5-3) that bridges this data for the users, while hiding the underlying structure and extraneous data.

A view of this sort is possible by taking advantage of the relationships between tables. In the case of the CDInventory and Labels tables, a foreign key has been defined on the LabelID column of the CDInventory table that references the LabelID column of the Labels table. The query that is contained in the CompactDiscPublishers view definition matches the values in the LabelID column of the CDInventory table to the values in the LabelID column of the Labels table. For every match that is found, a row is returned. For example, the Famous Blue Raincoat row includes a LabelID value of 5422. In the Labels table, you can see that this value matches the Private Music row. As a result, the view contains a row with the Famous Blue Raincoat value and the Private Music value.

NOTE

You don't necessarily have to use a foreign key relationship to join tables. Any two columns from different tables that store the same information can be used. This might mean using all the columns in a foreign key (if the foreign key includes multiple columns), using only one of the columns, or not using a foreign key at all. I discuss joining multiple tables in Module 11.

In addition to joining information from different tables, you can also use views to modify the data that is pulled from a table column and inserted in the view column. This allows you to take such actions as perform calculations, find averages, determine minimum and maximum values, and do countless other operations. You can then take the results of these operations and insert them into a column within the view. In Figure 5-4, for example, the CDDiscounts view deducts a 10 percent discount from the retail price and inserts the result in the DiscountPrice column.

The CDDiscounts view includes three columns. The CompactDisc column pulls data directly from the CDTitle column. The RetailPrice and DiscountPrice columns in the view both pull their data from the RetailPrice column in the Inventory table. The RetailPrice column in the view copies the values just as they are. However, before values are inserted into the DiscountPrice column, they are pulled from the RetailPrice column in the Inventory table, multiplied by .9, and inserted in their new form into the DiscountPrice column.

Inventory

CompactDiskID: INT	CDTitle: VARCHAR (60)	Copyright: INT	RetailPrice: NUMERIC (5,2)	InStock: INT
99301	Famous Blue Raincoat	1991	16.99	6
99302	Blue	1971	14.99	26
99303	Court and Spark	1974	14.99	18
99304	Past Light	1983	15.99	2
99305	Kojiki	1990	15.99	5
99306	That Christmas Feeling	1993	10.99	3
99307	Patsy Cline: 12 Greatest Hits	1988	16.99	25

CDDiscounts

CompactDisc	RetailPrice	DiscountPrice
Famous Blue Raincoat	16.99	15.29
Blue	14.99	13.49
Court and Spark	14.99	13.49
Past Light	15.99	14.39
Kojiki	15.99	14.39
That Christmas Feeling	10.99	9.89
Patsy Cline: 12 Greatest Hits	16.99	15.29

Figure 5-4 The CDDiscounts view, based on the Inventory table

As you can see, you can specify many types of operations in a view and then simply invoke the view when you need the information. Most of what can be included in a regular query can be included in a view. In fact, it is the query, or query expression, that forms the nucleus of the view. However, before we look at query expressions, I want to first discuss the syntax used for creating views.

Progress Check

1. How do views compare to persistent base tables and derived tables?

2. What are two advantages to using views?

3. What happens if you don't assign column names to a view?

Defining SQL Views

The simplest type of view to create is one that references only one table and that retrieves data from columns within the table without modifying that data. The more complicated the view, the more complicated the query expression underlying the view. At its most basic, the syntax for a view is as follows:

CREATE VIEW <view name> [(<view column names>)]
AS <query expression>
[WITH CHECK OPTION]

For now, we'll focus only on the first two lines of the syntax and leave the WITH CHECK OPTION for later, in the "Create Updateable Views" section. In the first line of the syntax, you must provide a name for the view. In addition, you must provide names for the columns in the following circumstances:

- If any column values are based on some sort of operation that calculates the value to be inserted in the column, rather than the value being copied directly from the table. (See Figure 5-4.)

- If table column names are duplicated, which can happen when joining tables together.

Even if you aren't required to provide column names, you still can. For example, you might find that you want to rename them for your own purposes so the names are more logical for your particular users. If, however, you do provide column names, you must provide them for all columns. You cannot specify column names for some columns and not others.

1. A view is like a persistent base table in that the view definition is stored as a schema object and has a unique name within that schema that can be invoked as you would a base table. A view is like a derived table in that no data is stored in association with the view.

2. You can define complex queries and store them within the view definition. That way, rather than having to re-create those queries every time you need them, you can instead invoke the view. You can also present information to users without providing them with more information than they need or information that they should not see.

3. The view columns inherit the names from the originating table.

The second line of the syntax includes the AS keyword, which is required, and the <query expression> placeholder. The <query expression> placeholder, although it appears straightforward, can imply a complex structure of query statements that can perform a number of operations, including retrieving data from multiple tables, calculating data, limiting the type of data returned, or performing most any other type of operation supported by a query expression. Because of the complexity of query expressions, I spend the better part of Part II in this book discussing various ways to query data. What this implies, then, is that it would be very difficult to condense a thorough discussion of query expressions into the topic of views. Still, I want to provide you with a number of examples that illustrate how you can create views that perform various functions. With each example, I'll include a cursory explanation of the query expression used in the view definition. Know, however, that I will be going into the details of query expressions in greater depth later in the book, beginning with Module 7.

The first example we'll look at is based on the view shown in Figure 5-1. The CompactDiscsInStock view derives data from the CompactDiscInventory table and includes three columns from that table. To create the view, use the following CREATE VIEW statement:

```
CREATE VIEW CompactDiscsInStock ( CompactDisc, Copyright, InStock )
AS SELECT CDTitle, Copyright, InStock FROM CompactDiscInventory ;
```

This view is the simplest of all types of views to create. It is based on one table and pulls three of the six columns from that table. In the first line of the statement, you provide a name for the view, CompactDiscsInStock, and then provide a name for each of the three columns: CompactDisc, Copyright, and InStock. If you did not include the column names, the view columns would inherit their names from the table columns.

The second line of the CREATE VIEW statement includes the AS keyword and the query expression, which in this case is the following SELECT statement:

```
SELECT CDTitle, Copyright, InStock FROM CompactDiscInventory
```

The SELECT statement is one of the most common statements (if not *the* most common statement) you'll be using as an SQL programmer. It also one of the most extensive and flexible statements you'll be using, allowing you to form intricate queries that can return exactly the type of data you want to retrieve from your database.

The SELECT statement used in the CompactDiscsInStock view definition is a SELECT statement at its most basic. The statement is divided into two clauses: the SELECT clause and the FROM clause. The SELECT clause identifies which columns to return (CDTitle, Copyright, and InStock), and the FROM clause identifies which table to pull the data from (CompactDiscInventory). When you invoke the CompactDiscsInStock view, you are essentially invoking the SELECT statement that is embedded in the view definition, which in turn pulls data from the applicable base table.

In the next example, which is based on the view in Figure 5-2, the CREATE VIEW statement is nearly the same as the previous example, except that an additional clause has been added to the statement:

```
CREATE VIEW CDsInStock1990s ( CompactDisc, Copyright, InStock )
AS SELECT CDTitle, Copyright, InStock FROM CompactDiscInventory
WHERE Copyright > 1989 AND Copyright < 2000 ;
```

The WHERE clause defines a condition that has to be met in order for data to be returned. As in the previous example, you're still pulling data from the CDTitle, Copyright, and InStock columns of the CompactDiscInventory table, only this time you're limiting the data to those rows whose Copyright values are greater than 1989 but less than 2000 (Copyright > 1989 AND Copyright < 2000). You might recognize the comparison operators greater than (>) and less than (<) from Module 4 in the discussion about CHECK constraints. They're used to limit which values will be included in the view.

NOTE

The operators used in the WHERE clause (or any condition defined in the clause) have no effect on the data stored in the base tables. They affect only the data returned when the view is invoked. I discuss these types of operators in greater detail in Module 9.

You can use the WHERE clause in a SELECT statement to define a wide variety of conditions. For example, the WHERE clause can be used to help join tables together, as shown in the following CREATE VIEW statement:

```
CREATE VIEW CompactDiscPublishers ( CompactDisc, Publisher )
AS SELECT CDInventory.CDTitle, Labels.CompanyName
FROM CDInventory, Labels
WHERE CDInventory.LabelID = Labels.LabelID ;
```

This statement creates the view that you see in Figure 5-3. The name of the view is CompactDiscPublishers and it includes the CompactDisc column and the Publisher column. The view pulls information from two sources: the CDTitle column in the CDInventory Table and the CompanyName column in the Labels table.

Let's first take a look at the SELECT clause. Notice that the name of each column is qualified by the name of its respective table (for example, CDInventory.CDTitle). When joining two or more tables, you must qualify the column names if there's any possibility that the column names could be confused, which would be the case if you included columns with the same name. If, however, there is no possibility the column names could be confused, then you can omit the table names. For example, the SELECT clause could read as follows:

```
SELECT CDTitle, CompanyName
```

Despite the fact that the qualified names are not always necessary, many programmers prefer to use them in all cases because it's easier to know what table is being referenced if you ever need to modify the database structure or the view definition at a later time.

The next clause in the SELECT statement is the FROM clause. When joining tables together, you must include the name of all the participating tables, separated by a comma. Other than the issue of multiple names, the FROM clause is similar to what you've seen in other examples.

The WHERE clause, which is the final clause in the SELECT statement, is what matches rows together. The WHERE clause is necessary because, without it, there would be no way of knowing how to match up the values from the different tables. The WHERE clause provides specific instructions how this is to be done. In the CompactDiscPublishers view definition, the value in the LabelID column of the CDInventory table must equal the value in the LabelID column of the Labels table for a row to be returned. For example, if you refer again to Figure 5-3, you can see that the Past Light row in the CDInventory table has a value of 5412 in the LabelID column, which is matched up with the Windham Hill Records row in the Labels table. Notice that, once again, the column names are qualified by the table names, which is essential in this case because the columns share the same name. Without the table names, SQL would not know whether it was comparing values with itself or with the other table.

You can also expand the WHERE clause to further qualify your query. In the following example, the WHERE clause limits the rows returned to only those that contain a value of 5403 in the LabelID column of the CDInventory table:

```
CREATE VIEW CompactDiscPublishers ( CompactDisc, Publisher )
AS SELECT CDInventory.CDTitle, Labels.CompanyName
FROM CDInventory, Labels
WHERE CDInventory.LabelID = Labels.LabelID
AND CDInventory.LabelID = 5403 ;
```

If you were then to invoke the CompactDiscPublishers view, you would see only the CDs that are produced by MCA Records.

Now let's look at another example, which is based on the view in Figure 5-4. Like the first two examples we looked at, this view derives data from only one table. However, this view actually performs calculations that return data that has been modified. The CREATE VIEW statement looks like this:

```
CREATE VIEW CDDiscounts ( CompactDisc, RetailPrice, DiscountPrice )
AS SELECT CDTitle, RetailPrice, RetailPrice * .9 FROM Inventory;
```

The CDDiscounts view includes three columns: CompactDisc, RetailPrice, and DiscountPrice. The DiscountPrice column contains the calculated values. The SELECT clause identifies the table columns that contain the source data. The first two columns are defined in the same manner as you've seen in previous examples. Data is copied from the CDTitle and RetailPrice columns in the Inventory table to the CompactDisc and RetailPrice columns of the CDDiscounts view. However, the third column definition (RetailPrice * .9) is a little different. Values are again taken from the RetailPrice column, only this time the values are multiplied by .9 (90 percent) to arrive at the discounted prices that appear in the DiscountPrice column of the view.

You can also add a WHERE clause to the SELECT statement used in the CDDiscounts view definition:

```
CREATE VIEW CDDiscounts ( CompactDisc, RetailPrice, DiscountPrice )
AS SELECT CDTitle, RetailPrice, RetailPrice * .9 FROM Inventory
WHERE InStock > 10 ;
```

The WHERE clause restricts the query to only those rows whose InStock value is greater than 10. Notice that you can use a comparison operator on a table column (InStock) whose values are not even returned by the view.

As you can see from all these examples of view definitions, there are a great many things that you can do with views as a result of the flexibility and extensibility of the SELECT statement. Later in the book, when you become more familiar with the various types of SELECT statements that you can create and the operations that you can perform, you will be able to create views that are far more complex than anything we've looked at so far.

CRITICAL SKILL
5.2 Create Updateable Views

In SQL, some types of views are updateable. In other words, you can use the view to modify the data in the underlying table. Whether a view is updateable depends on the SELECT statement that is defined within the view definition. Typically, the more complex the statement, the less likely the view will be updateable. There is no syntax within the CREATE VIEW statement that explicitly designates a view as being updateable. Instead, it is determined strictly by the nature of the SELECT statement, which must adhere to specific standards in order for the view to be updateable.

Up to this point in the module, I have implied that the <query expression> placeholder in the CREATE VIEW syntax is made up of a SELECT statement. To be more precise, a query expression can be one of several types of expressions. The most common of these, and the one you'll be concerned with in this book, is the query specification. A *query specification* is an SQL expression that begins with the SELECT keyword and includes a number of elements that form that expression, as you have seen in the view examples we've looked at. A query specification is updateable if it meets the numerous guidelines outlined in the SQL:1999 standard. For the sake of simplicity, I refer to the query specification as the SELECT statement, which is often how it's referred to in various types of SQL-related and product-related documentation.

The issue of query specifications and the complexity of the SQL standards aside, the point I'm trying to make is that the syntax rules that determine the updatability of a view are not simple, clear-cut guidelines, particularly in light of the fact that I have yet to cover the SELECT statement in depth (which I do beginning in Module 7). However, there are some logical underpinnings that can be gleaned from these guidelines:

- Data within the view cannot be summarized, grouped together, or automatically eliminated.

- At least one column in the source table must be updateable.

- Each column in the view must be traceable to exactly one source column in one table.

- Each row in the view must be traceable to exactly one source row in one table.

In many cases, you'll be able to determine the updatability of a view simply by applying common sense. Let's take a look at an example. Suppose that you decide to add information about your employees to your database because you want to track CD sale commissions earned by your employees. You decide to add the EmployeeCommissions table, shown in Figure 5-5, which lists the total amount of commissions each employee made during a three-year period.

Now suppose you want to know the average commission for each year for all the employees. You can create a view that determines the average for each year and displays those averages in three separate columns. To do so, you would use the following CREATE VIEW statement:

```
CREATE VIEW EmpComm ( Avg1999, Avg2000, Avg2001 )
AS SELECT AVG(Year1999), AVG(Year2000), AVG(Year2001)
FROM EmployeeCommissions ;
```

As you can see from the statement, the EmpComm view contains three columns: Avg1999, Avg2000, Avg2001. The SELECT clause pulls information from three columns

EmployeeCommissions

EmployeeID: INT	Year1999: NUMERIC (7,2)	Year2000: NUMERIC (7,2)	Year2001: NUMERIC (7,2)
99301	126.32	11.28	16.86
99302	16.27	90.20	198.14
99303	354.34	16.32	1237.56
99304	112.11	87.56	14.14

Figure 5-5 Annual commission earnings in the EmployeeCommissions table

EmpComm

Avg1999	Avg2000	Avg2001
152.26	51.34	366.68

Figure 5-6 The EmpComm view, based on the average of quarterly earnings

in the EmployeeCommissions table—Year1999, Year2000, and Year2001—and uses the AVG function to find the average for all the values in each column, as shown in Figure 5-6. For example, the AVG function first averages the four values in the Year1999 column and then enters that average in the Avg1999 column of the EmpComm view.

Now suppose you want to update the commission amounts in the EmployeeCommissions table. You could not do it through the view because values in the views are based on calculations performed on values in the table. For example, if you updated the value in the Avg1999 column, the RDBMS would not know how many rows were affected or how to distribute the values within those rows. In other words, the row in the view is not traceable back to exactly one source row.

You could, however, create a view that simply extracts information from the EmployeeCommissions table:

```
CREATE VIEW EmpComm
AS SELECT EmployeeID, Year1999, Year2000 FROM EmployeeCommissions ;
```

In this statement, you are creating a view that displays only three of the four columns of the table. No calculations are performed and only one table is used. Figure 5-7 shows what this view would look like.

This view, unlike the last one, is updateable. You can modify and insert data because no data has been summarized or grouped together, each column is traceable to exactly one source column in one table, and each row is traceable to exactly one source row in one table. In addition, no data is summarized or grouped together. Of course, if you were to update or insert data through the view, it is the data in the underlying table that is actually modified. That means any data modifications must still adhere to the constraints placed on that table. For example, you could not insert a row through the EmpComm view if null values were not allowed in the Year2001 column of the table. The view would not have the capacity to accept a value for that column, and the table would not allow you to insert a row without supplying that value.

EmpComm

EmployeeID	Year1999	Year2000
99301	126.32	11.28
99302	16.27	90.20
99303	354.34	16.32
99304	112.11	87.56

Figure 5-7 The EmpComm view, based on first and second quarterly earnings

You can often determine whether a table is updateable just by looking at the outcome of any modification attempts. If your goal is to create views that allow users to update data in the underlying tables, then you must consider the complexities of those views and the functions that they are to perform. Also keep in mind that the constraints placed on the underlying tables affect your ability to modify and insert data through a view.

Using the WITH CHECK OPTION Clause

Now let's return to the CREATE VIEW syntax that I introduced earlier in the section "Defining SQL Views." The last line of the syntax includes the following clause:

[WITH CHECK OPTION]

The WITH CHECK OPTION clause applies to updateable views that include a WHERE clause in the SELECT statement. The best way to illustrate how this works is through an example. Let's modify the last view definition we looked at:

```
CREATE VIEW EmpComm
AS SELECT EmployeeID, Year1999, Year2000 FROM EmployeeCommissions
WHERE Year1999 > 100 ;
```

The WHERE clause specifies that only rows with Year1999 values greater than 100 should be returned. This in itself is straightforward enough. However, suppose you want to update this view by setting a Year1999 value to be less than 100. Because the view is updateable, it will allow you to do that. However, if you were to then invoke the view, the row you updated would no longer be visible, nor could you update it further.

To work around this problem, you can add the WITH CHECK OPTION clause to your view definition, as in the following example:

```
CREATE VIEW EmpComm
AS SELECT EmployeeID, Year1999, Year2000 FROM EmployeeCommissions
WHERE Year1999 > 100 WITH CHECK OPTION ;
```

Now if you tried to update a Year1999 value to an amount less than 100, you would receive an error message telling you that the change could not be made. As you can see, the WITH CHECK OPTION is a handy way to ensure that your users don't perform updates that will prevent them from effectively using the views that you create.

Progress Check

1. You're creating a view that displays only the CDTitle and InStock columns of the CompactDiscs table. The view name is CDsInStock and the view column names are the same as the table column names. What SQL statement should you use to create your view?

2. You're creating a view with the following SELECT statement: SELECT AVG(Salary) FROM Employees. Why can't you update this view?

3. You're creating a view that contains a WHERE clause that limits the values returned in the view. Which additional clause should you include in a view definition to prevent users from updating data with values outside those limits?

---

1. You should use the following SQL statement:

```
CREATE VIEW CDsInStock AS SELECT CDTitle, InStock FROM CompactDiscs ;
```

2. The value returned is an average of the values in the Salary column. The RDBMS would not know how many rows in the table were affected or how to distribute the values within those rows. The row in the view is not traceable back to exactly one source row.

3. WITH CHECK OPTION

CRITICAL SKILL

5.3 Drop Views from the Database

You will no doubt run into situations when you want to remove a view definition from your database. The syntax for doing this is quite simple:

DROP VIEW <view name>

When you execute the DROP VIEW statement, the view definition is removed; however, none of the underlying data (which is stored in the base tables) is affected. Once the view is dropped, you can re-create the view or create a different view with the same name. Now let's look at a quick example:

```
DROP VIEW EmpComm ;
```

This statement removes the EmpComm view from your database but leaves the underlying data untouched.

Ask the Expert

Q: You discuss creating views and dropping views but you do not mention altering views. Does SQL support any sort of ALTER VIEW statement?

A: No, you cannot alter views in SQL. However, some RDBMSs support an ALTER VIEW statement. Be aware, though, that the functionality supported by these statements can vary from product to product. For example, the ALTER VIEW statement in SQL Server is fairly robust and allows you to change many aspects of the view definition, including the SELECT statement. On the other hand, the ALTER VIEW statement in Oracle is used to manually recompile a view to avoid runtime overhead. To actually alter a view, you must first drop it and then re-create it, as is the case with the SQL standard.

Q: In the examples that you use to show how views are created, you use one or two tables for your source data. Can views be based on more than two tables?

A: Yes, a view can be based on as many tables as can be logically queried in the SELECT statement. For example, suppose you want to create a view in the Inventory database. (The Inventory database is the one you've been working with for the projects in this book.) The view might match artists' names to CD titles. To do that, however, your SELECT statement would have to join together three tables. You would have to match the ArtistID values in the Artists table and the ArtistCDs table, and you would have to match the CompactDiscID values in the CompactDiscs table and the ArtistCDs table. The result will be that the view will display a list of artists and their CDs. (In Module 11, I discuss how you can join these tables together in your SELECT statement.)

Project 5-1 Adding Views to Your Database

`Prj05.txt` In this project, you will create two views in the Inventory database. The views will be based on tables you created in previous projects. The first view will be based on a single table, and the second view will be based on two tables. You'll create the second view two different times. You'll create it once, then drop the view definition from the database, and then re-create a modified version of the view. You can download the Prj05.txt file, which contains the SQL statements used in this project.

Step by Step

1. Open the client application for your RDBMS and connect to the Inventory database.

2. The first view that you'll create is named CDsInStock. The view is based on the CDTitle and InStock columns in the CompactDiscs table. You want the view to include only those rows whose values in the InStock column are greater than 10. The view will use the same column names as the table and will include the WITH CHECK OPTION to prevent values less than 10 from being added to the InStock column. Enter and execute the following SQL statement:

```
CREATE VIEW CDsInStock
AS SELECT CDTitle, InStock FROM CompactDiscs
WHERE InStock > 10 WITH CHECK OPTION ;
```

3. Next, you will create a view named CDPublishers that will contain the CDTitle column and the Publisher column. The view will be based on the CDTitle column in the CompactDiscs table and the CompanyName column of the CDLabels table. You will need to use a WHERE clause to match rows in the two tables. The WHERE clause will also limit the rows included in the view to those whose LabelID value in the CDLabels table is either 5403 or 5402. Enter and execute the following SQL statement:

```
CREATE VIEW CDPublishers ( CDTitle, Publisher )
AS SELECT CompactDiscs.CDTitle, CDLabels.CompanyName
FROM CompactDiscs, CDLabels
WHERE CompactDiscs.LabelID = CDLabels.LabelID
AND CDLabels.LabelID = 5403 OR CDLabels.LabelID = 5402 ;
```

4. You decide that you do not want to limit the rows to specific values in the LabelID column, so you must drop the view definition from the database and re-create the view without the value restrictions. Enter and execute the following SQL statement:

```
DROP VIEW CDPublishers ;
```

5. Now you can re-create the CDPublishers view. Enter and execute the following SQL statements:

```
CREATE VIEW CDPublishers ( CDTitle, Publisher )
AS SELECT CompactDiscs.CDTitle, CDLabels.CompanyName
FROM CompactDiscs, CDLabels
WHERE CompactDiscs.LabelID = CDLabels.LabelID ;
```

6. Close the client application.

Project Summary

In addition to the six tables created in earlier projects, your database should now include the CDsInStock view and the CDPublishers view. Later in this book, you'll use those views to query data from the base tables and update that data. Once you have a better understanding of how to create SELECT statements, you'll be able to define views that are even more extensive and provide an even greater level of detail than the views you've created so far.

Module 5 Mastery Check

1. What are the three types of stored tables supported by SQL?

2. How do you assign data types to view columns?

3. In what circumstances must you provide the view column names in a view definition?

4. You're creating a view named EmpBDays. The view is based on the EmpName column and the BDay column of the Employees table. The view column names will be the same as the table column names. What SQL code should you use to create the view?

5. You're creating a view based on the CompactDiscs table in the Inventory database. You want the view to include only those rows whose value in the LabelID column is 546. What clause—in addition to the SELECT clause and the FROM clause—should be included in the SELECT statement for the view?

6. You're creating a view that references the Employee table and the JobTitle table. The data in the two tables is matched together by the JobTitleID column in each table. How should you write the WHERE clause in the view's SELECT statement?

7. You're creating a view that references the Employee table and the JobTitle table. The data in the two tables is matched together by the JobTitleID column in each table. You want the view to display only those rows whose value in the JobTitleID column of the JobTitle table is 109. How should you write the WHERE clause in the view's SELECT statement?

(continued)

8. What is a query specification?

9. Which guidelines should you follow if you want to create an updateable view?

    A. Data within the view cannot be summarized, grouped together, or automatically eliminated.

    B. At least one column in the source table must be updateable.

    C. Each column in the view must be traceable to exactly one source column in one table.

    D. Each row in the view must be traceable to exactly one source row in one table.

10. You create the following view based on the CompactDiscs table in the Inventory database:

```
CREATE VIEW InStock(Average)
AS SELECT AVG(InStock) FROM CompactDiscs ;
```

How do you insert data through this view?

11. What type of view does the WITH CHECK OPTION clause apply to?

12. You create the following view definition:

```
CREATE VIEW EmpComm
AS SELECT EmployeeID, Year1999, Year2000 FROM EmployeeCommissions
WHERE Year1999 > 100 ;
```

You want to use the view to update data. What happens if you change the Year1999 value to an amount less than 100?

13. You want to alter the EmpComm view definition in your database. How do you alter that definition?

14. You want to drop the EmpBDays view definition from your database. What SQL statement should you use?

15. What happens to the SQL data when you drop a view from the database?

Module 6

Managing Database Security

A critical component of any database is the ability to protect the data from unauthorized access or malicious attacks. A database must ensure that no unauthorized users can view or change data that they should not be viewing or changing. At the same time, authorized users should not be prevented from accessing any information that should be available to them. In order to support these capabilities, SQL defines a security model that allows you to determine which users can access specific data and what they can do with that data. At the core of this model is the authorization identifier. An *authorization identifier,* as you learned in Module 2, is an object in the SQL environment that represents a user or group of users that are granted specific access privileges to objects and data within the SQL environment. Privileges are granted to authorization identifiers on schema objects. The type of privileges granted determines the type of access. In this module, we will look at the SQL security model, how it uses authorization identifiers, and how to set up privileges on objects in your SQL database.

CRITICAL SKILL
6.1 Understand the SQL Security Model

Authorization identifiers provide the foundation for your database's security. Access to all objects is permitted through these identifiers. If the authorization identifier doesn't have the appropriate privileges to access a specific object, such as a table, the data within that table is unavailable to that user. In addition, each authorization identifier can be configured with different types of privileges. For example, you can permit some authorization identifiers to view the data within a specific table, while permitting other authorization identifiers to modify that data.

SQL supports two types of authorization identifiers: user identifiers (or users) and role names (or roles). A *user identifier* is an individual security account that can represent an individual, an application, or a system service. The SQL standard does not specify how an SQL implementation should create a user identifier. The identifier might be tied to the operating system on which the relational database management system (RDBMS) is running, or it might be explicitly created within the RDBMS environment.

A *role name* is a defined set of privileges that can be assigned to a user or to another role. If a role name is granted access to a schema object and that role name is then specified as the authorization identifier, then all user identifiers and role names that have been assigned the specified role name have access to the same object as that role name. For example, in Figure 6-1 the MrktDept role name has been assigned to the AcctDept role name and to four user identifiers: Ethan, Max, Linda, and Emma. If the MrktDept role name is the current authorization identifier and it has been granted access to the Performers table, the AcctDept role name and all four user identifiers have access to the Performers table. Note that, unlike a user identifier, SQL *does* specify how to create a role name, which I discuss in the "Create and Delete Roles" section later in this module.

Performers

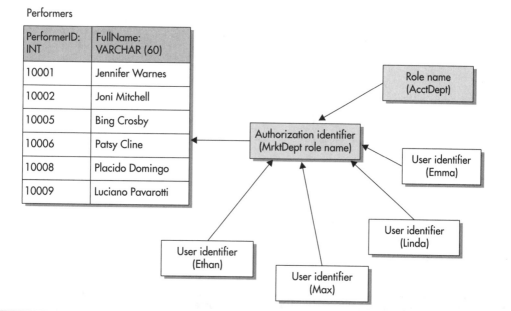

Figure 6-1 The MrktDept role assigned to four user identifiers and one role

In addition to user identifiers and role names, SQL supports a special authorization identifier named PUBLIC, which is an SQL built-in authorization identifier that includes everyone who uses the database. Just as with any other authorization identifier, you can grant access privileges to the PUBLIC account. For example, suppose you wanted any potential customers to be able to view your list of CDs. You could grant the necessary privileges to the PUBLIC account for the appropriate tables and column.

SQL Sessions

Each SQL session is associated with a user identifier and role name. An *SQL session* is the connection between some sort of client application and the database. The session provides the context in which the authorization identifier executes SQL statements during a single connection. Throughout this connection, the SQL session maintains its association with a user identifier/role name pair.

Let's take a look at Figure 6-2, which shows the user identifier/role name pair associated with a session. When a session is first established, the user identifier is always the *SQL session user identifier*, which is a special type of user identifier that remains associated with the session throughout the connection. It is up to the SQL implementation to determine how a specific

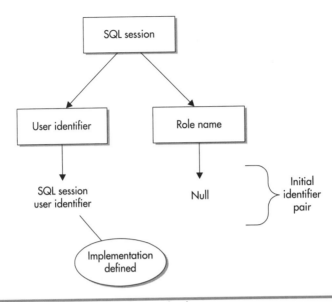

Figure 6-2 SQL session with user identifier and role name

account becomes the SQL session user identifier, although it can be an operating system user account or an account specific to the RDBMS. Whatever method is used to associate an account with the SQL session user identifier, it is this account that acts as the current user identifier.

As you can also see in Figure 6-2, the role name is a null value. The role name is always null when a session is first established. In other words, whenever you log onto an SQL database and establish a session, the initial user identifier will always be the SQL session user identifier and the role name will always be a null value.

At any instance during a connection, the session is associated with a user identifier/role name pair; however, it is not always the same pair throughout the length of the session. For example, embedded SQL statements, SQL client modules, and SQL-invoked routines can specify an authorization identifier. If a new identifier is specified, it becomes the current authorization identifier until the transactions have completed, and access to objects is granted based on the current user identifier/role name pair.

For any user identifier/role name pair that is current, one of the two values is almost always null. In other words, if a user identifier is specified, then the role name must be null; if a role name is specified, then the user identifier must be null. Whichever value is not null is the authorization identifier.

When more than one user identifier/role name pair is used during a session, an authorization stack is created that reflects the current authorization identifier. The pair at the top of the stack is the current authorization identifier. Figure 6-3 shows an example of an authorization stack that can be created during a session.

In this example, the initial user identifier/role name pair is at the bottom of the stack. As you would expect, the user identifier is the SQL session user identifier and the role name is a null value. Access to database objects is based on the privileges granted to the SQL session user identifier when it is current.

During the session, an embedded SQL statement specifies an authorization identifier of App_User, which is a user identifier. When the embedded statement is executed, App_User becomes the current authorization identifier, and access privileges are based on that account.

Suppose one of the embedded SQL statements then calls an SQL-invoked routine that specifies an authorization of Routine_Role, which is a role name. Routine_Role then becomes the current authorization identifier and is at the top of the authorization stack. Once the routine runs, the current authorization identifier reverts to App_User, until the embedded statements run, after which the authorization identifier reverts to the SQL session user identifier.

Notice that in each user identifier/role name pair shown in Figure 6-3, there is exactly one null value. The other value, the one that is not null, is the authorization identifier.

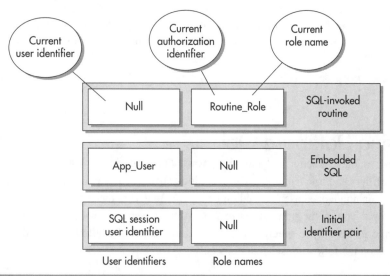

Figure 6-3 Authorization stack created during an SQL session

Ask the Expert

Q: You state that the current authorization identifier can change. How can you determine who the current authorization user and role name are at any time during a session?

A: SQL supports several special values that allow you to determine the current values of the various types of users. The special values act as placeholders for the actual user-related value. You can use these special values in expressions to return the value of the specific type of user. For example, you can use the CURRENT_USER special value to return the value of the current user identifier. SQL supports five of these special values: CURRENT_USER, USER, CURRENT_ROLE, SESSION_USER, and SYSTEM_USER. CURRENT_USER and USER mean the same thing and return a value equal to the current user identifier. CURRENT_ROLE returns the current role name, and SESSION_USER returns the SQL session user identifier. If the SQL session user identifier is the current user identifier, then CURRENT_USER, USER, and SESSION_USER all have the same value, which can occur if the initial identifier pair is the only active user identifier/role name pair (the pair at the top of the authorization stack). The last function, SYSTEM_USER, returns the operating system user who invoked an SQL module. As we get further into this module, you'll see how the CURRENT_USER and CURRENT_ROLE special values are used to identify the current authentication identifier when creating roles and granting privileges. (See the sections "Create and Delete Roles," "Grant and Revoke Privileges," and "Grant and Revoke Roles.") In addition, you'll find more information about special values in Module 10.

Accessing Database Objects

Now that you have a better understanding of what an authorization identifier is—along with user identifiers and role names—let's take a look at what you can do with these identifiers. Access to data in a database is based on being able to access the objects that contain the data. For example, you might grant access to some users to a specific set of tables, while other users have access only to specific columns within a table. SQL allows you to define access privileges on the following schema objects:

- Base tables
- Views
- Columns

- Domains

- Character sets

- Collations

- Translations

- User-defined types

- Triggers

- SQL-invoked routines

For each type of object, you can assign specific types of privileges that vary according to the type of object it is. These assigned privileges are associated with specific authorization identifiers. In other words, you can assign one or more privileges to an object for one or more authorization identifiers. For example, you can assign the SELECT privilege to a table for the PUBLIC authorization identifier. This would allow all database users to view the contents of that table.

SQL defines nine types of privileges that you can assign to a schema object. Table 6-1 describes each of these privileges and lists the types of objects that the privilege can be assigned to.

Privilege	Description	Objects
SELECT	Allows specified authorization identifiers to query data in the object. For example, if UserA is granted the SELECT privilege on the CDArtists table, that user can view data in that table.	Tables Views Columns Methods (in structured types)
INSERT	Allows specified authorization identifiers to insert data into the object. For example, if UserA is granted the INSERT privilege on the CDArtists table, that user can add data in that table.	Tables Views Columns
UPDATE	Allows specified authorization identifiers to update data in the object. For example, if UserA is granted the UPDATE privilege on the CDArtists table, that user can modify data in that table. However, this privilege does not allow the user to change the table definition.	Tables Views Columns
DELETE	Allows specified authorization identifiers to delete data from the object. For example, if UserA is granted the DELETE privilege on the CDArtists table, that user can remove data from that table. However, this privilege does not allow the user to drop the table definition from the database.	Tables Views

Table 6-1 Security Privileges Assigned to Database Objects

Privilege	Description	Objects
REFERENCES	Allows specified authorization identifiers to define tables that reference the table configured with the REFERENCES privilege. For example, if UserA is granted the REFERENCES privilege on the CDArtists table, that user can create other tables that reference the CDArtists table, as would be the case with foreign keys. (Note that UserA must also have the authorization to create other tables.)	Tables Views Columns
TRIGGER	Allows specified authorization identifiers to create triggers on the table. For example, if UserA is granted the TRIGGER privilege on the CDArtists table, that user can create triggers on that table.	Tables
USAGE	Allows specified authorization identifiers to use the object in a column definition. For example, if UserA is granted the USAGE privilege on the Money domain, that user can include the domain in a column definition when creating a table. (Note that UserA must also have the authorization to create a table.)	Domains Character sets Collations Translations User-defined types
EXECUTE	Allows specified authorization identifiers to invoke an SQL-invoked routine. For example, if UserA is granted the EXECUTE privilege on the sp_UpdateCDListing stored procedure, that user would be able to invoke that stored procedure.	SQL-invoked routines
UNDER	Allows specified authorization identifiers to define a direct subtype on a structured type. A *direct subtype* is a structured type that is associated with another structured type as a child object of that type. For example, if UserA is granted the UNDER privilege on the Employee structured type, that user can define direct subtypes such as Manager or Supervisor.	Structured types

Table 6-1 Security Privileges Assigned to Database Objects *(continued)*

Privileges are granted on database objects by using the GRANT statement to specify the objects as well as the authorization identifier that will have access to those objects. You can also revoke privileges by using the REVOKE statement. I will be going into greater detail about both these statements as we move through the module. However, before I discuss how to grant or revoke privileges, I want to first discuss how to create a role name. (Remember, SQL doesn't support the creation of a user identifier, only role names. The process for creating user identifiers is implementation-specific.)

Progress Check

1. What is an authorization identifier?

2. What two types of authorization identifiers does SQL support?

3. What is an SQL session?

4. Which privilege should you grant on an object if you want to allow an authorization identifier to query data in that object?

CRITICAL SKILL

6.2 Create and Delete Roles

For the most part, creating a role is a very straightforward process. The statement includes only one mandatory clause and one optional clause, as shown in the following syntax:

CREATE ROLE <role name>
[WITH ADMIN { CURRENT_USER | CURRENT_ROLE }]

Notice that the only required part of the syntax is the CREATE ROLE clause, which means that all you really need to do is specify a name for your role. The WITH ADMIN clause is optional and you will rarely need to use this. It is necessary only if the current user identifier/role name pair contains no null values. The clause allows you to designate either the current user identifier (CURRENT_USER) or the current role name (CURRENT_ROLE) as the authentication identifier allowed to assign the role to user identifiers or role names. If the WITH ADMIN clause is not specified, the current authentication identifier, whether the current user identifier or the current role name, is allowed to assign the role.

---

1. An authorization identifier is an object in the SQL environment that represents a user or group of users that are granted specific access privileges to objects and data within the SQL environment.

2. User identifiers and role names

3. An SQL session is the connection between some sort of client application to the database. The session provides the context in which the authorization identifier executes SQL statements during a single connection.

4. SELECT

NOTE

You'll probably find that you rarely need to use the WITH ADMIN clause, particularly as a beginning SQL programmer. As a result, I keep my discussion about the clause brief.

Now let's look at creating a role. In the following example, I use the CREATE ROLE statement to create the Customers role:

```
CREATE ROLE Customers ;
```

That's all there is to it. Once the role is created, you can grant the role to user identifiers or other role names. I discuss granting and revoking roles in the "Grant and Revoke Roles" section later in this module.

Dropping a role is just as easy as creating one. The syntax you use is as follows:

DROP ROLE <role name>

In this case, you merely need to identify the name of the role, as in the following example:

```
DROP ROLE Customers ;
```

The role is removed from the database. However, before removing a role, be sure that it is a role that you no longer need or that it is one you specifically want to delete (for security reasons).

As you can see, creating and dropping roles is a very simple process, and it can make managing your users a lot easier. Roles essentially allow you to group together those users who require the same privileges on the same object. Now let's take a look at granting and revoking privileges to authentication identifiers, including both user identifiers and role names.

NOTE

Support for the CREATE ROLE and DROP ROLE statements varies from implementation to implementation. For example, Oracle supports both statements, but SQL Server doesn't support either statement. However, SQL Server includes system stored procedures that you can use to create and delete roles. Ocelot, on the other, supports both statements, but when you execute them, you receive a message saying that the statement is not pure SQL-92 syntax.

CRITICAL SKILL
6.3 Grant and Revoke Privileges

When you grant privileges on an object, you are associating one or more privileges with one or more authorization identifiers. This set of privileges and authorization identifiers is assigned to the object, which allows the authorization identifiers to have access to the object according to the type of privileges defined. To grant privileges, you must use the GRANT statement, as shown in the following syntax:

6

```
GRANT { ALL PRIVILEGES | <privilege list> }
ON <object type> <object name>
TO { PUBLIC | <authorization identifier list> } [ WITH GRANT OPTION ]
[ GRANTED BY { CURRENT_USER | CURRENT_ROLE } ]
```

The statement, as you can see, includes three required clauses—GRANT, ON, and TO—and two optional clauses—WITH GRANT OPTION and GRANTED BY. I will discuss each clause individually except for the GRANTED BY clause. The GRANTED BY clause is similar to the WITH ADMIN clause in the CREATE ROLE statement. Like that clause, the GRANTED BY clause applies only in those situations where the current user identifier/role name pair contains no null values. As a beginner in SQL programming, you do not need to be concerned with the GRANTED BY clause.

NOTE

You must have the necessary privileges on an object to grant privileges on that object. If you created the object, then you are the owner, which means that you have complete access to the object. (All privileges have been granted to you, including the ability to assign privileges to other authorization identifiers.)

Now let's take a look at the GRANT clause. The clause includes two options: ALL PRIVILEGES and the <privilege list> placeholder. If you use the ALL PRIVILEGES keywords, you are granting all available privileges to that object according to the privileges that you have been granted on the object. For example, assume for a moment that you created a table and are the owner. As a result, you are automatically granted the SELECT, INSERT, UPDATE, DELETE, TRIGGER, and REFERENCES privileges. (These are the only privileges that apply to a table. Refer back to Table 6-1 for a list of privileges and the objects that they apply to.) You are also automatically granted the ability to assign these privileges. In this situation, if you use the ALL PRIVILEGES keywords, you would be granting these six privileges to the authorization identifiers in the GRANT statement.

If you decide not to use the ALL PRIVILEGES option, you must then list each privilege that should be applied to the user identifiers. However, you can list only those privileges that can be applied to the specific object. For example, you cannot list the DELETE privilege if you are granting a privilege on a domain. Also note, if you list more than one privilege, you must separate the privilege names by a comma.

The next clause we'll look at is the ON clause, which includes two placeholders: <object type> and <object name>. The <object type> placeholder simply refers to the type of object that you're granting permissions on. SQL supports the following values for the <object type> placeholder:

- TABLE

- DOMAIN

- COLLATION

- CHARACTER SET

- TRANSLATION

- TYPE

- Special designator for SQL-invoked routines

A value for the <object type> designator is required, unless the value is TABLE, in which case you can leave that off. (In fact, some implementations, such as SQL Server, require that you omit TABLE.) If you provide the name of an object without specifying a type, SQL assumes that the <object type> value is TABLE. However, you'll probably find that you'll want to include the keyword TABLE to keep your code consistent and easy to follow, unless the implementation prohibits it.

NOTE

The TABLE value includes views. As a result, you can include the name of the view without including the TABLE keyword.

The <object name> placeholder in the ON clause refers to the name of the specific object. This value is always required.

The next clause is the TO clause. Like the GRANT clause, the TO clause has two options: PUBLIC and the <authorization identifier list> placeholder. If you use PUBLIC, all database users are granted access to the object. If you use the <authorization identifier list> option, then you must provide the name of one or more authorization identifiers. If there are more than one, they must be separated by a comma.

The last clause that I am going to discuss is the WITH GRANT OPTION clause. This clause grants the authorization identifiers permission to grant whatever privileges they're being granted in the GRANT statement. For example, suppose you're granting the EmmaW user identifier the SELECT privilege on one of your tables. If you use the WITH GRANT OPTION, EmmaW will be able to grant the SELECT privilege to another user. If you do not use the WITH GRANT OPTION, EmmaW will not be able to grant the privilege to another user.

Now that we've taken a look at the syntax, let's look at a few examples. In the first example, we'll look at a GRANT statement that grants the SELECT privilege to the PUBLIC authorization identifier. The privilege is granted on a view named AvailableCDs, which lists the CDs that you currently have in stock. To grant the privilege, use the following statement:

```
GRANT SELECT ON TABLE AvailableCDs TO PUBLIC ;
```

The SELECT privilege allows all database users (PUBLIC) to view data in the AvailableCDs view. However, because PUBLIC has not been granted any other privileges, users can only view the data, but not take any action. In addition, because the WITH GRANT OPTION clause is not included in the statement, users cannot assign the SELECT privilege to any other users (which is a moot point in this case because everyone can already access the AvailableCDs view).

Now let's look at another example. This time, I'm granting the SELECT, UPDATE, and INSERT privileges to the Sales role and the Accounting role so that they have access to the CDInventory table:

```
GRANT SELECT, UPDATE, INSERT ON TABLE CDInventory
TO Sales, Accounting WITH GRANT OPTION ;
```

Notice that the privileges are separated by commas, as are the roles. As a result of this statement, the users associated with the Sales role and the Accounting role can view, update, and insert information into the CDInventory table. In addition, these users can assign the SELECT, UPDATE, and INSERT privileges to other users who need to access the CDInventory table.

The next example we will look at is a slight variation on this last one. Everything is the same, except that this time, I specify which column can be updated:

```
GRANT SELECT, UPDATE (CDTitle), INSERT ON TABLE CDInventory
TO Sales, Accounting WITH GRANT OPTION ;
```

Notice that you can add a column name after the specific privilege. You can add column names only to the SELECT, INSERT, UPDATE, and REFERENCES privileges. If you add more than one column name, you must separate them by a comma.

The GRANT statement in this example still allows the Sales and Accounting users to view and insert information into the CDInventory table, but they can update only the CDTitle value. They cannot update any other column values in the table. In addition, although they can still assign privileges to other users, they can assign the UPDATE privilege only on the CDTitle column.

Let's take a look at one more example that grants SELECT privileges to the PUBLIC authorization identifier:

```
GRANT SELECT (CDTitle, InStock) ON CDInventory TO PUBLIC ;
```

The PUBLIC authorization identifier allows all users to view data in the CDTitle and InStock columns of the CDInventory table, but they cannot view any other information in that table and they cannot modify the data in any way. Notice in this statement that the keyword TABLE isn't included. As I said earlier, TABLE is not required.

Ask the Expert

Q: You mention that, in certain situations, it's possible that the user identifier/role name pair contains no null values. When would that situation occur?

A: One way in which the user identifier and role name can both contain values (in other words, neither are null) is by manually assigning a value to the role name. The SET ROLE statement allows you to assign a value to the current role name. However, doing so has no effect on the current user identifier. As a result, if the current authorization identifier is based on a value for the current user identifier (in which case the role name is null) and you use the SET ROLE statement to assign a current role name value, you can end up with a user identifier/role name pair that contains no null values. Keep in mind, however, that even though SQL supports this possibility, your implementation might not, making it even more unlikely that this situation will come up for you. As a side note, the counterpart to the SET ROLE statement is the SET SESSION AUTHORIZATION statement, which sets the value for the current user authorization. However, this statement, unlike the SET ROLE statement, also sets the current role name to a null value, which means you won't run into the same situation as you can run into when using a SET ROLE statement.

The GRANT statement, when used in conjunction with the available privileges and the authorization identifiers, provides a strong foundation for your database security. However, each SQL implementation is different with regard to how security is implemented and maintained. Therefore, when it comes to matters of security, it is important that you work closely with network and database administrators and carefully read the product documentation.

Revoking Privileges

Now that you know how to grant privileges to authorization identifiers, it's time to learn how to revoke those privileges. The statement that you use to revoke privileges is the REVOKE statement, as shown in the following syntax:

```
REVOKE [ GRANT OPTION FOR ] { ALL PRIVILEGES | <privilege list> }
ON <object type> <object name>
FROM { PUBLIC | <authorization identifier list>
[ GRANTED BY { CURRENT_USER | CURRENT_ROLE } ]
{ RESTRICT | CASCADE }
```

You probably recognize many of the syntax elements from the GRANT statement or from other statements. In fact, the only new component, other than the REVOKE keyword, is the GRANT OPTION FOR clause. Let's take a look at that one first, since it's at the beginning of the REVOKE statement. This clause applies only when the WITH GRANT OPTION clause is used in the GRANT statement. If a privilege was granted with this clause, you can use the GRANT OPTION FOR clause to remove that particular permission. If you do use it, the privileges are reserved, but the user can no longer grant those privileges to other users.

Forgetting the GRANT OPTION FOR clause for a moment, let's look at the REVOKE clause itself, which is used to revoke either all privileges on an object (ALL PRIVILEGES) or only the defined privileges (<privilege list>). Both these options have the same meaning they did in the GRANT statement; you can either use ALL PRIVILEGES or you can list each privilege, separated by a comma.

The ON clause and GRANTED BY clause in the REVOKE statement are exactly the same as the ON clause and GRANTED BY clause in the GRANT statement. For the ON clause, you must specify values for the <object type> placeholder and the <object name> placeholder; however, if the <object type> value is TABLE, then you can leave that off. As for the GRANTED BY clause, you can choose one of two options (CURRENT_USER or CURRENT_ROLE).

The FROM clause in the REVOKE statement can also be compared to the GRANT statement. The only difference is that in the GRANT statement, you use the TO keyword, but in the REVOKE statement, you use the FROM keyword. In either case, you must choose PUBLIC as your authorization identifier, or you must list the specific user identifiers and role names.

The last elements of the statement to discuss are the RESTRICT keyword and the CASCADE keyword. You might recall these keywords from Module 2, Module 3, and Module 4. If you specify RESTRICT, the privilege will not be revoked if it had been passed on to other users—in other words, if there are any dependent privileges. (This would mean that the WITH GRANT OPTION had been used in the GRANT statement and that the authorization identifier that had been granted the privilege had then granted the privilege to someone else.) If you specify CASCADE, the privilege will be revoked as will any privileges that were passed on to other users.

Now let's take a look at some examples of revoking privileges. The following statement revokes a SELECT privilege that was granted to the PUBLIC authorization identifier on the AvailableCDs view:

```
REVOKE SELECT ON TABLE AvailableCDs FROM PUBLIC CASCADE ;
```

As you can see, this statement is very similar to what a GRANT statement might look like. You must identify the privileges, the authorization identifiers, and the object. In addition, you must specify RESTRICT or CASCADE.

The next example is based on privileges that have been granted on a table named CDInventory. The Sales role and Accounting role have been granted the following privileges on this table: GRANT, SELECT, and INSERT. To revoke these privileges, use the following REVOKE statement:

```
REVOKE SELECT, UPDATE, INSERT ON TABLE CDInventory
FROM Sales, Accounting CASCADE ;
```

Notice that you simply specify the privileges you want to revoke, the name of the objects, and the name of the authorization identifiers. However, since you are revoking all the privileges that had been granted, you could have simplified the statement by using the ALL PRIVILEGES keywords, as shown in the following example:

```
REVOKE ALL PRIVILEGES ON TABLE CDInventory
FROM Sales, Accounting CASCADE ;
```

If you do not want to revoke all privileges, but instead want to revoke only the UPDATE and INSERT privileges, you can specify only those privileges, as shown in the following example:

```
REVOKE UPDATE, INSERT ON TABLE CDInventory
FROM Sales, Accounting CASCADE ;
```

You can also choose to revoke privileges for only one of the role names, rather than both. In addition, you can use the RESTRICT keyword rather than CASCADE.

Now suppose the same privileges had been granted as in the preceding example but in addition to those, the WITH GRANT OPTION had been specified when granting privileges. If you want to revoke only the ability of the Sales and Accounting roles to grant privileges to other users, you can use the following statement:

```
REVOKE GRANT OPTION FOR ALL PRIVILEGES ON CDInventory
FROM Sales, Accounting CASCADE ;
```

This statement revokes only the ability to grant privileges; the Sales and Accounting roles still have access to the CDInventory table. If you want to revoke all their privileges, you would have to execute this statement without the GRANT OPTION FOR clause. Notice in this statement that the TABLE keyword wasn't used before the name of the table. The REVOKE statement, like the GRANT statement, doesn't require the TABLE keyword when specifying a table or view.

Progress Check

1. You are creating a role named AcctDept. What SQL statement should you use?

2. You are granting privileges on the CDInventory table. You are the owner of the table and you want to grant every privilege available on the table. What keywords can you use to specify every table privilege?

3. Which keyword should you use in a REVOKE statement to ensure that a privilege will not be revoked if there are any dependent privileges?

CRITICAL SKILL

 # Grant and Revoke Roles

Now that you know how to create and delete roles and grant and revoke privileges, let's look at granting and revoking roles. We'll start with granting roles. To grant a role, you must use a GRANT statement to assign one or more role names to one or more authorization identifiers, as shown in the following syntax:

```
GRANT <role name list>
TO { PUBLIC | <authorization identifier list> } [ WITH ADMIN OPTION ]
[ GRANTED BY { CURRENT_USER | CURRENT_ROLE } ]
```

By now, most of this syntax should look quite familiar to you, except for a few variations. The GRANT clause allows you to specify a list of one or more role names. If you specify more than one name, you must separate them by commas. The TO clause allows you to specify one or more authorization identifiers. Again, if there are more than one, you must separate them by a comma. You can also specify the PUBLIC authorization identifier to grant a role to all database users. The WITH ADMIN OPTION clause, which is optional, allows the authorization identifiers to grant the role to other users. And the GRANTED BY clause, which is also optional, is used in those rare instances when the user identifier/role name pair does not contain a null value.

---

1. You should use the following SQL statement:
CREATE ROLE AcctDept ;
2. ALL PRIVILEGES
3. RESTRICT

Let's look at an example. Suppose you have created a role named Managers and you want to assign that role to a user identifier named LindaN. You would use the following syntax:

```
GRANT Managers TO LindaN ;
```

Now suppose you want to give LindaN the ability to grant the Managers role to other users. To do this, you simply add the WITH ADMIN OPTION clause, as in the following example:

```
GRANT Managers TO LindaN WITH ADMIN OPTION ;
```

You can also grant multiple roles to multiple user identifiers. The user identifiers can be user identifiers or other role names. In the following example, I grant the Managers role and Accounting role to the LindaN user identifier and the Marketing role name:

```
GRANT Managers, Accounting TO LindaN, Marketing WITH ADMIN OPTION ;
```

Now that you know how to grant roles to authorization identifiers, it's time to learn how to revoke those roles.

Revoking Roles

Revoking roles is a lot like revoking privileges. The statement that you use to revoke privileges is the REVOKE statement, as shown in the following syntax:

```
REVOKE [ ADMIN OPTION FOR ] <role name list>
FROM { PUBLIC | <authorization identifier list> }
[ GRANTED BY { CURRENT_USER | CURRENT_ROLE } ]
{ RESTRICT | CASCADE }
```

As you can see, there is nothing new in the syntax except for the ADMIN OPTION FOR clause, which is similar to the GRANT OPTION FOR clause used when revoking privileges. It allows you to revoke the ability to assign roles to other users, without revoking the role itself.

Let's take a look at an example of revoking a role. Suppose you've granted the Managers role to the LindaN user identifier. You can revoke that role by using the following REVOKE statement:

```
REVOKE Managers FROM LindaN CASCADE ;
```

If you had granted the Managers role and the Accounting role to LindaN and the Marketing role, your REVOKE statement would look like the following:

```
REVOKE Managers, Accounting FROM LindaN, Marketing CASCADE ;
```

Now that we've looked at how to grant and revoke roles, you can see how similar this is to granting and revoking privileges. Again, I must stress that not all implementations are alike with regard to how they grant and revoke privileges and roles, so be sure to review your product documentation and work closely with the database administrator.

Project 6-1   Managing Roles and Privileges

Prj06.txt

In this project, you will create two roles in the Inventory database, grant privileges to the PUBLIC authorization identifier and to one of the roles you created, grant one of the roles to the other role, and then revoke all the privileges and roles. Finally, you will drop the two roles that you created. Your ability to follow all the steps in this project will depend on the type of security-related statements supported in the SQL implementation that you're using. However, the project is designed so that any roles you create or privileges you assign are dropped by the end of the project. You will not be using these roles for any projects later in the book. If for any reason this project might affect the security of the system on which you're working, you should discuss this project with a database administrator or skip it altogether. You can download the Prj06.txt file, which contains the SQL statements used in this project.

Step by Step

1. Open the client application for your RDBMS and connect to the Inventory database.

2. The first thing you'll do is create the Mrkt role. Enter and execute the following SQL statement:

```
CREATE ROLE Mrkt ;
```

3. Next you'll create the SalesStaff role. Enter and execute the following SQL statement:

```
CREATE ROLE SalesStaff ;
```

4. You'll now grant the SELECT privilege on the CDsInStock view. The privilege will be assigned to the PUBLIC authorization identifier. Enter and execute the following SQL statement:

```
GRANT SELECT ON TABLE CDsInStock TO PUBLIC ;
```

5. The next privileges you grant will be to the SalesStaff role that you created in step 3. You'll be granting the SELECT, INSERT, and UPDATE privileges on the CompactDiscs table. For the UPDATE privilege you will specify the CDTitle column. You will also allow the SalesStaff role to grant these privileges to other users. Enter and execute the following SQL statement:

```
GRANT SELECT, INSERT, UPDATE (CDTitle) ON TABLE CompactDiscs
TO SalesStaff WITH GRANT OPTION ;
```

(continued)

6. You'll now grant the SalesStaff role to the Mrkt role. Enter and execute the following SQL statement:

```
GRANT SalesStaff TO Mrkt ;
```

7. Your next step is to revoke the SELECT privilege that you granted to the PUBLIC authorization identifier. Enter and execute the following SQL statement:

```
REVOKE SELECT ON TABLE CDsInStock FROM PUBLIC CASCADE ;
```

8. Now you'll revoke the privileges that you granted to the SalesStaff role. Because you're revoking all privileges, you can use the ALL PRIVILEGES keyword. You also want to ensure that any dependent privileges are revoked, so you'll use the CASCADE keyword. Enter and execute the following SQL statement:

```
REVOKE ALL PRIVILEGES ON TABLE CompactDiscs FROM SalesStaff CASCADE ;
```

9. You can now revoke the SalesStaff role from the Mrkt role. Enter and execute the following SQL statement:

```
REVOKE SalesStaff FROM Mrkt CASCADE ;
```

10. Your next step is to drop the Mrkt role. Enter and execute the following SQL statements:

```
DROP ROLE Mrkt ;
```

11. Finally, you need to drop the SalesStaff role. Enter and execute the following SQL statements:

```
DROP ROLE SalesStaff ;
```

12. Close the client application.

Project Summary

The Inventory database should now be set up the same way it was before you started this project. The permissions and roles you granted should have been revoked, and the roles you created should have been dropped. This way, you will not have to worry about security considerations for other projects. For the remaining projects in the book, you should continue to work within the same security context in which you've been working for this project and for all projects preceding this one.

Module 6 Mastery Check

1. What is the difference between a user identifier and a role name?

2. What is the name of the special authorization identifier that grants access to all database users?

3. Each _____ is associated with a user identifier and role name.

4. An SQL session is associated with which of the following?

    A. Privilege

    B. User identifier

    C. PUBLIC

    D. Role name

5. When an SQL session is first established, the user identifier is always the _____.

6. What is the value of the current role name when an SQL session is first established?

7. What is an authorization identifier?

8. You establish an SQL session with your database. The current user identifier is EthanW. The current role name is null. What is the current authorization identifier?

9. On which schema objects can you define access privileges?

10. On which types of database objects can you assign the DELETE privilege?

    A. Tables

    B. Views

    C. Columns

    D. Domains

11. On which types of database objects can you assign the TRIGGER privilege?

    A. Tables

    B. Views

    C. Columns

    D. Domains

12. You're creating a role named Accounting. Which SQL statement should you use?

13. You're granting all privileges on the CDNames view to everyone who uses the database. Which SQL statement should you use?

14. You're granting the SELECT privilege to the SalesClerk role on a table in your database. You want the SalesClerk role to be able to assign the SELECT privilege to other users. What clause should you include in your GRANT statement?

15. You want to grant the Acct role to the MaxN user authorization. You do not want the user to be able to grant the role to other users. What SQL statement should you use to grant the role?

Part II

Data Access and Modification

Module 7

Querying SQL Data

Once the objects in a database have been created and the base tables populated with data, you can submit queries that allow you to retrieve specific information from the database. These queries, which usually take the form of SELECT statements, can range in complexity from a simple statement that returns all columns from a table to a statement that joins multiple tables, calculates values, and defines search conditions that restrict exactly which rows of data should be returned. The SELECT statement is made up of a flexible series of clauses that together determine which data will be retrieved. In this module, you will learn how to use each of these clauses in order to perform basic data retrieval, define search conditions, group query results, specify group search conditions, and order search results.

CRITICAL SKILL

7.1 Use a SELECT Statement to Retrieve Data

In Module 5, when discussing views, I introduce you to the SELECT statement. As you might recall, the SELECT statement allows you to form intricate queries that can return exactly the type of data you want to retrieve. It is one of the most common statements you'll be using as an SQL programmer, and it is also one of the most flexible and extensive statements in the SQL standard.

The SELECT statement is a query expression that begins with the SELECT keyword and includes a number of elements that form the expression. The basic syntax for the SELECT statement can be split into several specific clauses that each help to refine the query so that only the required data is returned. The syntax for the SELECT statement can be shown as follows:

```
SELECT [ DISTINCT | ALL ] { * | <select list> }
FROM <table reference> [ { , <table reference> } . . . ]
[ WHERE <search condition> ]
[ GROUP BY <grouping specification> ]
[ HAVING <search condition> ]
[ ORDER BY <order condition> ]
```

As you can see, the only required clauses are the SELECT clause and the FROM clause. All other clauses are optional.

The FROM, WHERE, GROUP BY, and HAVING clauses are referred to as the table expression. This portion of the SELECT statement is always evaluated first when a SELECT statement is processed. Each clause within the table expression is evaluated in the order listed in the syntax. The result of that evaluation is a virtual table that is used in the subsequent evaluation. In other words, the results from the first clause evaluated are used in the next clause. The results from that clause are then used in the following clause, until each clause in the table expression is evaluated. For example, the first clause to be evaluated in a SELECT statement is the FROM clause. Because this clause is required, it is always the first clause evaluated. The results from the FROM clause are then used in the WHERE clause, if a WHERE clause is specified. If the clause is not specified, then the results of the FROM clause are used in the next specified clause, either the GROUP BY clause or the HAVING clause. Once the final clause in the table expression is evaluated, the results are then used in the SELECT clause. After the SELECT clause is evaluated, the ORDER BY clause is evaluated.

To sum all this up, the clauses of the SELECT statement are applied in the following order:

- FROM clause

- WHERE clause (optional)

- GROUP BY clause (optional)

- HAVING clause (optional)

- SELECT clause

- ORDER BY clause (optional)

Having a basic understanding of the order of evaluation is important as you create more complex SELECT statements, especially when working with joins and subqueries (discussed in Module 11 and Module 12, respectively). This understanding is also helpful when discussing each clause individually because it explains how one clause relates to other clauses. As a result, it is a good idea for you to keep this order of evaluation in mind throughout this module and in subsequent modules that build upon various aspects of the SELECT statement.

The SELECT Clause and FROM Clause

Now that you have a basic overview of how the SELECT statement is executed, let's take a closer look at the SELECT clause and the FROM clause, the two required clauses in the statement. I'll discuss the other clauses in separate sections throughout the remainder of the module.

Let's begin with the SELECT clause. The SELECT clause includes the optional DISTINCT and ALL keywords. The DISTINCT keyword is used if you want to eliminate duplicate rows from the query results, and the ALL keyword is used if you want to return all rows in the query results. For example, suppose your database includes a table named PerformerCDs. The table includes the PerformerName column and the CDName column. Because a CD can include more than one performer, the CD name can appear more than one time in the table. Now suppose that you want to query the table for the name of the CDs only, but you don't want the names repeated. You can use the DISTINCT keyword to ensure that your query returns the name of each CD only one time, or you can use the ALL keyword to specify that all rows be returned, even if there are duplicates. If you don't specify either of the keywords, the ALL keyword is assumed.

Ask the Expert

Q: You state that you can use an asterisk to include all columns in the query result. Does this ever present a problem if the number of columns changes?

A: Yes, this can present a problem. In fact, it is generally recommended that you use the asterisk only when you're accessing an SQL database through direct invocation. If you use the asterisk in embedded SQL and the number of columns changes, you might find that your application no longer responds correctly because the application language was coded to expect a specific response. If an asterisk is used and specific columns are expected to be returned, then you could run into a number of surprises if the database has been changed. For this reason, you should avoid the asterisk unless directly invoking a SELECT statement. However, in the case of direct invocation, the asterisk is a handy way to return all columns without having to specify each one. In fact, many of the examples in the module use the asterisk to avoid having to repeat column names unnecessarily.

In addition to the DISTINCT and ALL keywords, the SELECT clause includes the asterisk (*) and the <select list> placeholder. You must specify one of these options in the clause. If you specify the asterisk, all applicable columns are included in the query result.

If you don't specify an asterisk in the SELECT clause, you must specify each column as it is derived from its source. The <select list> placeholder can be broken down into the following syntax:

<derived column> [[AS] <column name>]
[{ , <derived column> [[AS] <column name>] } . . .]

Let's take a look at the first line of this syntax. (The second line is merely a repeat—as many times as necessary—of the first line.) The <derived column> placeholder in most cases refers to the name of the column in the source table. If more than one column is specified, then they must be separated by a comma. However, the <derived column> placeholder might also refer to a column or set of columns that are in some way part of an expression. For instance, in Module 5 I discuss the AVG function, which averages the values in a specified column. The example I show in that module uses a SELECT statement to query data from the EmployeeCommissions table, which lists the total amount of commissions each employee made during a three-year period. The SELECT statement averages the values in three different columns, as shown in the following SELECT statement:

```
SELECT AVG(Year1999), AVG(Year2000), AVG(Year2001)
FROM EmployeeCommissions ;
```

In this case, there are three expressions that are used for the <derived column> placeholder: AVG(Year1999), AVG(Year2000), and AVG(Year2001). Notice that each derived column expression is separated by a comma, as would be the case if each value were simply a column name. The following example shows the same SELECT statement as in the preceding example, except that it uses only column names as the derived columns:

```
SELECT Year1999, Year2000, Year2001
FROM EmployeeCommissions ;
```

If you were to execute this SELECT statement, your query would return all the values in the three columns, rather than averaging those values.

The SELECT clause also allows you to provide a column name for each derived column. To do this, add the AS keyword and the new column name after the derived column, as shown in the following example:

```
SELECT AVG(Year1999) AS Average1999
FROM EmployeeCommissions ;
```

In this SELECT statement, the value that is returned from the Year1999 column is placed in a column named Average1999. This is the name of the column that's returned as part of a virtual table in the query results. If you don't specify an AS subclause, the column name in the virtual table is the same as the column name in the source table. If a column name cannot be inherited naturally (for example, when adding two column values together), you must use the AS subclause.

Notice that in the previous examples the FROM clause is used to specify the table (EmployeeCommissions) that contains the columns referred to in the SELECT clause. The FROM clause includes the FROM keyword and one or more table references. If there are more than one, they must be separated by a comma. In most cases, the table reference is either the name of a table or of joined tables, although it can also be a type of subquery. I discuss joined tables in Module 11 and subqueries in Module 12. For this module, the FROM clause is used primarily to reference table names, as I have defined the clause in the two previous examples (where <table reference> equals EmployeeCommissions).

Together the SELECT clause and the FROM clause form the foundation for the SELECT statement, which can be as simple as querying every row and every column of a table, as shown in the following example:

```
SELECT * FROM Performers ;
```

In this statement, I specify that every column should be returned for the Performers table. In addition, because no other clauses have been specified, every row will also be returned. Let's take a closer look at this. The Performers table includes the PerformerID, PerformerName, and PlaceOfBirth columns, as shown in Figure 7-1.

PerformerID: INT	PerformerName: VARCHAR (60)	PlaceOfBirth VARCHAR (60)
2001	Jennifer Warnes	Seattle, Washington, USA
2002	Joni Mitchell	Fort MacLeod, Alberta, Canada
2003	William Ackerman	Germany
2004	Kitaro	Toyohashi, Japan
2005	Bing Crosby	Tacoma, Washington, United States
2006	Patsy Cline	Winchester, Virginia, United States
2007	Jose Carreras	Barcelona, Spain
2008	Luciano Pavarotti	Modena, Italy
2009	Placido Domingo	Madrid, Spain

Figure 7-1 The PerformerID, PerformerName, and PlaceOfBirth columns of the
Performers table

If you execute the SELECT statement shown in the previous example, your query results
would look similar to the following:

```
PerformerID   PerformerName        PlaceOfBirth
--------      ------------------   ------------------------------
2001          Jennifer Warnes      Seattle, Washington, USA
2002          Joni Mitchell        Fort MacLeod, Alberta, Canada
2003          William Ackerman     Germany
2004          Kitaro               Toyohashi, Japan
2005          Bing Crosby          Tacoma, Washington, USA
2006          Patsy Cline          Winchester, Virginia, USA
2007          Jose Carreras        Barcelona, Spain
2008          Luciano Pavarotti    Modena, Italy
2009          Placido Domingo      Madrid, Spain
```

Notice that every row of every column is returned in the query results. If you use the asterisk
in your SELECT clause, you do not have to specify the column names.

Now suppose you want to return only the PerformerName and PlaceOfBirth columns.
You could modify your SELECT statement to look like the following:

```
SELECT PerformerName AS Name, PlaceOfBirth FROM Performers ;
```

Your query results will now contain only two columns, as shown in the following:

```
Name                  PlaceOfBirth
----------------      ------------------------------
Jennifer Warnes       Seattle, Washington, USA
Joni Mitchell         Fort MacLeod, Alberta, Canada
William Ackerman      Germany
Kitaro                Toyohashi, Japan
Bing Crosby           Tacoma, Washington, USA
Patsy Cline           Winchester, Virginia, USA
Jose Carreras         Barcelona, Spain
Luciano Pavarotti     Modena, Italy
Placido Domingo       Madrid, Spain
```

Notice that the name of the first column is Name, rather than PerformerName. This is because the AS subclause (specifying Name) is defined as part of the PerformerName derived column. If you were to specify the DISTINCT keyword in this particular situation, you would still receive the same number of rows, although they might not be returned in the same order as they were when you didn't use the keyword, depending on the SQL implementation. The reason that the DISTINCT keyword would make no difference in the query results is that there are no duplicate rows in the table. However, using the DISTINCT keyword can affect performance, particularly if your query has to sort through a large number of rows, so be sure to use the keyword only when necessary.

Now let's take a look at an example that uses the DISTINCT keyword. Suppose your database includes a table that matches performers to types of music, as shown in Figure 7-2.

PerformerName: VARCHAR (60)	Type: VARCHAR (10)
Jennifer Warnes	Folk
Jennifer Warnes	Pop
Joni Mitchell	Pop
Joni Mitchell	Folk
Joni Mitchell	Jazz
William Ackerman	New Age
Kitaro	New Age
Kitaro	International

Figure 7-2 The PerformerName and Type columns of the PerformerType table

If your SELECT statement includes both columns in the SELECT clause, as shown in the following example, your query will return all rows:

```
SELECT * FROM PerformerType ;
```

It does not matter if you specify the DISTINCT keyword in this case because your query results include no duplicate rows. The results would be the same whether you include the ALL keyword, rather than DISTINCT, or whether you specify neither of the two qualifiers. In either case, the query results would include the same information that is shown in the table in Figure 7-2.

Now let's take a look at the same statement, only this time it specifies the DISTINCT keyword and only one of the two columns:

```
SELECT DISTINCT PerformerName FROM PerformerType ;
```

Notice that this statement includes only the PerformerName column, which includes duplicate values. By using the DISTINCT keyword, your query results will include only one instance of each value. If you execute the SELECT statement in the preceding example, your query results will look similar to the following:

```
PerformerName
-------------------------
Jennifer Warnes
Joni Mitchell
Kitaro
William Ackerman
```

Although there are seven rows in the PerformerType table, only four rows are returned because there are only four unique values in the PerformerName column and the other values are duplicates.

As you can see, the SELECT clause and the FROM clause are fairly straightforward, at least at this level of coding. Once we get into more complex structures, you'll find that both these clauses can at times become more complicated. However, the important thing to remember right now is that these clauses act as the foundation for the rest of the SELECT statement. In terms of execution, the SELECT statement, for all practical purposes, begins with the FROM clause and ends with the SELECT clause. (The ORDER BY clause is used primarily for display purposes and doesn't affect which information is actually returned. The ORDER BY clause is discussed in more detail in the "Use the ORDER BY Clause to Sort Query Results" section later in this module.)

Progress Check

1. What are the six main clauses in a SELECT statement?

2. Which clauses in a SELECT statement are considered to be part of the table expression?

3. Which keyword should you include in the SELECT clause if you want to eliminate duplicate rows from the query results?

4. Which symbol can you use if you want to include all of a table's columns in the SELECT clause?

CRITICAL SKILL

7.2 Use the WHERE Clause to Define Search Conditions

The next clause in the SELECT statement is the WHERE clause. The WHERE clause takes the values returned by the FROM clause (in a virtual table) and applies the search condition that is defined within the WHERE clause. The WHERE clause acts as a filter on the results returned by the FROM clause. Each row is evaluated against the search condition. Those rows that evaluate to true are returned as part of the query result. Those that evaluate to unknown or false are not included in the results.

For a better understanding of how each row is evaluated, let's take a closer look at the <search condition> placeholder. The search condition is made up of one or more predicates that are used to test the contents returned by the FROM clause. A *predicate* is an SQL expression that defines a fact about any row returned by the SELECT statement. You have already seen examples of predicates in Module 4 and Module 5. For instance, one example of a view definition (in Module 5) includes the following SELECT statement:

```
SELECT CDTitle, Copyright, InStock FROM CompactDiscInventory
WHERE Copyright > 1989 AND Copyright < 2000 ;
```

---

1. SELECT, FROM, WHERE, GROUP BY, HAVING, and ORDER BY

2. FROM, WHERE, GROUP BY, and HAVING

3. DISTINCT

4. An asterisk (*)

This statement is querying three columns in the CompactDiscInventory table. The SELECT clause specifies the columns to be returned, and the FROM clause specifies the source table. The WHERE clause determines which rows (based on the FROM clause) are included in the results. In this case, the WHERE clause contains two predicates that are connected by the AND keyword. The first predicate (Copyright > 1989) specifies that all rows included in the query results must contain a value greater than 1989 in the Copyright column. The second predicate (Copyright < 2000) specifies that all rows included in the query results must contain a value less than 2000 in the Copyright column.

Each predicate is evaluated on an individual basis to determine whether it meets the condition defined by that predicate. Returning to the last example, the first predicate sets the condition that values must be greater than 1989. If the Copyright value for a particular row is more than 1989, the condition is met and the predicate evaluates to true. If the value is not greater than 1989, the predicate evaluates to false. If SQL cannot determine whether or not the value meets the condition (as would be the case if the value is null), the predicate evaluates to unknown.

Every predicate is evaluated to true, false, or unknown. If more than one predicate is included in the WHERE clause, they are joined together by the OR keyword or the AND keyword. If OR is used, then at least one of the predicates on either side of OR must evaluate to true. If AND is used, then predicates on either side must evaluate to true. For instance, the WHERE clause in the last example includes two predicates that are connected by the AND keyword. This means that the first predicate must evaluate to true *and* the second predicate must evaluate to true. If OR had been used instead of AND, then only one of the predicates must evaluate to true, which is a bit nonsensical because all values except null are either above 1989 or below 2000.

Ultimately, the WHERE clause as a whole must evaluate to true in order for a row to be included in the query results. If the WHERE clause includes more than one predicate, SQL follows specific guidelines for how the statement as a whole is evaluated. Let's start by looking at the OR keyword. Table 7-1 lists the evaluation of a search condition if the OR keyword is used to separate two predicates. To use the table, match a condition in the left column to a condition in the top row. The result (where the cells intersect) shows how the search condition is evaluated based on how each predicate is evaluated.

As the table shows, if both predicates evaluate to true, then the search condition evaluates to true. If both are false, then the search condition evaluates to false. A condition is provided

	True	False	Unknown
True	True	True	True
False	True	False	Unknown
Unknown	True	Unknown	Unknown

Table 7-1 Evaluating Predicates Connected by OR

for each possible match. For example, suppose your SELECT statement includes the following WHERE clause:

```
WHERE Type = 'Folk' OR Type = 'Jazz'
```

Now suppose that the first predicate in this example (Type = 'Folk') evaluates to true and the second predicate (Type = 'Jazz') evaluates to false. This means that the row being evaluated contains the Folk value in the Type column, but does not contain the Jazz value in that column. Now refer back to Table 7-1. If you select True from the first column, select False from the top row, and then match these two values together (by picking where they intersect), you can see that the search condition evaluates to true, so the row will be included in the query results.

You can do the same thing with the AND keyword as you did with the OR keyword. Table 7-2 matches the nine possible outcomes of two predicates.

Again, you simply match up how each predicate is evaluated to determine whether the search condition will be evaluated to true, false, or unknown. Remember, the search condition must evaluate to true for the row to be included in the query results. As you can see, the AND keyword is a lot less forgiving than the OR keyword. The only way for the search condition to evaluate to true is for both predicates to evaluate to true.

NOTE

Comparison operators and predicates in general are discussed in greater detail in Module 9.

If a search condition includes more than two predicates, the predicates are evaluated in the order they appear, unless parentheses are used to separate combinations of predicates. For example, you might have a SELECT statement that includes the following WHERE clause:

```
WHERE InStock = 6 OR InStock = 27 AND LabelID = 833 OR LabelID = 829
```

	True	False	Unknown
True	True	False	Unknown
False	False	False	False
Unknown	Unknown	False	Unknown

Table 7-2 Evaluating Predicates Connected by AND

Notice that there are four predicates in this clause. In order to evaluate to true, a row must contain one of the following values or set of values:

- InStock value of 6

- InStock value of 27 and LabelID value of 833

- LabelID value of 829

The WHERE clause would create the same results if parentheses were used for the predicate pair in the second bullet:

```
WHERE InStock = 6 OR (InStock = 27 AND LabelID = 833) OR LabelID = 829
```

If parentheses are used for other sets of predicates, the results will be different from what we've seen. For example, suppose you use parentheses as follows:

```
WHERE (InStock = 6 OR InStock = 27) AND (LabelID = 833 OR LabelID = 829)
```

The predicates are first evaluated within the context of the parentheses and then compared to other predicates accordingly. In this case, a row must contain one of the two InStock values *and* the row must contain one of the two LabelID values. As a result, a row must contain one of the following sets of values to evaluate to true:

- InStock value of 6 and LabelID value of 833

- InStock value of 6 and LabelID value of 829

- InStock value of 27 and LabelID value of 833

- InStock value of 27 and LabelID value of 829

In general, it's a good idea to use parentheses to clarify your search condition if there's any possibility for confusion.

NOTE

SQL includes three operators that you can use if a search condition becomes too complicated. These operators are IS TRUE, IS FALSE, and IS UNKNOWN. For example, you can specify the following search condition: (FirstName = 'Joni' AND LastName = 'Mitchell') IS TRUE. This means that the FirstName value of a returned row must be Joni *and* the LastName value must be Mitchell. In other words, they must evaluate to true. If you specify IS FALSE in this situation, the predicate pair would have to evaluate to false, meaning that at least one of the two predicates had to be false (could not be Joni *or* could not be Mitchell).

Another keyword that you might find useful is the NOT keyword, which can be used alone or along with the AND keyword and the OR keyword to specify the inverse of a predicate. For example, your SELECT statement might include the following WHERE clause:

```
WHERE PerformerName = 'Joni Mitchell' OR NOT PerformerName = 'Kitaro'
```

In this case, the PerformerName value can be Joni Mitchell or it can be any value other than Kitaro. By the way, you would get the same result if you used the not equal (<>) comparison operator, as shown in the following example:

```
WHERE PerformerName <> 'Kitaro'
```

Defining the WHERE Clause

Now that you have an overview of how to define a WHERE clause, let's put it together with the SELECT clause and FROM clause and take a look at a few examples. The examples that we'll be looking at are based on the Inventory table, shown in Figure 7-3. The Inventory table contains five columns, some of which we'll be using to define our search conditions.

The first example that we'll be looking at includes a WHERE clause that defines which rows can be returned based on the InStock values:

```
SELECT * FROM Inventory
WHERE InStock < 20 ;
```

CompactDiskID: INT	CDTitle: VARCHAR (60)	Copyright: INT	RetailPrice: NUMERIC (5,2)	InStock: INT
99301	Famous Blue Raincoat	1991	16.99	6
99302	Blue	1971	14.99	26
99303	Court and Spark	1974	14.99	18
99304	Past Light	1983	15.99	2
99305	Kojiki	1990	15.99	5
99306	That Christmas Feeling	1993	10.99	3
99307	Patsy Cline: 12 Greatest Hits	1988	16.99	25

Figure 7-3 The Inventory table containing CD-related data

If you execute this statement, your query results will be similar to the following:

```
CompactDiscID  CDTitle                  Copyright  RetailPrice  InStock
-------------  ----------------------   ---------  -----------  -------
99301          Famous Blue Raincoat     1991       16.99        6
99303          Court and Spark          1974       14.99        18
99304          Past Light               1983       15.99        2
99305          Kojiki                   1990       15.99        5
99306          That Christmas Feeling   1993       10.99        3
```

As you can see, all but two rows are included in the query results. The rows not included contain InStock values greater than 20. In other words, these two rows evaluated to false.

Now let's take that same SELECT statement and refine the WHERE clause even further. In the new statement, the WHERE clause includes two predicates that are connected by the AND keyword, as shown in the following example:

```
SELECT * FROM Inventory
WHERE InStock < 20 AND RetailPrice < 15.00 ;
```

When you execute this statement, you receive the following results:

```
CompactDiscID  CDTitle                  Copyright  RetailPrice  InStock
-------------  ----------------------   ---------  -----------  -------
99303          Court and Spark          1974       14.99        18
99306          That Christmas Feeling   1993       10.99        3
```

Notice that only two rows meet the search condition. In other words, only these two rows have an InStock value of less than 20 *and* a RetailPrice value of less than 15.00. Because the AND keyword is used, both predicates must evaluate to true, which they do for these two rows.

Now let's make one small modification to the SELECT statement. In the WHERE clause, I have changed the AND keyword to an AND NOT keywords, as shown in the following example:

```
SELECT * FROM Inventory
WHERE InStock < 20 AND NOT RetailPrice < 15.00 ;
```

The NOT keyword changes the query results. As you can see, three rows are returned:

```
CompactDiscID  CDTitle                  Copyright  RetailPrice  InStock
-------------  ----------------------   ---------  -----------  -------
99301          Famous Blue Raincoat     1991       16.99        6
99304          Past Light               1983       15.99        2
99305          Kojiki                   1990       15.99        5
```

The returned rows each contain an InStock value of less than 20 *and* a RetailPrice value that is *not* less than 15.00, or 15.00 or greater.

Next we'll look at the same SELECT statement, only this time the two predicates are connected by the OR keyword, as shown in the following example:

```
SELECT * FROM Inventory
WHERE InStock < 20 OR RetailPrice < 15.00 ;
```

The query results for this statement include many more rows than when the AND keyword was used. By its very nature, the OR keyword permits greater opportunities for a search clause to evaluate to true. As you can see, six rows have now been returned:

```
CompactDiscID  CDTitle                 Copyright  RetailPrice  InStock
-------------  ----------------------  ---------  -----------  -------
99301          Famous Blue Raincoat    1991       16.99        6
99302          Blue                    1971       14.99        26
99303          Court and Spark         1974       14.99        18
99304          Past Light              1983       15.99        2
99305          Kojiki                  1990       15.99        5
99306          That Christmas Feeling  1993       10.99        3
```

Each row in the query results contains an InStock value of less than 20 *or* a RetailPrice value of less than 15.00. Because the OR keyword is being used, only one of the predicates needs to evaluate to true, although it's acceptable if both predicates evaluate to true.

In the next example, I add one more predicate that limits the rows returned to those with an InStock value greater than 5:

```
SELECT * FROM Inventory
WHERE InStock < 20 AND InStock > 5 OR RetailPrice < 15.00 ;
```

For a row to be returned, the InStock value must fall between the range of 5 and 20 *or* the RetailPrice value must be less than 15.00. The query results from this SELECT statement would be as follows:

```
CompactDiscID  CDTitle                 Copyright  RetailPrice  InStock
-------------  ----------------------  ---------  -----------  -------
99301          Famous Blue Raincoat    1991       16.99        6
99302          Blue                    1971       14.99        26
99303          Court and Spark         1974       14.99        18
99306          That Christmas Feeling  1993       10.99        3
```

Now let's make one more change to the WHERE clause. Suppose you want the InStock value to be less than 20 and greater than 5 or the InStock value to be less than 20 and the RetailPrice value to be less than 15. One way to do this is to add parentheses around the last two predicates:

```
SELECT * FROM Inventory
WHERE InStock < 20 AND (InStock > 5 OR RetailPrice < 15.00) ;
```

The results you receive this time are slightly different because the Blue row no longer evaluates to true:

```
CompactDiscID  CDTitle                Copyright  RetailPrice  InStock
-------------  ---------------------  ---------  -----------  -------
99301          Famous Blue Raincoat   1991       16.99        6
99303          Court and Spark        1974       14.99        18
99306          That Christmas Feeling 1993       10.99        3
```

By combining predicates together, you can create a variety of search conditions that allow you to return exactly the data you need. The key to writing effective search conditions is a thorough understanding of predicates and the operators used to form those predicates. Module 9 takes you through many of the operators that you can use and the types of predicates that you can create. With that information, you can create effective, concise search conditions.

Progress Check

1. A WHERE clause applies a search condition to the values returned by which clause?

2. What is a predicate?

3. What two keywords can you use to join together predicates in the WHERE clause?

4. What keyword can you use to express the inverse of a predicate?

---

1. FROM
2. A predicate is an SQL expression that defines a fact about any row returned by the SELECT statement.
3. OR and AND
4. NOT

CRITICAL SKILL

7.3 Use the GROUP BY Clause
to Group Query Results

The next clause in the SELECT statement is the GROUP BY clause. The GROUP BY clause
has a function very different from the WHERE clause. As the name implies, the GROUP BY
clause is used to group together types of information in order to summarize related data. The
GROUP BY clause can be included in a SELECT statement whether or not the WHERE clause
is used.

As you saw in the "Use a SELECT Statement to Retrieve Data" section, the syntax for the
GROUP BY clause, as it appears in the SELECT statement syntax, looks like the following:

[GROUP BY <grouping specification>]

However, the <grouping specification> placeholder can be broken down into smaller elements:

<column name> [{ , <column name> } . . .]
| { ROLLUP | CUBE } (<column name> [{ , <column name> } . . .])

In actuality, the <grouping specification> syntax, like some of the other syntax in this book, is
even more complex than what I'm presenting here; however, for the purposes of this module,
this syntax will provide you with all the details that you need to use the GROUP BY clause
effectively.

Now let's look at the syntax itself. The first line should be self-explanatory. You specify
one or more column names that contain values that should be grouped together. This normally
applies to columns that represent some sort of categories whose values are repeated within
the table. For example, your database might include a table that lists the employees in your
organization. Suppose that for each employee the table includes a job title. You might find that
you want to group together information in the table by job title, perhaps to determine such things
as the average salary of each job or number of employees holding each job title. If you need to
specify more than one column name, be sure to separate them with a comma.

As you can see from the syntax, you can specify the second line rather than the first. In this
case, you can use either the ROLLUP or CUBE keyword, along with the name of the columns
in parentheses. Again, be sure to separate column names with a comma. With regard to ROLLUP
and CUBE, the best way to understand these operators is through the use of examples. In fact,
the best way to understand the entire GROUP BY clause is through examples. However, before
we get into those, let's take a look at the table on which the examples will be based. Figure 7-4
shows the CompactDiscStock table, which contains a list of CDs, whether they're vocal or
instrumental, the price, and how many of each title are currently in stock.

CompactDisc: VARCHAR (60)	Category: VARCHAR (15)	Price: NUMERIC (5,2)	OnHand: INT
Famous Blue Raincoat	Vocal	16.99	13
Blue	Vocal	14.99	42
Court and Spark	Vocal	14.99	22
Past Light	Instrumental	15.99	17
Kojiki	Instrumental	15.99	6
That Christmas Feeling	Vocal	14.99	8
Patsy Cline: 12 Greatest Hits	Vocal	16.99	32
Carreras Domingo Pavarotti in Concert	Vocal	15.99	27
After the Rain: The Soft Sounds of Erik Satie	Instrumental	16.99	21
Out of Africa	Instrumental	16.99	29
Leonard Cohen The Best of	Vocal	15.99	12
Fundamental	Vocal	15.99	34
Blues on the Bayou	Vocal	14.99	27
Orlando	Instrumental	14.99	5

Figure 7-4 CD information in the CompactDiscStock table

Now we can get on with the examples. In the first one we'll look at, I use the GROUP BY clause to group rows based on the Category column of the CompactDiscStock table, as shown in the following SELECT statement:

```
SELECT Category, SUM(OnHand) AS TotalOnHand
FROM CompactDiscStock
GROUP BY Category ;
```

First, let's take a look at the GROUP BY clause, which specifies that the rows should be grouped together based on the Category column. If you look at Figure 7-4, you'll see that the column contains only two values: Vocal and Instrumental. As a result, the SELECT statement will return only two rows, one for Instrumental and one for Vocal:

```
Category       TotalOnHand
------------   -----------
Instrumental   78
Vocal          217
```

Now let's look at the SELECT clause in the preceding SELECT statement example. Notice that the select list includes the SUM function, which adds data in the OnHand column. The resulting column is then named TotalOnHand. The only other column included in the select list is the Category column. The select list can include only those columns that are specified in the GROUP BY clause or that can somehow be summarized.

What this statement does, then, is add together the total OnHand values for each value in the Category column. In this case, there are 217 total CDs in stock that are categorized as Vocal, and 78 in stock that are categorized as Instrumental. If there were another category, then a row would appear for that one as well.

As I said earlier, you can still use the WHERE clause in a SELECT statement that includes a GROUP BY clause. For example, suppose you want to view totals only for CDs that sell for less than $16.00. To do this, simply modify your SELECT statement as follows:

```
SELECT Category, SUM(OnHand) AS TotalOnHand
FROM CompactDiscStock WHERE Price < 16.00
GROUP BY Category ;
```

Your query results from this statement will be slightly different than if the WHERE clause had not been included:

```
Category        TotalOnHand
------------    ----------
Instrumental    28
Vocal           172
```

Notice that your results now show only 28 Instrumental CDs for less than $16.00 and 172 Vocal CDs.

In the previous two examples, the GROUP BY clause specified only one column. However, you can specify additional columns as necessary. This allows you to create subgroups that group data within the scope of the main groups. For example, suppose you want to group data not only according to the values in the Category column, but also according to the values in the Price column. To do this, you should include the Price column in the select list as well as the GROUP BY clause, as shown in the following SELECT statement:

```
SELECT Category, Price, SUM(OnHand) AS TotalOnHand
FROM CompactDiscStock
GROUP BY Category, Price ;
```

Now your query results will include six rows, rather than two:

```
Category       Price   TotalOnHand
------------   -----   ----------
Instrumental   14.99   5
Vocal          14.99   99
```

```
Instrumental  15.99  23
Vocal         15.99  73
Instrumental  16.99  50
Vocal         16.99  45
```

Notice that for each Category value, there are three rows, one for each of the Price values. For example, in the Vocal group, there are 99 CDs at 14.99, 73 CDs at 15.99, and 45 CDs at 16.99. The number of rows depends on how many different values there are in the columns specified in the GROUP BY clause. In this example, there are two different values in the Category column and three different values in the Price column, which means that six rows will be returned.

NOTE

The way in which your query results are returned can vary from implementation to implementation. For example, some products might group all the Instrumental rows together and all the Vocal rows together. However, regardless of how the information appears in your user interface, the end results should be the same.

Now let's take a look at the ROLLUP and CUBE operators. Both operators are similar in function in that they return additional data in your query results when added to the GROUP BY clause. The main difference between the two is that the CUBE operator returns even more information than the ROLLUP operator. Let's start with an example of the ROLLUP operator so I can demonstrate the difference.

In the following SELECT statement, the GROUP BY clause applies the ROLLUP operator to the Category and Price columns:

```
SELECT Category, Price, SUM(OnHand) AS TotalOnHand
FROM CompactDiscStock
GROUP BY ROLLUP (Category, Price) ;
```

NOTE

Implementations can vary with regard to how they support the ROLLUP and CUBE operators. For example, in SQL Server, you must add WITH ROLLUP or WITH CUBE to the end of the GROUP BY clause, rather than defining the clause in the way that the SQL:1999 standard specifies. Be sure to check your product documentation to determine how these operators are supported.

Now when you execute the SELECT statement, the query results include an additional row for each value in the Category column:

```
Category        Price   TotalOnHand
-----------     -----   -----------
Instrumental    14.99   5
Instrumental    15.99   23
Instrumental    16.99   50
Instrumental    NULL    78
Vocal           14.99   99
Vocal           15.99   73
Vocal           16.99   45
Vocal           NULL    217
NULL            NULL    295
```

The two additional rows provide totals for each value in the Category column. For example, the Instrumental group includes a total of 78 CDs. Notice that the Price column includes a null value for these particular rows. A value cannot be calculated for this column because all three subgroups (from the Price column) are represented here.

The CUBE operator returns the same data as the ROLLUP operator, and then some. Notice that, in the following SELECT statement, I've merely replaced the CUBE keyword for ROLLUP:

```
SELECT Category, Price, SUM(OnHand) AS TotalOnHand
FROM CompactDiscStock
GROUP BY CUBE (Category, Price) ;
```

This statement returns the following query results:

```
Category        Price   TotalOnHand
-----------     -----   -----------
Instrumental    14.99   5
Instrumental    15.99   23
Instrumental    16.99   50
Instrumental    NULL    78
Vocal           14.99   99
Vocal           15.99   73
Vocal           16.99   45
Vocal           NULL    217
NULL            NULL    295
NULL            14.99   104
NULL            15.99   96
NULL            16.99   95
```

You can see that three additional rows have been added to the query results, one row for each different value in the Price column. Unlike the ROLLUP operator, the CUBE operator summarizes the values for each subgroup. Also notice that a null value is shown for the Category column. This is because both Vocal and Instrumental values are included in each subgroup summary.

As you can see, the GROUP BY clause can be a valuable tool when trying to summarize data, particularly when you make use of the many functions available in SQL, such as SUM and AVG. In Module 10, I discuss these and many other functions that you can use to make your SELECT statement more robust and applicable to your needs.

CRITICAL SKILL
7.4 # Use the HAVING Clause to Specify Group Search Conditions

The HAVING clause is similar to the WHERE clause in that it defines a search condition. However, unlike the WHERE clause, the HAVING clause is concerned with groups, not individual rows:

- If a GROUP BY clause is specified, the HAVING clause is applied to the groups created by the GROUP BY clause.

- If a WHERE clause is specified and no GROUP BY clause is specified, the HAVING clause is applied to the output of the WHERE clause and that output is treated as one group.

- If no WHERE clause and no GROUP BY clause are specified, the HAVING clause is applied to the output of the FROM clause and that output is treated as one group.

The best way to understand the HAVING clause is to remember that the clauses in a SELECT statement are processed in a definite order. A WHERE clause can receive input only from a FROM clause, but a HAVING clause can receive input from a GROUP BY, WHERE, or FROM clause. This is a subtle, yet important, distinction, and the best way to illustrate it is to look at a couple of examples.

In the first example, which is based on the CompactDiscStock table in Figure 7-4, I use a WHERE clause to specify that the query results should include only rows whose OnHand value is less than 20, as shown in the following SELECT statement:

```
SELECT Category, AVG(Price) AS AvgPrice
FROM CompactDiscStock
WHERE OnHand < 20
GROUP BY Category ;
```

The statement returns two columns: Category and AvgPrice, which is the average of all prices for each category. The averages include only those rows whose OnHand values are less than 20. If you executed this statement, the results would look similar to the following:

```
Category       AvgPrice
------------   --------
Instrumental   15.656666
Vocal          15.990000
```

As you would expect, the query result returns two rows—one for the Instrumental group and one for the Vocal group.

If you were to use the HAVING clause, rather than the WHERE clause, to limit values to less than 20, you might use the following SELECT statement:

```
SELECT Category, AVG(Price) AS AvgPrice
FROM CompactDiscStock
GROUP BY Category
HAVING OnHand < 20 ;
```

However, if you were to try to execute this statement, you would receive an error because you cannot apply individual OnHand values to the groups. For a column to be included in the HAVING clause, it must be a grouped column or it must be summarized in some way.

Now let's take a look at another example that uses the HAVING clause. In this case, the clause includes a summarized column:

```
SELECT Price, Category, SUM(OnHand) AS TotalOnHand
FROM CompactDiscStock
GROUP BY Price, Category
HAVING SUM(OnHand) > 10 ;
```

The HAVING clause in this statement will work because the OnHand values are being added together, which means they can work within the group structure. The query results would be as follows:

```
Price   Category        TotalOnHand
-----   ------------    -----------
15.99   Instrumental    23
16.99   Instrumental    50
14.99   Vocal           99
15.99   Vocal           73
16.99   Vocal           45
```

The HAVING clause is applied to the results after they have been grouped together (in the GROUP BY clause). For each group, the OnHand values are added together, but only groups with TotalOnHand values over 10 are included. If the HAVING clause were not included, the query results would include an additional row for the 14.99/Instrumental group.

For the most part, you'll probably find that you'll be using the HAVING clause in conjunction with the GROUP BY clause. By using these two together, you can group together relevant data and then filter that data to refine your search even further. The HAVING clause also has the advantage of allowing you to use set functions such as AVG or SUM, which you cannot use in a WHERE clause. The important points to keep in mind with the HAVING clause are that it is the last clause in the table expression to be applied and that it is concerned with grouped data, rather than individual rows.

Progress Check

1. You're creating a SELECT statement and you want to group together data based on the EmployeeTitle column. How should you create your GROUP BY clause?

2. What two operators can you use in a GROUP BY clause to return additional summary data in a query result?

3. What clause can you add to a SELECT statement to define a search condition on groups?

CRITICAL SKILL
7.5

Use the ORDER BY Clause to Sort Query Results

The ORDER BY clause, when it is used in a SELECT statement, is the last clause to be processed. The ORDER BY clause takes the output from the SELECT clause and orders the query results according to the specifications within the ORDER BY clause. The clause does not group rows together, as they're grouped by the GROUP BY clause, nor does it filter out rows, as they're filtered by the WHERE clause or the HAVING clause. You can, however, specify whether the rows are organized in an ascending order (by using the ASC keyword) or in descending order (by using the DESC keyword).

To use the ORDER BY clause, simply specify one or more columns and the optional ASC or DESC keywords (one per column). If a keyword is not specified, ASC is assumed. The rows are organized according to the column you specify. If you define more than one column in the ORDER BY clause, the rows are organized in the order in which the columns are specified.

Let's take a look at a few examples to clarify how the ORDER BY clause works. (The examples are based on the CompactDiscStock table in Figure 7-4.) In the first example, I order the rows based on the Price column:

```
SELECT * FROM CompactDiscStock
WHERE Price < 16.00
ORDER BY Price ;
```

---

1. GROUP BY EmployeeTitle
2. ROLLUP or CUBE
3. HAVING

Notice that the Price column is specified in the ORDER BY clause. Also notice that neither the ASC nor the DESC keyword has been specified, so the ASC keyword will be assumed. If you execute this query, you will receive the following results:

```
CompactDisc                              Category      Price  OnHand
-----------------------------------      ------------  -----  ------
Blue                                     Vocal         14.99  42
Court and Spark                          Vocal         14.99  22
That Christmas Feeling                   Vocal         14.99  8
Blues on the Bayou                       Vocal         14.99  27
Orlando                                  Instrumental  14.99  5
Carreras Domingo Pavarotti in Concert    Vocal         15.99  27
Leonard Cohen The Best Of                Vocal         15.99  12
Fundamental                              Vocal         15.99  34
Past Light                               Instrumental  15.99  17
Kojiki                                   Instrumental  15.99  6
```

The rows are listed according to the Price column. The values in the Price column appear in ascending order (lowest price to highest price). Because the WHERE clause was specified, no rows with prices above 15.99 are included in the query results.

In the next example, the SELECT statement is nearly the same as the last statement, except that an additional column is specified in the ORDER BY clause:

```
SELECT * FROM CompactDiscStock
WHERE Price < 16.00
ORDER BY Price, OnHand DESC ;
```

In this case, the OnHand column is followed by the DESC keyword, which means that the rows will be listed in descending order. However, because there are two columns, the rows are first ordered by the Price column and then by the OnHand column. If you execute this SELECT statement, you'll receive the following results:

```
CompactDisc                              Category      Price  OnHand
-----------------------------------      ------------  -----  ------
Blue                                     Vocal         14.99  42
Blues on the Bayou                       Vocal         14.99  27
Court and Spark                          Vocal         14.99  22
That Christmas Feeling                   Vocal         14.99  8
Orlando                                  Instrumental  14.99  5
Fundamental                              Vocal         15.99  34
Carreras Domingo Pavarotti in Concert    Vocal         15.99  27
Past Light                               Instrumental  15.99  17
Leonard Cohen The Best Of                Vocal         15.99  12
Kojiki                                   Instrumental  15.99  6
```

Ask the Expert

Q: How does the ORDER BY clause affect query results in embedded SQL and SQL modules?

A: You can use the ORDER BY clause only in direct invocation and when defining cursors. You cannot use an ORDER BY clause in other situations. This is because of the limitations on application languages that cannot handle an unknown number of rows in a query result. Application languages do not know what to do with this sort of uncertainty. And because the ORDER BY clause applies only to multirow query results, the clause is not applicable to environments that require rows to be returned one at a time. However, cursors offer a way for application languages to deal with that uncertainty, allowing the ORDER BY clause to be used in cursor definitions. Cursors are discussed in more detail in Module 15.

As you can see, the rows are listed according to the order of the Price values, which are in ascending order. In addition, the OnHand values are listed in descending order for each price. So for the set of 14.99 Price values, the rows start with a value of 42 in the OnHand column and end with a value of 5. Then we jump to the next group of Price values: 15.99. Once again, the largest OnHand value for the 15.99 Price range is listed first and the last row contains the smallest OnHand value for the 15.99 Price range.

Whenever you're using the ORDER BY clause, you must be aware of the order in which you list column names within that clause. In the preceding example, the Price column is listed first, so the rows are ordered first by the Price column and then by the OnHand column. However, you can reverse the column names, as shown in the following SELECT statement:

```
SELECT * FROM CompactDiscStock
WHERE Price < 16.00
ORDER BY OnHand, Price DESC ;
```

This time, the OnHand column is listed first and the Price column listed second, and the Price column is assigned the DESC keyword. As a result, the rows will be sorted by the OnHand column, as shown in the following query results:

CompactDisc	Category	Price	OnHand
Orlando	Instrumental	14.99	5
Kojiki	Instrumental	15.99	6
That Christmas Feeling	Vocal	14.99	8
Leonard Cohen The Best Of	Vocal	15.99	12
Past Light	Instrumental	15.99	17

```
Court and Spark                           Vocal        14.99   22
Carreras Domingo Pavarotti in Concert     Vocal        15.99   27
Blues on the Bayou                        Vocal        14.99   27
Fundamental                               Vocal        15.99   34
Blue                                      Vocal        14.99   42
```

Notice that the OnHand values are in ascending order. The rows are then ordered according to the Price value. However, because there are only two rows that share the same OnHand value (27), these are the only rows that the ORDER BY column affects, with regard to the Price column.

The ORDER BY clause is a convenient tool for organizing your query results, but remember, it doesn't affect which data is displayed. Only the other clauses can actually name, filter, and group data. The ORDER BY clause is merely an organizer for what already exists.

Project 7-1 Querying the Inventory Database

Prj07.txt

For the projects in previous modules, you created a number of persistent base tables that are capable of storing data. In this module, you learned how to create SELECT statements that allow you to query data in base tables. As a result, this project focuses on creating SELECT statements that query data in the tables that you created. However, before you can actually query those tables, data must be stored within them. Unfortunately, I do not cover inserting data until Module 8, but I do provide the statements you need to insert the data in the Prj07.txt file, which you can download from our web site. The file contains a series of INSERT statements—along with the SELECT statements used in this project—that allow you to populate the tables. You can also view these statements in Appendix C.

If you look at the Prj07.txt file, you'll see a series of INSERT statements that are grouped together according to the tables that you created in the Inventory database. For example, the first set of INSERT statements are for the CDLabels table, as shown in the following statements:

```
--Insert data into the CDLabels table
INSERT INTO CDLabels VALUES ( 827, 'Private Music' ) ;
INSERT INTO CDLabels VALUES ( 828, 'Reprise Records' ) ;
INSERT INTO CDLabels VALUES ( 829, 'Asylum Records' ) ;
INSERT INTO CDLabels VALUES ( 830, 'Windham Hill Records' ) ;
INSERT INTO CDLabels VALUES ( 831, 'Geffen' ) ;
INSERT INTO CDLabels VALUES ( 832, 'MCA Records' ) ;
INSERT INTO CDLabels VALUES ( 833, 'Decca Record Company' ) ;
INSERT INTO CDLabels VALUES ( 834, 'CBS Records' ) ;
INSERT INTO CDLabels VALUES ( 835, 'Capitol Records' ) ;
INSERT INTO CDLabels VALUES ( 836, 'Sarabande Records' ) ;
--End inserts for the CDLabels table
```

(continued)

You will need to copy these statements into your client application and execute them. Each INSERT statement adds one row of data to the applicable table. For example, the first INSERT statement listed in the preceding code adds one row of data to the CDLabels table. The values that are added are 827 (for the LabelID column) and Private Music (for the CompanyName column). Again, I will be going into the INSERT statement in greater detail in Module 8. If you are uncomfortable inserting this data before reading about the INSERT statement, I suggest that you review the information in Module 8 before working on this project and then return here to do each step. However, if you decide to do this project now, then you simply need to execute each statement, as described in the following steps.

NOTE

As you probably noticed, each block of INSERT statements begins and ends with a line that starts off with double hyphens (--). Double hyphens indicate that the line of text that follows is a comment. Your SQL implementation will not process these lines. The comments are there only to provide information to the SQL programmers so they can better understand the code.

Step by Step

1. Open the client application for your RDBMS and connect to the Inventory database.

2. Open the Prj07.txt file and copy the INSERT statements into your client application. Most applications will allow you to execute blocks of statements, rather than having to enter the data one row at a time. If your application supports executing multiple statements, execute the statements one table at a time. You should enter data for each table in the order that the data appears in the Prj07.txt file. For example, you should insert values into the CDLabels table before the CompactDiscs table.

   For each INSERT statement that you execute, you should receive a message acknowledging that the row has been inserted into the table. After you've populated each table with data, you're ready to move on to the next step.

3. You will now query all the data in the Artists table. Enter and execute the following SQL statement:

```
SELECT * FROM Artists ;
```

   Your query results should include the ArtistID, ArtistName, and PlaceOfBirth columns. There should be 18 rows of data in all.

4. Now let's create a query that specifies which columns to include in the query results. For the next SELECT statement, you will query the CompactDisc table, but return only the CDTitle and InStock columns. Enter and execute the following SQL statement:

```
SELECT CDTitle, InStock FROM CompactDiscs ;
```

Your query results should include only the two columns you specified in the SELECT statement. In addition, the query should return 15 rows of data.

5. In Module 5, Project 5-1, you created the CDsInStock view. The view returns the same data as specified in the SELECT statement in Step 4, except that it limits the results to rows with InStock values greater than 10. You will now query that view. Enter and execute the following SQL statement:

```
SELECT * FROM CDsInStock ;
```

Notice that your SELECT statement is the same as it would have been for a persistent base table. You can even specify the view column names if you want. (In fact, you should if you're querying the view in any way other than through direct invocation.) In the last SELECT statement, the query returned 15 rows, but this query returns only 12 rows because the InStock values must be over 10. The nice part about the view is that it is already set up to return exactly the information you want, without having to define the WHERE clause.

6. Now let's query the CompactDiscs table but refine our SELECT statement by using a WHERE clause. Enter and execute the following SQL statement:

```
SELECT CDTitle, InStock FROM CompactDiscs
WHERE InStock > 10 AND InStock < 30 ;
```

Because the WHERE clause has been added, your query results should now include only nine rows, and each row should contain an InStock value between 10 and 30.

7. The next SELECT statement that you create groups together information in the CompactDiscs table. Enter and execute the following SQL statement:

```
SELECT LabelID, SUM(InStock) AS TotalInStock
FROM CompactDiscs
GROUP BY LabelID ;
```

One row is returned for each different LabelID value, and for each of those values, the total for the InStock values is returned. There are 10 rows in all. Notice that, in your query results, the name of the column with the InStock totals is called TotalInStock. When you learn more about joining tables, you'll be able to group data based on more complex queries. Joining tables is discussed in Module 11.

(continued)

8. Now you'll add a HAVING clause to the SELECT statement you just executed. Enter and execute the following SQL statement:

```
SELECT LabelID, SUM(InStock) AS TotalInStock
FROM CompactDiscs
GROUP BY LabelID
HAVING SUM(InStock) > 10 ;
```

The HAVING clause limits the rows that are returned to those whose TotalInStock values are greater than 10. Now only eight rows are returned.

9. You can also execute a SELECT statement that orders the data returned by your query. Enter and execute the following SQL statement:

```
SELECT * FROM CompactDiscs
WHERE InStock > 10
ORDER BY CDTitle DESC ;
```

Your query results should be organized according to the CDTitle column, with the columns listed in descending order. Because the WHERE clause is used, only 12 rows should have been returned.

10. Close the client application.

Project Summary

In this project, you inserted data into the tables of the Inventory database. You then created SELECT statements that allowed you to query data in those tables. You should feel free to experiment with SELECT statements and try different types of queries. As you become more comfortable with using the SELECT statement and learn more advanced techniques for querying data, you'll be able to write SELECT statements that access multiple tables, calculate data, and summarize information. However, even the more advanced techniques rely on the basic foundation that you have demonstrated in this project. Everything else builds on this.

✓ *Module 7 Mastery Check*

1. Which clauses in a SELECT statement are part of the table expression?

    A. SELECT

    B. FROM

    C. WHERE

    D. ORDER BY

2. In what order are the clauses of a SELECT statement applied?

3. You are writing a SELECT statement that retrieves the CDTitle column and all rows from the Inventory table. Which SELECT statement should you use?

4. You are writing a SELECT statement that retrieves the CDTitle column and all rows from the Inventory table. You want the column in the query results to be named CompactDisc. Which SELECT statement should you use?

5. Which clauses in a SELECT statement are required?

    A. SELECT

    B. FROM

    C. WHERE

    D. GROUP BY

6. Which keyword should you add to the SELECT clause to ensure that each row of the query result is unique?

    A. ALL

    B. ROLLUP

    C. DISTINCT

    D. CUBE

7. You're creating a SELECT statement for the Inventory table and you want to ensure that only rows with a RetailPrice value of less than $16.00 are included in the query results. What WHERE clause should you use?

8. You're creating a SELECT statement that includes a WHERE clause. The WHERE clause contains two predicates. You want the condition of either one of the predicates to be met, but it's not necessary for both conditions to be met. What keyword should you use to connect the two predicates?

9. Each predicate in a WHERE clause is evaluated to which of the following?

    A. True

    B. Not

    C. False

    D. Unknown

10. Which clause allows you to group together values in a specified column?

    A. ROLLUP

    B. HAVING

C. ORDER BY

D. GROUP BY

11. Which two operators can you use in a GROUP BY clause to return additional summary data in a query result?

A. ROLLUP

B. HAVING

C. CUBE

D. DISTINCT

12. You're writing a SELECT statement that retrieves the Category and Price columns from the CompactDiscStock table. You want to group data together first by the Category column and then by the Price column. Which SELECT statement should you use?

13. You're writing a SELECT statement that retrieves the Category and Price columns from the CompactDiscStock table. You want to group together data first by the Category column and then by the Price column. You then want to filter out any groups that have a Price value over 15.99. Which SELECT statement should you use?

14. You're creating a SELECT statement that includes a SELECT clause, FROM clause, WHERE clause, GROUP BY clause, and HAVING clause. From which clause will the HAVING clause receive output?

A. SELECT

B. FROM

C. WHERE

D. GROUP BY

15. How does the HAVING clause differ from the WHERE clause?

16. From which clause does the ORDER BY clause receive output?

17. Which keyword should you add to an ORDER BY clause to sort data in descending order?

Module 8

Modifying SQL Data

One of the primary functions of any database is to be able to manipulate the data stored within its tables. Designated users must be able to insert, update, and delete data as necessary in order to keep the database current and ensure that only the appropriate data is being stored. SQL provides three statements for basic data manipulation: INSERT, UPDATE, and DELETE. In this module, I will examine each of these statements and demonstrate how they can be used in an SQL environment to modify data in the database.

CRITICAL SKILL
8.1 Insert SQL Data

In Module 7, Project 7-1, I introduce you briefly to the INSERT statement. As you can see from this project, the INSERT statement allows you to add data to the various tables in your database. The syntax for a basic INSERT statement is relatively straightforward:

```
INSERT INTO <table name>
[ ( <column name> [ { , <column name> } ... ] ) ]
VALUES ( <value> [ { , <value> } ... ] )
```

Only the first and last lines in the syntax are required. The second line is optional. Both the first and second lines are part of the INSERT INTO clause. In this clause, you must identify the name of the table in which you will be inserting data. The table name follows the INSERT INTO keywords. You then have the option of identifying the column names in the table that will be receiving the data. This is what the second line in the syntax is for. You can specify one or more columns, all of which must be enclosed in parentheses. If you specify more than one column, they must be separated by a comma. If you do specify column names, any columns within the target table that are *not* specified must support null values or must be defined with a default value; otherwise, the database will not know what values to insert into those columns.

In the third line of syntax, which is the VALUES clause, you must specify one or more values that will be inserted into the table. The values must be enclosed in parentheses and, if more than one is specified, must be separated by a comma. In addition, the values must meet the following requirements:

- If the column names are not specified in the INSERT INTO clause, then there must be one value for each column in the table and the values must be in the same order as they are defined in the table.

- If the column names are specified in the INSERT INTO clause, then there must be exactly one value per specified column and those values must be in the same order in which they are defined in the INSERT INTO clause. However, the column names and values do not have to be in the same order as the columns in the table definition.

- Each value with a character string data type must be enclosed in single quotes.

NOTE

Many SQL programmers prefer to specify the column names in the INSERT INTO clause, whether or not it's necessary to do so, because it provides a method for documenting which columns are supposed to be receiving data. This is especially useful if the database or applications accessing the database should need to change in any way.

Now let's take a look at some examples of the INSERT statement. For these examples, I will use the CDInventory table. The table is based on the following table definition:

```
CREATE TABLE CDInventory
( CDName VARCHAR (60) NOT NULL,
MusicType VARCHAR (15),
Publisher VARCHAR (50) DEFAULT 'Independent' NOT NULL,
InStock INT NOT NULL ) ;
```

The first example I'll show you inserts values into every column in the CDInventory table:

```
INSERT INTO CDInventory
VALUES ( 'Patsy Cline: 12 Greatest Hits', 'Country', 'MCA Records', 32 ) ;
```

Notice that the INSERT INTO clause includes only the name of the CDInventory table, but does not specify any columns. In the VALUES clause, four values have been specified. The values are separated by commas, and the values with character string data types are enclosed in single quotes. If you refer back to the table definition, you'll see that the values specified in the VALUES clause are in the same order as the column definitions.

When you execute the INSERT statement shown in the example, the data is added to the CDInventory table, as shown in Figure 8-1.

If you had tried to execute an INSERT statement like the last example, but included only three values, rather than four, you would have received an error. For example, you would not be able to execute the following statement:

```
INSERT INTO CDInventory
VALUES ( 'Patsy Cline: 12 Greatest Hits', 'MCA Records', 32 ) ;
```

In this example, only three values have been specified. In this case, the missing value is for the MusicType column. Even though this column accepts null values, the SQL implementation has no way of knowing which value is being omitted, so an error is returned.

CDName: VARCHAR (60)	MusicType: VARCHAR (15)	Publisher: VARCHAR (50)	InStock: INT
Patsy Cline: 12 Greatest Hits	Country	MCA Records	32

Figure 8-1 The CDInventory table with the new row of data

Instead of leaving the value out of the VALUES clause, you can specify a null value, as shown in the following example:

```
INSERT INTO CDInventory
VALUES ( 'Out Of Africa', null, 'MCA Records', 29 ) ;
```

If you execute the INSERT statement, your table will now include an additional row. Figure 8-2 shows what the table would look like, assuming that the two INSERT statements have been executed.

The null value was inserted into the MusicType column, and the other values were inserted into the appropriate columns. If a null value were not permitted in the MusicType column, you would have had to specify a value.

NOTE

Figure 8-2 shows the new row being inserted after the existing row in the table. However, the row can be inserted at any place in a table, depending on how the SQL implementation inserts rows. The SQL standard does not specify where a row should be inserted in a table.

Rather than having to insert a value for every column when you insert a row, you can specify which columns receive values. For example, you can specify values for the CDName, Publisher, and InStock columns of the CDInventory table, as shown in the following example:

```
INSERT INTO CDInventory ( CDName, Publisher, InStock )
VALUES ( 'Fundamental', 'Capitol Records', 34 ) ;
```

In this case, one value has been specified for each of the columns identified in the INSERT INTO clause, and the values are specified in the same order as the columns in the INSERT INTO clause. Notice that the INSERT statement doesn't include the MusicType column in the INSERT INTO clause or in the VALUES clause. You can omit this column because null values are permitted in that column. If you were to execute this statement, your CDInventory table would now have a third row (shown in Figure 8-3).

CDName: VARCHAR (60)	MusicType: VARCHAR (15)	Publisher: VARCHAR (50)	InStock: INT
Patsy Cline: 12 Greatest Hits	Country	MCA Records	32
Out of Africa	NULL	MCA Records	29

Figure 8-2 The CDInventory table with two rows of data

CDName: VARCHAR (60)	MusicType: VARCHAR (15)	Publisher: VARCHAR (50)	InStock: INT
Patsy Cline: 12 Greatest Hits	Country	MCA Records	32
Out of Africa	NULL	MCA Records	29
Fundamental	NULL	Capitol Records	34

Figure 8-3 The CDInventory table with three rows of data

Once again, the null value is automatically added to the MusicType column. If a default value had been defined for the column, that value would have been added. For example, the following INSERT statement omits the Publisher column, rather than the MusicType column:

```
INSERT INTO CDInventory ( CDName, MusicType, InStock )
VALUES ( 'Orlando', 'Soundtrack', 5 ) ;
```

When the row is added to the CDInventory table, the default value (Independent) is added to the Publisher column, as shown in Figure 8-4.

If you try to execute an INSERT statement that omits a column that does not permit null values or is not defined with a default value, you will receive an error.

NOTE

The values that you specify in the VALUES clause must conform to *all* restrictions placed on a table. This means that the values must conform to the data types or domains associated with a column. In addition, the values are limited by any constraints defined on the table. For example, a foreign key constraint would prevent you from adding any values that violate the constraint, or a check constraint may limit the range of values that can be inserted into the table. Be sure that you're familiar with the restrictions placed on a table before trying to insert data into that table. You can learn more about data types in Module 3. You can learn more about domains and constraints in Module 4.

CDName: VARCHAR (60)	MusicType: VARCHAR (15)	Publisher: VARCHAR (50)	InStock: INT
Patsy Cline: 12 Greatest Hits	Country	MCA Records	32
Out of Africa	NULL	MCA Records	29
Fundamental	NULL	Capitol Records	34
Orlando	Soundtrack	Independent	5

Figure 8-4 The CDInventory table with four rows of data

You can, of course, specify all columns in the INSERT INTO clause. If you do this, you must be sure to specify the same number of values, in the same order in which the columns are specified. The following INSERT statement inserts values into all columns of the CDInventory table:

```
INSERT INTO CDInventory ( CDName, MusicType, Publisher, InStock )
VALUES ( 'Court and Spark', 'Pop', 'Asylum Records', 22 ) ;
```

When you execute this statement, a row is added to the CDInventory table, with a value for each row, as shown in Figure 8-5. If you were to omit one of the values from the VALUES clause—even if null values were allowed for the related column—you would receive an error when you executed that statement.

Inserting Values from a SELECT Statement

Earlier in this module, at the beginning of the "Insert SQL Data" section, I say that the VALUES clause is mandatory and that you need to specify at least one value. There is, however, an alternative to the VALUES clause. You can use a SELECT statement to specify the values that you want to insert into a table. The key to using a SELECT statement, just as with using the VALUES clause, is to make sure that the number of values returned by the SELECT statement matches the required number of values and that those values conform to any restriction on the target table. Let's look at an example.

Suppose that, in addition to the CDInventory table I've been using in previous examples, your database includes a second table named CDInventory2, which includes two columns, as shown in the following table definition:

```
CREATE TABLE CDInventory2
( CDName2 VARCHAR (60) NOT NULL,
InStock2 INT NOT NULL ) ;
```

CDName: VARCHAR (60)	MusicType: VARCHAR (15)	Publisher: VARCHAR (50)	InStock: INT
Patsy Cline: 12 Greatest Hits	Country	MCA Records	32
Out of Africa	NULL	MCA Records	29
Fundamental	NULL	Capitol Records	34
Orlando	Soundtrack	Independent	5
Court and Spark	Pop	Asylum Records	22

Figure 8-5 The CDInventory table with five rows of data

The CDName2 column in the CDInventory2 table has the same data type as the CDName column in the CDInventory table, and the InStock2 column in the CDInventory2 table has the same data type as the InStock column in the CDInventory table. As a result, values taken from the two columns in one table can be inserted into the two columns in the second table.

NOTE

A column in one table does not have to be the same data type as a column in another table for values to be copied from one to the other, as long as the values inserted into the target table conform to the data restrictions of that table.

By using an INSERT statement, you can copy values from the CDInventory table to the CDInventory2 table. The following INSERT statement includes a SELECT statement that queries the CDInventory table:

```
INSERT INTO CDInventory2
SELECT CDName, InStock FROM CDInventory ;
```

As you can see, no columns are specified in the INSERT INTO clause; as a result, values will be inserted into both columns in the CDInventory2 table. In the second line of the statement, a SELECT statement is used to pull values from the CDName and InStock columns of the CDInventory table. The values will then be inserted into their respective columns in the CDInventory2 table, as shown in Figure 8-6.

Notice that the CDInventory2 table contains the same five rows of data that are shown in Figure 8-5, only the CDInventory2 table contains only two columns: CDName2 and InStock2.

Like any other SELECT statement, the SELECT statement that you use in an INSERT statement can contain a WHERE clause. In the following INSERT statement, the SELECT statement contains a WHERE clause that limits the InStock values to an amount greater than 10:

```
INSERT INTO CDInventory2
SELECT CDName, InStock FROM CDInventory
WHERE InStock > 10 ;
```

CDName2: VARCHAR (60)	InStock2: INT
Patsy Cline: 12 Greatest Hits	32
Out of Africa	29
Fundamental	34
Orlando	5
Court and Spark	22

Figure 8-6 The CDInventory2 table with five rows of data

If you were to execute this statement, only four rows would be added to the CDInventory2 table, rather than the five rows we saw in the previous example. The WHERE clause in this case works just like the WHERE clause in any SELECT statement. As a result, any row with an InStock value that is not greater than 10 is eliminated from the query results. Those new filtered results are then inserted into the CDInventory2 table.

Progress Check

1. What two clauses are mandatory in an INSERT statement?

2. You're creating an INSERT statement that inserts data into a table that has four columns. You do not specify the column names in your INSERT INTO clause. How many values must you include in your VALUES clause?

3. You're creating an INSERT statement for the CDInventory table, which includes four columns. Your INSERT INTO clause includes only three column names. How must the fourth column be configured to support this INSERT statement?

4. What type of statement can you use in place of a VALUES clause when inserting data into a table?

CRITICAL SKILL

8.2 Update SQL Data

As its name implies, the UPDATE statement allows you to update data in your SQL database. With the UPDATE statement, you can modify data in one or more rows for one or more columns. The syntax for the UPDATE statement can be shown as follows:

UPDATE <table name>
SET <set clause expression> [{ , <set clause expression> } . . .]
[WHERE <search condition>]

As you can see, the UPDATE clause and the SET clause are required, and the WHERE clause is optional. In the UPDATE clause, you must specify the name of the table that you're updating. In the SET clause, you must specify one or more set clause expressions, which I

---

1. INSERT INTO and VALUES
2. Four
3. The omitted column must support null values or must be defined with a default value.
4. SELECT

discuss in more detail later in this module. In the WHERE clause, as with the WHERE clause in a SELECT statement (see Module 7), you must specify a search condition. The WHERE clause works here in much the same way it does in the SELECT statement. You specify a condition or set of conditions that act as a filter for the rows that are updated. Only the rows that meet these conditions are updated. In other words, only rows that evaluate to true are updated.

Now let's return to the SET clause. As you can see, the clause includes the <set clause expression> placeholder. You must specify one or more set clause expressions. If you specify more than one, you must separate them with a comma. The syntax of the <set clause expression> placeholder can be broken down as follows:

<column name> = <value expression>

Basically, you must specify a column name (from the table that you're updating) and provide a value that the value in the column should equal. For example, suppose you want a value in the InStock column to be changed to 37. (It doesn't matter what the current value is.) The set clause expression would be as follows: InStock = 37. In this case, the value expression is 37; however, the value expression can be more complicated than that. For example, you can base the new value on an old value: InStock = (InStock + 1). In this case, the value expression is InStock + 1, which adds the current value in the InStock column to 1 to give you a new value. If the original value was 37, the new value will be 38.

Now that we've taken a look at the various parts of the UPDATE statement, let's put it all together in some examples. The examples we'll be looking at are based on the CDInventory table, which is shown in Figure 8-5.

In the first example, I use the UPDATE statement to change the values of the InStock column to 27, as shown in the following SQL statement:

```
UPDATE CDInventory SET InStock = 27 ;
```

This statement does exactly what you might expect: changes every row in the CDInventory table so that the InStock column for each row contains a value of 27. This is fine if that's what you want, but it will probably turn out to be unlikely that you'll want to change every row in a table so that one of its values is the same in every row. More likely than not, you'll want to qualify the update by using a WHERE clause.

In the next example, I modify the previous UPDATE statement to include a WHERE clause:

```
UPDATE CDInventory SET InStock = 27
WHERE CDName = 'Out of Africa' ;
```

The UPDATE statement still changes the InStock column to a value of 27, but it does so only for the rows that meet the search condition in the WHERE clause. In this case, only one row meets that condition: Out of Africa.

You might find that you want to change a value based on a value that already exists, such as the amount of inventory in stock. For example, you can add 2 to the value in the InStock column:

```
UPDATE CDInventory SET InStock = (InStock + 2)
WHERE CDName = 'Out of Africa' ;
```

If the Out of Africa row contains the value 27 in the InStock column, and you execute this UPDATE statement, the new value will be 29. If you execute this statement without the WHERE clause, 2 will be added to the InStock value for every row in the table.

The WHERE clause also allows you to specify more than one predicate, as you can do with a WHERE clause in a SELECT statement. In the following example, I subtract 2 from the InStock value for any row that contains a MusicType value of Country *and* an InStock value greater than 30:

```
UPDATE CDInventory SET InStock = (InStock - 2)
WHERE MusicType = 'Country' AND InStock > 30 ;
```

Only one row (Patsy Cline: 12 Greatest Hits) conforms to the search conditions specified in the WHERE clause. The InStock value for that row has been changed from 32 to 30.

You can also specify multiple expressions in the SET clause. In other words, you can change the values of more than one column at a time. For example, suppose you want to change the Publisher value and InStock value for the Orlando row. Your UPDATE statement might look something like the following:

```
UPDATE CDInventory
SET Publisher = 'Sarabande Records', InStock = (InStock * 2)
WHERE CDName = 'Orlando' ;
```

Notice that the two expressions in the SET clause are separated by a comma. When you execute this statement, the Publisher value is changed from Independent to Sarabande Records, and the InStock value is changed from 5 to 10. (The 5 value is multiplied by 2.)

One thing you cannot do, however, is change the value for the same column for two different rows if you're trying to insert different values in those rows. Let's look at an example to make this clearer. Suppose you want to update the MusicType value for the Out of Africa row and the Fundamental row, but you want to update these rows with different values. The Out of Africa row should have a MusicType value of Soundtrack, and the Fundamental row should have a MusicType value of Blues. As a result, you might try to execute a statement similar to the following:

```
UPDATE CDInventory
SET MusicType = 'Soundtrack', MusicType = 'Blues'
WHERE CDName = 'Out of Africa' OR CDName = 'Fundamental' ;
```

If you tried to execute this statement, the SQL implementation would not know which MusicType value to put into which row, and you would receive an error. To handle a situation like this, you would need to create two separate UPDATE statements:

```
UPDATE CDInventory SET MusicType = 'Soundtrack'
WHERE CDName = 'Orlando' ;
UPDATE CDInventory SET MusicType = 'Blues'
WHERE CDName = 'Fundamental' ;
```

Updating Values from a SELECT Statement

In the "Inserting Values from a SELECT Statement" section earlier in this module, I told you that you can use a SELECT statement in place of the VALUES clause. You can also use a SELECT statement in the SET clause of the UPDATE statement. The SELECT statement returns the value that is defined in the <value expression> portion of the set clause expression. In other words, the SELECT statement is added to the right of the equal sign.

Let's take a look at a few examples to see how this works. The following examples are based on the original data in the CDInventory table (shown in Figure 8-5) and the CDInventory2 table (shown in Figure 8-6). Suppose you want to update data in the CDInventory2 table by using values from the CDInventory table. You might create an UPDATE statement that is similar to the following:

```
UPDATE CDInventory2
SET InStock2 = ( SELECT AVG(InStock) FROM CDInventory ) ;
```

The SELECT statement calculates the average of the InStock values in the CDInventory table, which is 24, so the set clause expression can be interpreted as follows: InStock = 24. As a result, all InStock2 values in the CDInventory2 table are set to 24. Of course, you probably don't want all your InStock2 values to be the same, so you can limit which rows are updated by adding a WHERE clause to the UPDATE statement:

```
UPDATE CDInventory2
SET InStock2 = ( SELECT AVG(InStock) FROM CDInventory )
WHERE CDName2 = 'Orlando' ;
```

Now only the Orlando row will be updated and the InStock value will be changed to 24.

You can even add a WHERE clause to the SELECT statement, as shown in the following example:

```
UPDATE CDInventory2
SET InStock2 =
  ( SELECT InStock FROM CDInventory WHERE CDName = 'Orlando' )
WHERE CDName2 = 'Orlando' ;
```

In this case, the InStock value of 5 is taken directly from the Orlando row of the CDInventory and used as the <value expression> portion of the set clause expression. As a result, the set clause expression can be interpreted as the following: InStock2 = 5. (Of course, the value in the CDInventory won't change because it is already 5, but if it were something other than 5, it would have been updated to 5.)

You can add one more layer of complexity to the UPDATE statement by modifying the SET clause even further. For example, suppose you want to increase the value by 2 before inserting it into the InStock2 column. To do so, you can change the value expression to the following:

```
UPDATE CDInventory2
SET InStock2 =
   ( SELECT InStock FROM CDInventory WHERE CDName = 'Orlando' ) + 2
WHERE CDName2 = 'Orlando' ;
```

Again, the SELECT clause pulls the value of 5 from the InStock column of the CDInventory table, but this time, 2 is added to the value returned by the SELECT statement, resulting in a total of 7. As a result, the new set clause expression can be represented as follows: InStock2 = (5) + 2. If you execute this statement, the InStock2 value will be changed to 7 in the Orlando row of the CDInventory2 table.

By combining the SET clause with the WHERE clause, you can create UPDATE statements that can calculate very specific values that can be used to modify any number of rows and columns that you need to update. However, as with the INSERT statement, any values that you modify must conform to the restrictions of that table. In other words, the new values must abide by applicable data types, domains, and constraints.

Ask the Expert

Q: When you've discussed the INSERT statement, your examples showed only one statement at a time. What if you want to execute more than one INSERT statement at a time?

A: Many applications allow you to execute more than one INSERT statement at a time. You probably saw an example of that in Module 7, Project 7-1, in which you inserted a number of values in the tables in the Inventory database. However, if your application doesn't allow you to insert multiple INSERT statements, you might want to try a different approach. You can include each set of values in the VALUES clause, separated by a comma. For example, suppose you want to insert data into the CDInventory table that we've been using for the examples. Your INSERT statements might look something like the following:

```
INSERT INTO CDInventory VALUES
( 'Patsy Cline: 12 Greatest Hits', 'Country', 'MCA Records', 32 ),
( 'Out Of Africa', 'Soundtrack', 'MCA Records', 29 ),
```

(continued)

8

Modifying SQL Data

```
( 'Fundamental', 'Blues', 'Capitol Records', 34 ),
( 'Orlando', 'Soundtrack', 'Independent', 5 ),
( 'Court and Spark', 'Pop', 'Asylum Records', 22 ) ;
```

Notice that there are five sets of values, each separated by a comma. If you executed this statement, five rows would be added to the CDInventory table. Note that not all implementations support this method for adding values. However, if you're using the Ocelot RDBMS, you can use this method. (Another method that you can use is to enclose the statements in a BEGIN...END block, which I discuss in Module 13.)

Q: So far in this module, you have inserted and updated data in a table. Can you insert and update data through a view?

A: Yes, you can insert or update data through a view as long as the view is considered updateable. This means that data within the view cannot be summarized, grouped together, or automatically eliminated. In addition, at least one column in the source table must be updateable. Also, each column in the view must be traceable to exactly one source column in one table, and each row must be traceable to exactly one source row in one table. In other words, the view cannot use functions such as AVG or SUM because there is no way of knowing exactly what rows should be updated and what values to update. (See Module 5 for a more detailed discussion on updateable views.) However, if a view is updateable, then you simply treat it as you would a persistent base table. Instead of a table name, specify the view name in the UPDATE or INSERT INTO clause. In addition, if the view column names are different from the table column names, use the view column names in your UPDATE or INSERT statements.

Progress Check

1. Which clauses in an UPDATE statement are mandatory?

2. What clause can you add to an UPDATE statement to specify a condition that must be met in order for a row to be updated?

3. What are the components of a set clause expression?

4. What type of statement can you use as a value expression to query data from a table?

---

1. UPDATE and SET
2. WHERE
3. <column name> = <value expression>
4. SELECT

CRITICAL SKILL
8.3 Delete SQL Data

Of all the data modification statements supported by SQL, the DELETE statement is probably the simplest. It contains only two clauses, only one of which is mandatory. The following syntax shows you just how basic the DELETE statement is:

DELETE FROM <table name>
[WHERE <search condition>]

As you can see, the DELETE FROM clause requires that you specify the name of the table from which you are deleting rows. The WHERE clause, which is similar to the WHERE clause in a SELECT statement and an UPDATE statement, requires that you specify a search condition. If you don't include a WHERE clause in your DELETE statement, all rows are deleted from the specified table.

NOTE

The DELETE statement deletes only data from a table; it does not delete the table definition itself. To delete the data and the table definition, use the DROP TABLE statement. For more information about the DROP TABLE statement, see Module 3.

Notice in the DELETE statement that no column names are specified. This is because you cannot delete individual column values from a table. You can delete only rows. If you need to delete a specific column value, you should use an UPDATE statement to set the value to null. But you can do this only if null values are supported for that column.

Now let's take a look at a couple of examples of the DELETE statement. The first example deletes data from the CDInventory table, shown in Figure 8-5:

```
DELETE FROM CDInventory ;
```

That's all there is to it. Of course, you would use this statement only if you want to delete *all* data from the CDInventory. Although you might run into some occasions where it's necessary to delete every row from a table, it is more likely that you'll want to use the WHERE clause to specify which rows to delete. Let's modify the statement we just looked at to delete only rows where the MusicTypes values are Country:

```
DELETE FROM CDInventory
WHERE MusicType = 'Country' ;
```

When you execute this statement, all rows whose MusicType value is Country will be deleted from the CDInventory table, which in this case, is the Patsy Cline: 12 Greatest Hits row.

Now let's modify this DELETE statement a little further by including two predicates in the WHERE clause:

```
DELETE FROM CDInventory
WHERE MusicType = 'Pop' OR Publisher = 'Independent' ;
```

This statement will delete any rows in the CDInventory table that include a MusicType value of Pop *or* a Publisher value of Independent, which means that the Court and Spark row and Orlando row will be deleted.

As you can see, the number of rows that are deleted from any table depends on the search conditions defined within the WHERE clause. When a WHERE clause is not specified, all rows evaluate to true and are deleted from the table. The WHERE clause allows you to specify exactly which rows should be deleted from the table.

Project 8-1   Modifying SQL Data

Prj08.txt

In this project, you will use the data modification statements discussed in this module to modify data in the Inventory database. You will use the INSERT statement to add data, the UPDATE statement to modify data, and the DELETE statement to remove the data from the database. Because you will be working only with data, you will not affect the underlying structure of the tables. You can download the Prj08.txt file, which contains the SQL statements used in this project.

Step by Step

1. Open the client application for your RDBMS and connect to the Inventory database.

2. First you will add a new company to the CDLabels table. The company is DRG Records and it will have a LabelID value of 837. Enter and execute the following SQL statement:

```
INSERT INTO CDLabels VALUES ( 837, 'DRG Records' ) ;
```

One row will be added to the CDLabels table.

3. Now let's add a new CD to the CompactDiscs table. The CD is named *Ann Hampton Callaway,* which has a CompactDiscID value of 116. There are 14 of these CDs in stock and the LabelID value should be 836. (This is not the correct LabelID value, but we will use it here for the purposes of this project.) Enter and execute the following SQL statement:

```
INSERT INTO CompactDiscs
VALUES ( 116, 'Ann Hampton Callaway', 836, 14 ) ;
```

One row will be added to the CompactDiscs table. The LabelID value of 836 represents Sarabande Records.

(continued)

4. Now let's insert another row into the CompactDiscs table; only this time, your INSERT statement will specify the column names of the target table. You will insert a CD named *Rhythm Country and Blues*. The new row will contain a CompactDiscID value of 117, a LabelID value of 832 (MCA Records), and an InStock value of 21. Enter and execute the following SQL statement:

```
INSERT INTO CompactDiscs
VALUES ( 117, 'Rhythm Country and Blues', 832, 21 ) ;
```

One row will be inserted into the CompactDiscs table.

5. After you enter the Rhythm Country and Blues row, you realize that the InStock value is incorrect, and you want to update that value to 25. Enter and execute the following SQL statement:

```
UPDATE CompactDiscs SET InStock = 25
WHERE CompactDiscID = 117 ;
```

The InStock value of the Rhythm Country and Blues row will be changed to 25.

6. You now realize that you entered the wrong LabelID value for the Ann Hampton Callaway row. However, you want to be able to modify the existing value by specifying the company name rather than the LabelID value. The company name is DRG Records, which you added to the CDLabels table in Step 2. Enter and execute the following SQL statement:

```
UPDATE CompactDiscs
SET LabelID =
  ( SELECT LabelID FROM CDLabels WHERE CompanyName = 'DRG Records' )
WHERE CompactDiscID = 116 ;
```

In this statement, you used a SELECT statement to pull the LabelID value from the CDLabels table. The statement returned a value of 837. The value 837 was then used as the LabelID value for the CompactDiscs table. Note that you would not have been able to enter the value of 837 into the LabelID column of the CompactDiscs table if it did not already exist in the CDLabels table. Not only is this because a SELECT statement was used to pull that value, but also because the LabelID column in the CompactDiscs table is a foreign key that references the CDLabels table. As a result, the value must exist in the referenced table before it can be added to the referencing table. See Module 4 for more information about foreign keys.

7. Now let's take a look at the data that you've entered and updated. Enter and execute the following SQL statement:

```
SELECT * FROM CompactDiscs
WHERE CompactDiscID = 116 OR CompactDiscID = 117 ;
```

The SELECT statement requests data from all columns in the CompactDiscs table, but only for those rows that have a CompactDiscID value of 116 *or* 117. Your query results should include two rows. Verify that the information in those rows is correct. The Ann Hampton Callaway row should have a LabelID value of 837 and an InStock value of 14, and the Rhythm Country and Blues row should have a LabelID value of 832 and an InStock value of 25.

8. Now let's delete the two rows you added to the CompactDiscs table. Enter and execute the following SQL statement:

```
DELETE FROM CompactDiscs
WHERE CompactDiscID = 116 OR CompactDiscID = 117 ;
```

The Ann Hampton Callaway row and the Rhythm Country and Blues row should have been deleted from the CompactDiscs table.

9. Next delete the row you added to the CDLabels table. Enter and execute the following SQL statement:

```
DELETE FROM CDLabels WHERE LabelID = 837 ;
```

The DRG Records row should have been deleted from the CDLabels table.

NOTE

If you had tried to delete this row before deleting the Ann Hampton Callaway row in the CompactDiscs table, you would have received an error because the LabelID value in CompactDiscs references the DRG Records row in CDLabels. The Ann Hampton Callaway row had to be deleted first, or the LabelID value had to be changed to another value that conformed to the foreign key constraint.

10. Close the client application.

Project Summary

In this project, you added one row to the LabelID table and two rows to the CompactDiscs table. You then updated the two rows in the CompactDiscs table. After that, you deleted all the rows that you created. By the time you finished the project, the Inventory database should have been the same as when you began. As you can see, modifying data within tables is a very straightforward process; however, individual data modification statements can become far more complex. When you learn more advanced techniques for querying data, you'll be able to refine your statements to an even greater degree, providing you with more flexibility in inserting, updating, and deleting data.

Module 8 Mastery Check

1. Which SQL statement should you use to add data to a table?

   A. SELECT

   B. INSERT

   C. UPDATE

   D. DELETE

2. In which clause in the INSERT statement do you identify the table that will receive the new data?

3. You create the following INSERT statement to add data to the PerformingArtists table:

   ```
   INSERT INTO PerformingArtists VALUES ( 12, 'Frank Sinatra' ) ;
   ```

   The PerformingArtists table includes three columns. What will happen when you try to execute this statement?

4. What information must you specify in the VALUES clause of an INSERT statement?

5. What requirements must be met by the values in a VALUES clause?

6. You're creating an INSERT statement to insert data into the ArtistTypes table. The table includes only two columns: ArtID and TypeName. You want to insert one row that includes the ArtID value of 27 and the TypeName value of Gospel. Which SQL statement should you use?

7. You're creating an INSERT statement that inserts values taken from another table. Which type of statement or clause can you use in place of the VALUES clause to pull data from that other table?

   A. UPDATE

   B. SET

   C. SELECT

   D. WHERE

8. Which statement should you use to modify existing data in one or more rows in a table?

   A. SELECT

   B. INSERT

   C. UPDATE

   D. DELETE

9. What is the purpose of the WHERE clause in an UPDATE statement?

10. You're creating an UPDATE statement to update data in the PerformingArtists table. You want to update the ArtID value in the row that contains the PerfArtID value of 139. The new ArtID value is 27. Which SQL statement should you use?

11. You're creating an UPDATE statement to update data in the PerformingArtists table. You want to update the ArtID value of every row to 27. Which SQL statement should you use?

12. You're updating two columns in the CDInventory table. You want to change the Publisher value to MCA Records and you want to double the InStock value. Which SET clause should you use?

13. You're creating an UPDATE statement that includes a SET clause with one value expression. You want the value expression to pull a value from another table in the database. Which statement or clause can you use as a value expression to choose data from another table?

   A. SELECT

   B. WHERE

   C. UPDATE

   D. INSERT

14. Which clause in a DELETE statement is required?

15. Which statement or clause do you use in a DELETE statement to specify which rows are deleted from a table?

   A. SELECT

   B. WHERE

   C. UPDATE

   D. INSERT

Module 9

Using Predicates

U p to this point in the book, I have presented a great deal of information about various aspects of database objects and the data that they store. In relation to this, I discussed querying data (Module 7) and modifying data (Module 8). Now I want to take a step back and focus on one aspect of these discussions: the WHERE clause. The WHERE clause, as you might recall, allows you to specify a search condition that filters out those rows that you do not want returned by a SELECT statement or modified by an UPDATE or DELETE statement. The search condition includes one or more predicates that each state a fact about any row that is to be returned or modified. SQL supports a number of types of predicates, all of which allow you to test whether a condition is true, false, or unknown. In this module, I focus on those predicates that are most commonly used by SQL programmers, and I provide examples of how they're used to view and modify data in an SQL database.

CRITICAL SKILL
9.1 Compare SQL Data

The first types of predicates that I plan to discuss are those that compare data. These predicates, like any predicate, are included in the WHERE clause. You can include a WHERE clause in a SELECT, UPDATE, or DELETE statement, and in each case, the clause can contain one or more comparison predicates.

Each predicate in the WHERE clause (whether a comparison predicate or another type) is evaluated on an individual basis to determine whether it meets the condition defined by that predicate. After the predicates are evaluated, the WHERE clause is evaluated as a whole. The clause must evaluate to true in order for a row to be included in a search result, be updated, or be deleted. If the clause evaluates to false or unknown, the row is not included or is not modified. For a complete discussion of how predicates and the WHERE clause are evaluated, see Module 7.

A comparison predicate is a type of predicate that compares the values in a specified column to a specified value. A comparison operator is used to compare those values. You have already seen a number of comparison operators (and, subsequently, comparison predicates) throughout the book. Table 9-1 lists the six comparison operators supported by SQL and provides an example of each one.

You no doubt recognize several of these operators, and even those you don't recognize should be fairly self-explanatory. But let's take a quick look at the examples in Table 9-1 to make sure you understand how a comparison predicate works. In the first row in the table (the Equals row), the example predicate is InStock = 47. If this were to appear in a WHERE clause, it would look like the following:

```
WHERE InStock = 47
```

InStock is the name of the column in the table identified in the statement that contains the WHERE clause. The equals sign (=) is the comparison operator that is used to compare the

Operator	Symbol	Example
Equals	=	InStock = 47
Not equals	<>	InStock <> 47
Less than	<	InStock < 47
Greater than	>	InStock > 47
Less than or equals	<=	InStock <= 47
Greater than or equals	>=	InStock >= 47

Table 9-1 1999 Comparison Operators

values in the InStock column to the value to the right of the equals sign, which in this case is 47. Therefore, for a row to be evaluated to true, the InStock value for that row must be 47. All six comparison operators work in the same way. In each case, the WHERE clause must evaluate to true in order for the row to be returned in the query results or to be modified.

NOTE

As you learned in Module 7, you can combine predicates by using the AND keyword or the OR keyword to join together two or more predicates in a WHERE clause. You can also use the NOT keyword to create an inverse condition for a particular predicate. Remember, no matter how many predicates are included in the WHERE clause, the clause must still evaluate to true.

Now that you have an overview of the six types of comparison predicates, let's take a look at some examples. These examples are based on Figure 9-1, which shows the data stored in the CDsOnHand table.

In the first example we'll look at, the WHERE clause uses an equals operator to compare the values in the CDTitle column with one of the CD titles:

```
SELECT CDTitle, Copyright FROM CDsOnHand
WHERE CDTitle = 'Past Light' ;
```

This statement will return one row with only two values (one for each column specified in the SELECT clause), as shown in the following query results:

```
CDTitle      Copyright
----------   ---------
Past Light   1983
```

CDTitle: VARCHAR (60)	Copyright: INT	RetailPrice: NUMERIC (5,2)	Inventory: INT
Famous Blue Raincoat	1991	16.99	6
Blue	1971	14.99	26
Court and Spark	1974	14.99	18
Past Light	1983	15.99	2
Kojiki	1990	15.99	5
That Christmas Feeling	1993	10.99	3
Patsy Cline: 12 Greatest Hits	1988	16.99	25

Figure 9-1 Comparing data in the CDsOnHand table

Now let's change this SELECT statement a bit. Instead of using the equals operator, I'll use the not equals operator:

```
SELECT CDTitle, Copyright FROM CDsOnHand
WHERE CDTitle <> 'Past Light' ;
```

When you execute this statement, six rows are returned:

```
CDTitle                        Copyright
-----------------------------  ---------
Famous Blue Raincoat           1991
Blue                           1971
Court and Spark                1974
Kojiki                         1990
That Christmas Feeling         1993
Patsy Cline: 12 Greatest Hits  1988
```

Notice that all rows except the Past Light row are included in the query results. In this case, the WHERE clause evaluates to true only when the CDTitle value does not equal Past Light.

Now let's take a look at the less than operator and the greater than operator. In the next example, I join two comparison predicates together by using the AND keyword:

```
SELECT CDTitle, Inventory FROM CDsOnHand
WHERE Inventory > 2 AND Inventory < 25 ;
```

As you can see, the rows returned by this SELECT statement must contain an Inventory value between 2 and 25. If you execute this statement, four rows are returned:

```
CDTitle                 Inventory
--------------------    ---------
Famous Blue Raincoat    6
Court and Spark         18
Kojiki                  5
That Christmas Feeling  3
```

When defining the predicates in a WHERE clause, you're not limited to using only one column. For instance, suppose you want to modify the last SELECT statement to include a predicate that's based on the RetailPrice value, as shown in the following example:

```
SELECT CDTitle, Inventory FROM CDsOnHand
WHERE Inventory > 2 AND Inventory < 25 AND RetailPrice <> 16.99 ;
```

Any row returned in the query results must meet all three conditions defined in the WHERE clause. As a result, only three rows are returned when you execute this statement:

```
CDTitle                 Inventory
--------------------    ---------
Court and Spark         18
Kojiki                  5
That Christmas Feeling  3
```

Notice that the query results do not include the RetailPrice column. That is because this column is not specified in the SELECT clause. Even so, you can still use that column in a predicate in the WHERE clause to define a search condition.

Now let's take a look at the less than or equals operator and the greater than or equals operator. In the following example, both operators are used to limit the rows returned to those with a Copyright value that falls within the range of 1971 through 1989.

```
SELECT CDTitle, Copyright FROM CDsOnHand
WHERE Copyright >= 1971 AND Copyright <= 1989 ;
```

This statement will return slightly different results than what would be returned if you simply used the greater than and less than operators. By using the greater than or equals operator and the less than or equals operator, values that equal the specified value are also returned, as shown in the following query results:

```
CDTitle                        Copyright
--------------------------     ---------
Blue                           1971
Court and Spark                1974
Past Light                     1983
Patsy Cline: 12 Greatest Hits  1988
```

Notice that the Blue row includes a Copyright value of 1971. This would not have been included if you had merely used a greater than operator.

Up to this point, the examples I've shown you have all been based on SELECT statements. However, you can add a WHERE clause to an UPDATE statement or a DELETE statement. Suppose you want to increase the Inventory value for the That Christmas Feeling row. You can use the following UPDATE statement:

```
UPDATE CDsOnHand SET Inventory = 10
WHERE CDTitle = 'That Christmas Feeling' ;
```

When you execute this statement, the Inventory value is increased to 10 for the That Christmas Feeling row, but not for any other row because the WHERE clause evaluates to true only for that row. You could have just as easily added this WHERE clause to a DELETE statement, in which case the That Christmas Feeling row would have been deleted.

As with the WHERE clause in a SELECT statement, you can combine two or more predicates to form a search condition:

```
UPDATE CDsOnHand SET Inventory = 3
WHERE CDTitle = 'That Christmas Feeling' AND Copyright = 1993 ;
```

When you specify the AND keyword, both predicates must evaluate to true in order for the WHERE clause to evaluate to true. If you specify the OR keyword, instead of AND, then only one of the predicates must evaluate to true.

Using the BETWEEN Predicate

Strictly speaking, the BETWEEN predicate is not a comparison predicate, at least not as it is presented in the SQL:1999 standard. It is, however, so similar in function to the greater than or equals operator and the less than or equals operator (when used together) that it's worth discussing here.

The BETWEEN predicate is used in conjunction with the AND keyword to identify a range of values that can be included as a search condition in the WHERE clause. Values in the identified column must fall within that range in order to evaluate to true. When you use the BETWEEN clause, you must specify the applicable column, the low end of the range, and the high end of the range. The following example (which is based on the CDsOnHand table in Figure 9-1) specifies a range from 14 through 16:

```
SELECT CDTitle, RetailPrice FROM CDsOnHand
WHERE RetailPrice BETWEEN 14 AND 16 ;
```

The RetailPrice value for each row must fall within that range. If you execute this statement, only four rows are included in the query results:

```
CDTitle           RetailPrice
---------------   ---------
Blue              14.99
Court and Spark   14.99
Past Light        15.99
Kojiki            15.99
```

Now let's take a look at a query similar to the one in the last example, only this time using comparison predicates rather than the BETWEEN predicate:

```
SELECT CDTitle, RetailPrice FROM CDsOnHand
WHERE RetailPrice >= 14 AND RetailPrice <= 16 ;
```

Notice that two predicates are used: one with the greater than or equals operator and one with the less than or equals operator. This SELECT statement will produce the same query results as the previous SELECT statement.

Now let's return to the BETWEEN predicate. As with any predicate, you can combine the BETWEEN predicate with other predicates. In the following statement, the WHERE clause includes a BETWEEN predicate and a comparison predicate:

```
SELECT CDTitle, RetailPrice FROM CDsOnHand
WHERE RetailPrice BETWEEN 14 AND 16 AND Inventory > 10 ;
```

As a result of both predicates, the query results can include only those rows with a RetailPrice value that falls within the range of 14 through 16 *and* with an Inventory value greater than 10. When you execute this query, only two rows are returned:

```
CDTitle           RetailPrice
---------------   ----------
Blue              14.99
Court and Spark   14.99
```

Again, you will notice that the query results don't include the Inventory column even though that column is specified in a predicate in the WHERE clause. You'll also notice that more than one column is referenced in the WHERE clause.

In addition to what you've seen so far with the BETWEEN predicate, you can also use the clause to specify the inverse of a condition. This is done by using the NOT keyword within the predicate. For example, suppose you change the last example to the following:

```
SELECT CDTitle, RetailPrice FROM CDsOnHand
WHERE RetailPrice NOT BETWEEN 14 AND 16 ;
```

The rows returned in the query result will include all rows that do not have a RetailPrice value within the range of 14 through 16. When you execute the statement, three rows are returned:

```
CDTitle                          RetailPrice
---------------------------      -----------
Famous Blue Raincoat             16.99
That Christmas Feeling           10.99
Patsy Cline: 12 Greatest Hits    16.99
```

Notice that all values within the specified range have been excluded from the query results.

Progress Check

1. What are the six comparison operators?

2. Which symbol do you use to represent a not equals operator in a comparison predicate?

3. What type of predicate can you use in place of the greater than or equals operator and the less than or equals operator?

CRITICAL SKILL

9.2 Return Null Values

As you might recall from Module 4, a null value is used in place of a value when that value is undefined or not known. A null indicates that the value is absent. This is not the same as a zero, a blank, or a default value. By default, SQL allows nulls to be used in place of regular values (although you can override the default by using a NOT NULL constraint in your column definition). In those cases where null values are permitted, you might find it necessary to specify that null values be returned when you query a table. For this reason, SQL provides the NULL predicate, which allows you to define search conditions that return null values.

The NULL predicate is very straightforward to implement. Used in conjunction with the IS keyword, the predicate is added to a WHERE clause in the same way any other predicate is added, and it applies only to null values that might exist in the column that you query. The best way to illustrate this is through the use of examples. In these examples, I use the ArtistsBio table, shown in Figure 9-2.

1. Equals, not equals, less than, greater than, less than or equals, greater than or equals

2. <>

3. The BETWEEN predicate

PerformerName: VARCHAR (60)	PlaceOfBirth: VARCHAR (60)	YearBorn: INT
Jennifer Warnes	Seattle, Washington, USA	1947
Joni Mitchell	Fort MacLeod, Alberta, Canada	1943
William Ackerman	NULL	NULL
Kitaro	Toyohashi, Japan	NULL
Bing Crosby	NULL	1904
Patsy Cline	Winchester, VIrginia, United States	1932
Jose Carreras	Barcelona, Spain	NULL
Luciano Pavarotti	Modena, Italy	1935
Placido Domingo	Madrid, Spain	1941

Figure 9-2 Returning null values from the ArtistsBio table

The first example is a SELECT statement that returns rows with a PlaceOfBirth value of null:

```
SELECT * FROM ArtistsBio
WHERE PlaceOfBirth IS NULL ;
```

The statement returns all columns from the ArtistsBio table; however, it returns only two rows, as you can see in the following query results:

```
PerformerName      PlaceOfBirth   YearBorn
----------------   ------------   --------
William Ackerman   NULL           NULL
Bing Crosby        NULL           1904
```

The fact that the YearBorn column contains a null value for the William Ackerman row has no bearing on the fact that a NULL predicate is used. The NULL predicate in this case identifies the PlaceOfBirth column only, not the YearBorn column. You can, however, replace the PlaceOfBirth column with the YearBorn column, in which case the rows returned will be those with a YearBorn value of null.

According to the SQL:1999 standard, you can also specify both columns in the NULL predicate, as shown in the following example:

```
SELECT * FROM ArtistsBio
WHERE (PlaceOfBirth, YearBorn) IS NULL ;
```

When you include both columns, the PlaceOfBirth column and YearBorn column must both return null values in order for a row to be returned, which in the case of the ArtistsBio table would only be one row.

NOTE

Although the SQL standard permits you to specify multiple columns in the NULL predicate, many implementations do not support this. Instead you must specify two NULL predicates.

As an alternative to including both columns in one predicate, you can write your SELECT statement as follows:

```
SELECT * FROM ArtistsBio
WHERE PlaceOfBirth IS NULL AND YearBorn IS NULL ;
```

If you execute this statement, you'll receive the following query results:

```
PerformerName       PlaceOfBirth   YearBorn
----------------    ------------   --------
William Ackerman    NULL           NULL
```

SQL supports another feature in the NULL predicate. You can use the NOT keyword to find the inverse results of the predicate. For example, suppose you want to return all rows that include an actual value in the PlaceOfBirth column, rather than a null value. Your statement might look like the following:

```
SELECT * FROM ArtistsBio
WHERE PlaceOfBirth IS NOT NULL ;
```

Your query results will now include seven rows, all of which contain values in the PlaceOfBirth column:

```
PerformerName       PlaceOfBirth                      YearBorn
----------------    ------------------------------    --------
Jennifer Warnes     Seattle, Washington, USA          1947
Joni Mitchell       Fort MacLeod, Alberta, Canada     1943
Kitaro              Toyohashi, Japan                  NULL
Patsy Cline         Winchester, Virginia, USA         1932
Jose Carreras       Barcelona, Spain                  NULL
Luciano Pavarotti   Modena, Italy                     1935
Placido Domingo     Madrid, Spain                     1941
```

Notice that null values can still exist in other columns. Because only the PlaceOfBirth column is specified in the NULL predicate, only that column must contain a value in order for a row to be returned.

As with the predicates we looked at earlier in the module, you can combine the NULL predicate with other types of predicates. For example, you can modify the last example to limit the YearBorn values to certain years, as shown in the following example:

```
SELECT * FROM ArtistsBio
WHERE PlaceOfBirth IS NOT NULL AND YearBorn > 1940 ;
```

Now any rows returned must include a value in the PlaceOfBirth column *and* the YearBorn value must be greater than 1940. If you execute this query, you'll receive the following results:

```
PerformerName      PlaceOfBirth                          YearBorn
---------------    ----------------------------          --------
Jennifer Warnes    Seattle, Washington, USA              1947
Joni Mitchell      Fort MacLeod, Alberta, Canada         1943
Placido Domingo    Madrid, Spain                         1941
```

As you can see, only three rows are returned. No rows with a PlaceOfBirth value of null are returned because null evaluates to unknown, and only WHERE clauses that evaluate to true can be included in the query results.

CRITICAL SKILL
9.3 Return Similar Values

If any predicate can be fun, it is the LIKE predicate. The LIKE predicate provides a flexible environment in which you can specify values that are only *similar* to the values stored in the database. This is particularly advantageous if you know only the partial name of a value but still need to retrieve information based on that value. For example, suppose you don't know the entire title of a CD, but you do know part of that title. Or perhaps you know only part of a performer's name. By using the LIKE predicate, you can ask for values that are similar to what you do know and from those results determine if the information you need is there.

Before we take a look at the LIKE predicate itself, let's look at two symbols used within the predicate. The LIKE predicate uses two special characters—the percentage sign (%) and the underscore (_)—to help define the search condition specified in the predicate. The percentage sign represents zero or more unknown characters, and the underscore represents exactly one unknown character. You can use these characters at the beginning of a value, in the middle, or at the end, and you can combine them with each other as necessary. The way in which you use these two characters determines the type of data that is retrieved from your database. Table 9-2 provides a number of examples of how these special characters can be used in a LIKE predicate.

Sample Value	Possible Query Results
'J%'	Jennifer Warnes, Joni Mitchell, Jose Carreras
'%spark'	Court and Spark
'%blue%'	Famous Blue Raincoat, Blue, Blues on the Bayou
'%Cline%Hits'	Patsy Cline: 12 Greatest Hits
'194_'	1940, 1942, 1947
'19__'	1900, 1907, 1938, 1963, 1999
'_ue'	Blue
'9__01'	90201, 91401, 95501, 99301, 99901
'9_3%'	9032343, 903, 95312, 99306, 983393300333

Table 9-2 Using Special Characters in a LIKE Predicate

As you can see, the percentage sign and underscore special characters provide a great deal of flexibility and allow you to query a wide range of data.

Now that you have an understanding of the special characters, let's take a look at the LIKE predicate as a whole. The LIKE predicate includes the column name, the LIKE keyword, and a value enclosed in a set of single quotation marks, which is then enclosed in a set of parentheses. For example, the following WHERE clause includes one LIKE predicate:

```
WHERE CDID LIKE ('%01')
```

The predicate includes the CDID column, the LIKE keyword, and a value of %01. Only rows that contain the correct value in the CDID column are returned in the query results. The CDID column is part of the CDs table, which is shown in Figure 9-3. We will be using this table for the examples in this section. Notice that, based on the LIKE predicate defined in the preceding WHERE clause, only one row can be returned by this clause, the row with a CDID value of 99301.

Now let's take a look at a few examples of SELECT statements that include a LIKE predicate. Suppose you want to find any CDs that contain the word Christmas in the title. You can create the following SELECT statement to query the CDs table:

```
SELECT * FROM CDs
WHERE CDTitle LIKE ('%Christmas%') ;
```

Your query results will include only one row:

```
CDID    CDTitle
------  --------------------
99306   That Christmas Feeling
```

CDID: INT	CDTitle: VARCHAR (60)
99301	Famous Blue Raincoat
99302	Blue
99303	Court and Spark
99304	Past Light
99305	Kojiki
99306	That Christmas Feeling
99307	Patsy Cline: 12 Greatest Hits

Figure 9-3 Returning similar values from the CDs table

If you had included only one percentage sign, no rows would have been returned. For example, if you eliminated the first percentage sign, your SQL implementation would have interpreted this to mean that the value begins with the word Christmas, which it does not. The same is true for the other percentage sign. If you had eliminated that, your implementation would have assumed that Christmas was the last word in the character string. In addition, if no percentage signs were used, no rows would have been returned because no values would have matched Christmas exactly.

You can also add the NOT keyword to a LIKE predicate if you want all rows returned except those specified by the predicate. Take, for instance, the last example. If you add the NOT keyword, it will look like the following:

```
SELECT * FROM CDs
WHERE CDTitle NOT LIKE ('%Christmas%') ;
```

This time, your query results include all rows that do not include the word Christmas:

```
CDID    CDTitle
-----   --------------------
99301   Famous Blue Raincoat
99302   Blue
99303   Court and Spark
99304   Past Light
99305   Kojiki
99307   Patsy Cline: 12 Greatest Hits
```

Notice that the That Christmas Feeling row is now among the missing.

You can also combine one LIKE predicate with another LIKE predicate. Suppose, for example, you still want to exclude the Christmas value, but you want to include the Blue value, as shown in the following example:

```
SELECT * FROM CDs
WHERE CDTitle NOT LIKE ('%Christmas%') AND CDTitle LIKE ('%Blue%') ;
```

The WHERE clause in this SELECT statement eliminates any rows that have the word Christmas appearing anywhere in the CDTitle value. In addition, the CDTitle value should include the word Blue. As a result, only two rows are returned.

```
CDID    CDTitle
-----   -------------------
99301   Famous Blue Raincoat
99302   Blue
```

But what happens if the CD title includes both words? For example, Elvis Presley's *Blue Christmas* is now available in CD. In a case of this sort, the LIKE predicate containing NOT takes precedence over the one that doesn't contain NOT, regardless of the order in which the predicates are included in the WHERE clause. Even if a Blue Christmas row existed, it would not be included in the query results.

Progress Check

1. When is a null value used in a column?

2. What two keywords must you use in a NULL predicate?

3. What two special characters can you use in a LIKE predicate?

4. What components make up a LIKE predicate?

---

1. A null value is used in place of a value when that value is undefined or not known. A null indicates that the value is absent. This is not the same as a zero, a blank, or a default value.

2. IS NULL

3. A percentage sign and an underscore

4. A LIKE predicate is made up of a column name, the LIKE keyword, and a value enclosed in a set of single quotation marks, which is then enclosed in a set of parentheses.

Project 9-1   Using Predicates in SQL Statements

Prj09.txt Before we move on to other predicates, I think it's a good idea to review those predicates that have already been discussed. These include the six types of comparison predicates, the BETWEEN predicate, the NULL predicate, and the LIKE predicate. In this project, you will try a number of these predicates through the use of SELECT statements that will include the appropriate WHERE clauses. You will be querying tables that you created in the Inventory database. Because you will be using only SELECT statements, you won't be modifying the tables or the database structure in any way. You'll simply request data based on the predicates that you define. You can download the Prj09.txt file, which contains the SQL statements used in this project.

Step by Step

1. Open the client application for your RDBMS and connect to the Inventory database.

2. In the first statement that you create, you'll query the MusicTypes table to return the names of those rows whose TypeID value is equal to 11 or 12. Enter and execute the following SQL statement:

```
SELECT TypeID, TypeName FROM MusicTypes
WHERE TypeID = 11 OR TypeID = 12 ;
```

The statement should return two rows, one for Blues and one for Jazz. Notice that the OR keyword is used to indicate that either value is acceptable.

3. Now you'll query the Artists table and look for artists other than Patsy Cline and Bing Crosby. Enter and execute the following SQL statement:

```
SELECT ArtistName, PlaceOfBirth FROM Artists
WHERE ArtistName <> 'Patsy Cline' AND ArtistName <> 'Bing Crosby' ;
```

Your query should return 16 rows and should not include the Patsy Cline row or the Bing Crosby row.

4. Now let's combine a couple of comparison predicates to create a different sort of search condition. In this statement, you'll again query the Artists table, but you'll request only those rows whose ArtistID values lie between 2004 and 2014. Enter and execute the following SQL statement:

```
SELECT ArtistID, ArtistName FROM Artists
WHERE ArtistID > 2004 AND ArtistID < 2014 ;
```

Your query should return nine rows.

(continued)

5. Now let's modify the SELECT statement that you just executed. You should use a BETWEEN predicate rather than the two comparison predicates. Enter and execute the following SQL statement:

```
SELECT ArtistID, ArtistName FROM Artists
WHERE ArtistID BETWEEN 2004 AND 2014 ;
```

You should now see 11 rows, rather than the 9 that were returned in the previous step. Had you used the greater than or equals operator and the less than or equals operator in the last step, your query results would have been the same as in this step.

6. Now let's query the Artists table once more, only this time, we'll use the NULL predicate. Enter and execute the following SQL statement:

```
SELECT * FROM Artists
WHERE PlaceOfBirth IS NULL ;
```

Your query will return no results because the PlaceOfBirth column contains no null values.

7. Let's try the same query as in the last step, only this time we'll add the NOT keyword to the NULL predicate. Enter and execute the following SQL statement:

```
SELECT * FROM Artists
WHERE PlaceOfBirth IS NOT NULL ;
```

Your query should now return every row in the table (18 in all).

8. In the next statement, you will use the LIKE predicate to find CD titles that include the word Best or the word Greatest. Your predicate will reference the CDTitle column of the CompactDiscs table. Enter and execute the following SQL statement:

```
SELECT CDTitle, InStock FROM CompactDiscs
WHERE CDTitle LIKE ('%Greatest%') OR CDTitle LIKE ('%Best%') ;
```

Your query should return three rows. In all those rows, the CDTitle value should contain the words Greatest or Best.

9. Next you'll modify the statement in the previous step to include the NOT keyword in both predicates. You should also change the OR keyword to AND. Enter and execute the following SQL statement:

```
SELECT CDTitle, InStock FROM CompactDiscs
WHERE CDTitle NOT LIKE ('%Greatest%') AND CDTitle NOT LIKE
('%Best%') ;
```

Your query results should now include 12 rows. If you had not changed the OR keyword to AND, your results would have included all 15 rows. This is because connecting the two predicates with OR would have essentially cancelled out the NOT condition of each of the two predicates.

10. Close the client application.

Project Summary

In this project, you created a number of SELECT statements that included various predicates. The predicates were contained in WHERE clauses that were part of the SELECT statements; however, these clauses could also have been part of UPDATE and DELETE statements. As you move through the rest of this module, you will learn about other predicates and how they can be used in various types of statements. These predicates can be used in conjunction with the ones I've already discussed or used by themselves to create more complex search conditions and return more precise results.

CRITICAL SKILL

9.4 Reference Additional Sources of Data

SQL supports several types of predicates that allow you to reference sources other than the main table that you're querying or modifying. As a result, you can create search conditions that compare data between tables in order to determine which rows should be included in your query results, which rows should be updated, or which ones deleted. In this section, I look at two important predicates that you can use to reference other tables: the IN predicate and the EXISTS predicate.

Both predicates use subqueries to reference data in tables other than the main table being queried or modified. I first introduce the topic of subqueries in Module 4. As you might recall from that module, a subquery is an expression that is used as a component within another expression. In its most common usage, a subquery is simply a SELECT statement embedded within another statement. When used in a predicate, a subquery becomes part of that predicate and consequently is embedded in the WHERE clause of a SELECT, UPDATE, or DELETE statement. Although subqueries are discussed in detail in Module 12, I mention them here because they're an integral part of the predicates I'll be discussing in the remaining part of this module. In each of these predicates, subqueries are used to reference data in other tables. For the purposes of this module, I keep my examples of subqueries simple, but know that they can be far more elaborate than what you see here, and once you complete Module 12, you'll be able to apply that knowledge to the predicates you learn about in this module.

Using the IN Predicate

The IN predicate allows you to determine whether the values in the specified column of one table are contained in a defined list or contained within another table. In the first case, you specify the column name, the IN keyword, and a list of values that are compared to the values in the specified column. In the second case, you specify the column name, the IN keyword, and a subquery, which references the second table. In either case, if the column value matches one of the values in the list or in the subquery results, the predicate evaluates to true, and the row is returned in the query results.

The best way to illustrate both of these methods is through examples. However, before we look at those, refer to the tables shown in Figure 9-4. These are the tables I'll be using for the examples.

As I mentioned, the first method for using the IN predicate is to define a list. Your list should include all values that are to be compared to the values in the specified column. For example, suppose you want to limit your query results to rows in the CompactDiscInventory

CompactDiscInventory

CDName: VARCHAR (60)	InStock: INT
Famous Blue Raincoat	13
Blue	42
Court and Spark	22
Past Light	17
Kojiki	6
That Christmas Feeling	8
Out of Africa	29
Blues on the Bayou	27
Orlando	5

CompactDiscArtists

Title: VARCHAR (60)	Artist: VARCHAR (60)
Famous Blue Raincoat	Jennifer Warnes
Blue	Joni Mitchell
Court and Spark	Joni Mitchell
Past Light	William Ackerman
Kojiki	Kitaro
That Christmas Feeling	Bing Crosby
Patsy Cline: 12 Greatest Hits	Patsy Cline
After the Rain: The Soft Sounds of Erik Satie	Pascal Roge
Out of Africa	John Barry
Leonard Cohen The Best of	Leonard Cohen
Fundamental	Bonnie Raitt
Blues on the Bayou	B.B. King
Orlando	David Motion

Figure 9-4 Querying data from the CompactDiscInventory table and the CompactDiscArtists table

table that have an InStock value of 12, 22, 32, or 42. You can create a SELECT statement that looks like the following:

```
SELECT CDName, InStock FROM CompactDiscInventory
WHERE InStock IN ( 12, 22, 32, 42 ) ;
```

This statement returns only two rows because those are the only rows that have the correct InStock values:

```
CDName           InStock
---------------  -------
Blue             42
Court and Spark  22
```

As you can see, using the IN predicate to define a list is a fairly straightforward process and a useful one when you know exactly which values you want to compare your columns to. It also is a simpler method than defining separate predicates for each value, as in the following example:

```
SELECT CDName, InStock FROM CompactDiscInventory
WHERE InStock = 12 OR InStock = 22 OR InStock = 32 OR InStock = 42 ;
```

This statement will return the same results as the SELECT statement in the previous example; however, as you can see, it's much more cumbersome.

Now let's take a look at a SELECT statement that uses a subquery in the IN predicate. Suppose you want to create a query that returns CD names and their artists. You want your query results to include only those CDs in which there are more than 10 copies of each one. If you refer back to Figure 9-4, you'll see that the CompactDiscArtists table includes the CD names and their artists. However, as you can also see, the InStock values are stored in the CompactDiscInventory table, which means you'll need to reference that table in order to return the correct rows. To do so, you can create the following SELECT statement:

```
SELECT Title, Artist FROM CompactDiscArtists
WHERE Title IN
( SELECT CDName FROM CompactDiscInventory WHERE InStock > 10 ) ;
```

If you execute this statement, you'll receive the following results:

```
Title                 Artist
--------------------  ----------------
Famous Blue Raincoat  Jennifer Warnes
Blue                  Joni Mitchell
Court and Spark       Joni Mitchell
```

```
Past Light            William Ackerman
Out of Africa         John Barry
Blues on the Bayou    B.B. King
```

Notice that only six rows have been returned. These are the six CDs listed in the CompactDiscInventory table that have an InStock value greater than 10.

Now let's take a closer look at the SELECT statement in order to give you a better understanding of how the IN predicate works. The WHERE clause contains only one predicate. It begins with the name of the column (Title) whose values you want to verify. The Title column is followed by the IN keyword. The keyword is then followed by a subquery, which is enclosed in parentheses. The subquery consists of the following SELECT statement:

```
SELECT CDName FROM CompactDiscInventory WHERE InStock > 10
```

If you were to execute this statement on its own, you would receive the following results:

```
CDName
--------------------
Famous Blue Raincoat
Blue
Court and Spark
Past Light
Out of Africa
Blues on the Bayou
```

Each row in the query results, which are derived from the CompactDiscInventory table, contains an InStock value greater than 10. The values in the Title column of the CompactDiscArtists table are then compared against these results. Any row that contains a Title value that matches one of six CDName values (in the subquery results) is included in the query results of the main SELECT statement.

NOTE

When including a subquery in an IN predicate, you must specify only one column name in the SELECT clause. If you specify more than one column name or you specify an asterisk, you will receive an error.

Like many other predicates, the IN predicate allows you to specify the inverse of a condition by using the NOT keyword. Suppose you rewrite the SELECT statement in the last example to include the NOT keyword in the IN predicate:

```
SELECT Title, Artist FROM CompactDiscArtists
WHERE Title NOT IN
( SELECT CDName FROM CompactDiscInventory WHERE InStock > 10 ) ;
```

Your query results will include all those rows that were not returned by the last SELECT statement and will exclude all those rows that were returned, as shown in the following results:

```
Title                                            Artist
---------------------------------------------    ------------
Kojiki                                           Kitaro
That Christmas Feeling                           Bing Crosby
Patsy Cline: 12 Greatest Hits                    Patsy Cline
After the Rain: The Soft Sounds of Erik Satie    Pascal Roge
Leonard Cohen The Best Of                        Leonard Cohen
Fundamental                                      Bonnie Raitt
Orlando                                          David Motion
```

As you can see, the IN predicate is a very flexible tool for comparing values in a specified column to data in other tables. You'll find this extremely useful as you learn more about subqueries and can create more complex predicates.

Using the EXISTS Predicate

Although similar to an IN predicate, the EXISTS predicate has a slightly different focus. It is concerned only with determining whether or not the subquery returns any rows. If it returns one or more rows, the predicate evaluates to true. Otherwise, the predicate evaluates to false. The predicate is made up of the EXISTS keyword and a subquery. For the subquery to be of any real value (and subsequently the EXISTS predicate itself), it should include a predicate that matches two columns in different tables. For example, in Figure 9-4, the CompactDiscInventory table includes the CDName column, and the CompactDiscArtists table includes the Title column. The two columns can be matched together to ensure that only relevant rows are returned by the subquery. Let's take a look at an example to help clarify this issue.

Suppose you want to retrieve rows from the CompactDiscInventory table so you can determine how many Joni Mitchell CDs you have in stock. You want to display only the CD names and the number of CDs in stock. You do not want to display the artist's name, and you do not want to display CDs by other artists. To accomplish this, you can use the following SELECT statement:

```
SELECT * FROM CompactDiscInventory
WHERE EXISTS
( SELECT Title FROM CompactDiscArtists
WHERE Artist = 'Joni Mitchell'
AND CompactDiscInventory.CDName = CompactDiscArtists.Title ) ;
```

If you execute this statement, you'll receive the following query results:

```
CDName            InStock
--------------    -------
Blue              42
Court and Spark   22
```

The best way to understand how this statement works is to look at how individual rows are evaluated. Each row returned by the main SELECT statement is evaluated against the subquery. Because the subquery WHERE clause matches the CDName value to the Title value, the Title value in the row being evaluated (in the subquery) must match the CDName value in order for that row to be returned. For example, the first row in the CompactDiscInventory table contains a CDName value of Famous Blue Raincoat. When this row is tested against the EXISTS predicate, the Famous Blue Raincoat value is matched with the Famous Blue Raincoat value of the Title column in the CompactDiscArtists table. In addition, the Joni Mitchell value is matched against the Artist value for the Famous Blue Raincoat row. Because the Artist value is Jennifer Warnes, and not Joni Mitchell, the search condition specified in the subquery WHERE clause evaluates to false, so no subquery row is returned for the Famous Blue Raincoat row. As a result, the WHERE clause in the main SELECT statement evaluates to false for the Famous Blue Raincoat row of the CompactDiscInventory table, and the row is not included in the query results.

This process is repeated for each row in the CompactDiscInventory table. If the WHERE clause in the subquery evaluates to true, then the EXISTS predicate evaluates to true, which means that the WHERE clause in the main SELECT statement evaluates to true. In the case of our last example SELECT statement, only two rows meet this criteria.

NOTE

It does not matter what columns or how many columns you specify in the SELECT clause of the subquery in an EXISTS predicate. This type of predicate is concerned only with whether rows are being returned, not with the content of those rows. You can specify any column names or just an asterisk.

The EXISTS predicate, as you might expect, allows you to test the inverse of the predicate condition by using the NOT keyword:

```
SELECT * FROM CompactDiscInventory
WHERE NOT EXISTS
( SELECT Title FROM CompactDiscArtists
WHERE Artist = 'Joni Mitchell'
AND CompactDiscInventory.CDName = CompactDiscArtists.Title ) ;
```

In this case, all CDs *except* the Joni Mitchell CDs are included in the query results. This means that, if the WHERE clause of the subquery evaluates to true (which means that the subquery returns a row), the predicate itself evaluates to false, and no row is returned. On the other hand, if the subquery does not return a row, the predicate evaluates to true, and the row is returned in the query results of the main SELECT statement.

Ask the Expert

Q: You've provided examples that show that there is often more than one way to achieve the same outcome. How do you know which option to select when you're writing an SQL statement?

A: You'll find that, as you learn more about SQL programming and gain a better understanding of the nuances of each statement, there will often be more than one way to achieve the same results. In these cases, your choice of methods will often depend on which statement is the simplest to write or how performance is affected in a particular SQL implementation. As your understanding of SQL grows, so too will your ability to choose the method that's best for your situation. In many cases, the difference between one method over another will not be very great, and your choice might merely depend on your personal preference. However, you might also run into situations in which the SQL implementation in which you're working does not support all the methods provided in the SQL standard. Therefore, you must select the method that can be implemented in your particular environment. Whichever methods you might ultimately use in any given environment, it is best for now that you have as complete a foundation as necessary in the basics of SQL. That way you'll be more prepared for various situations and be better equipped to move from implementation to implementation. In addition, you should learn about performance issues related to the implementation with which you're working. You should consider issues of performance when making a decision about which SQL statements to use.

Q: When you provided examples of the EXISTS predicate, your subqueries always matched columns within the subquery WHERE clause. Is this necessary?

A: You can, if you want, create an EXISTS predicate that does not match columns in the subquery, such as in the following statement:

```
SELECT Title, Artist FROM CompactDiscArtists
WHERE EXISTS
( SELECT CDName FROM CompactDiscInventory WHERE InStock > 10 ) ;
```

(continued)

In this case, your subquery merely checks to see whether any rows exist in the CompactDiscInventory table with an InStock value greater than 10. If those rows exist, the predicate evaluates to true, which means the WHERE clause in the main SELECT statement evaluates to true. As a result, all rows in the CompactDiscArtists table are returned. Using this sort of subquery is generally not very useful because it offers little advantage over a simple SELECT statement. Matching columns from different tables is essential within the subquery to provide meaningful data to the main SELECT statement.

Progress Check

1. What is a subquery?

2. What type of predicate should you use to determine whether the values in the specified column of one table are contained in a defined list or contained within another table?

3. What type of predicate should you include in the subquery WHERE clause of an EXISTS predicate?

9.5 Quantify Comparison Predicates

SQL includes another type of predicate called a *quantified comparison predicate,* which is a type of predicate used in conjunction with a comparison operator to determine whether *any* or *all* returned values meet the search requirement. SQL supports three quantified comparison predicates: SOME, ANY, and ALL. The SOME and ANY predicates are referred to as *existential quantifiers* and are concerned with whether *any* returned values meet the search requirements. These two predicates are identical in meaning and can be used interchangeably. The ALL predicate is referred to as a *universal quantifier* and is concerned with whether *all* returned values meet the search requirements. Now let's take a closer look at each one.

---

1. A subquery is an expression that is used as a component within another expression. In its most common usage, a subquery is simply a SELECT statement embedded within another statement.
2. An IN predicate
3. A predicate that matches two columns in different tables

Using the SOME and ANY Predicates

As I mentioned, the SOME and ANY predicates return identical results. For each row, the predicates compare the value in a specified column to the results of a subquery. If the comparison evaluates to true for *any* of the results, the condition has been satisfied and that row is returned. To create one of these predicates, you must specify the column name that contains the values you want to compare, the comparison operator (see the "Compare SQL Data" section), the SOME or ANY keyword, and the subquery. Although you can use either keyword, I prefer ANY because it seems more intuitive to me, but feel free to use either one.

Now let's take a look at an example to give you a better feel for how these predicates work. The example is based on the CDRetail table and the CDSale table, which are shown in Figure 9-5.

In this example, I want to query data from the CDSale table. I want to return only those rows that have a Sale value less than some of the Retail values in the CDRetail table. The Retail values should be from rows that have an InStock value greater than 9. In other words, the query should return only those CDs whose sale price is less than *any* retail price of those CDs in which there are more than nine in stock. To accomplish this, I will use the following SELECT statement:

```
SELECT Title, Sale FROM CDSale
WHERE Sale < ANY
( SELECT Retail FROM CDRetail WHERE InStock > 9 ) ;
```

CDRetail

CDName: VARCHAR (60)	Retail: NUMERIC (5,2)	InStock: INT
Famous Blue Raincoat	16.99	5
Blue	14.99	10
Court and Spark	14.99	12
Past Light	15.99	11
Kojiki	15.99	4
That Christmas Feeling	10.99	8
Patsy Cline: 12 Greatest Hits	16.99	14

CDSale

Title: VARCHAR (60)	Sale: NUMERIC (5,2)
Famous Blue Raincoat	14.99
Blue	12.99
Court and Spark	14.99
Past Light	14.99
Kojiki	13.99
That Christmas Feeling	10.99
Patsy Cline: 12 Greatest Hits	16.99

Figure 9-5 Using quantified comparison predicates on the CDRetail and the CDSale tables

If you want, you can use the SOME keyword rather than the ANY keyword. The query results would be the same, as shown in the following results:

```
Title                        Sale
---------------------        -----
Famous Blue Raincoat         14.99
Blue                         12.99
Court and Spark              14.99
Past Light                   14.99
Kojiki                       13.99
That Christmas Feeling       10.99
```

Now let's look at the SELECT statement more closely. The ANY predicate contains the following subquery:

```
SELECT Retail FROM CDRetail WHERE InStock > 9
```

If you were to execute this subquery on its own, you would receive the following results:

```
Retail
-------
14.99
14.99
15.99
16.99
```

The Sale value in each row in the CDSale table is then compared to the subquery results. For example, the Past Light row has a Sale value of 14.99. This value is compared to the subquery results to see whether 14.99 is less than *any* value. Because it is less than 15.99 and 16.99, the predicate evaluates to true, and the row is returned. The only row that does not evaluate to true is the Patsy Cline: 12 Greatest Hits row because the Sale value is 16.99, and this is not less than any of the values returned by the query results.

You can use any of the six comparison operators in an ANY or SOME predicate. For example, if you had used the greater than operator, only the Patsy Cline: 12 Greatest Hits row would have been returned because it would have been the only row with a Sale value greater than any row in the subquery results.

NOTE

The quantified comparison predicates do not support an inverse condition like other predicates. In other words, you cannot add the NOT keyword before ANY or SOME. However, because you can use the not equals (<>) operator, you can achieve the same results.

Using the ALL Predicate

The ALL predicate works the same way as the ANY and SOME predicates. The ALL predicate compares column values to the subquery results. However, rather than the column values having to evaluate to true for *any* of the result values, the column values must evaluate to true for *all* the result values; otherwise, the row is not returned.

Let's return to the previous example we looked at, only this time substitute the keyword ALL for the keyword ANY. Your new SELECT statement will look like the following:

```
SELECT Title, Sale FROM CDSale
WHERE Sale < ALL
( SELECT Retail FROM CDRetail WHERE InStock > 9 ) ;
```

If you execute this statement, you'll find that your query results are quite different from what they were in the previous example:

```
Title                   Sale
--------------------    -----
Blue                    12.99
Kojiki                  13.99
That Christmas Feeling  10.99
```

This time, only three rows are returned because they are the only ones that meet the condition of the WHERE predicate.

If you take a closer look at the statement, you'll find that the subquery returns the same values as it does in the previous examples. However, the Sale value for each row in the CDSale table must now be less than all the values in the subquery results. For example, the Kojiki row contains a Sale value of 13.99. The subquery results include the values 14.99, 15.99, and 16.99. The 13.99 value is less than all three of the subquery result values, which means that the predicate evaluates to true, so that row is included in the query results. On the other hand, the Past Light row contains a Sale value of 14.99, which is not less than the 14.99 subquery value, so that row is not included in the query results.

Ask the Expert

Q: In your discussions about quantified comparison predicates, you included examples on how to use these predicates; however, the examples included only one predicate in the WHERE clause. Can you use multiple predicates when using a quantified comparison predicate?

(continued)

A: Yes, you can use multiple predicates. As with any other sort of predicate, you simply connect the predicates with the AND keyword or the OR keyword. But you must make sure that the logic you're using not only makes sense in terms of the data being returned, but also in the sense of being able to understand the statement itself. As a result, the best way to treat these sorts of situations is to set off each predicate in parentheses and then connect the parenthetical expressions with AND or OR. For example, suppose you want to take the example in the section "Using the SOME and ANY Predicates" and add a LIKE predicate to it. (The example is based on Figure 9-5.) You can create a SELECT statement similar to the following:

```
SELECT Title, Sale FROM CDSale WHERE
( Sale < ANY ( SELECT Retail FROM CDRetail WHERE InStock > 9 ) )
AND ( Title LIKE ('%Blue%') ) ;
```

Notice that each predicate has been enclosed in a set of parentheses and that they are joined together by AND. If you execute this statement, your query results will meet the condition of the ANY predicate *and* the LIKE predicate, which specifies that the Title value include the word Blue. If you wanted to, you could write these statements without enclosing the predicates in parentheses, but then the statements can start to get confusing and, in more complex structures, can start producing unexpected results.

As with the ANY and SOME predicates, you can use any of the six comparison operators in an ALL predicate. In addition, you can create any type of subquery, as long as it fits in logically with the main SELECT statement. The point to remember is that the column value must be true for all subquery results, not just some of them.

Project 9-2   Using Subqueries in Predicates

Prj09.txt   This project basically picks up where you left off in Project 9-1. Once more, you'll be working with predicates, only this time it will be those that use subqueries. These are the predicates that were discussed since the last project. They include the IN, EXISTS, ANY, and ALL predicates. As with the previous project, you'll apply these predicates to the tables you created in the Inventory database. You can download the Prj09.txt file, which contains the SQL statements used in this project.

Step by Step

1. Open the client application for your RDBMS and connect to the Inventory database.

2. In your first statement, you'll use an IN predicate to query data from the CompactDiscs table. You want to view CD and inventory information for CDs published by Decca Record

Company. To find out which CDs these are, you must create a subquery that queries data from the CDLabels table. Enter and execute the following SQL statement:

```
SELECT CDTitle, InStock FROM CompactDiscs
WHERE LabelID IN
( SELECT LabelID FROM CDLabels
WHERE CompanyName = 'Decca Record Company' ) ;
```

Your query results should include only two rows. Both these rows have a LabelID value of 833, which is the value returned by the subquery.

3. Now you will try a SELECT statement similar to the one in Step 2, only this time you'll use an EXISTS predicate to return data. In addition, you will have to add a predicate to the subquery WHERE clause that matches the LabelID value in the CompactDiscs table to the LabelID value in the CDLabels table. Enter and execute the following SQL statement:

```
SELECT CDTitle, InStock FROM CompactDiscs
WHERE EXISTS
( SELECT LabelID FROM CDLabels
WHERE CompactDiscs.LabelID = CDLabels.LabelID AND LabelID > 830 ) ;
```

Notice that one of the predicates in the subquery WHERE clause uses a comparison operator to look for LabelID values greater than 830. If you were to look at the CDLabels table, you would see that six rows contain LabelID values greater than 830. If you were then to match these six values to the LabelID values in the CompactDiscs table, you would find 11 rows that would evaluate to true. These are the 11 rows returned by your SELECT statement.

4. In this statement, you'll use an ANY predicate to compare LabelID values in the CDLabels table to LabelID values in the CompactDiscs table that are included in rows with an InStock value greater than 20. The LabelID values in the CDLabels table can match any values in the subquery results. Enter and execute the following SQL statement:

```
SELECT LabelID, CompanyName FROM CDLabels
WHERE LabelID = ANY
( SELECT LabelID FROM CompactDiscs WHERE InStock > 20 ) ;
```

Your query should return only five rows.

5. Now try creating the same SELECT statement in Step 4, only use an ALL predicate rather than an ANY predicate. Enter and execute the following SQL statement:

```
SELECT LabelID, CompanyName FROM CDLabels
WHERE LabelID = ALL
( SELECT LabelID FROM CompactDiscs WHERE InStock > 20 ) ;
```

Project 9-2

Using Subqueries in Predicates

(continued)

You'll find that no rows are returned by this query. This is because the subquery returns eight rows with five different values. The LabelID value for each row in the CDLabels table cannot match all values, only one or some of them. The only way you would return any rows in this case would be if the subquery returned only one row or returned multiple rows all with the same value.

6. Now try modifying the SELECT statement by changing the comparison predicate in the subquery WHERE clause to greater than 40. Enter and execute the following SQL statement:

```
SELECT LabelID, CompanyName FROM CDLabels
WHERE LabelID = ALL
( SELECT LabelID FROM CompactDiscs WHERE InStock > 40 ) ;
```

Your query results will now return one row. This is because the subquery returns only one row, which meets the condition of the ALL predicate.

7. Close the client application.

Project Summary

In this project, you used the IN, EXISTS, ANY, and ALL predicates to query data from the Inventory database. You could have also used the SOME predicate in place of the ANY predicate. Combined with the steps in Project 9-1, your statements here should have allowed you to try a large variety of predicates. As you learn more about subqueries, you will be able to create even more elaborate predicates, ones that you can use not only in SELECT statements, but in UPDATE and DELETE statements as well. In the meantime, I suggest that you experiment with various types of SELECT statements and try different predicates within those statements to see exactly what types of query results you can receive.

Module 9 Mastery Check

1. In which SELECT statement clause do you include predicates?

2. Which comparison operator symbol should you use to express a not equal condition?

A. <=

B. >=

C. <>

D. =<

3. Which keywords can you use to combine predicates in a WHERE clause?

4. You want to query a table that includes the Price column. You want to ensure that all rows returned have a Price value of 13.99. What predicate should you use?

5. You create the following SQL statement:

```
SELECT CDTitle, RetailPrice FROM CDsOnHand
WHERE RetailPrice >= 14 AND RetailPrice <= 16 ;
```

What predicate can you use in place of the two predicates shown in this statement?

6. What keyword can you add to a BETWEEN predicate to find the inverse of the condition specified by the predicate?

7. You want to query a table to determine which values are null. What type of predicate should you use?

8. You're creating a SELECT statement that queries the ArtistsBio table. You want to return all columns in the table, but you want to return only those rows that do not contain null values in the PlaceOfBirth column. Which SELECT statement should you use?

9. You're querying the CDInventory table. You want to view all columns, but you want to view only rows that contain the word Christmas in the name of the CD. The names are stored in the CDTitle column. Which SELECT statement should you use?

10. What is the difference between a percentage sign and an underscore when used in a LIKE predicate?

11. What two types of data sources can you use in an IN predicate?

12. Which type of predicate is concerned only with determining whether or not a subquery returns any rows?

13. What column names must be specified in an EXISTS predicate?

14. You're creating a SELECT statement that includes a predicate in the WHERE clause. You want to use a comparison operator to compare the values in one of the columns to

the results of a subquery. You want the predicate to evaluate to true for any of the subquery results. Which type of predicate should you use?

A. EXISTS

B. ANY

C. ALL

D. IN

15. What is the difference between a SOME predicate and an ANY predicate?

16. How does the ALL predicate differ from the SOME predicate?

Module 10

Working with Functions and Value Expressions

233

In earlier parts of the book, you have been briefly introduced to various value-related functions and expressions. These values and expressions are used in examples and projects in a number of modules in order to help demonstrate different components of SQL. In this module, I take a closer look at many of these values and expressions, focusing on those that you are most likely to use as a beginning SQL programmer. You should keep in mind, however, that this module covers only a portion of the many types of functions and expressions supported by SQL. In addition, SQL implementations can vary greatly with regard to which SQL functions and expressions they support, how those values and expressions are implemented, and what nonstandard functions and expressions they include in their products in addition to the standard ones. Be sure to check the product documentation to determine what functionality is supported. In general, I include in this module those functions and expressions most commonly supported by SQL implementations.

CRITICAL SKILL
10.1 Use Set Functions

In Module 3, I introduce the concept of a function. As you might recall, a function is a named operation that performs predefined tasks that you can't normally perform by using SQL statements alone. It is a type of routine that takes input parameters and returns values based on those parameters. You have already seen examples of functions, such as SUM and AVG. Both of these functions are known as set functions. A *set function,* sometimes referred to as an *aggregate function,* processes or calculates data and returns the appropriate values. Set functions require that the data be grouped in some way, such as would be the case if the GROUPED BY clause were used in a SELECT statement. If a table is not explicitly grouped in some way, the table as a whole is treated as one group.

In this section, I discuss five set functions, COUNT, MAX, MIN, SUM, and AVG. These functions are all commonly supported in SQL implementations. For all the set functions, I provide examples of how you would use them in the SELECT clause of a SELECT statement. The examples are based on the ArtistCDs table, shown in Figure 10-1.

Using the COUNT Function

The first set function that we'll look at is the COUNT function. As the name implies, the COUNT function counts the number of rows in a table or values in a column, as specified in a SELECT statement. When you use the COUNT function, you must specify a column name or an asterisk, which counts all the rows in a table. For example, if you want to know the total number of rows in the ArtistCDs table, you can use the following SELECT statement:

```
SELECT COUNT(*) AS TotalRows
FROM ArtistCDs ;
```

In this statement, the COUNT function is used with an asterisk—in parentheses— to return every row in the ArtistCDs table. The returned value is listed under the

ArtistName: VARCHAR (60)	CDName: VARCHAR (60)	NumberSold: INT
Jennifer Warnes	Famous Blue Raincoat	23
Joni Mitchell	Blue	45
Joni Mitchell	Court and Spark	34
William Ackerman	Past Light	12
Bing Crosby	That Christmas Feeling	34
Patsy Cline	Patsy Cline: 12 Greatest Hits	54
John Barry	Out of Africa	23
Leonard Cohen	Leonard Cohen The Best of	20
Bonnie Raitt	Fundamental	29
B.B. King	Blues on the Bayou	18

Figure 10-1 Using set functions on the ArtistCDs table

TotalRows column, a name given to the column returned in the query results, as shown in the following results:

```
TotalRows
---------
10
```

As you can see, the query results include only one value (one row with one column). The value of 10 indicates that the ArtistCDs table contains 10 rows.

As with any other sort of SELECT statement, you can qualify your query results by adding the necessary clauses to the statement. For example, suppose you want to find out how many rows include a NumberSold value greater than 20. You can modify your SELECT statement to include a WHERE clause:

```
SELECT COUNT(*) AS TotalRows
FROM ArtistCDs WHERE NumberSold > 20 ;
```

The value returned will now be 7, rather than 10, because only seven rows meet the search condition specified in the WHERE clause.

You might find that, instead of querying the number of rows in a table, you want to know the number of values in a given column. In this case, you would specify the column name rather than the asterisk. For example, suppose you modify the SELECT statement shown in the last example to count values in the ArtistName column:

```
SELECT COUNT(ArtistName) AS TotalArtists
FROM ArtistCDs WHERE NumberSold > 20 ;
```

When you execute this query, the value returned is again 7. This means that seven ArtistName values have a NumberSold value greater than 20. However, this statement doesn't account for ArtistName values that might be duplicated. If you want to arrive at a count that takes into consideration duplicate values, you can add the DISTINCT keyword to the COUNT function:

```
SELECT COUNT(DISTINCT ArtistName) AS TotalArtists
FROM ArtistCDs WHERE NumberSold > 20 ;
```

This time, a value of 6 is returned rather than 7. This is because the ArtistName column includes two instances of the Joni Mitchell value. The column contains only six unique values that meet the condition set forth in the search criteria.

NOTE

Keep in mind that the SELECT statement is processed in a specific order: first the FROM clause, then the WHERE clause, and then the SELECT clause. As a result, the COUNT function applies only to the rows that meet the search condition defined in the WHERE clause. Rows that are not included in the results of the WHERE clause have no bearing on the COUNT function. For more information about the SELECT statement, see Module 7.

If the column specified in the COUNT function contains null values, those values are not included in the count. For example, if the ArtistCDs table includes a row with an ArtistName value of null and a NumberSold value greater than 20, the SELECT statement shown in the previous example will still return a value of 6 because the null value will not be counted. However, if you use an asterisk rather than a column name in the COUNT function, all rows are counted, even if some contain null values.

Using the MAX and MIN Functions

The MAX and MIN functions are so similar that it is worth discussing them together. The MAX function returns the highest value from the specified column, and the MIN function returns the lowest value. Both functions require that you specify a column name. For example, suppose you want to return the highest value from the NumberSold column in the ArtistCDs table. Your SELECT statement would look like the following:

```
SELECT MAX(NumberSold) AS MaxSold FROM ArtistCDs ;
```

When you execute this statement, your query results will include only one value (one row and one column), as shown in the following results:

```
MaxSold
-------
54
```

This result, by itself, is not particularly helpful. It would be nice if your query results also include the name of the artist and the CD. However, SQL does not support a SELECT statement such as the following:

```
SELECT ArtistName, CDName, MAX(NumberSold) FROM ArtistCDs ;
```

Because set functions treat data as groups, you cannot specify the artist name and CD name without somehow grouping the data together. As it stands now, the MAX function treats the entire table as one group; however, neither the ArtistName values nor the CDName values are grouped together in any way, so the SELECT clause becomes illogical.

One way around this is to use a subquery in the WHERE clause to return the maximum value and then return the necessary information based on that value, as shown in the following example:

```
SELECT ArtistName, CDName, NumberSold FROM ArtistCDs
WHERE NumberSold = ( SELECT MAX(NumberSold) FROM ArtistCDs ) ;
```

The subquery finds the maximum value (54) and uses that value as a condition in the WHERE clause. The NumberSold value must equal 54 as long as that is the highest NumberSold value in the table. Once you define the necessary search condition in the WHERE clause, you can then use these results to return the information you need. If you execute this statement, one row is returned:

```
ArtistName    CDName                          NumberSold
------------  ------------------------------  ----------
Patsy Cline:  Patsy Cline 12 Greatest Hits    54
```

As you can see, you now have all the information you need to determine which artist and CD have sold the greatest number.

As I said earlier, the MAX and MIN functions are very similar. If you replace MIN for MAX in the previous example, your query results will look like the following:

```
ArtistName        CDName        NumberSold
----------------  ----------    ----------
William Ackerman  Past Light    12
```

The Past Light row is returned because that is the row with the lowest NumberSold value.

The MAX and MIN functions are not limited to integers. You can also use them to compare character strings. For example, suppose you want to know which artist comes first alphabetically. The following statement will return B.B. King:

```
SELECT MIN(ArtistName) AS LowName FROM ArtistCDs ;
```

If you use the MAX function, the statement will return William Ackerman.

NOTE

It is quite likely that the tables in your database will separate first names from last names. I've included both names in one column to provide you with simple examples of how various statements work. If names were separated into two columns, the MIN or MAX function would need to be used with the appropriate column.

Now let's back up a little and return to the idea of grouping data. As I mentioned, a set function treats a table as one group if no grouping has been implemented. However, you can easily use a GROUP BY clause to group data. Suppose you want to know the maximum amount sold by each artist. You can group data based on the ArtistName values:

```
SELECT ArtistName, MAX(NumberSold) AS MaxSold
FROM ArtistCDs WHERE NumberSold > 30
GROUP BY ArtistName ;
```

The WHERE clause returns only those rows with a NumberSold value greater than 30. These rows are then grouped together according to the ArtistName values. Once they're grouped together, the maximum amount is returned for each artist, as shown in the following query results:

```
ArtistName      MaxSold
------------    -------
Bing Crosby     34
Joni Mitchell   45
Patsy Cline     54
```

The GROUP BY clause creates three groups, one for each artist that meets the search condition defined in the WHERE clause. Of these three groups, only one is made up of duplicate values: Joni Mitchell. Because there are two Joni Mitchell rows in the ArtistCDs table, there are two NumberSold values: 45 and 34. As you can see, the highest value is 45, which is the value that's included in the query results for the Joni Mitchell group. If the MIN function had been used in the SELECT statement, the 34 value would have been returned. As for the other two artist groups, because there is only one value for each of them, the same value is used regardless of whether the MAX or the MIN function is used.

Using the SUM Function

Unlike the MIN and MAX functions, which select the lowest and highest values from a column, the SUM function adds those values together. This is particularly handy when you want to find the totals for grouped data (although the SUM function, like any other set function, treats the table as one group if data hasn't been explicitly grouped together).

To better understand the SUM function, let's take the last example we looked at and modify it slightly:

```
SELECT ArtistName, SUM(NumberSold) AS TotalSold
FROM ArtistCDs WHERE NumberSold > 30
GROUP BY ArtistName ;
```

As you saw before, the WHERE clause returns only those rows with a NumberSold value greater than 30. These rows are then grouped together according to the ArtistName values. Once they're grouped together, the total amount for each artist group is returned in the query results:

```
ArtistName      TotalSold
-------------   ---------
Bing Crosby     34
Joni Mitchell   79
Patsy Cline     54
```

Notice that the query results include the same three groups that were returned in the previous example. The only difference is that the TotalSold value in the Joni Mitchell row is 79, as opposed to 45 or 34. The SUM function adds these two values together and returns a value of 79. Because the other two groups are each made up of only one entry, their TotalSold values are the same as their NumberSold values in the ArtistCDs table.

You do not have to use a GROUP BY clause in a SELECT statement that uses a SUM function. You can create a SELECT statement as simple as the following:

```
SELECT SUM(NumberSold) AS TotalSold FROM ArtistCDs ;
```

This statement merely adds together all the values in the NumberSold column and returns a value of 292. By itself, this is not always the most helpful information, which is why using the function along with a GROUP BY clause is far more effective.

Using the AVG Function

As you probably realize, the AVG function merely averages the values in a specified column. Like the SUM function, it is most effective when used along with a GROUP BY clause, although it can be used without the clause, as shown in the following example:

```
SELECT AVG(NumberSold) AS AvgSold FROM ArtistCDs ;
```

This statement returns a value of 29, which is based on the NumberSold values in the ArtistCDs table. This means that, for all the CDs listed in the table, an average of 29 for each one has been sold. Although you might find this information helpful, it might be more useful to you if you were to create a statement that groups data together:

```
SELECT ArtistName, AVG(NumberSold) AS AvgSold
FROM ArtistCDs WHERE NumberSold > 30
GROUP BY ArtistName ;
```

If you execute this statement, you will receive the following query results:

```
ArtistName      AvgSold
-------------   -------
Bing Crosby     34
Joni Mitchell   39
Patsy Cline     54
```

As in the previous examples, three groups are created, and for each group, an average is calculated based on the values in the NumberSold column. For the Joni Mitchell row, this average is based on the NumberSold values of 45 and 34. For the other two rows, the average is the same as the NumberSold value because there is only one row for each artist.

NOTE

The precision of the values returned by the AVG function depends on the column's data type, whether decimals are used, and how the SQL implementation averages numerics. For example, the exact average for the Joni Mitchell row is 39.5, but because the NumberSold column is configured with an INT data type, only whole numbers are used. For some implementations, the .5 is dropped and not rounded up, as shown in my latest sample query results.

Progress Check

1. Which set function should you use if you want to find the total number of rows in a table?

2. Which set functions can you use to find the highest and lowest values within a column of numerical values?

3. How does a set function treat a table if the data is not explicitly grouped?

1. COUNT(*)

2. MAX and MIN

3. The table is treated as one group.

CRITICAL SKILL
10.2 Use Value Functions

Value functions are a type of function that allow you to return a value that in some way calculates or derives information from the data stored within your tables or from the SQL implementation itself. Value functions are similar to set functions in the sense that they perform some sort of behind-the-scenes action to arrive at that value. However, value functions are different from set functions in that they do not require that data be grouped together.

SQL supports a number of value functions. Which functions are supported in which SQL implementations can vary widely. In addition, the meaning of a function name can sometimes vary from one implementation to the next. Still, there are some consistencies among the various implementations, and those are the value functions on which I focus.

The value functions that I discuss fall into two categories: string value functions and datetime value functions. In order to illustrate how these functions work, I use the SalesDates table, shown in Figure 10-2.

Working with String Value Functions

A string value function allows you to manipulate character string data to produce a precise value that is based on the original character string. When using a string value function, you must supply the character string as a parameter of the function. That parameter is then converted to a new value according to the purpose of that function and any other parameters that might be specified. In this section, I introduce you to three string value functions: SUBSTRING, UPPER, and LOWER.

CompactDisc: VARCHAR (60)	DateSold: TIMESTAMP
Famous Blue Raincoat	2002-12-22 10:58:05.120
Blue	2002-12-22 12:02:05.033
Court and Spark	2002-12-22 16:15:22.930
Past Light	2002-12-23 11:29:14.223
That Christmas Feeling	2002-12-23 13:32:45.547
Patsy Cline: 12 Greatest Hits	2002-12-23 15:51:15.730
Out of Africa	2002-12-23 17:01:32.270
Leonard Cohen The Best of	2002-12-24 10:46:35.123
Fundamental	2002-12-24 12:19:13.843
Blues on the Bayou	2002-12-24 14:15:09.673

Figure 10-2 Using value functions on the SalesDates table

Using the SUBSTRING String Value Function

The SUBSTRING string value function extracts a defined number of characters from an identified character string in order to create a new string. That original character string can be derived from a column or can be explicitly stated. In both cases, the character string is passed as a parameter of the SUBSTRING function, along with a start point and, optionally, a length specification. For example, suppose you want to return only the first 10 characters of the values in the CompactDisc column in the SalesDates table. You can create a SELECT statement similar to the following:

```
SELECT SUBSTRING(CompactDisc FROM 1 FOR 10) AS ShortName
FROM SalesDates ;
```

The SUBSTRING function includes three parameters. The first is the name of the column, CompactDisc, which identifies the source used for the character string. The next parameter, FROM 1, indicates that the function will start counting at the first character. The third parameter, 10, follows the FOR keyword. The FOR 10 parameter, which is optional, indicates that up to 10 characters will be included in the new character string.

If you execute this SELECT statement, you'll receive the following query results:

```
ShortName
----------
Famous Blu
Blue
Court and
Past Light
That Chris
Patsy Clin
Out of Afr
Leonard Co
Fundamenta
Blues on t
```

Notice that only the first 10 characters of each CompactDisc value are included in the results. For those values less than 10 characters, the full name appears.

NOTE

In SQL Server, you do not use the FROM and FOR keywords when specifying a SUBSTRING function. Instead, you simply separate the parameters by using a comma. In addition, all three parameters are required. Oracle does not support the SUBSTRING function, but does support a similar function called SUBSTR.

The FROM parameter can accept a negative number or a zero as a parameter. When using a negative number or a zero, keep in mind that 1 represents what you would think of as a normal starting position. The next character to the left of 1 is 0. The character to the left of 0 is –1, and so on. The FOR parameter counts characters starting at the starting point. If a zero or a negative number is used, the SUBSTRING function acts as though characters actually exist in those places. For example, suppose you modify the preceding SELECT statement as follows:

```
SELECT SUBSTRING(CompactDisc FROM -2 FOR 10) AS ShortName
FROM SalesDates ;
```

If you execute this statement, only the first seven characters of each name would be returned. If you use a zero instead, only the first nine characters will be returned. It is only when you use a FROM parameter of 1 that you return exactly the number of characters (from the character string) that are specified by the FOR parameter.

The SUBSTRING function is not limited to the SELECT clause. In fact, using it in a WHERE clause can be quite useful when defining a search condition. For example, the following SELECT statement uses the SUBSTRING function to return rows that start with Blue:

```
SELECT CompactDisc, DateSold FROM SalesDates
WHERE SUBSTRING(CompactDisc FROM 1 FOR 4) = 'Blue' ;
```

In this statement, the SUBSTRING function returns the first four characters of the CompactDisc values and compares them to the Blue value. Only two rows are included in the query results:

```
CompactDisc          DateSold
------------------   -----------------------
Blue                 2002-12-22 12:02:05.033
Blues on the Bayou   2002-12-24 14:15:09.673
```

Both rows in the query results have a CompactDisc value that starts with Blue. No other rows meet the search condition specified in the WHERE clause.

Using the UPPER and LOWER String Value Functions

The UPPER and LOWER string value functions are quite similar in that they are both used to convert characters from one case to another. The UPPER function allows you to convert a character string to all uppercase. The LOWER function allows you to convert a string to all lowercase. For example, suppose you want to modify the SELECT statement shown in the last example to return all CompactDisc values in uppercase. Your SELECT statement would now include an UPPER function:

```
SELECT UPPER(CompactDisc) AS Title, DateSold FROM SalesDates
WHERE SUBSTRING(CompactDisc FROM 1 FOR 4) = 'Blue' ;
```

Your query results are the same as in the last example, only this time the CD titles are all in uppercase, as shown in the following results:

```
Title              DateSold
-----------------  -----------------------
BLUE               2002-12-22 12:02:05.033
BLUES ON THE BAYOU 2002-12-24 14:15:09.673
```

If you had used the LOWER function, instead of the UPPER, the CD titles would all be in lowercase, with no initial capitalization at the beginning of the words.

Working with Datetime Value Functions

Datetime value functions provide information about the current date and time. Each function returns a value based on the time or date (or both) as they are configured in the operating system. SQL:1999 supports five datetime value functions, which are described in Table 10-1.

NOTE

SQL implementations vary widely with regard to how they implement datetime functionality; consequently, the implementation of datetime functions also varies. For example, SQL Server supports only the CURRENT_TIMESTAMP datetime value function. On the other hand, Oracle supports the CURRENT_DATE, CURRENT_TIMESTAMP, and LOCALTIMESTAMP datetime value functions, but not the CURRENT_TIME and LOCALTIME functions. In addition, the exact values generated by these functions can also vary from implementation to implementation. For example, the query results will not always include information about the current time zone, and some might represent time using a 24-hour clock rather than A.M. and P.M.

Because the CURRENT_TIMESTAMP datetime value function is supported by both SQL Server and Oracle, let's take a closer look at implementing that one. However, keep in mind that implementing any of the SQL datetime functions is the same process, depending on which functions are supported by the specific SQL implementation in which you're working.

Value Function	Description
CURRENT_DATE	Returns a value that represents the current date.
CURRENT_TIME	Returns a value that represents the current time. The value includes information about the current time zone, relative to Universal Coordinated Time (UCT), which used to be called Greenwich Mean Time (GMT).
CURRENT_TIMESTAMP	Returns a value that represents the current date and time. The value includes information about the current time zone, relative to UCT.
LOCALTIME	Returns a value that represents the current time.
LOCALTIMESTAMP	Returns a value that represents the current date and time.

Table 10-1 Datetime Value Functions Supported by SQL: 1999

By understanding how the CURRENT_TIMESTAMP function works, you'll gain a better understanding of how all functions work. However, be sure to check your implementation's documentation for more information on any of the functions that are supported by that product.

Depending on the SQL implementation, you can use the CURRENT_TIMESTAMP function in a SELECT statement to simply retrieve the current timestamp information. As you might expect with anything related to datetime functionality, the way in which you call a function can vary. However, in some cases you might be able to use a statement as basic as the following:

```
SELECT CURRENT_TIMESTAMP
```

This statement will retrieve the current time and date in some implementations. In other implementations, you might have to add a FROM clause to the statement in order to retrieve this information. Regardless of how you need to write your SELECT statement, in all likelihood using a CURRENT_TIMESTAMP function in this way is not very useful. You'll probably make better use of datetime functions by using them to compare data or to insert data automatically.

For example, suppose you wanted the SalesDates table (shown in Figure 10-2) to insert the current time and date automatically in your table each time you add another row. Your table definition might look something like the following:

```
CREATE TABLE SalesDates
( CompactDisc VARCHAR (60),
DateSold DATETIME DEFAULT CURRENT_TIMESTAMP ) ;
```

In this table definition, the DateSold column has been assigned a default value that is based on the CURRENT_TIMESTAMP function. Each time a row is added to the table, the datetime value is inserted into the DateSold column for that row. As a result, you can create INSERT statements that specify only the CompactDisc value. The current date and time are then automatically added to the DateSold column at the time that the row is added.

Progress Check

1. Which function do you use to extract a defined number of characters from an identified character string in order to create a new string?

2. How does the UPPER function differ from the LOWER function?

3. Which datetime function returns only the current date?

---

1. SUBSTRING

2. The UPPER function allows you to convert a character string to all uppercase. The LOWER function allows you to convert a string to all lowercase.

3. CURRENT_DATE

CRITICAL SKILL

10.3 Use Value Expressions

A value expression is a type of expression that returns a data value. The expression can include column names, values, mathematical operators, keywords, or other elements that together create a sort of formula, or expression, that returns a single value. For example, you can combine the values in two columns to create one value, or you can perform operations on the value in one column to create a new value.

In this section, we will look at numeric value expressions as well as the CASE and CAST value expressions. To demonstrate how several of these expressions work, we will use the CDTracking table, shown in Figure 10-3.

Working with Numeric Value Expressions

Numeric value expressions are expressions that use mathematic operators to perform calculations on numeric data values stored in your tables. You can use these operators to add, subtract, multiply, and divide these values. Table 10-2 shows the four operators that you can use to create numeric value expressions.

You can build numeric value expressions in much the same way as you build mathematical formulas. The basic principles are the same. For example, multiplication and division take precedence over addition and subtraction, and elements that should be calculated first are enclosed in parentheses; otherwise, each operation is calculated according to precedence and

CDName: VARCHAR (60)	CDCategory: CHAR (4)	InStock: INT	OnOrder: INT	Sold: INT
Famous Blue Raincoat	FROK	19	16	34
Blue	CPOP	28	22	56
Court and Spark	CPOP	12	11	48
Past Light	NEWA	6	7	22
That Christmas Feeling	XMAS	14	14	34
Patsy Cline: 12 Greatest Hits	CTRY	15	18	54
Out of Africa	STRK	8	5	26
Leonard Cohen The Best of	FROK	6	8	18
Fundamental	BLUS	10	6	21
Blues on the Bayou	BLUS	11	10	17

Figure 10-3 Using value expressions on the CDTracking table

Expression	Operator	Example
Addition	+	InStock + OnOrder
Subtraction	-	Sold - (InStock + OnOrder)
Multiplication	*	InStock * 2
Division	/	Sold / 2

Table 10-2 Using Numeric Value Expressions to Calculate Data

the order in which it is written. For example, the formula 2 + 2 * 5 / 4 equals 4.5; however, the formula (2 + 2) * 5 / 4 equals 5. In the first formula, 2 is multiplied by 5, then divided by 4, and then added to 2. In the second formula, 2 is added to 2, then multiplied by 5, and then divided by 4.

Now let's take a look at an example of a numeric value expression. Suppose you want to add the InStock column to the OnOrder column in the CDTracking table. You can create a SELECT statement similar to the following:

```
SELECT CDName, InStock, OnOrder, (InStock + OnOrder) AS Total
FROM CDTracking
```

As you can see, the SELECT clause first specifies three column names: CDName, InStock, and OnOrder. These are then followed by a numeric value expression: (InStock + OnOrder). Values from the InStock and OnOrder columns are added together and included in the query results under a column named Total, as shown in the following results:

```
CDName                          InStock  OnOrder  Total
-----------------------------   -------  -------  -----
Famous Blue Raincoat            19       16       35
Blue                            28       22       50
Court and Spark                 12       11       23
Past Light                      6        7        13
That Christmas Feeling          14       14       28
Patsy Cline: 12 Greatest Hits   15       18       33
Out of Africa                   8        5        13
Leonard Cohen The Best Of       6        8        14
Fundamental                     10       6        16
Blues on the Bayou              11       10       21
```

For each row, a value has been added to the Total column that adds together the values in the InStock column and the OnOrder column.

Numeric value expressions are not limited to the SELECT clause. For example, you can use one in a WHERE clause to specify a search condition. Suppose you want to return the same results as in the previous SELECT statement but only for those CDs with a Total value greater than 25. You can modify your statement as follows:

```
SELECT CDName, InStock, OnOrder, (InStock + OnOrder) AS Total
FROM CDTracking WHERE (InStock + OnOrder) > 25
```

Now your search results include only four rows, as shown in the following:

```
CDName                        InStock  OnOrder  Total
----------------------------  -------  -------  -----
Famous Blue Raincoat            19       16       35
Blue                            28       22       50
That Christmas Feeling          14       14       28
Patsy Cline: 12 Greatest Hits   15       18       33
```

Numeric value operators can also be combined with each other to create more complex expressions. In the next example, I include an additional expression that calculates three sets of values and combines them into one column in the query results:

```
SELECT CDName, InStock, OnOrder, (InStock + OnOrder) AS Total,
Sold, (Sold - (InStock + OnOrder)) AS Shortage
FROM CDTracking WHERE (InStock + OnOrder) > 25
```

This statement allows you to calculate how many CDs you have available (InStock + OnOrder) as compared to how many you sold. The difference is then added to the Shortage column in the query results. If you have sold more CDs than are available, a positive number is added to the Shortage column. If, on the other hand, there are enough CDs available, a negative number is added. The following query results show the amounts calculated when you execute the SELECT statement:

```
CDName                        InStock  OnOrder  Total  Sold  Shortage
----------------------------  -------  -------  -----  ----  --------
Famous Blue Raincoat            19       16       35    34     -1
Blue                            28       22       50    56      6
That Christmas Feeling          14       14       28    34      6
Patsy Cline: 12 Greatest Hits   15       18       33    54     21
```

The query results now include two calculated columns: Total and Shortage. All other values (InStock, OnOrder, and Sold) are taken directly from the table.

As you can see, numeric value expressions are quite flexible and can be used in many different ways. In addition to the methods we've looked at so far, you can also combine column values with specified values. For example, suppose you want to see how many CDs you would have available if you doubled the amount you had on order for those CDs where there are fewer than 15 available:

```
SELECT CDName, InStock, OnOrder, (InStock + OnOrder) AS Total,
(InStock + OnOrder * 2) AS DoubleOrder
FROM CDTracking WHERE (InStock + OnOrder) < 15
```

The second numeric value expression in this statement multiplies the OnOrder value by 2, adds it to the InStock value, and inserts the total into the DoubleOrder column of the query results, as shown in the following results:

```
CDName                     InStock  OnOrder  Total  DoubleOrder
-----------------------    -------  -------  -----  -----------
Past Light                 6        7        13     20
Out of Africa              8        5        13     18
Leonard Cohen The Best Of  6        8        14     22
```

The query results include only three rows that meet the condition of the WHERE clause. For each of these rows, the InStock and OnOrder columns are calculated to provide you with data that can be useful to you, depending on your needs. The nice part is that these values do not have to be stored in the database. Instead, they're calculated when you execute the SELECT statement, rather than having to maintain tables with additional data.

Using the CASE Value Expression

A CASE value expression allows you to set up a series of conditions that modify specified values returned by your SQL statement. You can change the way a value is represented or calculate a new value. Each value is modified according to the condition specified within the CASE expression. A CASE value expression includes the CASE keyword and a list of conditions. The last condition provides a default condition if none of the previous conditions have been met. The value expression is then closed by using the END keyword.

Let's take a look at an example to give you a better idea of how this works. Suppose you want to increase the number of CDs you have on order, but you want to increase the amount for only certain CDs. In addition, you want to base how many CDs you add to the order on the current amount. Before you actually update the table, you can look at what the new values would be by creating a SELECT statement that queries the CDTracking table, as shown in the following example:

```
SELECT CDName, OnOrder, NewOrders  =
CASE
  WHEN OnOrder < 6 THEN OnOrder + 4
  WHEN OnOrder BETWEEN 6 AND 8 THEN OnOrder + 2
  ELSE OnOrder
END
FROM CDTracking WHERE OnOrder < 11 ;
```

In this statement, three columns are specified: CDName, OnOrder, and NewOrders. The NewOrders column is the column created for the query results. It will contain the values updated by the CASE value expression. The expression itself is made up of the column name (NewOrders), the equals sign, the CASE keyword, two WHEN/THEN clauses, one ELSE clause, and the END keyword. Each WHEN/THEN clause represents one of the conditions. For example, the first clause specifies that if the OnOrder value is less than 6, then 4 should be added to the value. The second WHEN/THEN clause specifies that if the OnOrder value falls within the range of 6 though 8, then 2 should be added to the value.

After the WHEN/THEN clauses, the ELSE clause specifies the final condition. If the value does not meet the conditions defined in the WHEN/THEN clauses, then the ELSE clause specifies a default condition. In the case of the preceding SELECT statement, the ELSE clause merely refers to the OnOrder column, without specifying any modifications. (It would be the same as saying OnOrder + 0.) In other words, if none of the WHEN/THEN conditions are met, the OnOrder value stays the same. If you were to execute the SELECT statement, you would receive the following results:

```
CDName                        OnOrder  NewOrders
----------------------        -------  ---------
Past Light                    7        9
Out of Africa                 5        9
Leonard Cohen The Best Of     8        10
Fundamental                   6        8
Blues on the Bayou            10       10
```

As you can see, the Out of Africa row is increased by 4, the Blues on the Bayou row is not increased at all, and the other three rows are increased by 2.

In addition to modifying values, you can use a CASE value expression to rename values. This is particularly useful if your query results include values that are not easily recognizable. For example, suppose you want to create a query that returns data from the CDCategory column of the CDTracking table. You can rename the values in the column so that the information returned is more understandable to users, as shown in the following SELECT statement:

```
SELECT CDName, CDCategory =
CASE
   WHEN CDCategory = 'FROK' THEN 'Folk Rock'
   WHEN CDCategory = 'CPOP' THEN 'Classic Pop'
   WHEN CDCategory = 'NEWA' THEN 'New Age'
   WHEN CDCategory = 'XMAS' THEN 'Christmas'
   WHEN CDCategory = 'CTRY' THEN 'Country'
   WHEN CDCategory = 'STRK' THEN 'Soundtrack'
   WHEN CDCategory = 'BLUS' THEN 'Blues'
   ELSE NULL
END
FROM CDTracking ;
```

NOTE

You do not have to put the various components of the CASE value expression on separate lines, as I have done here. I do it this way in order to clearly show you each component. It also makes the code more readable to anyone reviewing it.

In this SELECT statement, the different values in the CDCategory column are renamed to more useful names. Notice that you do not need to repeat the column names to the right of the THEN keyword. The predicate construction is assumed by the context of the clause. When you execute this statement, you receive the following query results:

```
CDName                           CDCategory
-------------------------------  ----------
Famous Blue Raincoat             Folk Rock
Blue                             Classic Pop
Court and Spark                  Classic Pop
Past Light                       New Age
That Christmas Feeling           Christmas
Patsy Cline: 12 Greatest Hits    Country
Out of Africa                    Soundtrack
Leonard Cohen The Best Of        Folk Rock
Fundamental                      Blues
Blues on the Bayou               Blues
```

As you can see, only user-friendly names appear in the CDCategory column. If any of the original values had not met the condition defined in the WHEN/THEN clauses, a null value would be inserted in the query results.

Ask the Expert

Q: Can you use a CASE value expression anywhere other than a SELECT statement?

A: Another handy use for the CASE value expression is in the SET clause of an UPDATE statement. For example, suppose you want to update the values in the OnOrder column in the CDTracking table (shown in Figure 10-3). You can update those values by specifying specific conditions in a CASE expression:

```
UPDATE CDTracking
SET OnOrder =
CASE
   WHEN OnOrder < 6 THEN OnOrder + 4
   WHEN OnOrder BETWEEN 6 AND 8 THEN OnOrder + 2
   ELSE OnOrder
END
```

(continued)

This statement will add 4 to the OnOrder values that are less than 6, and it will add 2 to the OnOrder values that fall within the range of 6 through 8. Otherwise, no additional rows will be changed.

Q: **Can you reference more than one column in a CASE value expression?**

A: Yes, you can reference more than one column. Suppose you want to update OnOrder values, but base those updates on CDCategory values. You can create a statement similar to the following:

```
UPDATE CDTracking
SET OnOrder =
CASE
  WHEN CDCategory = 'CPOP' THEN OnOrder * 3
  WHEN CDCategory = 'BLUS' THEN OnOrder * 2
  ELSE OnOrder
END
```

In this statement, OnOrder values are multiplied by 3 when CDCategory values equal CPOP, and OnOrder values are multiplied by 2 when CDCategory values equal BLUS. Otherwise, no values are changed.

Using the CAST Value Expression

The CAST value expression serves a much different purpose than the CASE expression. The CAST expression allows you to change a value's data type when retrieving that value from your database. However, it does not change the data type of the source column. This is particularly useful when working with programming languages in which data types do not match up and you need to use a common denominator to work with the value.

To use the CAST value expression, you must specify the CAST keyword, and, in parentheses, provide the column name, the AS keyword, and the new data type, in that order. To illustrate this, let's return to the SalesDates table shown in Figure 10-2. The table includes the CompactDisc column and the DateSold column. The DateSold column is configured with the TIMESTAMP data type. Suppose you want to change the datetime values to character strings. You can use the CAST expression in your SELECT clause, as shown in the following statement:

```
SELECT CompactDisc, CAST(DateSold AS CHAR (25)) AS CharDate
FROM SalesDates WHERE CompactDisc LIKE ('%Blue%')
```

This statement converts the DateSold values from TIMESTAMP values to CHAR values. As you can see, all you need to do is specify the CASE keyword, followed by the parenthetical parameters that identify the source column and the new data type, along with the AS keyword. When you execute this statement, you receive query results similar to what you would see if you had not used CAST:

```
CompactDisc              CharDate
--------------------     --------------------
Famous Blue Raincoat     Dec 22 2002 10:58AM
Blue                     Dec 22 2002 12:02PM
Blues on the Bayou       Dec 24 2002  2:15PM
```

Notice that you can assign a name to the column that contains the new datetime results. In this case, the new column name is CharDate.

NOTE

You might find that, in your SQL implementation, when a datetime value is converted, the format changes slightly. For example, in SQL Server, a date value is expressed numerically and a time value is expressed in a 24-hour clock (military time), but when the value is converted to a CHAR data type, the time value is expressed in alphanumeric characters, and the time is expressed in a 12-hour clock (A.M. and P.M.).

Progress Check

1. What type of operators are used in numeric value expressions?

2. What is a CASE value expression?

3. What is the last word in a CASE value expression?

4. What does a CAST value expression do?

---

1. Mathematic operators

2. A CASE value expression is a type of expression that allows you to set up a series of conditions that modify specified values returned by your SQL statement.

3. END

4. A CAST value expression changes a value's data type when retrieving that value from the data base. It does not change the data type of the source column.

Working with Functions and Value Expressions

Use Special Values

In Module 6, I discuss special values that SQL supports that allow you to determine the current users. A special value exists for each type of user. These values act as placeholders for the actual user-related value. You can use them in expressions to return the value of the specific user. SQL supports five special values, which are described in Table 10-3. (See Module 6 for more information about the various types of SQL users.)

The special values can be used in different ways in an SQL database, such as for establishing connections or running a stored procedure. The special value, rather than the actual user name, is embedded in the code to allow the code to remain flexible from one situation to another. Another way in which a special value can be used is to store user data in a table. To illustrate this, let's take a look at the CDOrders table in Figure 10-4.

Each time a row is added to the table, a value for CURRENT_USER is inserted into the OrderedBy column. This makes it handy to track which user has placed the order. If you were to look at the table definition, you would see that a default value had been defined for the OrderedBy column, as shown in the following CREATE TABLE statement:

```
CREATE TABLE CDOrders
( CDTitle VARCHAR (60), Ordered INT,
OrderedBy CHAR (30) DEFAULT CURRENT_USER ) ;
```

If you were to insert data into this table, you would have to specify only a CDTitle value and an Ordered value. The OrderedBy value would be inserted automatically, and that value would be the current user identifier. If you do not specify a default value for the OrderedBy

Value	Description
CURRENT_USER	Identifies the current user identifier. If the SQL-session user identifier is the current user identifier, then CURRENT_USER, USER, and SESSION_USER all have the same value, which can occur if the initial identifier pair is the only active user identifier/role name pair (the pair at the top of the authentication stack).
USER	Identifies the current user identifier. USER means the same thing as CURRENT_USER.
SESSION_USER	Identifies the current SQL-session user identifier.
CURRENT_ROLE	Identifies the current role name.
SYSTEM_USER	Identifies the current operating system user who invoked an SQL module.

Table 10-3 Using SQL: 1999 Special Values

CDTitle: VARCHAR (60)	Ordered: INT	OrderedBy: CHAR (30)
Famous Blue Raincoat	16	Mngr
Blue	22	AsstMngr
Court and Spark	11	Mngr
Past Light	7	AsstMngr
That Christmas Feeling	14	Mngr
Patsy Cline: 12 Greatest Hits	18	AsstMngr
Out of Africa	5	AsstMngr
Leonard Cohen The Best of	8	Mngr
Fundamental	6	Mngr
Blues on the Bayou	10	Mngr

Figure 10-4 Using the CURRENT_USER special value in the CDOrders table

column, you can use the special value to insert the user. For example, the following INSERT statement inserts a row into the CDOrders table:

```
INSERT INTO CDOrders
VALUES ( 'Rhythm Country and Blues', 14, CURRENT_USER ) ;
```

When you execute the statement, a value representing the current user identifier (such as Mngr) is inserted into the OrderedBy column.

To determine the extent to which you can use the special values, you should review the product documentation for your SQL implementation. You'll find that the ways in which you can use these values will vary from one implementation to the next; however, once you're comfortable with using special values in your implementation, you'll find them a useful tool as you become more proficient with programming SQL.

Project 10-1 Using Functions and Value Expressions

Prj10.txt

In this module, you learned about many of the functions and value expressions supported by SQL. Now you will try out these functions and expressions by querying data from the Inventory database. Specifically, you will create SELECT statements that contain

(continued)

the COUNT, MIN, SUM, SUBSTRING, and UPPER functions and ones that contain numerical, CASE, and CAST value expressions. You can download the Prj10.txt file, which contains the SQL statements used in this project.

Step by Step

1. Open the client application for your RDBMS and connect to the Inventory database.

2. In the first statement, you will determine the number of unique ArtistName values in the Artists table. Enter and execute the following SQL statement:

```
SELECT COUNT(DISTINCT ArtistName) AS Artists FROM Artists ;
```

Your query should return 18 rows, one for each artist.

3. In the next statement, you will determine the minimum number of CDs in stock, as listed in the CompactDiscs table. You'll name the column in the query results MinStock. Enter and execute the following SQL statement:

```
SELECT MIN(InStock) AS MinStock FROM CompactDiscs ;
```

Your query results should include only one column and one row, and show a value of 5. That means that five is the least number of CDs you have in stock for any one CD.

4. Now you will determine the total number of CDs in stock. However, this time you will group these totals according to the LabelID values. Enter and execute the following SQL statement:

```
SELECT LabelID, SUM(InStock) AS Total
FROM CompactDiscs GROUP BY LabelID ;
```

Your query should return 10 rows, one for each LabelID value. The Total value for each row represents the total number of CDs for that particular LabelID group.

5. In the preceding steps, you used set functions when querying data from the Inventory database. You'll now try a couple of value functions. The first of these is SUBSTRING. In this SELECT statement, you'll extract data from the PlaceOfBirth column in the Artists table. You want to extract eight characters, starting with the first character in the string. Enter and execute the following SQL statement:

```
SELECT ArtistName, SUBSTRING(PlaceOfBirth FROM 1 FOR 8) AS Birthplace
FROM Artists ;
```

Your query results should return 18 rows and include two columns: ArtistName and Birthplace. The Birthplace column contains the extracted values, which are based on the table's PlaceOfBirth column.

6. The next value function you'll try is the UPPER function. In this SELECT statement, you'll convert the names of the CDs to all uppercase. Enter and execute the following SQL statement:

```
SELECT UPPER(CDTitle) AS CDName FROM CompactDiscs ;
```

This statement should return 15 rows with only one column that lists the name of the CDs in the CompactDiscs table. The CD titles should all be in uppercase.

7. Now you will move on to numeric value expressions. The next statement you try creates two columns in the query results that double and triple the values in the InStock column of the CompactDiscs table. However, the statement returns values only for those rows with an InStock value less than 25. Enter and execute the following SQL statement:

```
SELECT CDTitle, InStock,
(InStock * 2) AS Doubled, (InStock * 3) AS Tripled
FROM CompactDiscs WHERE InStock < 25 ;
```

Your SELECT statement should return nine rows that each include InStock values that have been multiplied by 2 and by 3.

8. The next value expression you'll try is the CASE expression. The statement will provide updated InStock values in the ToOrder column of the query results. For InStock values less than 10, the values will be doubled. For InStock values that fall within the range of 10 through 15, 3 will be added to the values. All other InStock values will remain the same. The statement operates only on those rows whose original InStock value is less than 20. Enter and execute the following SQL statement:

```
SELECT CDTitle, InStock, ToOrder =
CASE
  WHEN InStock < 10 THEN InStock * 2
  WHEN InStock BETWEEN 10 AND 15 THEN InStock + 3
  ELSE InStock
END
FROM CompactDiscs WHERE InStock < 20 ;
```

Your query results should include only seven rows, and the ToOrder column of the query results should contain the updated values.

9. Now you will try the CAST value expression. You will query the MusicTypes table but will convert the data type of the TypeName column in your query results. Enter and execute the following SQL statement:

```
SELECT TypeID, CAST(TypeName AS CHAR (20)) AS CharType
FROM MusicTypes ;
```

Your query should return 11 rows. The query results should include a CharType column that contains the converted values.

10. Close the client application.

(continued)

Project Summary

You should now be fairly comfortable with the various functions and value expressions that we reviewed in this module. Remember that each SQL implementation supports different functions and value expressions, usually many more than what you have seen here. In fact, in many cases, the functions and value expressions you saw in this module represent only the tip of the iceberg. Be sure to review your product documentation to find out what functions and value expressions are supported and how they're implemented. You'll find them useful tools in a variety of situations and well worth the effort you invest now.

✔ Module 10 Mastery Check

1. What is a set function?

2. You're creating a SELECT statement that queries the ArtistCDs table. The table includes the ArtistName and CDName columns. You want your statement to return the total number of rows in the table. Which COUNT function should you include in your SELECT clause?

    A. COUNT(*)

    B. COUNT(ArtistName)

    C. COUNT(CDName)

    D. COUNT(ArtistName, CDName)

3. Which set function should you use to add together the values in a column?

    A. MAX

    B. COUNT

    C. SUM

    D. AVG

4. Set functions require that the data be _____ in some way.

5. What are value functions?

6. You're using the SUBSTRING function to extract characters from the CompactDisc column of the SalesDates table. You want to start with the third character and extract eight characters. What parameters should you use in the SUBSTRING function?

7. You're using the LOWER function on the Past Light value of the CDName column. What value will be returned?

8. Which function returns a value that represents the current date and time as well as information related to UCT?

    A. LOCALTIMESTAMP

    B. CURRENT_DATE

    C. LOCALTIME

    D. CURRENT_TIMESTAMP

9. What are four types of operators that you use in a numeric value expression?

10. You are querying data from the CDTracking table. You want to add values in the InStock column to values in the OnOrder column. You then want to double the column totals. How do you set up the numeric value expression?

11. Which value expression do you use to set up a series of conditions that modify values?

12. You're creating a SELECT statement that includes a CASE value expression. You want one of the conditions to specify that any OnOrder values greater than 10 should be increased by 5. How should you set up the WHEN/THEN clause?

13. What is a CAST value expression?

14. You're querying the DateSold column in the SalesDates table. You want to convert the values to a CHAR (25) data type, and you want the data displayed in the CharDate column in the query results. How do you define the CAST value expression?

15. Which special value can you use to identify the current SQL session user identifier?

Module 11

Accessing Multiple Tables

A n important component of any relational database is the relationship that can exist between any two tables. This relationship allows you to tie data in one table to data in another table. These sorts of relationships are particularly useful when you want to query related data from more than one table and you want to retrieve that data in a meaningful way so that the relationships between the tables are, for all practical purposes, invisible. One method that SQL:1999 supports for querying data in this manner is to join the tables in one statement. SQL defines several types of join operations. The type that you can use in any given situation depends on your SQL implementation (with regard to statements supported and how performance might be impacted), on which data you want returned, and on how the tables have been defined. In this module, I discuss a number of join operations and provide details about how they're implemented and what results you can expect when you use them.

CRITICAL SKILL

11.1 Perform Basic Join Operations

One of the simplest types of joins to implement is the comma-separated join. In this type of operation, you're required only to supply a list of tables (separated by commas) in the FROM clause of the SELECT statement. You can, of course, qualify the join in the WHERE clause—which you would want to do if you want to extract meaningful data from the tables—but you're not required to do so. However, before I discuss the WHERE clause, let's first take a look at the comma-separated join at its most basic.

Suppose you want to display data from the CDInventory table and the Performers table, shown in Figure 11-1. (The figure also includes the PerfType table, which we'll be using in the "Creating Joins with More than Two Tables" section.) You can view the data in the CDInventory and Performers tables by querying each table separately, or you can join the tables in one statement.

To join the two tables, you can create a SELECT statement as simple as the following one:

```
SELECT * FROM CDInventory, Performers ;
```

The query results returned by this statement produce what is known as a *Cartesian product table*, which is a list of each row in one table joined together with each row in the other table, as shown (in part) in the following query results:

```
CDName                   PerfID  InStock  PerfID  PerfName          TypeID
-----------------------  ------  -------  ------  ---------------   ------
Famous Blue Raincoat     102     12       102     Jennifer Warnes   12
Blue                     101     24       102     Jennifer Warnes   12
Court and Spark          101     17       102     Jennifer Warnes   12
Past Light               105     9        102     Jennifer Warnes   12
Fundamental              104     22       102     Jennifer Warnes   12
Blues on the Bayou       103     19       102     Jennifer Warnes   12
```

```
Longing in Their Hearts  104   18     102   Jennifer Warnes  12
Luck of the Draw         104   25     102   Jennifer Warnes  12
Deuces Wild              103   17     102   Jennifer Warnes  12
Nick of Time             104   11     102   Jennifer Warnes  12
Both Sides Now           101   13     102   Jennifer Warnes  12
Famous Blue Raincoat     102   12     101   Joni Mitchell    10
Blue                     101   24     101   Joni Mitchell    10
Court and Spark          101   17     101   Joni Mitchell    10
Past Light               105   9      101   Joni Mitchell    10
```

In actuality, the preceding SELECT statement would return far more rows than are shown here. These results represent only a partial list. Because the CDInventory table contains 11 rows and the Performers table contains 9 rows, the entire query results would contain 99 rows. Let's take a closer look at this. The Famous Blue Raincoat row in the CDInventory table has been joined with each row in the Performers table, which totals 9 rows. Each of the remaining 10 rows in the CDInventory table is matched to each row in the Performers table in the same way. As a result, there are 99 rows ($11 \times 9 = 99$).

As you can see, these query results are not the most useful. However, you can generate more meaningful results if you use a WHERE clause to create an *equi-join,* which is a type of join that equates the values in one or more columns in the first table to the values in one or

CDInventory

CDName: VARCHAR (60)	PerfID: INT	InStock: INT
Famous Blue Raincoat	102	12
Blue	101	24
Court and Spark	101	17
Past Light	105	9
Fundamental	104	22
Blues on the Bayou	103	19
Longing in Their Hearts	104	18
Luck of the Draw	104	25
Deuces Wild	103	17
Nick of Time	104	11
Both Sides Now	101	13

Performers

PerfID: INT	PerfName: VARCHAR (60)	TypeID: INT
101	Joni Mitchell	10
102	Jennifer Warnes	12
103	B.B. King	11
104	Bonnie Raitt	10
105	William Ackerman	15
106	Bing Crosby	16
107	Patsy Cline	17
108	John Barry	18
109	Leonard Cohen	12

PerfType

TypeID: INT	TypeName: CHAR (20)
10	Popular
11	Blues
12	Folk
13	Rock
14	Classical
15	New Age
16	Classic Pop
17	Country
18	Soundtrack

Figure 11-1 Joining the CDInventory, Performers, and PerfType tables

more corresponding columns in the second table. For example, you can qualify the previous SELECT statement in the following way:

```
SELECT * FROM CDInventory, Performers
WHERE CDInventory.PerfID = Performers.PerfID ;
```

Now your query results will include only those rows in which the values in the PerfID column of the CDInventory table match the values in the PerfID column of the Performers table. Notice that you have to qualify the column names by adding the table names. You must do this whenever columns from different tables have the same name. If you execute this statement, you'll receive the following query results:

```
CDName                    PerfID  InStock  PerfID  PerfName           TypeID
----------------------    ------  -------  ------  ----------------   ------
Famous Blue Raincoat      102     12       102     Jennifer Warnes    12
Blue                      101     24       101     Joni Mitchell      10
Court and Spark           101     17       101     Joni Mitchell      10
Past Light                105     9        105     William Ackerman   15
Fundamental               104     22       104     Bonnie Raitt       10
Blues on the Bayou        103     19       103     B.B. King          11
Longing in Their Hearts   104     18       104     Bonnie Raitt       10
Luck of the Draw          104     25       104     Bonnie Raitt       10
Deuces Wild               103     17       103     B.B. King          11
Nick of Time              104     11       104     Bonnie Raitt       10
Both Sides Now            101     13       101     Joni Mitchell      10
```

The data returned by this query is now a lot more meaningful. Each CD is matched with the appropriate performer, and only 11 rows are displayed, rather than 99. However, even these query results include repetitive data (the PerfID column). In addition, you might find that not only do you want to eliminate duplicate columns, but you also want to display only certain columns and perhaps qualify your search condition even further.

Let's modify the SELECT statement we've been looking at even further by specifying column names in the SELECT clause and adding another predicate to the WHERE clause, as shown in the following example:

```
SELECT CDInventory.CDName, Performers.PerfName, CDInventory.InStock
FROM CDInventory, Performers
WHERE CDInventory.PerfID = Performers.PerfID
  AND CDInventory.InStock < 15 ;
```

In this statement, I have specified that three columns should be included in the query results. Notice that I've qualified the column names by including the table names. Notice also that the WHERE clause includes an additional predicate, separated from the first predicate by the AND keyword. Now any rows that are returned must also have InStock values less than 15. If you execute this statement, you'll receive the following query results:

CDName	PerfName	InStock
Famous Blue Raincoat	Jennifer Warnes	12
Both Sides Now	Joni Mitchell	13
Past Light	William Ackerman	9
Nick of Time	Bonnie Raitt	11

As you can see, we've refined the query down to just the most essential information. Of course, you can create all sorts of queries, depending on your needs, as long as you follow the basic guidelines for creating a comma-separated join:

● Your FROM clause should include all table names.

● Your WHERE clause should define an equi-join.

● Your column references should be qualified when column names are shared among tables.

Aside from these guidelines, you're free to create whatever sort of SELECT statement is necessary to extract the information you need from the participating tables. But keep in mind that there needs to be some sort of logical connection between the tables. This connection is often seen in the form of a foreign key, but that doesn't have to be the case. (For more information about foreign keys, see Module 4.) Whether or not a foreign key exists, you must be able to join columns logically through an equi-join condition.

Using Correlation Names

As I stated earlier, you must qualify your column references by adding table names to those columns that share a name. However, as a general policy, it's a good idea to always qualify column references when joining tables, whether or not it's necessary. This makes referencing the code at a later time much easier if the statement is fully self-documented. However, as your queries become more complex, it can become increasingly tedious to re-enter table names every time you reference a column. Because of this, SQL supports correlation names, or aliases, that can be used for the duration of a statement. A *correlation name* is simply a shortened version of the actual table name that is used to simplify code and make it more readable.

Take, for example, the last SELECT statement that we looked at. You can recast this statement by using correlation names for the two tables:

```
SELECT c.CDName, p.PerfName, c.InStock
FROM CDInventory AS c, Performers AS p
WHERE c.PerfID = p.PerfID
  AND c.InStock < 15 ;
```

The SELECT statement produces exactly the same results as the preceding statement, only now the tables are referenced by different names, except in the FROM clause. In fact, you use the FROM clause to define the aliases that are used in the rest of the statement. In this case, the CDInventory table is renamed c, and the Performers table is renamed p. As a result, c and p must be used everywhere else in the SELECT statement when referring to those tables. Once a correlation name has been defined, you cannot use the actual table name.

To better understand how the renaming process works, let's revisit the issue of how SELECT statements are processed. As you might recall from Module 7, the FROM clause is processed first and the SELECT clause is processed last. That is why the correlation names are defined in the FROM clause. Once they are defined, all other clauses can use those aliases when qualifying column references. The correlation names are used throughout the remainder of the statement. If you create a new SELECT statement, you must redefine those names.

As you can see in the previous SELECT statement, a correlation name is defined immediately after the actual table name. The new name follows the AS keyword. However, the AS keyword is not required. In most implementations, you can also use the following convention to rename the tables:

```
SELECT c.CDName, p.PerfName, c.InStock
FROM CDInventory c, Performers p
WHERE c.PerfID = p.PerfID
  AND c.InStock < 15 ;
```

Notice that only the new name is specified, without the AS keyword. This makes the SQL statement that much simpler. In fact, some implementations, such as Oracle, do not allow you to use the AS keyword at all, even though it is part of the SQL standard. Again, this last SELECT statement will provide the same query results that you saw in the two previous examples. Only the statement itself has been changed.

Creating Joins with More than Two Tables

Up to this point, the examples that we've looked at have joined only two tables. However, you can use a comma-separated join to display data from more than two tables. If you refer again to Figure 11-1, you'll see that the PerfType table is included in the illustration. You can, if you want, join all three tables in a single SELECT statement, as shown in the following example:

```
SELECT c.CDName, p.PerfName, t.TypeName
FROM CDInventory c, Performers p, PerfType t
WHERE c.PerfID = p.PerfID
  AND p.TypeID = t.TypeID
  AND TypeName = 'Popular' ;
```

In this statement, the FROM clause includes all three tables. In addition, the WHERE clause provides two equi-join conditions: one that maps the PerfID columns and one that maps the TypeID columns. If you execute this statement, you'll receive the following query results:

```
CDName                    PerfName        TypeName
----------------------    -------------   --------
Blue                      Joni Mitchell   Popular
Court and Spark           Joni Mitchell   Popular
Fundamental               Bonnie Raitt    Popular
Longing in Their Hearts   Bonnie Raitt    Popular
Luck of the Draw          Bonnie Raitt    Popular
Nick of Time              Bonnie Raitt    Popular
Both Sides Now            Joni Mitchell   Popular
```

Notice that information from all three tables is included in the results: the name of the CD, the name of the performer, and the category of performer. Even though a relationship might exist between the CDInventory table and the Performers table, as well as between the Performers table and the PerfType table, your query results provide a seamless display that hides these relationships and shows only the information that you need.

Creating the Cross Join

In addition to the comma-separated join, SQL supports another type of operation called the cross join. The cross join is nearly identical to the comma-separated join. The only difference is that, instead of separating column names with a comma, you use the CROSS JOIN keywords. For example, let's take a statement we used earlier and modify it by replacing the comma with the CROSS JOIN keywords:

```
SELECT c.CDName, p.PerfName, c.InStock
FROM CDInventory c CROSS JOIN Performers p
WHERE c.PerfID = p.PerfID
  AND c.InStock < 15 ;
```

This statement returns three columns from two tables, and the WHERE clause contains an equi-join condition. If you execute the statement, you'll receive the same results as if you were using a comma-separated join. Using one over the other may simply be a matter of determining which statement your SQL implementation supports and, if both are supported, which provides better performance. In all likelihood, it will come down to a matter of personal preference, with little advantage of one over the other.

Ask the Expert

Q: If you're joining tables, it seems likely that in some cases you will return duplicate rows in your query results, depending on how your SELECT statement is constructed. How can you avoid duplicate rows?

A: As with most queries, it is possible to return duplicate rows. For example, the following statement will return duplicate performer names and types:

```
SELECT p.PerfName, t.TypeName
FROM CDInventory c, Performers p, PerfType t
WHERE c.PerfID = p.PerfID
  AND p.TypeID = t.TypeID ;
```

For those performers who made more than one CD, the query results will contain a row for each of those CDs. However, as with any other SELECT statement, you can add the DISTINCT keyword to your SELECT clause, as shown in the following example:

```
SELECT DISTINCT p.PerfName, t.TypeName
FROM CDInventory c, Performers p, PerfType t
WHERE c.PerfID = p.PerfID
  AND p.TypeID = t.TypeID ;
```

This statement will return fewer rows than the previous statement (5 compared to 11), and no rows will be duplicated.

Creating the Self-Join

Another type of join that you can create is the self-join, which can be either a comma-separated join or a cross join. In a self-join, you create a join condition that merely references the same table. For example, suppose you add an Employees table to your database, as shown in Figure 11-2. The Employees table includes a list of employee IDs, employee names, and the employee IDs of their managers, who are also listed in the table. For example, the manager of Mr. Jones (EmpID 102) is Ms. Smith (EmpID 101).

To create a self-join on this table, you must create a join that treats the table as two separate tables with the same name, same columns, and same data:

```
SELECT a.EmpID, a.EmpName, b.EmpName AS Manager
FROM Employees a, Employees b
WHERE a.Mngr = b.EmpID ORDER BY a.EmpID ;
```

EmpID: INT	EmpName: VARCHAR (60)	Mngr: INT
101	Ms. Smith	NULL
102	Mr. Jones	101
103	Mr. Roberts	101
104	Ms. Hanson	103
105	Mr. Fields	102
106	Ms. Lee	102
107	Mr. Carver	103

Figure 11-2 Self-joining the Employees table

In this statement, each instance of the table is given a correlation name. As a result, you now have table a and table b. You pull the EmpID value and EmpName value from table a, but you pull the Manager value from table b. The equi-join condition is defined in the WHERE clause by equating the Mngr value in table a with the EmpID value in table b. This provides the link that treats one physical table as two logical tables. When you execute this statement, you receive the following query results:

```
EmpID   EmpName       Manager
-----   -----------   -----------
102     Mr. Jones     Ms. Smith
103     Mr. Roberts   Ms. Smith
104     Ms. Hanson    Mr. Roberts
105     Mr. Fields    Mr. Jones
106     Ms. Lee       Mr. Jones
107     Mr. Carver    Mr. Roberts
```

The results include the employee ID and name of each employee, along with the name of the employee's manager. As you can see, the self-join can be a handy tool to use in cases such as this where one table references itself.

Progress Check

1. What type of table does a comma-separated join return if an equi-join condition is not specified in the WHERE clause?

2. What constitutes an equi-join condition in a WHERE clause?

3. If two columns from two different tables share the same name, what must you do with that name in a SELECT statement?

4. What is a correlation name?

CRITICAL SKILL
11.2 Join Tables with Shared Column Names

SQL provides two methods for setting up joins that you can use when you're working with columns that have the same names. These two methods—the natural join and the named column join—allow you to easily specify a join condition between two tables when one or more columns within those tables are the same. In order to use either of these two methods, the tables must meet the following conditions:

- The joined columns must share the same name and have compatible data types.

- The names of the joined columns cannot be qualified with table names.

When you're using either the natural join or the named column join, each table must share at least one column in common. For example, the TitlesInStock and the TitleCosts tables, shown in Figure 11-3, have two columns that are the same: CDTitle and CDType. Notice that each set of matching columns is configured with the same data type.

You can use a natural join or a named column join to join these two tables. I describe each of these types of join operations in the next several sections, and I use the tables in Figure 11-3 to illustrate how each of these methods work.

---

1. Cartesian product table

2. The values in one or more columns in the first table are equated with the values in one or more corresponding columns in the second table.

3. You must qualify the name by adding the table name.

4. A correlation name is a shortened version of the actual table name that is used to simplify code and make it more readable.

TitlesInStock

CDTitle: VARCHAR (60)	CDType: CHAR (20)	Inventory: INT
Famous Blue Raincoat	Folk	12
Blue	Popular	24
Past Light	New Age	9
Blues on the Bayou	Blues	19
Luck of the Draw	Popular	25
Deuces Wild	Blues	17
Nick of Time	Popular	11
Both Sides Now	Popular	13

TitleCosts

CDTitle: VARCHAR (60)	CDType: CHAR (20)	Wholesale: NUMERIC (5,2)	Retail: NUMERIC (5,2)
Famous Blue Raincoat	Folk	8.00	16.99
Blue	Popular	7.50	15.99
Court and Spark	Popular	7.95	15.99
Past Light	New Age	6.00	14.99
Fundamental	Popular	8.25	16.99
Blues on the Bayou	Blues	7.25	15.99
Longing in their Hearts	Popular	7.50	15.99
Deuces Wild	Blues	7.45	14.99
Nick of Time	Popular	6.95	14.99

Figure 11-3 Joining the TitlesInStock and TitleCosts tables

NOTE

Not all SQL implementations support natural joins or named column joins. For example, SQL Server does not support either of these methods, although Oracle supports both.

Creating the Natural Join

The natural join automatically matches rows for those columns with the same name. You do not have to specify any sort of equi-join condition for natural joins. The SQL implementation determines which columns have the same names and then tries to form a match. The drawback to this is that you cannot specify which columns are matched up, although you can specify which columns are included in the query results.

In the following example, a natural join is used to join the TitlesInStock table to the TitleCosts table:

```
SELECT CDTitle, CDType, c.Retail
FROM TitlesInStock s NATURAL JOIN TitleCosts c
WHERE s.Inventory > 15 ;
```

In this statement, the tables are joined through the CDTitle and CDType columns. Notice that neither column names are qualified. If either of these column names had been included in the WHERE clause, they still would not be qualified. When you execute this statement, you receive the following query results:

```
CDTitle              CDType   Retail
-------------------- -------- ------
Blues on the Bayou   Blues    15.99
Deuces Wild          Blues    14.99
Blue                 Popular  15.99
```

As you can see, only three rows are returned. These are the rows in which the CDTitle values in both tables are equal *and* the CDType values are equal. In addition, the Inventory values are greater than 15.

Creating the Named Column Join

Although natural joins can be handy for simple join operations, you might find that you do not always want to include every matching column as part of the join condition. The way around this is to use a named column join, which allows you to specify which matching columns to include. For example, suppose you want to include only the CDTitle in the join condition. You can modify the previous example as follows:

```
SELECT CDTitle, s.CDType, c.Retail
FROM TitlesInStock s JOIN TitleCosts c
USING (CDTitle)
WHERE s.Inventory > 15 ;
```

In this statement, I've removed the NATURAL keyword and added a USING clause, which identifies the matching columns. Notice that the CDType column name has now been qualified, but the CDTitle column has not. Only the columns identified in the USING clause are not qualified. This statement returns the same results as the preceding example, although this does not necessarily have to be the case, depending on the data in the tables. If, however, you include both matching columns in the USING clause, you would definitely see the same results as you saw in the natural join. By identifying all matching columns in the USING clause, you are performing the same function as a natural join.

CRITICAL SKILL
11.3 Use the Condition Join

So far in this module, we've looked at comma-separated joins, cross joins, natural joins, and named column joins. In comma-separated and cross joins, the equi-join condition is defined in the WHERE clause. In natural joins, the equi-join condition is automatically assumed on all matching columns. And in named column joins, the equi-join condition is placed on any matching columns defined in the USING clause. The condition join takes an approach different from any of these. In a condition join, the equi-join condition is defined in the ON clause, which works in a way very similar to the WHERE clause. However, despite the use of the ON clause, a basic condition join is similar in many ways to the previous join operations we've looked at, except that, unlike the natural join and named column join, the condition join allows you to match any compatible columns from one table against those in another table. Column names do not have to be the same.

A condition join can be separated into two types of joins: inner joins and outer joins. The difference between the two is the amount of data returned by the query. An inner join returns only those rows that meet the equi-join condition defined in the SELECT statement. In other words, the inner join returns only matched rows. An outer join, on the other hand, returns matched rows and some or all of the unmatched rows, depending on the type of outer join.

NOTE

According to the SQL:1999 standard, natural joins and named column joins support both inner and outer joins. However, this can vary from SQL implementation to implementation, so be sure to check the product documentation. By default, a join is processed as an inner join unless specifically defined as an outer join.

Creating the Inner Join

Now that you have a general overview of the condition join, let's take a closer look at the inner join. The inner join is the most common of the condition joins and is specified by using the INNER JOIN keywords. However, the INNER keyword is not required. If JOIN is used alone, an inner join is assumed. In addition to the JOIN keyword (specified in the FROM clause), you must also define an ON clause, which immediately follows the FROM clause. Let's take a look at an example to see how this works.

Suppose you want to join the CDTitles table and the TitlesArtists table, shown in Figure 11-4. In the following example, an inner join has been created that is based on the TitleID columns in the two tables:

```
SELECT t.Title, ta.ArtistID
FROM CDTitles t INNER JOIN TitlesArtists ta
  ON t.TitleID = ta.TitleID
WHERE t.Title LIKE ('%Blue%') ;
```

The statement uses the INNER JOIN keywords to join the CDTitles and TitlesArtists tables. The equi-join condition is defined in the ON clause, using the TitleID column in each table. Notice that correlation names have been defined on both tables. The SELECT statement is further qualified by the WHERE clause, which returns only those rows that contain Blue in

CDTitles

TitleID: INT	Title: VARCHAR (60)
101	Famous Blue Raincoat
102	Blue
103	Court and Spark
104	Past Light
105	Kojiki
106	That Christmas Feeling
107	Patsy Cline: 12 Greatest Hits
108	Carreras Domingo Pavarotti in Concert
109	Out of Africa
110	Leonard Cohen The Best of
111	Fundamental
112	Blues on the Bayou
113	Orlando

TitlesArtists

TitleID: INT	ArtistID: INT
101	2001
102	2002
103	2002
104	2003
105	2004
106	2005
107	2006
108	2007
108	2008
108	2009
109	2010
110	2011
111	2012
112	2013
113	2014
113	2015

CDArtists

ArtistID: INT	Artist: VARCHAR (60)
2001	Jennifer Warnes
2002	Joni Mitchell
2003	William Ackerman
2004	Kitaro
2005	Bing Crosby
2006	Patsy Cline
2007	Jose Carreras
2008	Luciano Pavarotti
2009	Placido Domingo
2010	John Barry
2011	Leonard Cohen
2012	Bonnie Raitt
2013	B.B. King
2014	David Motion
2015	Sally Potter

Figure 11-4 Joining the CDTitles, TitlesArtists, and CDArtists tables

the Title column of the CDTitles table. When you execute this query, you receive the following query results:

```
Title                ArtistID
-------------------- --------
Famous Blue Raincoat 2001
Blue                 2002
Blues on the Bayou   2013
```

As you can see, the results include information from both tables: the Title column from the CDTitles table and the ArtistID column from the TitlesArtists table. Although this information can be useful, it might be better for some users if they can view the actual names of the artists, rather than numbers. The way to achieve this is to include a third table in the join.

Let's return to the previous example and add a second join condition to the CDArtists table (shown in Figure 11-4). In the following example, the second condition is added immediately after the original ON clause:

```
SELECT t.Title, a.Artist
FROM CDTitles t INNER JOIN TitlesArtists ta
  ON t.TitleID = ta.TitleID
INNER JOIN CDArtists a
  ON ta.ArtistID = a.ArtistID
WHERE t.Title LIKE ('%Blue%') ;
```

Notice that the INNER JOIN keywords are repeated, followed by the name of the third table, which is then followed by another ON clause. In this clause, the equi-join condition is defined on the ArtistID columns in the TitlesArtists and CDArtists tables. Keep in mind that you do not need to include the INNER keyword, nor do the columns specified in the ON clause need to have the same name.

If you execute this statement, you'll receive the following query results:

```
Title                 Artist
-------------------   ------
Famous Blue Raincoat  Jennifer Warnes
Blue                  Joni Mitchell
Blues on the Bayou    B.B. King
```

Notice that the artist names are now listed in the results. Also notice that the fact that three tables have been used to retrieve this information is invisible to whoever views the query results.

Creating the Outer Join

As I mentioned earlier in this section, an outer join returns all matched rows and some or all unmatched rows, depending on the type of outer join you create. SQL supports three types of outer joins:

- **Left** Returns all matched rows and all unmatched rows from the left table—the table to the left of the JOIN keyword.

- **Right** Returns all matched rows and all unmatched rows from the right table—the table to the right of the JOIN keyword.

- **Full** Returns all matched and unmatched rows from both tables.

An outer join follows the same syntax as an inner join, except that, rather than using the INNER JOIN keywords (or just the JOIN keyword), you use LEFT OUTER JOIN, RIGHT OUTER JOIN, or FULL OUTER JOIN. Note that the OUTER keyword is optional. For example, you can specify LEFT JOIN instead of LEFT OUTER JOIN.

The best way to illustrate the differences between the types of outer joins is to show you the query results for each type. To illustrate the differences, I use the CDInfo table and the CDType table, shown in Figure 11-5.

In the first example, I define an inner join on the two tables, just to show you what the query results would normally look like:

```
SELECT i.Title, t.TypeName, i.Stock
FROM CDInfo i JOIN CDType t
  ON i.TypeID = t.TypeID ;
```

This statement returns the following query results:

```
Title                TypeName     Stock
-------------------- -----------  -----
Famous Blue Raincoat Folk Rock    19
Blue                 Classic Pop  28
Past Light           New Age      6
Out of Africa        Soundtrack   8
Blues on the Bayou   Blues        11
```

CDInfo

Title: VARCHAR (60)	TypeID: CHAR (4)	Stock: INT
Famous Blue Raincoat	FROK	19
Blue	CPOP	28
Past Light	NEWA	6
Out of Africa	STRK	8
Fundamental	NPOP	10
Blues on the Bayou	BLUS	11

CDType

TypeID: CHAR (4)	TypeName: CHAR (20)
FROK	Folk Rock
CPOP	Classic Pop
NEWA	New Age
CTRY	Country
STRK	Soundtrack
BLUS	Blues
JAZZ	Jazz

Figure 11-5 Joining the CDInfo and CDType tables

In most cases, the inner join will provide all the information you need. But suppose you want to include the unmatched rows from the CDInfo table. In that case, you would create a left outer join, as shown in the following example:

```
SELECT i.Title, t.TypeName, i.Stock
FROM CDInfo i LEFT OUTER JOIN CDType t
  ON i.TypeID = t.TypeID ;
```

Notice that I've replaced JOIN (for INNER JOIN) with LEFT OUTER JOIN. As I mentioned earlier, you can omit the OUTER keyword. If you execute this statement, you'll receive the following query results:

```
Title                  TypeName     Stock
-------------------    ----------   -----
Famous Blue Raincoat   Folk Rock    19
Blue                   Classic Pop  28
Past Light             New Age      6
Out of Africa          Soundtrack   8
Fundamental            NULL         10
Blues on the Bayou     Blues        11
```

As you may have noticed, the Fundamental row is now included in the query results. Although this row doesn't include matched columns, it is still included in the query results because it is part of the *left* table. For this row, the TypeName column is assigned a null value because no logical value can be returned for this column. The null value serves as a placeholder.

You can also return the unmatched rows from the CDType table, which is the table to the right of the JOIN keyword:

```
SELECT i.Title, t.TypeName, i.Stock
FROM CDInfo i RIGHT OUTER JOIN CDType t
  ON i.TypeID = t.TypeID ;
```

This statement is nearly the same as the preceding statement, except that RIGHT has been specified. The statement returns the following query results:

```
Title                  TypeName     Stock
-------------------    ----------   -----
Famous Blue Raincoat   Folk Rock    19
Blue                   Classic Pop  28
Past Light             New Age      6
NULL                   Country      NULL
Out of Africa          Soundtrack   8
Blues on the Bayou     Blues        11
NULL                   Jazz         NULL
```

This time the unmatched columns from the *right* table are included in the results, and null values are shown for the Title and Stock column.

If you want to return all unmatched rows, then you would need to modify the statement to define a full outer join:

```
SELECT i.Title, t.TypeName, i.Stock
FROM CDInfo i FULL OUTER JOIN CDType t
  ON i.TypeID = t.TypeID ;
```

This statement will return the following query results:

```
Title                   TypeName      Stock
-------------------     -----------   -----
Famous Blue Raincoat    Folk Rock     19
Blue                    Classic Pop   28
Past Light              New Age       6
Out of Africa           Soundtrack    8
Fundamental             NULL          10
Blues on the Bayou      Blues         11
NULL                    Jazz          NULL
NULL                    Country       NULL
```

As you can see, all matched and unmatched rows are included in the query results. Notice that all six rows are included from the CDInfo table and all seven rows are included from the CDType table.

Progress Check

1. Which type of join operations can you use only when the joined columns share the same name?

2. In which clause of a named column join is the equi-join condition specified?

3. In which clause of a condition join is the equi-join condition specified?

4. Which type of condition join returns all matched and unmatched rows?

---

1. Natural joins and named column joins
2. USING clause
3. ON clause
4. Full outer join

CRITICAL SKILL
11.4 Perform Union Operations

SQL provides yet one more method to join data from different tables. The UNION operator is a method that you can use to join similar columns from different tables. In order to use the UNION operator, the source columns must be compatible and the same number of columns must be extracted from each table. In other words, you can join information, but the operation is very limited in scope.

Let's take a look at an example to show you what I mean. If you take a look at Figure 11-6, you can see that it shows two tables: the CDsContinued table and the CDsDiscontinued table. The tables are nearly identical in structure but serve two different purposes.

Suppose that you want to join together the data in these two tables so that you can view information from both tables. You can, of course, execute two separate SELECT statements, or you can combine those statements into one statement that joins the information, as shown in the following example:

```
SELECT * FROM CDsContinued
UNION
SELECT * FROM CDsDiscontinued ;
```

As you can see, the two SELECT statements are joined together with the UNION operator. If you execute this statement, you'll receive the following results:

```
CDName                        CDType  InStock
---------------------------   ------  -------
Blue                          CPOP    28
Blues on the Bayou            BLUS    11
Court and Spark               FROK    3
Famous Blue Raincoat          FROK    19
Fundamental                   NPOP    10
Kojiki                        NEWA    2
Leonard Cohen The Best Of     FROK    3
Orlando                       STRK    1
Out of Africa                 STRK    8
Past Light                    NEWA    6
Patsy Cline: 12 Greatest Hits CTRY    4
That Christmas Feeling        XMAS    2
```

CDsContinued

CDName: VARCHAR (60)	CDType: CHAR (4)	InStock: INT
Famous Blue Raincoat	FROK	19
Blue	CPOP	28
Past Light	NEWA	6
Out of Africa	STRK	8
Fundamental	NPOP	10
Blues on the Bayou	BLUS	11

CDsDiscontinued

CDName: VARCHAR (60)	CDType: CHAR (4)	InStock: INT
Court and Spark	FROK	3
Kojiki	NEWA	2
That Christmas Feeling	XMAS	2
Patsy Cline: 12 Greatest Hits	CTRY	4
Leonard Cohen The Best of	FROK	3
Orlando	STRK	1

Figure 11-6 Joining the CDsContinued and CDsDiscontinued tables

The results include 12 rows of data, six rows from each table. You can limit the results even further by specifying search conditions in WHERE clauses. You can also specify that your search return only specific columns, such as is the case in the following statement:

```
SELECT CDType FROM CDsContinued
UNION
SELECT CDType FROM CDsDiscontinued ;
```

Now when you generate your query, only values from the CDType column are displayed:

```
CDType
------
BLUS
CPOP
CTRY
FROK
NEWA
NPOP
STRK
XMAS
```

Notice that only 8 rows are returned, rather than 12. This is because duplicate rows are filtered out. If you want all rows included in the query results, regardless of whether there are duplicate values, you can add the ALL keyword after the UNION operator, as shown in the following example:

```
SELECT CDType FROM CDsContinued
UNION ALL
SELECT CDType FROM CDsDiscontinued ;
```

Ask the Expert

Q: Are there any types of joins that are comparable to using a UNION operator?

A: SQL:1999 actually supports a union join that performs many of the same functions as the UNION operator. The union join is similar to the full outer join, in terms of how query results are consolidated. However, the full outer join allows you to specify (in the ON clause) which columns will be matched. A union join does not. In addition, the union join has generally not been implemented in SQL relational database management systems (RDBMSs), and it has been *deprecated* in the SQL:1999 standard, which means that it is a candidate for deletion from future versions of SQL. So for all practical purposes, the union join is not something you need to be concerned with.

This statement will return 12 rows rather than 8, with several values duplicated.

As you can see, the UNION operator is useful only in very specific cases. If you want more control over your query results, you should use one of the several types of joins supported by SQL.

Project 11-1 Querying Multiple Tables

Prj11.txt

Project
11-1

In this module, you have been introduced to a variety of join operations as well as the UNION operator, which, technically, is not considered a join. Now you will have the opportunity to practice several of these join techniques by querying data from the Inventory database. Specifically, you will query some of the tables that are configured with foreign key relationships, which are the sort of relationships that tie data from one table to data in another table. Because you will not be changing any data, you should feel free to try out various types of join operations, beyond what we review in this project. You can download the Prj11.txt file, which contains the SQL statements used in this project.

Step by Step

1. Open the client application for your RDBMS and connect to the Inventory database.

2. The first type of operation you'll perform is a comma-separated join on the Artists and ArtistCDs tables. The join will use the ArtistID column to establish the equi-join condition. Enter and execute the following SQL statement:

```
SELECT * FROM Artists a, ArtistCDs c
WHERE a.ArtistID = c.ArtistID ;
```

(continued)

Your query results should include 19 rows and should include the ArtistID columns from both tables as well as the ArtistName, PlaceOfBirth, and CompactDiscID columns.

3. You will now modify the preceding statement so that it also joins the CompactDiscs table. That way, you can display the actual name of the CDs. In addition, you will specify the names of the columns that should be returned. Enter and execute the following SQL statement:

```
SELECT d.CDTitle, a.ArtistName, a.PlaceOfBirth
FROM Artists a, ArtistCDs c, CompactDiscs d
WHERE a.ArtistID = c.ArtistID AND d.CompactDiscID = c.CompactDiscID ;
```

Your query results should again include 19 rows. However, this time the results will display only the CDTitle, ArtistName, and PlaceOfBirth columns.

4. Now let's turn the last SELECT statement into a cross join. Enter and execute the following SQL statement:

```
SELECT d.CDTitle, a.ArtistName, a.PlaceOfBirth
FROM Artists a CROSS JOIN ArtistCDs c CROSS JOIN CompactDiscs d
WHERE a.ArtistID = c.ArtistID AND d.CompactDiscID = c.CompactDiscID ;
```

You should receive the same query results as you did in the preceding SELECT statement.

5. The next type of statement that you'll try is a condition join. As you probably recall, a condition join can be either an inner join or an outer join. The first type you'll try is the inner join. In this statement, you'll join together three tables: CompactDiscs, CompactDiscTypes, and MusicTypes. Enter and execute the following SQL statement:

```
SELECT d.CDTitle, t.TypeName
FROM CompactDiscs d JOIN CompactDiscTypes dt
  ON d.CompactDiscID = dt.CompactDiscID
JOIN MusicTypes t
  ON dt.MusicTypeID = t.TypeID ;
```

Your query results should include 24 rows. Only the CDTitle column and the TypeName column should be displayed.

6. Now let's modify the last SELECT statement to create a full outer join on both join conditions. Enter and execute the following SQL statement:

```
SELECT d.CDTitle, t.TypeName
FROM CompactDiscs d FULL JOIN CompactDiscTypes dt
  ON d.CompactDiscID = dt.CompactDiscID
FULL JOIN MusicTypes t
  ON dt.MusicTypeID = t.TypeID ;
```

Your query results should now include 26 rows rather than 24. This is because the MusicTypes table includes two rows that are unmatched: the Jazz row and the International row. In other words, no CDs match up to either of these two music types.

7. Close the client application.

Project Summary

In this project, you created comma-separated, cross, and condition joins. The condition joins included inner and outer joins. As you can see, join operations provide a great deal of flexibility when querying data from the tables in your database. However, they're not the only solution when accessing data from more than one table. A subquery will often provide the same functionality as a join. In Module 12, I discuss subqueries in great detail. As you will see, they provide yet one more way for you to access data from multiple tables.

✓
Module 11 Mastery Check

1. You are using a comma-separated join operation to join two tables. The first table contains five rows and the second table contains three rows. How many rows will the Cartesian product table contain?

2. Which clause contains the equi-join condition in a comma-separated join?

3. What basic guidelines should you follow when creating a comma-separated join?

4. You're creating a join on two tables. You assign correlation names to each of these tables. Which names should you use in the SELECT clause: the correlation names or the actual table names?

5. Which type of join is nearly identical to the comma-separated join?

   A. Condition join

   B. Natural join

   C. Cross join

   D. Named column join

6. How many tables are contained in a self-join?

7. What guidelines must you follow when creating natural joins or named column joins?

8. What is the difference between a natural join and a named column join?

9. Which type of join contains a USING clause to specify the equi-join condition?

10. What are the two types of condition joins?

11. What are the three types of outer joins?

12. Which type of condition join should you use if you want to return only matched rows?

    A. Inner join

    B. Left outer join

    C. Right outer join

    D. Full outer join

13. Which type of join contains an ON clause?

    A. Cross join

    B. Comma-separated join

    C. Natural join

    D. Condition join

14. A(n) _____ operator allows you to combine separate SELECT statements into one statement in order to join data in a query result.

15. What keyword can you use with a UNION operator to return all rows in the query results, regardless of whether there are duplicate values?

Module 12

Using Subqueries to Access and Modify Data

CRITICAL SKILLS

12.1 Create Subqueries That Return Multiple Rows

12.2 Create Subqueries That Return One Value

12.3 Work with Correlated Subqueries

12.4 Use Nested Subqueries

12.5 Use Subqueries to Modify Data

Subqueries, like joins, provide a way to access data in multiple tables with a single query. A subquery can be added to a SELECT, INSERT, UPDATE, or DELETE statement in order to allow that statement to use the query results returned by the subquery. The subquery is essentially an embedded SELECT statement that acts as a gateway to data in a second table. The data returned by the subquery is used by the primary statement to meet whatever conditions have been defined for that statement. In this module, I discuss how subqueries are used in various statements, particularly SELECT statements, and provide examples that demonstrate how to create subqueries and what type of query results to expect.

CRITICAL SKILL
12.1
Create Subqueries That Return Multiple Rows

In Module 9, I include several examples of subqueries that are used to demonstrate certain types of predicates, such as IN and EXISTS. This module, in many ways, is an extension of that discussion because of the way in which subqueries are most commonly implemented—in the WHERE clause of a SELECT statement. An understanding of these types of subqueries goes hand in hand with an understanding of how certain predicates are formulated to create specific search conditions, search conditions that rely on those subqueries to return data from a referenced table.

You can divide subqueries in a WHERE clause into two general categories: those that can return multiple rows and those that can return only one value. In this section, I discuss the first of these categories. In the next section, "Create Subqueries That Return One Value," I discuss the second category. As I expand on each subject, you'll no doubt recognize the statement formats from my discussion of predicates. Although this information might seem a bit repetitive (which is why I keep it brief), it is presented here not only to provide a cohesive overview of subqueries, but also to provide a different perspective. In other words, rather than looking at subqueries through the perspective of the predicate, we'll look at them through the subquery itself.

Despite the fact that my discussion focuses on subqueries that are implemented through the WHERE clause, the use of subqueries is not limited to that clause. Indeed, you can include subqueries in a SELECT clause or HAVING clause. However, using subqueries in a SELECT clause is not very common. In addition, you would use subqueries in a HAVING clause only when defining search conditions on grouped data. Even so, the principles for using subqueries in a HAVING clause are similar to using them in a WHERE clause. For these reasons, my discussion here focuses on using subqueries in the WHERE clause. As you become a more advanced SQL programmer, you might find that you want to try using subqueries in other places within a SELECT statement.

Using the IN Predicate

The first type of subquery that we'll look at is the type used within the IN predicate. As you might recall from Module 9, the IN predicate compares values from a column in the primary table to values returned by the subquery. If the column value is in the subquery results, that row (from the primary table) is returned in the query results of the SELECT statement. For example, suppose you want to query data from the CDStock table, shown in Figure 12-1.

Your query results should include only those rows whose CDTitle values match the values returned by the subquery. The subquery results should include only those rows that contain an ArtistName value of Joni Mitchell (from the CDArtists table). The following SELECT statement will return this data:

```
SELECT * FROM CDStock
WHERE CDTitle IN
( SELECT Title FROM CDArtists WHERE ArtistName = 'Joni Mitchell' ) ;
```

CDStock

CDTitle: VARCHAR (60)	Stock: INT
Famous Blue Raincoat	13
Blue	42
Court and Spark	22
Past Light	17
Kojiki	6
That Christmas Feeling	8
Out of Africa	29
Blues on the Bayou	27
Orlando	5

CDArtists

Title: VARCHAR (60)	ArtistName: VARCHAR (60)
Famous Blue Raincoat	Jennifer Warnes
Blue	Joni Mitchell
Court and Spark	Joni Mitchell
Past Light	William Ackerman
Kojiki	Kitaro
That Christmas Feeling	Bing Crosby
Patsy Cline: 12 Greatest Hits	Patsy Cline
After the Rain: The Soft Sounds of Erik Satie	Pascal Roge
Out of Africa	John Barry
Leonard Cohen The Best of	Leonard Cohen
Fundamental	Bonnie Raitt
Blues on the Bayou	B.B. King
Orlando	David Motion

Figure 12-1 Querying the CDStock and CDArtists tables

Let's take a closer look at the subquery in this statement. As you can see, it is included in the IN predicate, after the IN keyword. The subquery is basically a SELECT statement that includes a search condition defined in the WHERE clause:

```
SELECT Title FROM CDArtists WHERE ArtistName = 'Joni Mitchell'
```

If you were to execute only the subquery, you would receive the following query results:

```
Title
---------------
Blue
Court and Spark
```

These results are then used by the IN predicate to compare them to the CDTitle values in the CDStock table. When you execute the entire SELECT statement, you receive the following results:

```
CDTitle          Stock
---------------  -----
Blue             42
Court and Spark  22
```

Notice that only two rows are returned from the CDStock table. These rows represent the two CDs performed by Joni Mitchell. Even though the CDStock table does not include artist information, you can still tie data from the two tables together because they include similar columns, allowing you to use the data returned by a subquery.

NOTE

In the case of the example table shown in Figure 12-1, it is conceivable that a foreign key would be configured on the CDTitle column of the CDStock table to reference the Title column of the CDArtists table. However, a foreign key relationship is not required. The primary requirement that a subquery must meet is that it return results that are logically comparable to the referencing column values. Otherwise, the subquery serves no purpose, and no rows will be returned by the primary SELECT statement because the condition of the IN predicate cannot be met.

Using the EXISTS Predicate

In some circumstances, you might want your subquery to return only a value of true or false. The content of the data itself is unimportant, in terms of meeting a predicate condition. In this case, you can use an EXISTS predicate to define your subquery. The EXISTS predicate evaluates to true if one or more rows are returned by the subquery; otherwise, it evaluates to false.

For an EXISTS predicate to be useful, it should include in the subquery a search condition that matches values in the two tables that are being linked through the subquery. This search condition is similar to the equi-join condition used in certain join operations. (See Module 11 for information about joins and equi-join conditions.) For example, returning to the CDStock table and the CDArtists tables (shown in Figure 12-1), we can create a SELECT statement that uses an EXISTS predicate to query the CDArtists table:

```
SELECT * FROM CDStock s
WHERE EXISTS
( SELECT Title FROM CDArtists a
WHERE a.ArtistName = 'Joni Mitchell' AND s.CDTitle = a.Title ) ;
```

In this statement, each row returned by the primary SELECT statement is evaluated against the subquery. If the condition specified in the EXISTS predicate is true, the row is included in the query results; otherwise, the row is omitted. When the specified condition is true, that means at least one row has been returned by the subquery. In this case, the row returned will include an ArtistName value of Joni Mitchell. In addition, the CDTitle value in the CDStock table will be the same as the Title value in the CDArtists table. As a result, only two rows will be returned by the entire SELECT statement:

```
CDTitle          Stock
---------------  -----
Blue             42
Court and Spark  22
```

As was the case with the IN predicate, the EXISTS predicate allows you to use a subquery to access information in another table. Even though the CDStock table doesn't include information about the performing artists, the subquery allows you to return data that is based on artist information.

NOTE

The manner in which an EXISTS predicate is processed can sometimes be a little unclear. Be sure to refer to Module 9 for a more complete discussion of that predicate.

Using Quantified Comparison Predicates

The IN and EXISTS predicates are not the only predicates that rely on the type of subqueries that can return one or more rows for the search condition to evaluate to true. Quantified comparison predicates—SOME, ANY, and ALL—also use subqueries that can return multiple rows. These predicates are used in conjunction with comparison operators to determine whether any or all returned values (from the subquery) meet the search condition set by the predicate. The SOME and ANY predicates, which perform the same function, check to see whether *any* returned values meet the search requirement. The ALL predicate checks to see whether *all* returned values meet the search requirement.

When a quantified comparison predicate is used, the values in a column from the primary table are compared to the values returned by the subquery. Let's take a look at an example to clarify how this works. Suppose your database includes the RetailPrices table and the SalesPrices table, shown in Figure 12-2.

Now suppose that you decide to query the RetailPrices table, but you want to return only those rows with an RPrice value greater than *all* values in the SPrice column in the SalesPrices table, for those SPrice values less than 15.99. To set up this query, you can create a statement similar to the following:

```
SELECT CDName, RPrice FROM RetailPrices
WHERE RPrice > ALL
( SELECT SPrice FROM SalesPrices WHERE SPrice < 15.99 ) ;
```

Notice that the subquery returns only one column of data—the SPrice values that are less than 15.99. The values in the RPrice column are then compared to the subquery results. If a specific RPrice value is greater than *all* the subquery results, that row is returned. When you execute the entire SELECT statement, you receive the following results:

```
CDName                             RPrice
-----------------------------      ------
Famous Blue Raincoat               16.99
Past Light                         15.99
Kojiki                             15.99
Patsy Cline: 12 Greatest Hits      16.99
```

As you can see, only four rows are returned. For each row, the RPrice value is greater than the highest price returned by the subquery, which in this case would be 14.99.

RetailPrices

CDName: VARCHAR (60)	RPrice: NUMERIC (5,2)	Amount: INT
Famous Blue Raincoat	16.99	5
Blue	14.99	10
Court and Spark	14.99	12
Past Light	15.99	11
Kojiki	15.99	4
That Christmas Feeling	10.99	8
Patsy Cline: 12 Greatest Hits	16.99	14

SalesPrices

CDTitle: VARCHAR (60)	SPrice: NUMERIC (5,2)
Famous Blue Raincoat	14.99
Blue	12.99
Court and Spark	14.99
Past Light	14.99
Kojiki	13.99
That Christmas Feeling	10.99
Patsy Cline: 12 Greatest Hits	16.99

Figure 12-2 Querying the RetailPrices and SalesPrices tables

Ask the Expert

Q: You state that a SELECT clause can include a subquery. How would you include the subquery in that clause?

A: You can include the subquery in a SELECT clause just as you would a column name. The values returned from the subquery are inserted in the query results in the same way column values would be inserted. For example, you can insert a subquery in a SELECT clause of a statement that is used to query the CDStock table (shown in Figure 12-1). The subquery pulls data from the CDArtists table, as shown in the following example:

```
SELECT CDTitle,
( SELECT ArtistName FROM CDArtists a
  WHERE s.CDTitle = a.Title ) AS Artist ,
Stock FROM CDStock s ;
```

In the main part of this statement, values are pulled from the CDTitle and Stock columns. In addition to these values, a list of artists is returned by the subquery. The artists' names are matched up to their CDs by using a comparison predicate to compare values in the CDTitle and Title columns.

When using a subquery in a SELECT clause, you must be careful not to create a subquery that returns only one value when multiple values are needed. When you return only one value, that value might be inserted into all rows returned by the main SELECT statement, depending on how you've constructed your query.

CRITICAL SKILL
12.2 Create Subqueries That Return One Value

So far, we have looked at subqueries that can return one or more rows of data. This is fine in many circumstances; however, there might be times when you want your subquery to return only one value so that you can compare the values in one column with a single subquery value. In these cases, you can use comparison operators.

As you learned in Module 9, the comparison operators include equals (=), not equals (<>), less than (<), greater than (>), less than or equals (<=), and greater than or equals (>=). For example, let's take another look at the RetailPrices and SalesPrices tables (shown in Figure 12-2). Suppose you want to retrieve data from the RetailPrices table. You want the RPrice values to equal the maximum price listed in the SPrice column of the SalesPrices table. The following query allows you to return the necessary data:

```
SELECT CDName, RPrice FROM RetailPrices
WHERE RPrice =
( SELECT MAX(SPrice) FROM SalesPrices ) ;
```

Notice that the subquery returns only one value, which in this case is 16.99. As a result, only rows with an RPrice value of 16.99 are returned by the SELECT statement, as shown in the following query results:

```
CDName                          RPrice
----------------------------    ------
Famous Blue Raincoat            16.99
Patsy Cline: 12 Greatest Hits   16.99
```

You do not have to use an aggregate function (such as MAX) to return a single value in a subquery. For example, the subquery WHERE clause might include a condition that will return only one value. The important point to remember is that you must be sure that your subquery returns only one value; otherwise, you will receive an error when using a comparison operator. However, if you've set up your subquery properly, you can use any of the comparison operators to compare column values. In addition, you're not limited to numbers. Character strings can also be compared in comparison predicates.

NOTE

In many cases, you can use predicates such as IN with subqueries that return only one value. However, these predicates can support only the conditions equal or not equal, not the conditions lesser than or greater than, which you can use with comparison operators.

Progress Check

1. Which types of predicates can you use with subqueries that return multiple rows?

2. Which types of predicates are you prevented from using with subqueries that return multiple rows?

3. What should be included in a subquery's search condition when using an EXISTS predicate?

4. What are the three quantified comparison predicates?

---

1. IN, EXISTS, ANY, SOME, and ALL
2. Comparison predicates
3. The subquery of an EXISTS predicate should include a search condition that matches values in the two tables that are being linked through the subquery.
4. SOME, ANY, and ALL

CRITICAL SKILL
12.3 Work with Correlated Subqueries

In the "Using the EXISTS Predicate" section earlier in this module, I mention that, for the
EXISTS predicate to be useful, it should include in the subquery a search condition that
matches values in the two tables that are being linked through the subquery. To illustrate this
point, I include in that section an example SELECT statement that contains such a subquery.
I'll repeat that statement here for your convenience:

```
SELECT * FROM CDStock s
WHERE EXISTS
( SELECT Title FROM CDArtists a
WHERE a.ArtistName = 'Joni Mitchell' AND s.CDTitle = a.Title ) ;
```

This statement references the CDStock and CDArtists tables in Figure 12-1. Notice that
the subquery includes a predicate that matches CDTitle values in the CDStock table to Title
values in the CDArtists table. This matching of values is similar to the equi-join conditions
you define when joining tables.

The reason I've returned to this statement is that it includes a type of subquery I have not
discussed before—the correlated subquery. A *correlated subquery* is one that is dependent on
the outer statement in some way. In this case, the outer statement is the main SELECT statement
that includes a SELECT clause, a FROM clause, and a WHERE clause, which itself contains
a subquery. Because that subquery references the CDStock table, which is a component of the
outer statement, the subquery is dependent on that statement in order to return data.

In most of the subquery examples we've looked at in this module, the subqueries have
stood independent of the outer statement. For example, in the following SELECT statement
(which was used as an example in the "Using the IN Predicate" section earlier in this module),
the subquery is not dependent on the outer statement:

```
SELECT * FROM CDStock
WHERE CDTitle IN
( SELECT Title FROM CDArtists WHERE ArtistName = 'Joni Mitchell' ) ;
```

In this case, the subquery merely returns results, which are then used in an outer statement. The
subquery is evaluated just once, and the results are used by the main statement as necessary. However,
with a correlated subquery, the subquery must often be re-evaluated for each row returned by the
outer statement. The correlated subquery cannot be evaluated just once because at least one of the
values changes for each row. For example, looking again at the SELECT statement that contains
the correlated subquery (as part of the EXISTS predicate), you can see that the CDTitle value
changes for each row returned by the outer SELECT statement. This can have a severe impact on
performance, particularly when you are returning a large number of values. In these cases, you
might find that creating a join provides better performance than a correlated subquery.

Ask the Expert

Q: You state that creating a join might be a better alternative to creating a correlated subquery. How would you restate the preceding SELECT statement as a join?

A: In the preceding SELECT statement, you've already identified your equi-join condition in the subquery, and you already know the names of the two tables that are being joined. One way you can modify this statement is to use a comma-separated join, as shown in the following example:

```
SELECT CDTitle, Stock
FROM CDStock s, CDArtists a
WHERE a.ArtistName = 'Joni Mitchell' AND s.CDTitle = a.Title ;
```

Notice that the CDTitle and Title columns are still equated with each other. This statement produces the same results as the statement that included the correlated subquery, only the SQL implementation is not being forced to reprocess a subquery for each row returned by the outer statement. Instead, the WHERE clause merely takes the results returned by the FROM clause and applies the search conditions defined in the two predicates. For more information about join operations, see Module 11.

CRITICAL SKILL
12.4 Use Nested Subqueries

Up to this point, we have looked at SELECT statements that included only one subquery. However, a SELECT statement can contain multiple subqueries. The SQL:1999 standard does not limit the number of subqueries that can be included in a statement, although practical application, performance, and the limitations of the SQL implementation all play an important role in determining what a reasonable number might be. Make certain that you refer to the documentation for your SQL implementation to determine what restrictions might apply to the use of subqueries.

One way you can include multiple subqueries in a SELECT statement is to include them as different components of the statement. For example, your WHERE clause might include two predicates, each of which contains a subquery. Another way in which multiple subqueries can be included in a SELECT statement is to nest one subquery into the other. These are the types of subqueries we'll look at in this section.

A *nested subquery* is one that is a component of another subquery. The "outer" subquery acts as a primary SELECT statement that includes a subquery within one of its clauses. In most cases, the nested subquery will be part of a predicate in the WHERE clause of the outer subquery. Let's take a look at an example to help clarify this concept. The example uses the DiscInventory, DiscArtists, and DiscTypes tables, shown in Figure 12-3.

DiscInventory

DiscName: VARCHAR (60)	ArtistID: INT	StockAmount: INT
Famous Blue Raincoat	102	12
Blue	101	24
Court and Spark	101	17
Past Light	105	9
Fundamental	104	22
Blues on the Bayou	103	19
Longing in Their Hearts	104	18
Luck of the Draw	104	25
Deuces Wild	103	17
Nick of Time	104	11
Both Sides Now	101	13

DiscArtists

ArtistID: INT	ArtistName: VARCHAR (60)	DiscTypeID: INT
101	Joni Mitchell	10
102	Jennifer Warnes	12
103	B.B. King	11
104	Bonnie Raitt	10
105	William Ackerman	15
106	Bing Crosby	16
107	Patsy Cline	17
108	John Barry	18
109	Leonard Cohen	12

DiscTypes

DiscTypeID: INT	DiscTypeName: CHAR (20)
10	Popular
11	Blues
12	Folk
13	Rock
14	Classical
15	New Age
16	Classic Pop
17	Country
18	Soundtrack

Figure 12-3 Querying the DiscInventory, DiscArtists, and DiscTypes tables

Suppose that you want to display the names of CDs and the amount in stock for CDs that are performed by blues artists. The DiscInventory table contains the names of the CDs and the amount in stock of each one, the DiscArtists table contains the names of the artists, and the DiscTypes table contains the names of the artist types. The DiscInventory and DiscArtists tables are related through the ArtistID column in each table. The DiscArtists and DiscTypes tables are related through the DiscTypeID column in each table. In order to return the information you need, you must query all three tables, as shown in the following SELECT statement:

```
SELECT DiscName, StockAmount FROM DiscInventory
WHERE ArtistID IN
( SELECT ArtistID FROM DiscArtists WHERE DiscTypeID IN
  ( SELECT DiscTypeID FROM DiscTypes WHERE DiscTypeName = 'Blues' ) ) ;
```

In this statement, the primary SELECT statement queries the DiscInventory table. The statement includes a subquery in an IN predicate in the WHERE clause. The subquery is a SELECT statement that queries the DiscArtists table. The subquery, like the primary SELECT statement, includes an IN predicate in the WHERE clause. This predicate also includes a subquery. As is the case with the outer subquery, the inner subquery includes a SELECT statement. However, in this case, the statement is querying the DiscTypes table.

To better understand how the entire SELECT statement works, let's first look at the inner subquery. If you were to execute this statement alone, it would return a value of 11, which is the DiscTypeID value for the DiscTypeName value of Blues. The outer subquery uses this value in the IN predicate to return those rows with a DiscTypeID value of 11. In this case, the only row returned is the B.B. King row, which has an ArtistID value of 103. The ArtistID value is then used in the IN predicate of the primary SELECT statement to return only those rows that contain an ArtistID value of 103. If you execute the entire SELECT statement, you'll receive the following query results:

```
DiscName            StockAmount
------------------  -----------
Blues on the Bayou  19
Deuces Wild         17
```

As you can see, only two rows are returned. Notice that the results don't include any information from the DiscArtists table or the DiscTypes table, although these two tables are integral to arriving at these results. If you had wanted, you could have nested additional subqueries in your statement. Each one would have been processed in the same manner as the subqueries shown in the previous example.

Progress Check

1. What type of subquery is dependent on the outer statement in some way?

2. How many subqueries can you include in a SELECT statement?

3. What is a nested subquery?

CRITICAL SKILL
12.5 Use Subqueries to Modify Data

At the beginning of this module, I told you that you can use subqueries to modify data as well as query data. We'll now look at the three primary data modification statements—INSERT, UPDATE, and DELETE—and how they use subqueries to modify data in your database. For each statement, I provide an example that modifies data in the TitleTypes table, shown in Figure 12-4. Each example includes a subquery that returns data from the TitlesInventory table. This information is used as a basis for the data modification in the TitleTypes table.

---

1. Correlated subquery

2. The SQL:1999 standard does not limit the number of subqueries that can be included in a statement, although practical application, performance, and the limitations of the SQL implementation all play an important role in determining what a reasonable number might be.

3. A nested subquery is one that is a component of another subquery.

TitlesInventory

TitleID: INT	Title: VARCHAR (60)	Stock: INT
101	Famous Blue Raincoat	12
102	Blue	24
103	Past Light	9
104	Blues on the Bayou	19
105	Luck of the Draw	25
106	Deuces Wild	17
107	Nick of Time	11
108	Both Sides Now	13

TitleTypes

CDTitle: VARCHAR (60)	CDType: CHAR (20)
Famous Blue Raincoat	Folk
Blue	Popular
Court and Spark	Popular
Past Light	New Age
Fundamental	Popular
Blues on the Bayou	Blues
Longing in their Hearts	Popular
Deuces Wild	Blues
Nick of Time	Popular

Figure 12-4 Modifying the TitleTypes table

NOTE

This section focuses on the subqueries used in the INSERT, UPDATE, and DELETE statements. For more information about the statements themselves, see Module 8.

Using Subqueries to Insert Data

An INSERT statement, as you no doubt recall, allows you to add data to an existing table. You can add that data directly to the table or through a view that allows you to insert data into the underlying table. If you use a subquery in an INSERT statement, you must include it as one of the values defined in the VALUES clause. For example, suppose you want to insert data into the TitleTypes table. The VALUES clause should include a value for the CDTitle column and the CDType column. Now suppose that you know the TitleID value (from the TitlesInventory table), but you don't know the exact name of the CD. You can create an INSERT statement that pulls the name of the CD from the TitlesInventory table and inserts that value into the TitleTypes table, as shown in the following example:

```
INSERT INTO TitleTypes VALUES
( ( SELECT Title FROM TitlesInventory WHERE TitleID = 108 ), 'Popular' ) ;
```

Notice that the subquery appears as one of the values in the VALUES clause. The subquery returns the value of Both Sides Now. This value and the value Popular are inserted into the TitleTypes table.

For the most part, using a subquery in an INSERT statement is a relatively simple process. However, you must be sure that your subquery returns only one value; otherwise, you will receive an error. In addition, the value must be compatible with the data type and any other constraints defined on the target column.

NOTE

Not all SQL implementations support the use of a subquery as a value in the INSERT statement. For example, SQL Server does not allow you to insert values in this manner, although Oracle does.

Using Subqueries to Update Data

An UPDATE statement allows you to modify existing data in a table. As with an INSERT statement, you can modify data directly or through a view, if that view is updatable. To use a subquery in an UPDATE statement, you can include it in a predicate in the WHERE clause, as you did with the SELECT statements we looked at earlier in this module. For example, if you want to update the Both Sides Now row that was inserted in the preceding INSERT statement example, you can create an UPDATE statement similar to the following:

```
UPDATE TitleTypes
SET CDType = 'Folk'
WHERE CDTitle IN
( SELECT Title FROM TitlesInventory WHERE TitleID = 108 ) ;
```

In this statement, the IN predicate compares the values in the CDTitle column of the TitleTypes table with the value returned by the subquery. The subquery is a simple SELECT statement that returns data from the TitlesInventory table. The subquery here works the same way as you saw in earlier SELECT statement examples. In this case, the subquery returns a value of Both Sides Now. This value is then used to determine which row in the TitleTypes table to update. Once this row is determined, the CDType value is changed to Folk.

Subqueries are not limited to the WHERE clause of an UPDATE statement. You can also use a subquery in the SET clause to provide a value for the identified column. For example, suppose you want to once again update the Both Sides Now row that was inserted in the preceding INSERT statement example. You can pull a value from the TitlesInventory table to use as the new value for the TitleTypes table, as shown in the following UPDATE statement:

```
UPDATE TitleTypes
SET CDTitle =
  ( SELECT Title FROM TitlesInventory WHERE TitleID = 108 )
WHERE CDTitle = 'Both Sides Now' ;
```

Notice that, instead of specifying a value in the SET clause (to the right of the equal sign), you can specify a subquery. The subquery returns a value of Both Sides Now and inserts that value into the TitleTypes table.

NOTE
In the preceding example, all we've done is insert the same value over the existing one. The purpose of this statement is only to demonstrate how a subquery can be used in a SET clause. Even if a new value were being added, the principles would be the same. For example, if the title had changed in the TitlesInventory table, the preceding statement would update the title in the TitleTypes table.

Using Subqueries to Delete Data

A DELETE statement is similar to an UPDATE statement, in terms of how a subquery can be used in the WHERE clause. You simply include a predicate that contains a subquery. In the following example, I delete the Both Sides Now row that I modified in the previous UPDATE statement example. To determine which row to delete, I use a subquery to return the appropriate Title value from the TitlesInventory table:

```
DELETE TitleTypes
WHERE CDTitle IN
( SELECT Title FROM TitlesInventory WHERE TitleID = 108 ) ;
```

As you would expect, the subquery returns the value of Both Sides Now. The IN predicate compares this value to the values in the CDTitle column of the TitleTypes table. Every row with matching values is deleted. In this case, only one row has a CDTitle value of Both Sides Now, so that is the row that is deleted.

Project 12-1   Working with Subqueries

`Prj12.txt`

In this module, I discussed how you can use subqueries to query and modify data. The subqueries we looked at, for the most part, relied on the use of predicates to define the subquery condition. In this project, you will create a number of SELECT statements that include WHERE clauses. Those clauses will each include a predicate that defines a subquery, allowing you to access data from more than one table. You will also modify data by using an UPDATE statement that contains subqueries in the SET clause and the WHERE clause. For this project, as with previous projects, you will be using the Inventory database. You can download the Prj12.txt file, which contains the SQL statements used in this project.

(continued)

Step by Step

1. Open the client application for your RDBMS and connect to the Inventory database.

2. The first SELECT statement that you'll create allows you to return the name and number of CDs that are produced by MCA Records. Enter and execute the following SQL statement:

```
SELECT CDTitle, InStock FROM CompactDiscs
WHERE LabelID IN
( SELECT LabelID FROM CDLabels WHERE CompanyName = 'MCA Records' ) ;
```

   This statement uses a subquery to return the LabelID value for MCA Records, which is stored in the CDLabels table. The value is then used in the IN predicate to compare it to the LabelID values in the CompactDiscs table. Your query should return four rows.

3. In the next statement, you will use an EXISTS predicate to define a subquery. The predicate determines whether the CompactDiscs table contains any rows with a CDTitle value of Out of Africa. Enter and execute the following SQL statement:

```
SELECT CompanyName FROM CDLabels l
WHERE EXISTS
( SELECT * FROM CompactDiscs d
  WHERE l.LabelID = d.LabelID AND CDTitle = 'Out of Africa' ) ;
```

   The statement will return the name of the company that produces the *Out of Africa* CD, which in this case is MCA Records. The MCA Records row in the CDLabels table is the only row that evaluates to true for the subquery in the EXISTS predicate.

4. In the next statement you create, you'll determine the distributor names for those CDs in which the LabelID value in the CDLabels table is equal to any LabelID values returned by the subquery. Enter and execute the following SQL statement:

```
SELECT CompanyName FROM CDLabels
WHERE LabelID = ANY
( SELECT LabelID FROM CompactDiscs WHERE InStock > 30 ) ;
```

   The subquery returns only those LabelID values for rows that contain an InStock value greater than 30. When you execute this statement, the names of only three companies should be returned.

5. Now you'll create a SELECT statement that uses a comparison predicate to define a subquery. The subquery returns the LabelID value (from the CDLabels table) for Capitol Records. That value is then compared to the LabelID values in the CompactDiscs table. Enter and execute the following SQL statement:

```
SELECT CDTitle, InStock FROM CompactDiscs
WHERE LabelID =
( SELECT LabelID FROM CDLabels WHERE CompanyName = 'Capitol Records' ) ;
```

This statement should return only two rows.

6. Now let's redo the statement in Step 5 and turn it into a comma-separated join. Remember that you should assign correlation names to the tables to simplify the code. Also remember that the WHERE clause should include an equi-join condition that matches up LabelID values. Enter and execute the following SQL statement:

```
SELECT CDTitle, InStock FROM CompactDiscs d, CDLabels l
WHERE d.LabelID = l.LabelID AND CompanyName = 'Capitol Records' ;
```

As you can see, this statement is a lot simpler than the subquery used in the preceding statement, and it returns the same results.

7. In the next statement that you'll create, you will use a nested subquery to return values to the outer subquery. Enter and execute the following SQL statement:

```
SELECT ArtistName FROM Artists
WHERE ArtistID IN
( SELECT ArtistID FROM ArtistCDs WHERE CompactDiscID IN
  ( SELECT CompactDiscID FROM CompactDiscs WHERE CDTitle = 'Past Light' ) ) ;
```

The inner subquery returns the CompactDiscID value for the *Past Light* CD. The outer subquery then uses this value to determine the ArtistID value for that CD. This value is then used in the main SELECT statement, which returns one value: William Ackerman. He is the artist on the *Past Light* CD.

8. Now we're going to move on to using subqueries in an UPDATE statement. However, let's first take a look at the table we're going to update, which is the CompactDiscTypes table. In order to know what to update, we're going to use values from the CompactDiscs table and the MusicTypes table to help identify the IDs used in the CompactDiscTypes table. Enter and execute the following SQL statement:

```
SELECT CDTitle, TypeName
FROM CompactDiscs d, CompactDiscTypes t, MusicTypes m
WHERE d.CompactDiscID = t.CompactDiscID AND t.MusicTypeID = m.TypeID
  AND CDTitle = 'Kojiki' ;
```

In this statement, you join three tables to return the CDTitle value and TypeName value for the *Kojiki* CD. The CD is classified as New Age.

Project 12-1

Working with Subqueries

(continued)

9. In this step, you will update the row in the CompactDiscTypes table that matches the CompactDiscID for the *Kojiki* CD with the MusicTypeID value for the New Age music type. You'll change the music type from New Age to Classical. Enter and execute the following SQL statement:

```
UPDATE CompactDiscTypes
SET MusicTypeID =
  ( SELECT TypeID FROM MusicTypes WHERE TypeName = 'Classical' )
WHERE CompactDiscID =
  ( SELECT CompactDiscID FROM CompactDiscs WHERE CDTitle = 'Kojiki' )
AND MusicTypeID =
  ( SELECT TypeID FROM MusicTypes WHERE TypeName = 'New Age' ) ;
```

The statement uses a subquery in the SET clause to pull the TypeID value from the MusicTypes table. The statement also uses two subqueries in the WHERE clause of the UPDATE statement to determine which row to update in the CompactDiscTypes table. The first subquery in the WHERE clause returns the CompactDiscID value for the *Kojiki* CD. The second subquery returns the TypeID value for the Classical music type.

10. Now let's query the CompactDiscTypes table to view the changes. Enter and execute the following SQL statement:

```
SELECT CDTitle, TypeName
FROM CompactDiscs d, CompactDiscTypes t, MusicTypes m
WHERE d.CompactDiscID = t.CompactDiscID AND t.MusicTypeID = m.TypeID
  AND CDTitle = 'Kojiki' ;
```

The TypeName value should now be Classical.

11. Finally, you will return the CompactDiscTypes table to its original state. Enter and execute the following SQL statement:

```
UPDATE CompactDiscTypes
SET MusicTypeID =
  ( SELECT TypeID FROM MusicTypes WHERE TypeName = 'New Age' )
WHERE CompactDiscID =
  ( SELECT CompactDiscID FROM CompactDiscs WHERE CDTitle = 'Kojiki' )
AND MusicTypeID =
  ( SELECT TypeID FROM MusicTypes WHERE TypeName = 'Classical' ) ;
```

This statement is similar to the preceding UPDATE statement that you used, only now the New Age music type will be used (which was the original music type).

12. Let's check the table one more time. Enter and execute the following SQL statement:

```
SELECT CDTitle, TypeName
FROM CompactDiscs d, CompactDiscTypes t, MusicTypes m
WHERE d.CompactDiscID = t.CompactDiscID AND t.MusicTypeID = m.TypeID
  AND CDTitle = 'Kojiki' ;
```

The CompactDiscTypes table should now contain the same values as it did when you started this project.

13. Close the client application.

Project Summary

In this project, you created several SELECT statements that contained subqueries. These subqueries were included in predicates that permit the subqueries to return one or more rows. Specifically, the WHERE clauses included the IN, EXISTS, and ANY predicates. In addition, you created a SELECT statement that included a comparison predicate, which permits the subquery to return only one row. You also created a SELECT statement that included nested subqueries. These subqueries used the IN predicate. In addition to querying data in the Inventory database, you updated the CompactDiscTypes table by using subqueries that accessed other tables. As you can see, subqueries provide you with a versatile tool for accessing data in your database. However, when creating statements that include subqueries, you should always try to determine whether a join would perform better in any given situation.

✓

Module 12 Mastery Check

1. In which types of statements can you include subqueries?

A. SELECT

B. INSERT

C. UPDATE

D. DELETE

2. What is a subquery?

3. In which clauses of a SELECT statement can you include a subquery?

A. SELECT

B. WHERE

C. GROUP BY

D. HAVING

4. Into what two general categories can you divide subqueries in a WHERE clause?

5. Which types of predicates are you prevented from using with subqueries that return multiple rows? .

   A. IN and EXISTS predicates

   B. SOME, ANY, and ALL predicates

   C. Comparison predicates

   D. Quantified comparison predicates

6. When does an EXISTS condition evaluate to true?

7. In addition to numbers, _____ data can be compared in comparison predicates.

8. Which types of predicates allow you to use subqueries that return multiple rows?

   A. IN and EXISTS predicates

   B. SOME, ANY, and ALL predicates

   C. Comparison predicates

   D. Quantified comparison predicates

9. What is a correlated subquery?

10. How often is a correlated subquery evaluated when a SELECT statement is processed?

11. A(n) _____ is a subquery that is a component of another subquery.

12. How many subqueries can be included in a SELECT statement, as specified by the SQL standard?

13. Which clause in an INSERT statement can contain a subquery?

14. How many values can a subquery return if it is used in an INSERT statement?

15. Which clauses in an UPDATE statement can contain a subquery?

Part III

Advanced Data Access

Module 13

Creating SQL-Invoked Routines

P rior to the release of SQL:1999, the American National Standards Institute (ANSI) and the
International Organization for Standardization (ISO) published an interim standard in 1996 that
added procedures and functions, along with related language, to the existing SQL standard. This
new publication, referred to as SQL/PSM, or PSM-96 (PSM standing for *persistent stored module*),
represented the first step toward including procedural capabilities within SQL itself. These new
capabilities, which were later incorporated into the SQL:1999 standard, define, among other
components, the creation of SQL-invoked routines—specifically, SQL-invoked procedures and
SQL-invoked functions. In this module, we'll take a close look at both procedures and functions,
including how to create them and how to call them once they're created. We'll also take a look
at a number of examples that demonstrate the various types of procedures and functions and the
components that make up each.

CRITICAL SKILL
13.1
Understand SQL-Invoked Routines

I first introduced you to the concept of SQL-invoked routines in Module 2, where I describe
the schema objects that can exist within an SQL environment. As you might recall, an
SQL-invoked routine is a function or procedure that can be invoked from SQL. Both functions
and procedures are stored sets of predefined SQL statements that perform some sort of action
on the data in your database. For example, you can define a SELECT statement and store it as
an SQL-invoked procedure. Once you have created that procedure, you can call it simply by
calling its name and, if appropriate, supplying the necessary parameters.

All SQL-invoked routines support the use of *parameters,* which are values passed to and
from a routine when you invoke that routine. A function can receive input parameters and return
a value based on the expression included in the function definition. A procedure can pass input
and output parameters. Regardless of whether it's a procedure or function, an SQL-invoked
routine can be a schema object or can be embedded in an SQL server module, which is also a
schema object. (A *module* is an object that contains SQL statements or routines.)

NOTE

SQL:1999 also supports a third type of SQL-invoked routine—the SQL-invoked
method. A method, which is used in user-defined types, is a type of function that performs
predefined tasks. SQL supports two types of user-defined types: structured types and
distinct types. Methods are used in structured types. The subject of structured user-defined
types is beyond the scope of the book, so I won't be covering methods in this module.

Most SQL implementations support some form of the SQL-invoked routine in their products.
Within various SQL implementations, SQL-invoked procedures are often referred to as *stored
procedures,* and SQL-invoked functions are often referred to as *user-defined functions*. Regardless

of the names used, the fundamental concepts are the same, and the basic functionality supported is similar from product to product. However, while concepts and functionality are similar, the implementation of SQL-invoked routines can vary widely, and the specifics of how SQL-invoked routines are created and called differ not only between the SQL standard and the individual product, but also between the products themselves. The main reason for this is that many products had already implemented PSM technology prior to the publication of the SQL/PSM standard in 1996. As a result, proprietary functionality has persisted among the different implementations, with few SQL products conforming to the actual SQL/PSM standard, or, consequently, the PSM-related portion of the SQL:1999 standard.

Despite the product differences, it is still worthwhile to take a look at the basic concepts behind SQL-invoked routines, as they are defined in the SQL standard. The standard provides insight into the underlying structure used by the various SQL implementations and can give you a cohesive overview of the basic concepts shared by all products that implement SQL-invoked procedures and functions. However, as with other SQL-related technology, you should refer to the product documentation for your specific SQL implementation. In few cases will you be able to use pure SQL to create an implementation-specific SQL-invoked routine.

SQL-Invoked Procedures and Functions

As I mentioned earlier, an SQL-invoked routine can be either an SQL-invoked procedure or an SQL-invoked function (or, in the case of user data types, an SQL-invoked method). SQL-invoked procedures and functions are similar in many ways, although there are some basic differences. Table 13-1 provides an overview of the main differences and similarities.

The easiest way to distinguish between SQL-invoked procedures and functions is to think of a procedure as a set of one or more stored SQL statements, similar to how a view stores a SELECT statement (as described in Module 5) and to think of a function as a type of operation that returns a value, similar to set functions such as SUM or AVG (as described in Module 10).

Procedures	Functions
Invoked from SQL statements, not from a programming language.	Invoked from SQL statements, not from a programming language.
Can be written in SQL or another programming language.	Can be written in SQL or another programming language.
Invoked by using the CALL statement.	Invoked as a value in an expression.
Support input and output parameters, although neither are required.	Support input parameters, although none are required. You cannot define output parameters for a function. The function returns a single output value.

Table 13-1 Comparing SQL-Invoked Procedures and Functions

Working with the Basic Syntax

There are many similarities between the syntax used to create procedures and that used to create functions. In fact, they're defined as one syntactic element in SQL:1999. In addition, the syntax is, at its most basic level, similar to how procedures are created in most SQL implementations. Let's take a look at the syntax for each one to better understand their basic elements.

Using the CREATE PROCEDURE Statement

The first syntax we'll look at is that for creating a procedure. At its most basic, the CREATE PROCEDURE statement looks like the following:

```
CREATE PROCEDURE <procedure name>
( [ <parameter declaration> [ { , <parameter declaration> } . . . ] ] )
[ <routine characteristic> . . . ]
<routine body>
```

As you can see, you must provide a name for the procedure—in the CREATE PROCEDURE clause—followed by zero or more parameter declarations, which are enclosed in parentheses. If no declarations are defined, you must still provide the parentheses. If more than one declaration is defined, you must separate them by commas. Following the parameter declarations, you have the option of defining one or more routine characteristics. For example, you can specify whether the routine is an SQL routine or one written in another language.

NOTE

The type of routine characteristics that you can define vary greatly among the SQL implementations, not only in terms of which options are supported, but also with regard to how they're defined. Consequently, I will keep my discussion of these options short, but be sure to check the product documentation for more information.

After you've defined the procedure's characteristics, you're ready to add the SQL statements, which are represented by the <routine body> placeholder. Many of the statements you'll use in this section will be similar to those you've already seen in this book. However, the SQL/PSM standard introduced new language elements that make procedures more dynamic. As we continue through this module, we'll look at many of these elements and how they're used to extend the functionality of SQL-invoked procedures.

Using the CREATE FUNCTION Statement

Now let's take a look at the statement used for creating an SQL-invoked function. As you can see in the following syntax, a function contains a few more elements than a procedure:

```
CREATE FUNCTION <function name>
( [ <parameter declaration> [ { , <parameter declaration> } . . . ] ] )
RETURNS <data type>
[ <routine characteristic> . . . ]
[ STATIC DISPATCH ]
<routine body>
```

As with procedures, you must first provide a name for your function, followed by the parameter declaration list. Functions support only input parameters, and if none are provided, you must still use the parentheses. If more than one is provided, you must separate them by commas. Following the parameter declarations is the RETURNS clause. You must provide the data type for the value that's returned by the parameter. After that, you can include any of the optional routine characteristics, depending on what options your SQL implementation supports. Next comes the STATIC DISPATCH clause. You must specify this clause if you use a user-defined type, a reference data type, or an array data type. Because these types are all beyond the scope of this book, you do not need to be concerned with the STATIC DISPATCH clause at this time.

The last thing that you must include in the procedure definition is, of course, the routine body. As with procedures, these are the SQL statements that make up the core of your procedure. However, there is one additional element you'll find in the routine body that is not included in a procedure's routine body—a RETURN statement. The RETURN statement specifies the value that will be returned by the function. Later in this module, in the "Create SQL-Invoked Functions" section, I'll discuss the RETURN statement and other elements of the CREATE FUNCTION statement in more detail.

Progress Check

1. What are the two primary types of SQL-invoked routines supported by SQL?

2. Which type of SQL-invoked routine is invoked by using a CALL statement?

3. What two clauses are included in a CREATE FUNCTION statement that are not included in a CREATE PROCEDURE statement?

4. What type of parameters can you declare in a CREATE FUNCTION statement?

---

1. SQL-invoked procedures and functions
2. SQL-invoked procedure
3. The RETURNS clause and the STATIC DISPATCH clause
4. Input parameters only

Create SQL-Invoked Procedures

Now that you have an overview of SQL-invoked routines and the syntax used to create them, let's take a closer look at how to create SQL-invoked procedures. A procedure can perform most functions that you can perform by using SQL statements directly. In addition, procedures can be used to pass parameters and define variables, which we'll get into later in this module. For now, let's look at a procedure at its most basic, one that includes no parameters or special types of SQL statements.

Suppose you need to query the data in the CDInventory and CDTypes tables shown in Figure 13-1. You want your query results to return the CD names and number in stock for all New Age CDs.

To view this information, you can create a SELECT statement that joins the two tables, as shown in the following example:

```
SELECT CDTitle, CDStock FROM CDInventory i, CDTypes t
WHERE i.CDTypeID = t.CDTypeID AND CDTypeName = 'New Age' ;
```

Of course, every time you want to view this information, you would have to re-create the SELECT statement. However, another option is to store the SELECT statement within the schema. That way, all you need to do is call that statement whenever you want to view the New Age CDs. One way to store the SELECT statement is within a view definition:

```
CREATE VIEW NewAge AS
SELECT CDTitle, CDStock FROM CDInventory i, CDTypes t
WHERE i.CDTypeID = t.CDTypeID AND CDTypeName = 'New Age' ;
```

CDInventory

CDTitle: VARCHAR (60)	CDTypeID: CHAR (4)	CDStock: INT
Famous Blue Raincoat	FROK	19
Blue	CPOP	28
Past Light	NEWA	6
Out of Africa	STRK	8
Fundamental	NPOP	10
Blues on the Bayou	BLUS	11
Kojiki	NEWA	10

CDTypes

CDTypeID: CHAR (4)	CDTypeName: CHAR (20)
FROK	Folk Rock
CPOP	Classic Pop
NEWA	New Age
CTRY	Country
STRK	Soundtrack
BLUS	Blues
JAZZ	Jazz

Figure 13-1 Using procedures to access the CDInventory and CDTypes tables

Once the view is created, you can use a SELECT statement to call the view, as shown in the following statement:

```
SELECT * FROM NewAge ;
```

However, views are very limited with regard to the types of statements and functionality that are supported. For example, you cannot include an UPDATE statement in a view, nor can you pass parameters. As a result, a better way to store this SELECT statement is as an SQL-invoked procedure. To do this, you must create a schema object by using the CREATE PROCEDURE statement, as shown in the following example:

```
CREATE PROCEDURE NewAgeCDs ( )
SELECT CDTitle, CDStock FROM CDInventory i, CDTypes t
WHERE i.CDTypeID = t.CDTypeID AND CDTypeName = 'New Age' ;
```

This statement represents the minimum amount of information that you must provide in order to create a procedure; it includes a CREATE PROCEDURE clause that names the procedure (NewAgeCDs), a set of parentheses, and a routine body, which is the SELECT statement. If you were defining parameters, their declarations would be enclosed in the parentheses.

As you might well imagine, a CREATE PROCEDURE statement can be far more complex than what you see here. However, the statement in the example represents the basic structure on which you would build more extensive statements. Before I discuss more complicated procedures, let's first touch on the issue of how this statement is created in various SQL implementations.

Earlier in the module, I told you that SQL implementations can vary widely with regard to the specifics of how SQL-invoked routines are created and called. As a result, few implementations support pure SQL when attempting to define your procedures. For example, both SQL Server and Oracle require that you use the AS keyword before the routine body. In addition, SQL Server does not use parentheses after the procedure name, whether or not parameters are being defined. Oracle, on the other hand, does. As a result, you must consult your product documentation whenever you're creating a procedure to determine how the product-specific language differs from the SQL standard.

Invoking SQL-Invoked Procedures

Once you've created your procedure, you can call it by using a CALL statement. The basic syntax for the CALL statement is as follows:

```
CALL <procedure name>
( [ <value> [ { , <value> } . . . ] ] )
```

As you can see, you must identify the name of the procedure in the CALL clause and follow that with the values (in parentheses) that are passed into the procedure as parameters. If no parameters are defined for the procedure, you must still use the parentheses. If more than one parameter is defined for the procedure, you must separate them with commas. In addition, you must follow these guidelines when entering values:

● Your CALL statement must include the same number of values as the number of parameters defined in the procedure.

● The values must be entered in the same order as the order in which they are defined in the procedure.

● The values must conform to the data types that are assigned to the parameters.

I'll be discussing parameters in more detail in the next section, "Add Input Parameters to Your Procedures."

Now let's look at an example of the CALL statement. If you want to call the procedure that was created in the preceding example, you can use the following statement:

```
CALL NewAgeCDs ( ) ;
```

In this statement, the name of the procedure follows the CALL keyword. Notice the use of parentheses even though no parameters were defined for the procedure. Had parameters been defined, they would have been enclosed in the parentheses. When you call this statement, you'll receive the same results as you would have if you had executed the SELECT statement separately, as shown in the following query results:

```
CDTitle       CDStock
----------    -------
Past Light    6
Kojiki        10
```

The CALL statement, like the CREATE PROCEDURE statement, can vary from SQL implementation to implementation in how it is used and whether it is supported. In fact, you'll probably find that, for most implementations, you must use an EXECUTE statement, rather than CALL, to invoke a procedure.

Progress Check

1. What are two types of schema objects that you can use to store a SELECT statement?

2. Which SQL statement do you use to invoke a procedure?

3. You're calling a procedure named GetTotals. The procedure does not include any parameters, but does include a SELECT statement that queries the CDInventory table. What SQL statement should you use to invoke this parameter?

---

1. Views and SQL-invoked procedures
2. CALL
3. You should use the following SQL statement: `CALL GetTotals ( ) ;`

CRITICAL SKILL
13.3 Add Input Parameters to Your Procedures

The NewAgeCDs procedure that we looked at in the previous examples can be very handy because it saves you having to create an SQL statement each time you want to view information about New Age CDs. However, in order to return information about other types of CDs, such as Blues or Country, you must create a new query or set up a procedure for the specific type of music. But there is another alternative. You can create a procedure that does not specifically define the music type but instead allows you to enter that type whenever you call that procedure. That way, you need only one procedure to check each type of music.

To support this type of procedure, you must declare a parameter within the procedure definition that allows you to accept input values when you call that procedure. Let's return to the CDInventory table and CDTypes table shown in Figure 13-1. If we modify the language of the procedure we created earlier, we can create a new procedure that includes the necessary input parameter, as shown in the following CREATE PROCEDURE statement:

```
CREATE PROCEDURE CDsByType ( IN p_CDType CHAR (20) )
SELECT CDTitle, CDStock FROM CDInventory i, CDTypes t
WHERE i.CDTypeID = t.CDTypeID AND CDTypeName = p_CDType ;
```

In the first line of code, a parameter is defined after the CREATE PROCEDURE clause. The parameter declaration includes the IN keyword, the name of the parameter (p_CDType), and the data type for that parameter (CHAR (20)), all of which are enclosed in parentheses.

NOTE

The "p_" convention used to name the parameters is not necessary. However, I like to use some type of naming convention to set parameters apart to make them easier to pick out in the code.

SQL supports three types of parameters: input, output, and input/output. The three types are represented by the parameter mode keywords IN, OUT, and INOUT, respectively. Input parameters allow you to provide values when you invoke a procedure. Those values are then used within the routine body when the SQL statements are executed. Output parameters allow your procedure to provide values as a result of invoking the procedure. Input/output parameters are those that provide the functionality of both input and output parameters. You do not have to specify one of the parameter mode keywords when you define your parameters. However, if you don't specify one of the keywords, SQL assumes that you're defining an input parameter.

As with many other aspects of the CREATE PROCEDURE statement, parameter declarations can vary from product to product. In SQL Server, for example, parameter names must be preceded by the at (@) symbol, as in "@p_CDType," the parameter declarations are not enclosed in parentheses, and the IN keyword is not used. Oracle, on the other hand, does not require the at symbol and does use parentheses. Oracle also uses the IN keyword, but it is positioned *after* the name of the parameter, as in "p_CDType IN CHAR (20)."

Now let's return to the CDsByType procedure that is defined in the previous CREATE PROCEDURE statement. Once you define your input parameter, you'll want to use it in some meaningful way within the routine body. In this case, the p_CDType parameter is used in the second predicate in the WHERE clause (CDTypeName = p_CDType). This means that the value you enter when you invoke the procedure is compared to the CDTypeName values of the CDTypes table when the SELECT statement is executed. As a result, your query results will include CD information about the specified music type.

Once you create your procedure, you can invoke it by using a CALL statement that specifies a value for the parameter. For example, if you want to return information about Folk Rock CDs, you can use the following CALL statement:

```
CALL CDsByType ('Folk Rock') ;
```

Notice that you include the value for the parameter in parentheses after the name of the procedure. The value must conform to the data type assigned to the parameter, which in this case is CHAR (20). As with any other instance in which you're working with character string values, you must enclose the value in single quotes. When you invoke this procedure, the Folk Rock value is inserted into the predicate in the WHERE clause and the procedure returns the following query results:

```
CDTitle              CDStock
-------------------  -------
Famous Blue Raincoat 19
```

As you can see, you now have a procedure that you can use to return CD information on any music type. You simply provide the name of the music type when you call the procedure. However, procedures are not limited to only one parameter. You can include multiple parameters in any procedure definition. For example, suppose you want to modify the preceding procedure definition to allow you to enter an amount. You want to use that amount to return CD information for only those CDs with a CDStock value that exceeds the specified amount. At the same time, you still want to return CD information for only the specified music type. As a result, you need to define two parameters, as shown in the following CREATE PROCEDURE statement:

```
CREATE PROCEDURE CDsByType ( IN p_CDType CHAR (20), IN p_Amount INT )
SELECT CDTitle, CDStock FROM CDInventory i, CDTypes t
WHERE i.CDTypeID = t.CDTypeID
  AND CDTypeName = p_CDType AND CDStock > p_Amount ;
```

Notice that the parameter declaration clause now includes two input parameters: p_CDType and p_Amount. The p_Amount parameter is configured with the INT data type. The p_Amount parameter, like the p_CDType parameter, is used in a predicate in the WHERE clause (CDStock > p_Amount). As a result, the rows returned by the procedure must include CDStock values greater than the amount specified when calling the procedure.

Once you've created the procedure, you can call it by using a CALL statement that includes values for both parameters, as shown in the following example:

```
CALL CDsByType ('New Age', 5) ;
```

Now your CALL statement includes two values (separated by a comma) within the parentheses. The values must be listed in the order in which the parameters are defined in the CREATE PROCEDURE statement. When you invoke this statement, the New Age value is inserted in the p_CDType parameter, and the 5 value is inserted in the p_Amount parameter, making the SELECT statement embedded in the procedure definition behave as though you entered the values directly, as shown in the following example:

```
SELECT CDTitle, CDStock FROM CDInventory i, CDTypes t
WHERE i.CDTypeID = t.CDTypeID
  AND CDTypeName = 'New Age' AND CDStock > 5 ;
```

If you were to execute this statement, you would return the same query results as you would if you were to execute the CALL statement using the New Age value and 5 value, as shown in the following results:

```
CDTitle      CDStock
----------   -------
Past Light   6
Kojiki       10
```

Now let's modify the CALL statement to see how specifying a different value might affect your results. Suppose you use a numeric value of 8, rather than 5, as shown in the following statement:

```
CALL CDsByType ('New Age', 8) ;
```

If you were to execute this statement, only one row would be returned:

```
CDTitle      CDStock
----------   -------
Kojiki       10
```

If you refer back to the CDInventory table in Figure 13-1, you'll see that only the Kojiki row is a New Age CD with a CDStock value that exceeds 8, the value you specified in your CALL statement. As you can see, using multiple parameters can provide you with a variety of options that make procedures a useful and flexible tool that can eliminate the need to write multiple statements that are meant to provide similar results. If you define the necessary parameters, users simply plug in the necessary values to achieve the results they desire.

Using Procedures to Modify Data

Up to this point, the SQL-invoked procedures that we've looked at have contained SELECT statements that query data. However, procedures are not limited to only SELECT statements. You can include data modification statements such as INSERT, UPDATE, and DELETE. Let's return to the CDInventory table and CDTypes table, shown in Figure 13-1. You might have noticed that the CDInventory table includes a row for the *Fundamental* CD. The music type for that CD is New Pop, which is represented by NPOP (the value in the CDTypeID column). You might also have noticed that there is no corresponding entry in the CDTypes table for the New Pop type. You can create a procedure that allows you to insert values into that table. You simply need to define that procedure with the appropriate input parameters and INSERT statement, as shown in the following example:

```
CREATE PROCEDURE InsertType ( IN p_Type CHAR (4), IN p_Name CHAR (20) )
INSERT INTO CDTypes VALUES ( p_Type, p_Name ) ;
```

Notice that the procedure definition includes two input parameters: p_Type and p_Name, both of which are defined with the CHAR data type. These parameters are then used in the INSERT statement, in the same way in which you would normally specify values to be inserted into a table. Any parameter that you declare for this purpose must be defined with a data type that is compatible with the data type defined on the column that contains the data to be modified. Once you create the procedure, you can use a CALL statement similar to the following example to invoke the procedure:

```
CALL InsertType ('NPOP', 'New Pop') ;
```

Notice that the CALL statement includes NPOP and New Pop values. These values are passed to the two parameters defined in the InsertType procedure. As a result, they are inserted into the CDTypes table as though you had executed the INSERT statement directly.

In the same way that you create the InsertType procedure, you can create procedures that update and delete data by defining procedures that include the appropriate UPDATE and DELETE statement, rather than an INSERT statement. Simply create the necessary input parameters and pass the appropriate values to those parameters when you call the procedure. However, keep in mind that the value you pass to the parameters must conform not only to the data types defined in the parameter declarations, but also to the data types and constraints on the columns that contain the data you're trying to modify.

Ask the Expert

Q: Up to this point, you've shown us how to create SQL-invoked procedures, but not how to modify them. Is there a way to alter or delete procedures?

A: The SQL standard supports both an ALTER PROCEDURE statement and a DROP PROCEDURE statement. The ALTER PROCEDURE statement allows you to alter some of the routine characteristics of the procedure, but it does not allow you to alter the routine body. However, the functionality supported by the ALTER PROCEDURE statement can vary so widely from one SQL implementation to another that you'll need to check the product documentation to see whether the statement is supported and what you can do with that statement. In SQL Server, for example, the ALTER PROCEDURE statement allows you to modify most aspects of the procedure, whereas the same statement in Oracle is used primarily to recompile the procedure to avoid runtime compiling (which saves on runtime overhead). As for the DROP PROCEDURE statement, most implementations support this and it is usually fairly straightforward. You simply provide the name of the procedure in the statement and, depending on the SQL implementation, the RESTRICT or CASCADE keywords, as you've seen them used in other DROP statements. Note that the same is true for the ALTER FUNCTION and DROP FUNCTION statements. Although supported by many implementations, the ALTER FUNCTION statement can vary from one product to the next, and the DROP FUNCTION statement is fairly similar.

CRITICAL SKILL
13.4 Add Local Variables to Your Procedures

In addition to allowing you to pass parameters into a procedure, SQL also provides a way for you to create local variables in the procedure definition that can be used within the body of the procedure. You can think of a *local variable* as a type placeholder that holds a value in memory during the execution of the statements in the routine body. Once the statements are executed, the variable ceases to exist.

When you define a local variable, you must first declare the variable and then set an initial value for it. You can then use that variable in the remaining block of statements. The basic syntax for defining a variable is as follows:

DECLARE <variable name> <data type> ;

As you can see, the syntax is very straightforward. You must provide a name for the variable and assign a data type. Once you've declared the variable, you must then assign an initial value to it. To do so, you can use the SET statement, which is shown in the following syntax:

SET <variable name> = <value expression> ;

In this statement, you must first provide the variable name and then provide the initial value, which can be any sort of value expression, such as a number, a character string, or a subquery.

After you've declared the variable and assigned the initial value, you're ready to use the variable in your routine body. The best way to illustrate this is to show you an example of a procedure that uses a variable. For this example, we'll again use the CDInventory table, shown in Figure 13-1. The following statement creates a procedure that retrieves CD information for a specific music type:

```
CREATE PROCEDURE CDAmount ( IN p_TypeID CHAR (4) )
BEGIN
  DECLARE v_Amount INT ;
  SET v_Amount = ( SELECT AVG(CDStock) FROM CDInventory ) ;
  SELECT CDTitle, CDStock FROM CDInventory
    WHERE CDTypeID = p_TypeID AND CDStock < v_Amount ;
END ;
```

Let's go through this statement line by line. In the first line, we create a procedure named CDAmount and an input parameter named p_TypeID. The second line contains the keyword BEGIN. The BEGIN keyword is paired with the END keyword in the last line. Together they enclose a block of statements that are processed as a unit. We'll take a closer look at the BEGIN...END block later in the "Working with Control Statements" section.

The third line of the procedure definition includes a DECLARE statement that declares the v_Amount variable, which is defined with the INT data type. The next line uses a SET statement to assign an initial value to the parameter. This value is derived from a subquery that finds the average for all the CDStock values. The average is about 13. In the next two lines of the procedure definition, a SELECT statement retrieves data from the CDInventory table based on the values supplied by the parameter and variable.

Once you've created your procedure, you can retrieve it by using a CALL statement and providing a value for the parameter, as shown in the following example:

```
CALL CDAmount ('NEWA') ;
```

When the procedure is processed, it inserts the NEWA value from the parameter and the CDStock average from the variable into the SELECT statement defined in the procedure definition. It would be similar to executing the following statement:

```
SELECT CDTitle, CDStock FROM CDInventory
WHERE CDTypeID = 'NEWA' AND CDStock < 13 ;
```

This SELECT statement, like the procedure itself, will return the following query results:

```
CDTitle     CDStock
----------  -------
Past Light  6
Kojiki      10
```

Notice that both rows contain CDStock values less than the average amount (13) and both are New Age CDs.

You're not limited to only one variable in a procedure definition. You can create a DECLARE statement for each variable that you want to include. You can also include multiple variables in one statement, if those variables are assigned the same data type. For example, suppose you want to declare several variables with an INT data type, as shown in the following DECLARE statement:

```
DECLARE Var1, Var2, Var3 INT ;
```

This statement declares the Var1, Var2, and Var3 variables, and each one is assigned the INT data type. Once you assign initial values to the variables, you can use them in the routine body in the same way as any other local variables.

CRITICAL SKILL
13.5 Working with Control Statements

When the SQL/PSM standard was released in 1996, it included not only language that supported SQL-invoked routines, but language that could be used within those routines to make them more robust. Such characteristics as grouping statements into blocks and looping statements so that they could be executed multiple times—behavior traditionally associated with procedural type languages—made procedures and functions even more valuable to users needing to access and manipulate data in their databases. The SQL:1999 standard refers to these new language elements as *control statements* because they affect how you can control data in SQL-invoked routines. In this section, we'll look at several of these control statements, including those that allow you to group statements into a block, create conditional statements, and set up statements into a loop.

Create Compound Statements

The most basic of the control statements is the compound statement, which allows you to group statements into a block. The compound statement starts with the BEGIN keyword and finishes with the END keyword. Everything between the two keywords is part of the block. The compound statement is made up of one or more individual SQL statements, which can include statements such as DECLARE, SET, SELECT, UPDATE, INSERT, DELETE, or other control statements.

You've already seen an example of a compound statement in the preceding CREATE PROCEDURE statement that defines the CDAmount procedure. (This is the example shown in the "Add Local Variables to Your Procedures" section.) If you take another look at that example, you'll see that the procedure definition includes a compound statement. As you would expect, it starts with the BEGIN keyword and finishes with the END keyword. The block created by these keywords includes a DECLARE statement, a SET statement, and a SELECT statement. Notice that each statement is terminated with a semicolon. Although the BEGIN...END statement is considered one statement, the statements enclosed in the keywords are individual statements in their own right.

NOTE

In some SQL implementations, the compound statement might not be necessary under certain circumstances. In these cases, the semicolon terminator might be enough to signal to the implementation that one statement has ended and another has begun. Even those implementations that don't require the semicolon, such as SQL Server, will sometimes process multiple statements as a block even if the BEGIN...END construction has not been used. When the implementation reaches the end of one statement, it simply continues on to the next. However, as a general rule, you should use the compound construction to keep together those statements that should be processed as a unit. When you don't use it, you can sometimes experience unpredictable behavior, depending on the implementation.

You can use the compound statement wherever you need to keep SQL statements together. That means that they can be embedded within other compound statements or within other types of control statements. The BEGIN and END keywords do not affect how data might be passed from one statement to the next, as in the case of parameters.

The good news about compound statements and the BEGIN...END construction is that they're supported by most SQL implementations, although there can be slight variations from one product to the next, in terms of the specifics of how they're implemented. Be sure to check the product documentation when using these statements.

Create Conditional Statements

The next type of control statement we'll look at is the conditional statement. This statement determines whether a statement is executed based on whether a specified condition evaluates to true. The statement uses the IF, THEN, and ELSE keywords to establish the conditions and define the actions to take: *if* the condition is met, *then* the SQL statement is executed, or *else* another action is taken.

NOTE

The conditional statement is sometimes referred to as an IF statement, an IF...ELSE statement, an IF...END IF statement, or an IF...THEN...ELSE statement.

Let's take a look at an example that uses a conditional statement to define different courses of action, depending on the condition. In the following procedure definition, I modified the routine body of the CDAmount procedure (which we used in the preceding example) to include a conditional statement:

```
CREATE PROCEDURE CDAmount ( IN p_TypeID CHAR (4) )
BEGIN
  DECLARE v_Amount INT ;
  SET v_Amount = ( SELECT SUM(CDStock) FROM CDInventory
    WHERE CDTypeID = p_TypeID ) ;
  IF v_Amount < 20 THEN
    SELECT CDTitle, CDStock FROM CDInventory
    WHERE CDTypeID = p_TypeID ;
  ELSE
    SELECT * FROM CDInventory ;
  END IF ;
END ;
```

Notice that the BEGIN...END block now includes an IF...END IF statement. The IF clause introduces the statement and sets up the condition. For the condition to evaluate to true, the value of the v_Amount variable must be less than 20. If the condition evaluates to true, the first SELECT statement is executed. This is the SELECT statement that follows the THEN keyword. If the condition is false, then the second SELECT statement is executed. This is the statement that follows the ELSE keyword. To sum this all up, if v_Amount is less than 20, the CDTitle and CDStock values from the CDInventory table are returned for those rows that contain the TypeID specified by the p_TypeID parameter. If v_Amount is not less than 20, all rows from the CDInventory table are returned.

Once you create your procedure, you can invoke it by using a CALL statement, as you have for previous procedures. For example, if you want to return New Age (NEWA) CDs, you can use the following CALL statement:

```
CALL CDAmount ('NEWA') ;
```

This statement will return both New Age rows: Past Light and Kojiki. This is because the total number of New Age CDs (16) is less than 20, so the first SELECT statement is executed. If you had specified the Classic Pop category (CPOP) when you invoked the CDAmount procedure, all rows would have been returned. This is because the total number of Classic Pop CDs (28) exceeds 20. As a result the IF condition would not be met, so the ELSE statement would be executed.

If you want to create a conditional statement that includes more than one SQL statement in either the IF clause or the ELSE clause, you can enclose those statements in a control statement. For example, if we add an UPDATE statement to the condition in the preceding example and use a control statement to enclose the UPDATE and SELECT statements, your procedure definition will look like the following:

```
CREATE PROCEDURE CDAmount ( IN p_TypeID CHAR (4) )
BEGIN
  DECLARE v_Amount INT ;
  SET v_Amount = ( SELECT SUM(CDStock) FROM CDInventory
```

```
      WHERE CDTypeID = p_TypeID ) ;
    IF v_Amount < 20 THEN
      BEGIN
        UPDATE CDInventory SET CDStock = CDStock + 1
          WHERE CDTypeID = p_TypeID ;
        SELECT CDTitle, CDStock FROM CDInventory
          WHERE CDTypeID = p_TypeID ;
      END ;
    ELSE
      SELECT * FROM CDInventory ;
    END IF ;
END ;
```

The compound statement groups the two statements into one block of code. This way, the tables will be updated and the results of the update will be displayed in your query results.

Create Looping Statements

Now let's take a look at another type of control statement—the looping statement. SQL actually supports several types of looping statements. We'll be looking at two of them: the LOOP statement and the WHILE statement, both of which perform similar functions.

The LOOP statement uses the LOOP and END LOOP keywords to enclose a block of statements that are executed repeatedly until the loop is explicitly ended, usually through the use of the LEAVE keyword. Let's take a look at an example to illustrate how this looks. Once again using the tables in Figure 13-1, we'll use a LOOP statement to update the CDInventory table.

Ask the Expert

Q: The condition statement in the preceding example shows only two conditions and courses of action: the condition/action defined in the IF clause and the condition/action defined in the ELSE clause. What if you want to include more conditions?

A: The SQL:1999 standard supports more than two condition/action constructions in a conditional statement. If more than two are needed, you treat the IF clause and the ELSE clause as shown in the example. The additional conditions are inserted between the two clauses by adding an ELSE IF clause or an ELSEIF clause. The syntax for this would be as follows:

IF <condition> THEN <action>
ELSE IF <condition> THEN <action>
ELSE <action>

The exact way you implement the third condition/action depends on your implementation. In addition, not all implementations support ELSEIF, and some use the ELSIF keyword. As always, be sure to refer to your product documentation.

NOTE

If you created and tested the CDAmount procedure in the preceding example, assume that the CDInventory table has been returned to its original condition shown in Figure 13-1 and that no data has been modified.

In the following procedure definition, I include a LOOP statement that continues to update the CDStock column until it reaches an amount greater than 14:

```
CREATE PROCEDURE UpdateStock ( IN p_Title CHAR (20) )
BEGIN
  DECLARE v_Amount INT ;
  SET v_Amount = ( SELECT CDStock FROM CDInventory
    WHERE CDTitle = p_Title ) ;
  Loop1:
  LOOP
    SET v_Amount = v_Amount + 1 ;
    UPDATE CDInventory SET CDStock = v_Amount
      WHERE CDTitle = p_Title ;
    IF v_Amount > 14
      THEN LEAVE Loop1 ;
    END IF ;
  END LOOP ;
END ;
```

In this statement, the loop is first assigned a name (Loop1:). You must include a colon with the name when you first assign it. Next you create your loop block, which begins with the LOOP keyword and finishes with the END LOOP keywords. Within the block are SET and UPDATE statements. These two statements are executed until the loop is terminated. Notice that the CDStock value is increased by an increment of 1 each time the statements in the loop are executed. These two statements are followed by an IF statement, which specifies the condition in which the loop is terminated. *If* the value for the v_Amount variable exceeds 14, *then* the loop is terminated (LEAVE Loop1). The IF statement is then ended with the END IF keywords.

NOTE

If you did not include the IF statement in here (with the LEAVE termination operator), the loop would continue to increase the CDStock value until it fills all available storage or some other event terminates the operation.

You can then call the statement by providing the procedure name and a value for the parameter. For example, suppose you want to update the Fundamental row in the CDInventory table. You can invoke the procedure with the following CALL statement:

```
CALL UpdateStock ('Fundamental') ;
```

When the procedure is executed, a value of 1 is repeatedly added to the CDStock column until the value reaches 15, and then the loop is terminated.

You can receive the same results by using a WHILE statement. In the following example, I modified the UpdateStock procedural definition by replacing the LOOP statement with a WHILE statement:

```
CREATE PROCEDURE UpdateStock ( IN p_Title CHAR (20) )
BEGIN
  DECLARE v_Amount INT ;
  SET v_Amount = ( SELECT CDStock FROM CDInventory
    WHERE CDTitle = p_Title ) ;
  WHILE v_Amount < 15 DO
    SET v_Amount = v_Amount + 1 ;
    UPDATE CDInventory SET CDStock = v_Amount
      WHERE CDTitle = p_Title ;
  END WHILE ;
END ;
```

NOTE

Again, if you tested the procedure created in the example preceding this one, assume that the table has been returned to its original condition shown in Figure 13-1 and that no data has been modified.

The WHILE statement sets up the same type of loop condition as the LOOP statement. However, instead of using an IF statement to terminate the loop, a condition is specified in the WHILE clause that terminates the loop automatically when the condition evaluates to false. In this case, the parameter value for v_Amount must be less than 15 for the WHILE condition to evaluate to true. As long as it does evaluate to true, the SET statement and UPDATE statement are executed. If the condition evaluates to false, the WHILE loop is terminated.

Project 13-1 Creating SQL-Invoked Procedures

Prj13.txt

In this project you will apply what you have learned about creating SQL-invoked procedures to the Inventory database. You'll create procedures, invoke procedures, and drop procedures. One of the procedures will include a parameter and one will include a variable. For this project, even more so than most projects, you'll need to reference the product documentation for your SQL implementation to ensure that you take into account the variations in how a procedure is created, called, and dropped. As I said earlier in this module, procedure implementation can vary widely between the SQL standard and the individual product. You can download the Prj13.txt file, which contains the SQL statements used in this project.

Step by Step

1. Open the client application for your RDBMS and connect to the Inventory database.

2. The first procedure that you'll create is a very basic one that queries information from the CompactDiscs, ArtistCDs, and Artists tables. You'll join the three tables in order to display the CD names and artist names. Your procedure will include no parameters or variables. Enter and execute the following SQL statement:

```
CREATE PROCEDURE GetCDArtists ( )
SELECT cd.CDTitle, a.ArtistName
FROM CompactDiscs cd, ArtistCDs ac, Artists a
WHERE cd.CompactDiscID = ac.CompactDiscID AND ac.ArtistID = a.ArtistID ;
```

You should receive a message indicating that the GetCDArtists procedure has been created.

3. Next, you'll call the GetCDArtists procedure. Enter and execute the following SQL statement:

```
CALL GetCDArtists ( ) ;
```

When you invoke the procedure, you should receive query results that include a list of all the CDs and their artists.

4. Now you'll drop the procedure from the database. Enter and execute the following SQL statement:

```
DROP PROCEDURE GetCDArtists CASCADE ;
```

You should receive a message indicating that the GetCDArtists procedure has been dropped from the database.

5. Your next step is to create a procedure similar to the last one, only this time you'll define a parameter that allows you to enter the name of the CD. The SELECT statement will include a predicate that compares the CDTitle value to the value in the p_CD parameter. Enter and execute the following SQL statement:

```
CREATE PROCEDURE GetCDArtists ( IN p_CD VARCHAR (60) )
SELECT cd.CDTitle, a.ArtistName
FROM CompactDiscs cd, ArtistCDs ac, Artists a
WHERE cd.CompactDiscID = ac.CompactDiscID
  AND ac.ArtistID = a.ArtistID AND cd.CDTitle = p_CD ;
```

You should receive a message indicating that the GetCDArtists procedure has been created.

(continued)

6. Now you'll call the GetCDArtists procedure. The CALL statement will include the Fundamental value to insert into the parameter. Enter and execute the following SQL statement:

```
CALL GetCDArtists ('Fundamental') ;
```

Your query results should now include only the Fundamental row.

7. The next procedure that you'll create is one that uses a variable to hold a number based on the average of the InStock values. The procedure definition will include a compound statement that groups together the other statements in the routine body. Enter and execute the following SQL statement:

```
CREATE PROCEDURE GetCDAmount ( )
BEGIN
  DECLARE v_InStock INT ;
  SET v_InStock = ( SELECT AVG(InStock) FROM CompactDiscs ) ;
  SELECT CDTitle, InStock FROM CompactDiscs WHERE InStock < v_InStock ;
END ;
```

You should receive a message indicating that the procedure has been created.

8. Now you'll call the procedure. Enter and execute the following SQL statement:

```
CALL GetCDAmount ( ) ;
```

Your query results should include a list of CDs that have an InStock value less than the average for all InStock values.

9. Close the client application.

Project Summary

In this project, you created three procedures. The first procedure, GetCDArtists, included no parameters or variables. After you dropped that procedure, you modified the original GetCDArtists procedure to include a parameter. You then created a new procedure (GetCDAmount) that included no procedures but did include one variable. The Inventory database should now contain these two procedures. Because both procedures only retrieve SQL data, you can invoke them at any time.

CRITICAL SKILL
13.6 Add Output Parameters to Your Procedures

Up to this point, we've looked only at procedures that take input parameter values. However, SQL-invoked procedures also support output parameters. Output parameters provide a way to create a procedure that returns a value (or multiple values).

The process of defining an output parameter is similar to that of defining an input parameter, only you use the OUT keyword rather than IN. However, you must still provide a parameter name and assign a data type. In addition, you must assign a value to that parameter by using a SET statement.

A procedure definition can include both input and output parameters (and input/output parameters if your implementation supports them). You can also include variables or any other elements that we've looked at so far in this module.

Now let's take a look at an example of an output parameter. The following CREATE PROCEDURE statement creates a procedure that includes one output parameter (but no input parameters or variables):

```
CREATE PROCEDURE NewAgeTotal ( OUT p_Total INT )
BEGIN
  SET p_Total = ( SELECT SUM(CDStock) FROM CDInventory i, CDTypes t
    WHERE i.CDTypeID = t.CDTypeID AND CDTypeName = 'New Age' ) ;
END ;
```

The output parameter (p_Total) is assigned the INT data type. The SET statement defines a value for the parameter. In this case, the value is equal to the total number of New Age CDs. This is the value that is returned by the procedure when you invoke it.

The process of invoking a procedure is different from what you've seen so far. When invoking a procedure with an output parameter, you must first declare a variable that is then used in the CALL statement, as shown in the following example:

```
BEGIN
  DECLARE p_Total INT ;
  CALL NewAgeTotal ( p_Total ) ;
END ;
```

In this case, I used the same name for the variable as the name of the parameter that was defined in the procedure definition. However, the variable and parameter are not required to have the same name, although they must be defined with the same data type.

Progress Check

1. What component can you include in a procedure definition that will allow you to accept input values when you call that procedure?

2. What types of parameters are supported by SQL?

3. You create a procedure named GetCDInfo. The procedure includes one input parameter. You want to call that procedure with the value Bonnie Raitt. What SQL statement should you use to invoke the procedure?

4. What statement should you use to declare a variable?

---

1. Input parameter
2. Input, output, and input/output parameters
3. You should use the following SQL statement: CALL GetCDInfo ('Bonnie Raitt') ;
4. DECLARE statement

CRITICAL SKILL
13.7 Create SQL-Invoked Functions

Earlier in the module, in the "Understand SQL-Invoked Routines" section, I introduced you to the two types of SQL-invoked routines—procedures and functions—and I described the differences and similarities between the two. The main differences are that procedures support the definition of input and output parameters and are invoked by using the CALL statement. Functions, on the other hand, support the definition of input parameters only and are invoked as a value in an expression. The function's output is the value returned by the execution of the function, and not through the explicit definition of an output parameter.

To create a function, you must use a CREATE FUNCTION statement. The statement is similar to a CREATE PROCEDURE statement, except for a few critical differences:

● The input parameter definitions cannot include the IN keyword.

● A RETURNS clause must follow the parameter definitions. The clause assigns a data type to the value returned by the function.

● The routine body must include a RETURN statement that defines the value returned by the parameter.

NOTE
SQL Server also uses a RETURNS clause to assign a data type to the returned value, and Oracle uses a RETURN clause. In both cases this clause is followed by the AS keyword. Both SQL Server and Oracle use a RETURN statement in the routine body to define the value returned by the parameter.

A function definition can include many of the elements that have been described throughout this module. For example, you can define local variables, create compound statements, and use conditional statements. In addition, you can define and use input parameters in the same way you define and use input parameters in procedures (except that you do not use the IN keyword).

Now that you have an overview of how to create a function, let's look at an example, which is based on the InStockCDs and Performers tables, shown in Figure 13-2.

The following CREATE FUNCTION statement defines a function that returns the artist name for a specified CD, as it appears in the InStockCDs table:

```
CREATE FUNCTION CDArtist ( p_Title VARCHAR (60) )
RETURNS VARCHAR (60)
BEGIN
  RETURN
  ( SELECT ArtistName FROM InStockCDs s, Performers p
  WHERE s.Title = p.Title AND s.Title = p_Title ) ;
END ;
```

InStockCDs

Title: VARCHAR (60)	Stock: INT
Famous Blue Raincoat	13
Blue	42
Court and Spark	22
Past Light	17
Kojiki	6
That Christmas Feeling	8
Out of Africa	29
Blues on the Bayou	27
Orlando	5

Performers

Title: VARCHAR (60)	ArtistName: VARCHAR (60)
Famous Blue Raincoat	Jennifer Warnes
Blue	Joni Mitchell
Court and Spark	Joni Mitchell
Past Light	William Ackerman
Kojiki	Kitaro
That Christmas Feeling	Bing Crosby
Patsy Cline: 12 Greatest Hits	Patsy Cline
After the Rain: The Soft Sounds of Erik Satie	Pascal Roge
Out of Africa	John Barry
Leonard Cohen The Best of	Leonard Cohen
Fundamental	Bonnie Raitt
Blues on the Bayou	B.B. King
Orlando	David Motion

Figure 13-2 Using functions to retrieve values from the InStockCDs and Performers tables

In the first line of the statement, the CDArtist function and the p_Title parameter have been defined. In the next line, the RETURNS clause assigns the VARCHAR (60) data type to the value returned by the function. In the routine body, you can see that a RETURN statement has been defined. The statement includes a subquery that uses the value of the input parameter to return the name of the artist.

As you can see, defining a function is not much different from defining a procedure; however, calling the function is another matter. Instead of using the CALL statement to invoke the function, you use the function as you would any of the SQL predefined functions. (You saw some of these functions in Module 10.) For example, suppose you want to find the name of an artist based on the CD name and you want to know what other CDs that artist has made. You can create a SELECT statement similar to the one shown in the following example to retrieve the data:

```
SELECT Title, ArtistName FROM Performers
WHERE ArtistName = CDArtist ('Blue') ;
```

The CDArtist function returns the Joni Mitchell value (the artist of the *Blue* CD), which is then compared to the ArtistName values. As a result, two rows are returned by the statement, as shown in the following query results:

```
Title            ArtistName
---------------  ----------
Blue             Joni Mitchell
Court and Spark  Joni Mitchell
```

As you can see, functions help to simplify your queries by storing part of the code as a schema object (in the form of an SQL-invoked routine) and then invoking that code as necessary by calling the function as a value in your SQL statement. Functions provide you with a wide range of possibilities for returning values that make your queries less complex and more manageable.

Project 13-2 Creating SQL-Invoked Functions

Prj13.txt

In this project you will create a function named CDLabel in the Inventory database. The function will provide the name of the company that publishes a specified CD. Once you create the function, you will invoke it by using it as a value in a SELECT statement. When you are finished, you will drop that function from your database. You can download the Prj13.txt file, which contains the SQL statements used in this project.

Step by Step

1. Open the client application for your RDBMS and connect to the Inventory database.

2. You will create a function that returns the name of the company that publishes a specified CD. The function will include an input parameter that allows you to pass the name of the CD into the function. Enter and execute the following SQL statement:

```
CREATE FUNCTION CDLabel ( p_CD VARCHAR (60) )
RETURNS VARCHAR (60)
BEGIN
  RETURN
  ( SELECT CompanyName FROM CompactDiscs d, CDLabels l
  WHERE d.LabelID = l.LabelID AND CDTitle = p_CD ) ;
END ;
```

You should receive a message indicating that the CDLabel function has been created.

3. Now that the function has been created, you can use it in your SQL statements as a value in an expression. The next statement that you'll create is a SELECT statement that returns the name of the CD and the company that publishes the CD for those CDs published by the same company as the specified CD. Enter and execute the following SQL statement:

```
SELECT CDTitle, CompanyName FROM CompactDiscs d, CDLabels l
WHERE d.LabelID = l.LabelID
  AND CompanyName = CDLabel ('Blues on the Bayou') ;
```

Your query results should include a list of four CDs, all of which were published by MCA Records, the company that publishes *Blues on the Bayou*.

4. Try executing the same statement by using various names of CDs to see what sort of results are returned.

5. Now you can drop the CDLabel function from your database. Enter and execute the following SQL statement:

```
DROP FUNCTION CDLabel CASCADE ;
```

You should receive a message indicating that the CDLabel function has been dropped from the database.

6. Close the client application.

Project Summary

The project had you create a function (CDLabel) that includes one parameter (p_CD). The parameter passes the value of a CD name to the SELECT statement defined in the RETURN statement of the parameter. The statement uses this information to determine the name of the company that publishes the CD. You then used the CDLabel function in a SELECT statement to retrieve the names of all CDs that are published by the same company that published the specified CD. After that, you dropped the function from the database. Once you've completed this project, try creating other functions in the database, and then use the functions in SELECT statements to see what sort of data you can return.

✓ *Module 13 Mastery Check*

1. Which statement do you use to invoke an SQL-invoked procedure?

A. RETURN

B. CALL

C. SET

D. DECLARE

2. A(n) _____ is a value passed to a statement in a procedure when you invoke that procedure.

3. Which types of parameters can you use in an SQL-invoked function?

A. Input

B. Output

C. Input/output

D. Variable

4. What is another name for an SQL-invoked procedure?

5. What are the two primary differences between procedures and functions?

6. What information must you include in a CALL statement when invoking a procedure?

7. Which types of statements can you include in a procedure?

A. SELECT

B. INSERT

C. UPDATE

D. DELETE

8. Which statement do you use to assign an initial value to a variable?

A. DECLARE

B. RETURN

C. SET

D. CALL

9. A(n) _____ statement allows you to group SQL statements into blocks.

10. Which keyword do you use to begin a conditional statement?

A. IF

B. BEGIN

C. THEN

D. ELSE

11. What keyword do you use in a LOOP statement to end that loop?

12. What is the difference between a conditional statement and a compound statement?

13. What are two types of looping statements?

    A. BEGIN...END

    B. IF...END IF

    C. LOOP...END LOOP

    D. WHILE...END WHILE

14. Which type of parameter can return a value when you invoke a procedure?

15. What step must you take when calling a procedure that includes an output parameter?

16. How does a CREATE FUNCTION statement differ from a CREATE PROCEDURE statement?

Module 14

Creating SQL Triggers

Up to this point in the book, you have learned to create a number of schema objects that you can access or invoke by using SQL statements. For example, you learned how to create tables, views, and SQL-invoked routines. In each case, once you create these objects, you need to take some sort of action to interact directly with them, such as executing a SELECT statement to retrieve data from a table or using a CALL statement to invoke a procedure. However, SQL supports objects that perform actions automatically. These schema objects, which are known as *triggers*, respond to modifications made to data within a table. If a specified modification is made, the trigger is automatically invoked, or *fired*, causing an additional action to occur. As a result, you never have to directly invoke the trigger, only take an action that causes the invocation. In this module, we'll explore triggers and how they're used when table data is modified. We'll also look at examples of how to create the three basic types of triggers—insert, update, and delete—and how they can be defined to extend your database's functionality and help to ensure the integrity of the data.

CRITICAL SKILL
14.1 Understand SQL Triggers

If you've worked around any SQL products before, you've no doubt seen triggers implemented in one of your organization's databases, or at least heard the term tossed about. Most relational database management systems (RDBMSs) implemented triggers in their products long ago, although it wasn't until SQL:1999 that triggers were added to the standard. The result of the products preceding the standard is that trigger implementations are very proprietary among the SQL products and, as a result, support different types of functionality and are implemented in different ways. For example, SQL Server triggers are somewhat limited in scope, compared to the SQL standard, whereas Oracle triggers are more robust—and neither product implements triggers according to the specifications of the SQL standard. Despite this, there are a number of similarities among the products (such as the use of a CREATE TRIGGER statement to create a trigger), and the implementations of triggers in the various products share some basic characteristics, particularly that of being able to fire automatically to perform an action secondary to the primary action that invoked the trigger.

NOTE

The functionality supported by triggers is sometimes referred to as *active database*. In fact, this term is used to describe one of the optional packages that are included in the SQL standard. The package—PKG008—defines how triggers are implemented in SQL. (A *package* is a set of features that a product can claim conformance to in addition to Core SQL.) For more information about SQL:1999 conformance, see Module 1.

Before we get into the specifics of how to implement triggers, let's take a look at the trigger itself, which, as I said, is a schema object (in the same sense as a table or view). A trigger definition defines the characteristics of the trigger and what actions are taken when the trigger is invoked.

These actions, which are specified in one or more SQL statements (referred to as the *triggered SQL statements*), can include such events as updating tables, deleting data, invoking procedures, or performing most tasks that you can perform with SQL statements. Any limitations placed on those statements are usually the ones placed by the SQL implementation.

Triggers are invoked when you insert data into a table, update data, or delete data. By defining one or more triggers on a table, you can specify which data-modification actions will cause the trigger to fire. The trigger is never invoked unless the specified action is taken. As you can probably conclude from this, SQL supports three types of triggers: insert, update, and delete. Each type corresponds with the applicable data modification statement. For example, an insert trigger is fired when the INSERT statement is executed against the specified table.

Although a trigger is a schema object, separate from table objects, it can be associated with only one table, which you specify when you create your trigger definition. When the applicable data modification statement is invoked against that table, the trigger fires, but it will not fire if a similar statement is invoked against a different table or if a statement other than the specified type is invoked against the same table. In this sense, a trigger can be thought of as a table object, despite the fact that it is created at the schema level.

Trigger Execution Context

Before we move on to discussing how a trigger is created, I want to touch on the subject of how triggers are executed, with regard to the *trigger execution context,* a type of SQL execution context. You can think of an *execution context* as a space created in memory that holds a statement process during the execution of that statement. SQL supports several types of execution contexts, triggers being one of them.

A trigger execution context is created each time a trigger is invoked. If multiple triggers are invoked, an execution context is created for each one. However, only one execution context can be active in a session at any one time. This is important when a trigger in one table causes a trigger in a second table to be fired. Let's take a look at Figure 14-1 to help illustrate this point.

Notice that the figure contains three tables. An update trigger is defined on Table 1, and an insert trigger is defined on Table 2. When an UPDATE statement is executed against Table 1, the update trigger fires, creating a trigger execution context that becomes active. However, the update trigger, which is defined to insert data into Table 2, invokes the insert trigger on Table 2 when the first trigger attempts to insert data into that table. As a result, a second execution context is created, which becomes the active one. When the second trigger execution has completed, the second execution context is destroyed, and the first execution context becomes active once more. When the first trigger execution has completed, the first trigger execution context is destroyed.

A trigger execution context contains the information necessary for the trigger to be executed correctly. This information includes details about the trigger itself and the table on which the trigger was defined, which is referred to as the subject table. In addition, the execution context includes one or two transition tables, as shown in Figure 14-1. The transition tables are virtual tables that hold data that is updated in, inserted into, or deleted from the subject table. If data is

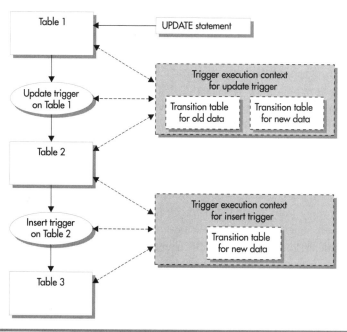

Figure 14-1 Trigger execution contexts for two triggers

updated, then two transition tables are created, one for the old data and one for the new data. If data is inserted, one transition table is created for the new data. If data is deleted, one transition table is created for the old data. The transition tables and some of the other information in the trigger execution context are used by the SQL statements that perform the triggered action. You'll learn more about how this information is used in the following section, when we look at the CREATE TRIGGER syntax.

Progress Check

1. What is a trigger?
2. What are the three types of triggers?
3. How many tables can a trigger be associated with?
4. What is a trigger execution process?

---

1. A trigger is a schema object that is invoked automatically when a specified data modification is made. Once invoked, the trigger takes a predefined action, which is specified in one or more SQL statements.

2. Insert, update, and delete

3. Only one

4. A trigger execution context is a space created in memory that holds a trigger process during the execution of that trigger.

CRITICAL SKILL
14.2 Create SQL Triggers

Now that you have a general overview of triggers, let's take a look at the syntax you use to create them. Most of the syntax is concerned with defining the characteristics of the trigger, such as the name of the trigger and the type. Only at the end of the statement do you define the triggered SQL statements that specify the actions taken by the trigger when it is invoked.

The basic syntax for creating a trigger definition is as follows:

```
CREATE TRIGGER <trigger name>
{ BEFORE | AFTER }
{ INSERT | DELETE | UPDATE [ OF <column list> ] }
ON <table name> [ REFERENCING <alias options> ]
[ FOR EACH { ROW | STATEMENT } ]
[ WHEN ( <search condition> ) ]
<triggered SQL statements>
```

Now let's take a look at each line of the syntax. The first line is fairly straightforward. You simply provide a name for the trigger following the CREATE TRIGGER keywords. In the second line, you must designate whether the trigger is invoked before or after the data modification statement is applied to the subject table. For example, if you're defining an insert trigger, you can specify whether the triggered SQL statements are executed before the data is inserted into the subject table (by using the BEFORE keyword) or after the data is inserted into the subject table (by using the AFTER keyword). This feature is particularly useful when one of the tables is configured with a referential integrity constraint and cannot contain data before that data exists in the other table. (For information about referential integrity, see Module 4.) Depending on the nature of the triggered action that is defined, it may not matter whether you designate BEFORE or AFTER because the triggered action may have no direct relation to the data modified in the subject table.

In the third line of syntax, you specify whether the trigger is an insert, delete, or update trigger. If it is an update trigger, you have the option of applying the trigger to one or more specific columns. If more than one column is specified, you must separate the column names with commas. In the next line of syntax, you must specify an ON clause that includes the name of the subject table. This is the table on which the trigger is applied. The trigger can be applied to only one table.

Up to this point, all the syntax we've looked at is required, except for specifying column names in update trigger definitions, which is optional. However, the next several clauses are not mandatory, but they add important capabilities to your trigger. The first of these clauses is the REFERENCING clause. This clause allows you to specify how data that is held in the trigger execution context is referenced within the WHEN clause or the triggered SQL statements. We'll look at the REFERENCING clause in more detail in the following section, "Referencing Old and New Values."

The next line of syntax contains the FOR EACH clause, which includes two options: ROW or STATEMENT. If you specify ROW, the trigger is invoked each time a row is inserted, updated, or deleted. If you specify STATEMENT, the trigger is invoked only one time for each applicable data modification statement that is executed, no matter how many rows are affected. If you do not include this clause in your trigger definition, the STATEMENT option is assumed, and the trigger fires only once for each statement.

Next in the syntax is the optional WHEN clause. The WHEN clause allows you to define a search condition that limits the scope of when the trigger is invoked. The WHEN clause is similar to the WHERE clause of a SELECT statement. You specify one or more predicates that define a search condition. If the WHEN clause evaluates to true, the trigger fires; otherwise, no trigger action is taken. However, this doesn't affect the initial data modification statement that was executed against the subject table; only the triggered SQL statements defined in the trigger definition are affected.

Finally, the last component that your CREATE TRIGGER statement must include is one or more SQL statements that are executed when the trigger is invoked and, if a WHEN clause is included, that clause evaluates to true. If the trigger definition includes more than one triggered SQL statement, those statements must be enclosed in a BEGIN...END block, like those you saw in Module 13. However, there is one difference from what you saw before. When used in a trigger definition, the BEGIN keyword must be followed by the ATOMIC keyword to notify the SQL implementation that the statements within the block must be handled as a unit. In other words, either all the statements must be executed successfully, or none of the results of any statement executions can persist. Without the ATOMIC keyword, it would be possible for some statements to be executed while others fail to be executed.

NOTE

Many implementations do not support the use of the ATOMIC keyword in the BEGIN...END block of the triggered SQL statements. This includes both SQL Server and Oracle.

Aside from the issue of the ATOMIC keyword, the triggered SQL statements, including the BEGIN...END block, can consist of almost any SQL statements, depending on the limitations of your SQL implementation. Be sure to check the product documentation to determine what limitations might be placed on the triggered SQL statements and how triggers are generally created and implemented.

Referencing Old and New Values

Now let's return to the REFERENCING clause of the CREATE TRIGGER statement. The purpose of this clause is to allow you to define correlation names for the rows stored in the transition tables or for the transition tables as a whole. As you'll recall from the "Understand SQL Triggers" section earlier in this module, the transition tables hold the data that has been updated, inserted, or deleted in the subject table. The correlation names, or aliases, can then be used in the triggered SQL statements to refer back to the data that is being held in the transition tables. This can be particularly handy when trying to modify data in a second table based on the data modified in the subject table. (This will be made clearer when we look at examples later in the module.)

If you refer back to the syntax in the previous section, you'll notice that the optional REFERENCING clause includes the <alias options> placeholder. SQL supports four options for this clause:

- REFERENCING OLD [ROW] [AS] <alias>

- REFERENCING NEW [ROW] [AS] <alias>

- REFERENCING OLD TABLE [AS] <alias>

- REFERENCING NEW TABLE [AS] <alias>

Notice that, in the first two options, the ROW keyword is not mandatory. If you don't specify ROW, it is assumed. Notice too that the AS keyword is optional in all cases. However, for the purposes of maintaining clear, self-referencing code, I recommend that you use the complete option whenever you include it in a trigger definition.

Depending on the type of trigger (update, insert, or delete) and the FOR EACH option (ROW or STATEMENT), you can include up to four REFERENCING options in your trigger definition, one of each type. However, you cannot include more than one of any single type. For example, you cannot include two OLD ROW options in your trigger definition. When adding REFERENCING options to your trigger definition, you must follow these guidelines:

- You cannot use the NEW ROW and NEW TABLE options for delete triggers because no new data is created.

- You cannot use the OLD ROW and OLD TABLE options for insert triggers because no old data exists.

- You can use all four options in an update trigger because there is old data and new data when you update a table.

- You can use the OLD ROW and NEW ROW options only when you specify the FOR EACH ROW clause in the trigger definition.

Once you define your REFERENCING clauses and assign the appropriate aliases, you're ready to use those aliases in your triggered SQL statements, in the same way you used correlation names in your SELECT statements.

Dropping SQL Triggers

Although the SQL standard does not support any sort of statement that allows you to alter a trigger, it does support a way to delete a trigger, which you achieve by using the DROP TRIGGER statement. As you can see in the following syntax, this statement is quite basic:

DROP TRIGGER <name>

All you need to do is provide the name of the trigger, along with the DROP TRIGGER keywords. Because no other objects are dependent on the trigger, you do not need to specify any additional keywords, such as CASCADE or RESTRICT. When you execute the DROP TRIGGER statement, the trigger definition is deleted from the schema.

Progress Check

1. What keywords can you use to designate whether the triggered SQL statements are executed before or after the data modification statement is applied to the subject table?

2. Which type of trigger allows you to specify the column names of the subject table?

3. Which REFERENCING clause option allows you to define an alias for an old row of data?

4. Which statement can you use to delete a trigger from the schema?

CRITICAL SKILL
14.3 Create Insert Triggers

So far in this module, I've provided you with background information about triggers and the syntax used to create triggers. Now we'll look at examples of how triggers are created and what happens when they're invoked. We'll begin with the insert trigger, which, as you know, is invoked when an INSERT statement is executed against the subject table (the table on which the trigger has been defined). In the first example, we'll create a trigger on the RetailInventory table (subject table), shown in Figure 14-2. The trigger, when invoked, will insert data into the InventoryLog table.

---

1. BEFORE or AFTER
2. Update trigger
3. REFERENCING OLD [ROW] [AS] <alias>
4. DROP TRIGGER statement

RetailInventory

CDName: VARCHAR (60)	RPrice: NUMERIC (5,2)	Amount: INT
Famous Blue Raincoat	16.99	5
Blue	14.99	10
Court and Spark	14.99	12
Past Light	15.99	11
Kojiki	15.99	4
That Christmas Feeling	10.99	8
Patsy Cline: 12 Greatest Hits	16.99	14

InventoryLog

ActionType: CHAR (6)	DateModified: TIMESTAMP
INSERT	2002-12-22 10:58:05.120
UPDATE	2002-12-22 12:02:05.033
UPDATE	2002-12-22 16:15:22.930
DELETE	2002-12-23 11:29:14.223
INSERT	2002-12-23 13:32:45.547
INSERT	2002-12-23 15:51:15.730
UPDATE	2002-12-23 17:01:32.270
UPDATE	2002-12-24 10:46:35.123
DELETE	2002-12-24 12:19:13.843
UPDATE	2002-12-24 14:15:09.673

Figure 14-2 Creating an insert trigger on the RetailInventory table

The following CREATE TRIGGER statement defines an INSERT trigger that fires after the data is inserted into the subject table:

```
CREATE TRIGGER InsertLog
AFTER INSERT ON RetailInventory
FOR EACH ROW
BEGIN ATOMIC
  INSERT INTO InventoryLog (ActionType)
  VALUES ('INSERT') ;
END ;
```

NOTE

As I mentioned at the beginning of the module, SQL implementations can vary widely with regard to the semantics of the CREATE TRIGGER statement. For example, SQL Server does not allow you to specify a FOR EACH clause, nor does it support the use of the ATOMIC keyword in the BEGIN...END statement. On the other hand, the basic Oracle trigger definition is a lot closer to the SQL standard, although Oracle also does not support the use of the ATOMIC keyword in a trigger definition.

Let's take a look at this statement one element at a time. In the first line, the CREATE TRIGGER clause defines a trigger named InsertLog. In the next line, the AFTER keyword is used to specify that the triggered SQL statements will be executed *after* the data has been inserted into the subject table. The AFTER keyword is followed by the INSERT keyword, which defines the trigger as an insert trigger. Next comes the ON clause, which specifies the name of the subject table. In this case, the subject table is RetailInventory.

As we move through the statement, we come to the FOR EACH clause, which specifies the ROW keyword. This clause, when used with ROW, indicates that the trigger will be invoked for each row that is inserted into the table, rather than for each INSERT statement that is executed against the table. Following the FOR EACH clause are the triggered SQL statements.

The triggered SQL statements include a BEGIN...END statement and an INSERT statement. I did not need to include the BEGIN...END statement in the trigger definition because, without it, there is only one triggered SQL statement. However, I wanted to demonstrate how the block would be used had there been more than one statement. Notice that the block includes the ATOMIC keyword following the BEGIN keyword. According to the SQL standard, ATOMIC is required, although it will depend on your SQL implementation whether the keyword is supported.

The BEGIN...END block encloses an INSERT statement that adds data to the InventoryLog table when the trigger is invoked. Each time a row is inserted into the RetailInventory table, a row is inserted into the InventoryLog table. The InventoryLog row will contain the INSERT value for the ActionType column. A timestamp value is then added automatically to the DateModified column, which is defined with the default CURRENT_TIMESTAMP.

You can, if you want, create other triggers on the RetailInventory table. For example, you might want to create update and delete triggers that insert rows into the InventoryLog table when the applicable data modifications are made. In that case, you would simply create a trigger definition for each additional trigger that you need.

NOTE

The SQL standard does not place a limit on the number of triggers that can be defined on any one table; however, SQL implementations can have many restrictions, so check the product documentation. In addition to these limitations, various implementations might support different ways in which multiple triggers can be implemented. For example, SQL Server allows you to define an insert, update, and delete trigger in one statement.

Now let's take a look at what happens when you insert a row into the RetailInventory table. Suppose you want to insert information on the *Fundamental* CD. You would create an INSERT statement as you would normally do, as shown in the following example:

```
INSERT INTO RetailInventory
VALUES ( 'Fundamental', 15.99, 18 ) ;
```

If you were to execute the statement, the rows would be inserted into the RetailInventory table. To verify this, you can execute the following SELECT statement:

```
SELECT * FROM RetailInventory ;
```

The SELECT statement will return the same rows shown in the RetailInventory table in Figure 14-2, plus an additional row for the *Fundamental* CD, exactly as you would expect. The trigger has no effect on the data modifications you make to the RetailInventory table. However, as you'll recall from the trigger definition that was defined on the RetailInventory table, the triggered SQL statements should insert data into the InventoryLog table when the trigger is invoked, which should occur when you inserted a row into the RetailInventory table. To verify this, you can execute the following SELECT statement:

```
SELECT * FROM InventoryLog ;
```

The query results should include not only the rows shown in the InventoryLog table in Figure 14-2, but also an additional row that includes an ActionType value of INSERT and a DateModified value for the current date and time. Each time a row is inserted into the RetailInventory table, a row is inserted in the InventoryLog table. You could have defined your triggered SQL statements to take any sort of action, not just log events in a log table. Depending on your needs and the database in which you work, you have a great many possibilities for the type of actions that your triggers will support.

CRITICAL SKILL
14.4 Create Update Triggers

Now that you've seen an example of an insert trigger, let's take a look at a couple of update triggers. The update trigger is invoked when an UPDATE statement is executed against the subject table. As with any other type of trigger, when the trigger is invoked, the triggered SQL statements are executed and an action is taken. To illustrate how the update trigger works, we'll use the TitlesInStock and TitleCosts tables shown in Figure 14-3.

The first example that we'll look at is created on the TitlesInStock table and includes triggered SQL statements that update the TitleCosts table, as shown in the following CREATE TRIGGER statement:

```
CREATE TRIGGER UpdateTitleCosts
AFTER UPDATE ON TitlesInStock
REFERENCING NEW ROW AS New
FOR EACH ROW
```

```
BEGIN ATOMIC
  UPDATE TitleCosts c
  SET Retail = Retail * .9
  WHERE c.CDTitle = New.CDTitle ;
END ;
```

As you can see, this trigger definition is similar in many ways to the insert trigger we looked at in the preceding example. The update trigger definition includes the name of the trigger (UpdateTitleCosts) and specifies the AFTER and UPDATE conditions. The ON clause then follows the UPDATE keyword and provides the name of the target table. Following all this is a line of code we did not see in the preceding example—a REFERENCING clause.

The REFERENCING clause uses the NEW ROW option to define a correlation name for the row that has been updated in the TitlesInStock table. However, the REFERENCING clause, and subsequently the search condition or triggered SQL statements that might refer to the alias defined in this clause, are not directly referencing the TitlesInStock table. Instead, they're referencing the transition table for new data in the trigger execution context. In other words, the correlation name defined in the REFERENCING clause references the updated row that is copied to the transition table. In this case, the correlation name is New. As a result, the New correlation name can be used in the search condition in the WHEN clause or in the triggered SQL statements to refer back to the data in the transition table.

Once you've defined the correlation name in the REFERENCING clause, you must use it to qualify the column names of the modified row when they are referenced in the WHEN clause or in the triggered SQL statements. In the CREATE TRIGGER statement in the preceding example, you can see that the alias is used in the WHERE clause of the UPDATE statement. Notice that the word New precedes the column name and that the two are separated

TitlesInStock

CDTitle: VARCHAR (60)	CDType: CHAR (20)	Inventory: INT
Famous Blue Raincoat	Folk	12
Blue	Popular	24
Past Light	New Age	9
Blues on the Bayou	Blues	19
Luck of the Draw	Popular	25
Deuces Wild	Blues	17
Nick of Time	Popular	11

TitleCosts

CDTitle: VARCHAR (60)	Wholesale: NUMERIC (5,2)	Retail: NUMERIC (5,2)
Famous Blue Raincoat	8.00	16.99
Blue	7.50	15.99
Past Light	6.00	14.99
Blues on the Bayou	7.25	15.99
Luck of the Drive	7.50	15.99
Deuces Wild	7.45	14.99
Nick of Time	6.95	14.99

Figure 14-3 Creating an update trigger on the TitlesInStock table

by a period. This is typical of how you would qualify a name. It is similar to the way in which you use the qualified name c.CDTitle for the CDTitle column in the TitleCosts table. If you had specified a different NEW ROW correlation name or used the name in the WHEN clause or in another part of the triggered SQL statement, you would still qualify the name of the column with the alias that references the rows in the transition table or the table itself.

NOTE

SQL Server does not support the REFERENCING clause. However, it supports similar functionality by automatically assigning the names Inserted and Deleted to the transition tables (Inserted for new data and Deleted for old data). In addition, there are some cases in which you must declare a variable to use values from the Inserted and Deleted tables, rather than qualifying column names, as you do in the SQL standard. Oracle, on the other hand, does support the REFERENCING clause, but it also automatically assigns the names New and Old to the transition tables, which you can use in the WHEN clause and triggered SQL statements without specifying a REFERENCING clause. When you do use the aliases in the triggered SQL statements of an Oracle trigger definition, you must precede the alias name with a colon, as in :New. This is not the case for the WHEN clause, in which the alias name is used without the colon. Also, you cannot use the keyword ROW in the REFERENCING clause of an ORACLE trigger definition.

In addition to the REFERENCING clause, the CREATE TRIGGER statement also includes a FOR EACH clause, which specifies the ROW option. Also notice that the triggered SQL statements include a BEGIN...END statement, which encloses an UPDATE statement. As you can see, the UPDATE statement modifies the Retail value in the TitleCosts table for the CD that was updated in the TitlesInStock table.

Now let's take a look at what happens when you update the TitlesInStock column. The following UPDATE statement changes the Inventory value for the Famous Blue Raincoat row:

```
UPDATE TitlesInStock
SET Inventory = 30
WHERE CDTitle = 'Famous Blue Raincoat' ;
```

When the UPDATE statement is executed, the UpdateTitleCosts trigger is invoked, causing the TitleCosts table to be updated. As a result, not only is the Inventory value in the TitlesInStock table changed to 30, but the Retail value in the TitleCosts table is reduced to 15.29 (Retail * .9). Any time you update the TitlesInStock table, the corresponding row or rows in the TitleCosts table will be reduced by 10 percent.

You might find that you want to limit when the triggered SQL statements are executed. For example, you might want to reduce the price of CDs only when the inventory exceeds a certain amount. As a result you decide to change your trigger definition to include a WHEN clause that defines the necessary search condition. However, as I said earlier, SQL does not support an ALTER TRIGGER statement, so you would need to first delete the trigger from the database. The way to do that is to use the following DROP TRIGGER statement:

```
DROP TRIGGER UpdateTitleCosts ;
```

When you execute this statement, the trigger definition is removed from the schema and you can now re-create the trigger with the necessary modifications. The following example again creates the UpdateTitleCosts trigger, but this time a WHEN clause has been added to the statement:

```
CREATE TRIGGER UpdateTitleCosts
AFTER UPDATE ON TitlesInStock
REFERENCING NEW ROW AS New
FOR EACH ROW
WHEN ( New.Inventory > 20 )
BEGIN ATOMIC
  UPDATE TitleCosts c
  SET RETAIL = Retail * .9
  WHERE c.CDTitle = New.CDTitle ;
END ;
```

As you can see, the WHEN clause specifies that the Inventory value must be greater than 20; otherwise, the triggered SQL statements will not be invoked. Notice that the Inventory column name is qualified with the New correlation name in the same way that the CDTitle column name is qualified in the WHERE clause of the UPDATE statement. As a result, the WHEN clause will reference the transition table for new data in the trigger execution context when comparing values.

Now let's take a look at what happens when you update the TitlesInStock table. The following UPDATE statement changes the Inventory value for the Past Light row:

```
UPDATE TitlesInStock
SET Inventory = 25
WHERE CDTitle = 'Past Light' ;
```

As you would expect, the Inventory value in the TitlesInStock column is changed to 25. In addition, because the condition specified in the WHEN clause is met (New.Inventory > 20), the triggered SQL statements are executed and the TitleCosts table is updated. If you were to query the TitleCosts table, you would see that the Retail value for the Past Light row has been changed to 13.49.

Now let's take a look at an UPDATE statement that sets the Inventory value to an amount less than 20:

```
UPDATE TitlesInStock
SET Inventory = 10
WHERE CDTitle = 'Past Light' ;
```

Ask the Expert

Q: When describing trigger execution contexts, you discussed how one trigger can cause another trigger to be invoked. Is there a point at which multiple triggers can become a problem if too many are invoked?

A: Problems can arise when multiple triggers are invoked and they cause a cascading effect from one table to the next. For example, an attempt to update one table might invoke a trigger that updates another table. That update, in turn, invokes another trigger that modifies data in yet another table. This process can continue on as one trigger after the next is invoked, creating undesirable results and unplanned data modifications. The condition can be made even worse if a loop is created in which a trigger causes a data modification on a table for which another trigger has fired. For example, a data modification on one table might invoke a trigger that causes a second modification. That modification invokes another trigger, which in turn invokes another trigger, which invokes yet another trigger. The last trigger might then modify data in the original table, causing the first trigger to fire again, repeating the process over and over until the system fails or an implementation-specific process ends the loop. The best way to prevent unwanted modifications or trigger loops is through careful planning in the database design. Triggers should not be implemented unless you're sure of their impact. In addition to careful planning, you should look to the SQL implementation to determine what sorts of safety nets might be in place to prevent trigger looping or unwanted cascading. For example, some implementations allow you to control whether cascading triggers are allowed, and some limit the number of cascading triggers that can fire. Make sure that you read your product's documentation before creating multiple triggers in your database.

Q: Earlier, you mentioned that SQL allows you to define multiple triggers on a table. How are triggers processed if multiple triggers are invoked?

A: In SQL, processing of multiple triggers is a concern only if the triggers are defined to fire at the same time (BEFORE or AFTER) and if they're the same type of trigger (INSERT, UPDATE, or DELETE). For example, a multiple trigger scenario would exist if two or more triggers are defined (on the same table) with the AFTER UPDATE keywords. If this condition exists, then the triggers are invoked in the order in which they were defined. Let's take a look at an example to show you what I mean. If you create Trigger1 and then create Trigger2 and then create Trigger3, Trigger1 is invoked first, then Trigger2, and then Trigger3. The problem with this is that SQL does not define any way in which you can change that order. For example, if you decide that you

(continued)

want Trigger3 invoked before Trigger1, your only option—based on the SQL standard—is to delete Trigger1 and Trigger2 from the schema and then re-create the triggers in the order you want them invoked. Because you did not delete Trigger3, it will move into the top spot and be the first to be invoked because it will then be seen as the first to have been created.

This statement will still update the Inventory value in the TitlesInStock table, but it will not cause the triggered SQL statements to be executed because the search condition in the WHEN clause is not met. As a result, no changes are made to the TitleCosts table, although the TitlesInStock table is still updated.

CRITICAL SKILL
14.5 Create Delete Triggers

The final type of trigger that we'll look at is the delete trigger. As you would expect, the delete trigger is invoked when a DELETE statement is executed against the subject table, and as with other triggers, the triggered SQL statements are executed and an action is taken. Now let's take a look at an example that uses the CDStock table and CDOut table, as shown in Figure 14-4.

Suppose you want to create a trigger on the CDStock table. You want the trigger to insert the deleted values into the CDOut table. The following CREATE TRIGGER statement uses a REFERENCING clause to allow the triggered SQL statement to know which data to insert into the CDOut table:

```
CREATE TRIGGER InsertCDout
AFTER DELETE ON CDStock
REFERENCING OLD ROW AS Old
FOR EACH ROW
   INSERT INTO CDOut
   VALUES ( Old.CDName, Old.CDType ) ;
```

In this statement, you are creating a trigger named InsertCDOut. The statement is defined with the AFTER DELETE keywords, meaning that the old values are inserted into the CDOut table after they have been deleted from the CDStock table. The ON clause identifies the CDStock table as the subject table.

Following the ON clause is the REFERENCING clause. The REFERENCING clause uses the OLD ROW option to assign a correlation name of Old. Remember that you can use only the OLD ROW and OLD TABLE options in the REFERENCING clause of a delete trigger definition. This is because there is no new data, only the old data that's being deleted.

The FOR EACH clause follows the REFERENCING clause. The FOR EACH clause uses the ROW option. As a result, a row will be inserted into the CDOut table for each row deleted from the CDStock table.

CDStock

CDName: VARCHAR (60)	CDType: CHAR (4)	InStock: INT
Famous Blue Raincoat	FROK	19
Blue	CPOP	28
Past Light	NEWA	6
Out of Africa	STRK	8
Fundamental	NPOP	10
Blues on the Bayou	BLUS	11

CDOut

CDName: VARCHAR (60)	CDType: CHAR (4)
Court and Spark	FROK
Kojiki	NEWA
That Christmas Feeling	XMAS
Patsy Cline: 12 Greatest Hits	CTRY
Leonard Cohen The Best of	FROK
Orlando	STRK

Figure 14-4 Creating a delete trigger on the CDStock table

Next comes the triggered SQL statement. Notice that in this example, a BEGIN...END statement is not used. Because there is only one triggered statement, you do not have to use the BEGIN...END block. The triggered statement in this case is an INSERT statement that specifies two values, each of which is based on the values deleted from the CDStock table. The Old alias is used to qualify each column name. As a result, the deleted values can be inserted directly into the CDOut table.

Now let's take a look at an example of what happens when you delete a row from the CDStock table. The following DELETE statement deletes the Past Light row from the table:

```
DELETE CDStock
WHERE CDName = 'Past Light' ;
```

Once you execute this statement, the row is deleted and the trigger is invoked. The row is then inserted into the CDOut table. You can verify the deletion by using the following SELECT statement to view the contents of the CDStock table:

```
SELECT * FROM CDStock ;
```

The query results from this statement should no longer include the Past Light row. However, if you execute the following SELECT statement, you'll see that a row has been inserted into the CDOut table:

```
SELECT * FROM CDOut ;
```

Each time a row is deleted from the CDStock table, two values from that row will be inserted into the CDOut table. As with other trigger definitions, you could have included a

WHEN clause in your CREATE TRIGGER statement so that the triggered SQL statements are executed only when the search condition specified in the WHEN clause evaluates to true. Otherwise, the statements are not executed. The row will still be deleted from the CDStock table, but nothing will be inserted into the CDOut table.

Project 14-1   Creating SQL Triggers

`Prj14.txt`

Throughout this module, we have looked at how to create the three basic types of triggers—insert, update, and delete triggers. You will now create your own triggers (one of each of the three types) in the Inventory database. The triggers will be defined to log data modification activity that occurs in the Artists table. Whenever data is modified in the Artists table, a row will be inserted into a log table, which you will create. The log table will record the type of action taken (insert, update, delete), the ArtistID value for the modified row, and a timestamp of when the row was inserted into the table. As a result, whenever you execute an INSERT, UPDATE, or DELETE statement against the Artists table, a row will be inserted into the new table for each row that is modified. As with other projects in this book (particularly Module 13, when you created stored procedures), you should refer to the documentation for your SQL implementation when creating triggers to make certain you follow that product's standards. There are a lot of variations among the SQL implementations. You can download the Prj14.txt file, which contains the SQL statements used in this project.

Step by Step

1. Open the client application for your RDBMS and connect to the Inventory database.

2. Before you create the actual triggers on the Artists table, you must create a table that will log the data modifications you make to the Artists table. The log table, named ArtistLog, will include three columns to record data modification events. One of the columns will be configured with a default value that records the current date and time. Enter and execute the following SQL statement:

```
CREATE TABLE ArtistLog
( ActionType CHAR (6), ArtistID INT,
    ModDate TIMESTAMP DEFAULT CURRENT_TIMESTAMP ) ;
```

You should receive a message indicating that the table was successfully created.

3. Now you will create an insert trigger on the Artists table. The trigger definition will include a REFERENCING clause that specifies a correlation name (New) for the new row that is inserted into the Artists table. That correlation name will then be used in the triggered SQL statement as a value inserted into the ArtistLog table. Enter and execute the following SQL statement:

```
CREATE TRIGGER InsertLog
AFTER INSERT ON Artists
REFERENCING NEW ROW AS New
FOR EACH ROW
BEGIN ATOMIC
   INSERT INTO ArtistLog ( ActionType, ArtistID )
   VALUES ( 'INSERT', New.ArtistID ) ;
END ;
```

You should receive a message indicating that the trigger was successfully created.

4. Next you will create an update trigger. This trigger definition is similar to the one in Step 3, except that you are specifying that it is an update trigger. Enter and execute the following SQL statement:

```
CREATE TRIGGER UpdateLog
AFTER UPDATE ON Artists
REFERENCING NEW ROW AS New
FOR EACH ROW
BEGIN ATOMIC
   INSERT INTO ArtistLog ( ActionType, ArtistID )
   VALUES ( 'UPDATE', New.ArtistID ) ;
END ;
```

You should receive a message indicating that the trigger was successfully created.

5. Now you will create a delete trigger. This trigger definition is a little different than the last two triggers because the REFERENCING clause specifies a correlation name for the old values, rather than the new. This is because new values are not created when you delete data from a table. The correlation name (Old) is then used in the VALUES clause of the INSERT statement. Enter and execute the following SQL statement:

```
CREATE TRIGGER DeleteLog
AFTER DELETE ON Artists
REFERENCING OLD ROW AS Old
FOR EACH ROW
BEGIN ATOMIC
   INSERT INTO ArtistLog ( ActionType, ArtistID )
   VALUES ( 'DELETE', Old.ArtistID ) ;
END ;
```

You should receive a message indicating that the trigger was successfully created.

6. Now you can begin to test the triggers that you created. The first step is to insert data into the Artists table. In this statement, values are specified for the ArtistID column and the

(continued)

ArtistName column, but not the PlaceOfBirth column. As a result, the default value of Unknown will be inserted in that column. Enter and execute the following SQL statement:

```
INSERT INTO Artists ( ArtistID, ArtistName )
VALUES ( 2019, 'John Lee Hooker' ) ;
```

You should receive a message indicating that the row was successfully inserted into the Artists table.

7. Now you will update the row that you just inserted by providing a value for the PlaceOfBirth column. Enter and execute the following SQL statement:

```
UPDATE Artists
SET PlaceOfBirth = 'Clarksdale, Mississippi, USA'
WHERE ArtistID = 2019 ;
```

You should receive a message indicating that the row was successfully updated into the Artists table.

8. Your next step is to delete the row that you just created. Enter and execute the following SQL statement:

```
DELETE Artists
WHERE ArtistID = 2019 ;
```

You should receive a message indicating that the row was successfully deleted from the Artists table.

9. Now that you've modified data in the Artists table, you will look at the ArtistLog table to verify that rows have been entered into the table to record your data modifications of the Artists table. Enter and execute the following SQL statement:

```
SELECT * FROM ArtistLog ;
```

Your query results should include three rows, one for each action type (INSERT, UPDATE, and DELETE). The rows should all have the same ArtistID value (2019) and include the current dates and times.

10. Your next step will be to drop the triggers from the database. The first trigger that you'll drop is the insert trigger. Enter and execute the following SQL statement:

```
DROP TRIGGER InsertLog ;
```

You should receive a message indicating that the trigger was successfully dropped from your database.

11. Next you will drop the update trigger. Enter and execute the following SQL statement:

```
DROP TRIGGER UpdateLog ;
```

You should receive a message indicating that the trigger was successfully dropped from the database.

12. Now drop the delete trigger. Enter and execute the following SQL statement:

```
DROP TRIGGER DeleteLog ;
```

You should receive a message indicating that the trigger was successfully dropped from the database.

13. Finally, you will drop the ArtistLog table that you created in Step 2. Enter and execute the following SQL statement:

```
DROP TABLE ArtistLog ;
```

You should receive a message indicating that the table was successfully dropped from the database.

14. Close the client application.

Project Summary

In this project, you created the ArtistLog table, which was set up to store information about data modifications to the Artists table. Next you created three triggers on the Artists table—an insert trigger, an update trigger, and a delete trigger. All three triggers used REFERENCING clauses to allow you to pass the ArtistID value of the modified row to the ArtistLog table. After the triggers were created, you inserted, updated, and deleted data in the Artists table to test the triggers. You then viewed the contents of the ArtistLog table to verify that the data modifications had been properly recorded. After that, you dropped the three triggers and the ArtistLog table. By the time you completed the project, the Inventory database should have been returned to the same state it was in when you began.

✓

Module 14 Mastery Check

1. What type of actions can be performed by the triggered SQL statements?

2. Which actions can invoke a trigger?

   A. Updating data

   B. Querying data

   C. Deleting data

   D. Inserting data

3. When is an insert trigger invoked?

4. A trigger can be defined on how many tables?

   A. Only one

   B. One or more

   C. One to three

   D. Any number of tables

5. A(n) _____ is a space created in memory that holds a trigger process during the execution of that trigger.

6. You insert data into Table 1, which invokes an insert trigger defined on that table. The trigger updates information in Table 2, which invokes an update trigger defined on that table. The update trigger deletes information in Table 3, which invokes a delete trigger defined on that table. Which trigger execution context is active at this point?

   A. The trigger execution context for the insert trigger

   B. The trigger execution context for the update trigger

   C. The trigger execution context for the delete trigger

7. If three triggers are invoked during a session, how many trigger execution contexts are created in that session?

8. What information is included in a trigger execution context?

9. In which clause of the CREATE TRIGGER statement do you assign correlation names to old and new data?

   A. FOR EACH

   B. ON

   C. REFERENCING

   D. WHEN

10. In which clause of the CREATE TRIGGER statement do you specify whether the triggered SQL statements are executed once for each row or once for each statement?

   A. FOR EACH

   B. ON

   C. REFERENCING

   D. WHEN

11. You're creating a trigger definition for an insert trigger. Which REFERENCING clauses can you include in your CREATE TRIGGER statement?

   A. REFERENCING OLD ROW AS Old

   B. REFERENCING NEW ROW AS New

   C. REFERENCING OLD TABLE AS Old

   D. REFERENCING NEW TABLE AS New

12. A(n) _____ trigger allows you to specify the column names of a subject table.

13. You're creating an update trigger on the CDInventory table. The table includes a column named InStock. You want the triggered SQL statements to be executed only when the InStock value of the updated row exceeds 20. Which clause should you include in your CREATE TRIGGER statement to restrict when the statements are executed?

   A. WHERE

   B. HAVING

   C. FOR EACH

   D. WHEN

14. What statement must you include in your CREATE TRIGGER statement if the trigger definition includes more than one triggered SQL statement?

15. What SQL statement do you use to alter a trigger definition?

Module 15

Using SQL Cursors

A s we have looked at different aspects of SQL throughout this book, we have used direct invocation to create and access various data objects. *Direct invocation,* or *interactive SQL,* is a type of data access method that supports the ad hoc execution of SQL statements, usually through some sort of client application. For example, you can use SQL Server Query Analyzer or Oracle SQL*Plus Worksheet to interact directly with your SQL database. However, direct invocation generally represents only a small percentage of users. A far more common method used to access SQL databases is *embedded SQL,* a data access model in which SQL statements are embedded in an application programming language, such as C and COBOL. To support embedded SQL, the SQL standard allows you to declare cursors that act as pointers to specific rows of data in your query results. This module explains why cursors are used and how cursors can be declared, opened, and closed within an SQL session. You'll also learn how to retrieve data from within the cursor so that your programming language can work with SQL data in a format that the application can process.

Understand SQL Cursors

One of the defining characteristics of SQL is the fact that data in an SQL database is managed in sets. In fact, query results returned by SELECT statements are often referred to as *result sets.* These result sets are each made up of one or more rows extracted from one or more tables.

When working with SQL data interactively, having data returned in sets rarely presents a problem because you can normally scroll through the query results to find the information you need. If the size of the results is too great to easily filter through, you can narrow the focus of your query expression to return a more manageable result set. However, most data access is through means other than direct invocation (despite the fact that we access data interactively throughout the book). One of the most common methods, embedded SQL, accesses data through embedded SQL statements. The data elements returned by the SQL statements are used by the outer programming language—the host language—to support specific application processes.

The problem we run into with this system is that the application programming languages are generally not equipped to deal with data returned in sets. As a result, an impedance mismatch exists between SQL and the programming languages. *Impedance mismatch* refers to differences between SQL and other programming languages. As you might recall from Module 3, one example of impedance mismatch is the way in which SQL data types differ from data types in other programming languages. These differences can lead to the loss of information when an application extracts data from an SQL database. Another example of impedance mismatch is the fact that SQL returns data in sets but other programming languages cannot handle sets. Generally, they can process only a few pieces of data at the same time. The way in which SQL deals with this type of impedance mismatch is through the use of cursors.

A cursor serves as a pointer that allows the application programming language to deal with query results one row at a time. Although the cursor can traverse all the rows of a query result, it focuses on only one row at a time. A cursor still returns a full result set, but allows the programming language to call only one row from that set. For example, suppose your query results are derived from the following SELECT statement:

```
SELECT PerformerName, PlaceOfBirth FROM Performers
```

The query results from this statement will return all rows from the Performers table, which includes the PerformerName column and the PlaceOfBirth column. However, your application programming language can deal with only one row at a time, so the cursor is declared as an embedded SQL statement within the application programming language. The cursor is then opened and a row is retrieved from the query results. Figure 15-1 illustrates how a cursor acts as a pointer to retrieve only one row of data.

In this case, the row that is retrieved through the cursor is the Bing Crosby row. However, you can retrieve any row from the query results, and you can continue to retrieve rows, as long as they're retrieved one at a time and the cursor remains open. Once you close the cursor, you cannot retrieve any more rows from the query results.

Declaring and Opening SQL Cursors

Most application programming languages support the use of cursors to retrieve data from an SQL database. The cursor language is embedded in the programming code in much the same way you would embed any SQL statement. When using a cursor in a programming language, you must first declare the cursor—similar to how you would declare a variable—and then use

PerformerName: VARCHAR (60)	PlaceOfBirth: VARCHAR (60)
Jennifer Warnes	Seattle, Washington, USA
Joni Mitchell	Fort MacLeod, Alberta, Canada
William Acherman	Germany
Kitaro	Toyohashi, Japan
Bing Crosby	Tacoma, Washington, United States
Patsy Cline	Winchester, Virginia, United States
Jose Carreras	Barcelona, Spain
Luciano Pavarotti	Modena, Italy
Placido Domingo	Madrid, Spain

(Cursor →)

Figure 15-1 Using a cursor to access the Performers table

the declaration name (the name you've assigned to the cursor) in other embedded SQL statements to open the cursor, retrieve individual rows through the cursor, and close the cursor.

NOTE

You can also use cursors in *SQL client modules,* which are sets of SQL statements that can be called from within an application programming language. Client modules, along with embedded SQL and interactive SQL, provide one more method to invoke SQL statements. Because client modules are not implemented as widely as embedded SQL, I focus on using cursors in embedded SQL. For more information about SQL client modules, see Module 17.

Although declaring a cursor is pivotal in using that cursor in your application, the declaration alone is not enough to extract data from an SQL database. In fact, full cursor functionality is supported through the use of four SQL statements, each of which are embedded in the application programming language, or host language. The following descriptions provide an overview of these four statements:

- **DECLARE CURSOR**   Declares the SQL cursor by defining the cursor name, the cursor's characteristics, and a query expression that is invoked when the cursor is opened.

- **OPEN**   Opens the cursor and invokes the query expression, making the query results available to FETCH statements.

- **FETCH**   Retrieves data into variables that pass the data to the host programming language or to other embedded SQL statements.

- **CLOSE**   Closes the cursor. Once the cursor is closed, data cannot be retrieved from the cursor's query results.

The four statements are called from within the host language. Figure 15-2 illustrates how the cursor-related statements are used. The embedded SQL statements are shown in the boxes that are shaded gray.

As you can see, you must first declare the cursor, and then you open it. Once you've opened the cursor, you can use the FETCH statement to retrieve rows of data. You can use this statement as many times as necessary, usually within some sort of looping structure defined by the host language. Once you've retrieved the necessary data, you should close the cursor.

NOTE

For most application programming languages, an embedded SQL statement is preceded by EXEC SQL. This signals to a preprocessor that the following statement is SQL and must be processed separately from the host language. The preprocessor, provided by the RDBMS vendor, analyzes the SQL code and converts it into a form that can be used by the SQL implementation. The host language is compiled in the normal way. For more information about embedded SQL, see Module 17.

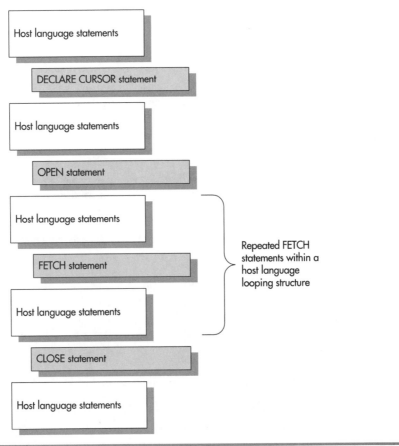

Figure 15-2 Embedding cursor-related SQL statements

Progress Check

1. Which invocation methods support the use of cursors?

2. What do you call the differences between SQL and other programming languages?

3. What is a cursor?

---

1. Embedded SQL and SQL client modules

2. Impedance mismatch

3. A cursor serves as a pointer that allows the application programming language to deal with query results one row at a time. Although the cursor can traverse all the rows of a query result, it focuses on only one row at a time.

CRITICAL SKILL

15.2 Declare a Cursor

The first statement that we'll look at is the DECLARE CURSOR statement. The cursor must be declared before you can use the cursor to retrieve data. You can declare a cursor at any point in your application code, as long as it's declared before using the cursor in any other statements.

NOTE

Many programmers prefer to declare all cursors and variables at the beginning of the program so that all declarations are kept together. The cursors and variables can then be referenced at any point in the program.

The syntax for a cursor declaration includes many elements, as shown in the following syntax:

```
DECLARE <cursor name>
[ SENSITIVE | INSENSITIVE | ASENSITIVE ]
[ SCROLL | NO SCROLL ] CURSOR
[ WITH HOLD | WITHOUT HOLD ]
[ WITH RETURN | WITHOUT RETURN ]
FOR <query expression>
[ ORDER BY <sort specification> ]
[ FOR { READ ONLY | UPDATE [ OF <column list> ] } ]
```

As you can see, most of the elements that make up the declaration are optional. We'll look at these in greater detail in the following section. For now, let's focus on those elements that are required. To do so, we can synthesize the syntax down to the following basic elements:

```
DECLARE <cursor name> CURSOR FOR <query expression>
```

This syntax shows only those parts of the cursor declaration that are mandatory. As you can see, this is a much more manageable chunk of code. All you're required to provide is a name for the cursor and the query expression that is invoked when the cursor is opened. The name must be different from the name of any other cursor declared within the same program. The query expression is basically a SELECT statement, as you have seen throughout this book.

That's all there is to the basic syntax. In the following section, we'll take a look at each of the optional elements that make up the cursor declaration. After that, we'll look at some examples.

Working with Optional Syntax Elements

If you refer back to the full syntax for a cursor declaration (shown in the previous section), you'll see that the majority of the elements are optional. In this section, we'll look at each of these elements. Later in the module, after we've completed this discussion, you might find that you'll want to refer back to this section for details about specific options.

Cursor Sensitivity

The first optional element of the DECLARE CURSOR statement that we'll look at is cursor sensitivity, which is represented with the following syntax:

[SENSITIVE | INSENSITIVE | ASENSITIVE]

Cursor sensitivity is concerned with statements outside the cursor that affect the same rows as those returned by the cursor. For example, suppose your cursor returns rows from the CDsInStock table. While the cursor is open, another statement within the same transaction deletes some of the same rows in the CDsInStock table that were returned by the cursor. Whether or not the cursor can see these deletions depends on the cursor sensitivity.

As you can see in the syntax, SQL supports three cursor sensitivity options:

- **SENSITIVE**   Significant changes made by statements outside the cursor immediately affect the query results within the cursor.

- **INSENSITIVE**   Significant changes made by statements outside the cursor do not affect the query results within the cursor.

- **ASENSITIVE**   Cursor sensitivity is implementation-defined. Significant changes may or may not be visible within the cursor.

If no cursor sensitivity option is specified, ASENSITIVE is assumed, in which case the SQL implementation can take whatever action it has been designed to take.

Cursor Scrollability

The next optional element in the DECLARE CURSOR statement that we'll look at is cursor scrollability, as shown in the following syntax:

[SCROLL | NO SCROLL]

Scrollability is directly tied to the FETCH statement and the options that the FETCH statement can use to retrieve data. If the SCROLL option is specified, the FETCH statement can be defined with one of several options that extend its ability to move through the query results and return specific rows. The SCROLL option allows the FETCH statement to skip around through the query results as needed to retrieve the specific row. If NO SCROLL is specified in the cursor declaration, the FETCH statement cannot make use of the additional scrolling options and can retrieve only the next available row from the query results. If neither option is specified, NO SCROLL is assumed. For more information about the FETCH options, see the "Retrieve Data from a Cursor" section later in this module.

Cursor Holdability

The next item that we'll look at in the DECLARE CURSOR syntax is related to cursor holdability, as shown in the following syntax:

[WITH HOLD | WITHOUT HOLD]

Cursor holdability refers to a characteristic in cursors that is concerned with whether a cursor is automatically closed when the transaction in which the cursor was opened is committed. A *transaction* is an atomic unit of work. This means that all statements within the transaction must succeed or none of them are used. If some statements within a transaction are executed and then one statement fails, all executed statements are rolled back and the database remains unchanged. (Transactions are discussed in more detail in Module 16.)

SQL provides two options that allow you to define cursor holdability: WITH HOLD and WITHOUT HOLD. If you specify WITH HOLD, your cursor will remain open after you commit the transaction, until you explicitly close it. If you specify WITHOUT HOLD, your cursor will be automatically closed when the transaction is committed. If neither option is specified, WITHOUT HOLD is assumed and your cursor is automatically closed.

NOTE

Even if your cursor is defined as a WITHOUT HOLD cursor—whether explicitly or by default—it is still generally considered good practice to explicitly close your cursor when it is no longer needed. This can free up system resources, and it helps to ensure that your code is clearly self-documented.

The advantage of defining a holdable cursor (one that is defined with the WITH HOLD option) is that there might be times after a transaction is committed in which you want your cursor to persist in order to maintain its position within the query results returned by that cursor. Closing a cursor and reopening it can often make it difficult to restore conditions to exactly what they were when you first closed the cursor.

Cursor Returnability

Cursor returnability, the next option we'll look at in the cursor declaration definition, uses the following syntax:

[WITH RETURN | WITHOUT RETURN]

The returnability option applies only to cursors that are opened in an SQL-invoked procedure. As you'll recall from Module 13, an *SQL-invoked procedure* is a type of routine that is invoked by using the CALL statement. The CALL statement is an SQL statement that retrieves procedures and allows you to pass parameter values to those procedures. If the cursor is not opened within a procedure, the returnability option has no effect.

As the syntax shows, SQL supports two returnability options: WITH RETURN and WITHOUT RETURN. If you specify WITH RETURN, the cursor is considered a result set cursor. If you then open the cursor within an SQL-invoked procedure, the cursor's result set is returned to the procedure's invoker, which might be another SQL-invoked routine or a programming host language. If you specify WITHOUT RETURN, the cursor's result set is returned in the normal manner, whether or not it is opened with an SQL-invoked procedure. If neither option is specified, WITHOUT RETURN is assumed.

Cursor Ordering

The DECLARE CURSOR statement includes an optional ORDER BY clause, as shown in the following syntax:

[ORDER BY <sort specification>]

You'll no doubt recognize this clause from Module 7, when we looked at the basic clauses of the SELECT statement. You might recall from that discussion that the ORDER BY clause can be used when directly invoking SQL, but not in an embedded SQL statement, unless that statement is contained within a cursor declaration.

The ORDER BY clause allows you to sort the query results returned by your query specification. In the clause, you can specify which columns form the basis for sorting the rows. If you use an ORDER BY clause, your cursor's SELECT statement cannot contain a GROUP BY clause or a HAVING clause. In addition, the SELECT clause portion of the statement cannot specify the DISTINCT keyword or use a set function.

If your ORDER BY clause includes calculated columns in the query results (such as ColumnA + ColumnB), you should define an alias for the result column, as in (ColumnA + ColumnB) AS ColumnTotals. In addition, you can also use the ASC and DESC keywords for any column included in the sort specification to specify that the column be sorted in ascending or descending order, respectively. (For more information about the ORDER BY clause, see Module 7.)

Cursor Updatability

The last optional element of the DECLARE CURSOR statement that we'll look at is cursor updatability, as shown in the following syntax:

[FOR { READ ONLY | UPDATE [OF <column list>] }]

Cursor updatability refers to the ability to use an UPDATE or DELETE statement to modify data returned by the cursor's SELECT statement. As you can see from the syntax, you must use the FOR keyword along with the READ ONLY or UPDATE option. Let's first go over the READ ONLY option. If you specify READ ONLY, you cannot execute an UPDATE or DELETE statement against the query results returned by the cursor's SELECT statement. On the other hand, if you specify UPDATE, you can execute the statements. If you specify neither option, UPDATE is assumed, unless another option overrides the UPDATE default.

NOTE

In some cases, even if no updatability option is specified, the cursor will be defined as a read-only cursor because other options might prevent the cursor from being updated. For example, if you specify the INSENSITIVE option, the cursor will be read-only. The same is true if you specify an ORDER BY clause or SCROLL keyword.

You'll notice that the UPDATE option also allows you to specify which columns in the underlying table can be updated. To do this, you must include the OF keyword, followed by one or more column names. If more than one column is specified, they must be separated by a comma. If you do not specify any column names (and the OF keyword), the UPDATE option applies to all columns in the underlying table.

Creating a Cursor Declaration

Now that we've looked at each component of the DECLARE CURSOR statement, let's take a look at a few examples that help illustrate how to declare a cursor. For these examples, we'll use the CDInventory table, shown in Figure 15-3.

The first example that we'll review is a basic cursor declaration that includes only the required elements plus an ORDER BY clause, as shown in the following DECLARE CURSOR statement:

```
DECLARE CD1 CURSOR
FOR
  SELECT * FROM CDInventory
  ORDER BY CompactDisc ;
```

In this statement, I've declared a cursor named CD1 and defined a SELECT statement. The cursor name follows the DECLARE keyword. After the cursor name, I've included the CURSOR keyword and the FOR keyword. The only additional element is the SELECT statement, which includes an ORDER BY clause. The statement returns all rows and columns from the CDInventory table. The rows are then ordered according to the values in the CompactDisc column. Because I did not specify the ASC or DESC keyword, the rows are returned in ascending order.

CompactDisc: VARCHAR (60)	Category: VARCHAR (15)	Price: NUMERIC (5,2)	OnHand: INT
Famous Blue Raincoat	Vocal	16.99	13
Blue	Vocal	14.99	42
Court and Spark	Vocal	14.99	22
Past Light	Instrumental	15.99	17
Kojiki	Instrumental	15.99	6
That Christmas Feeling	Vocal	14.99	8
Patsy Cline: 12 Greatest Hits	Vocal	16.99	32
Carreras Domingo Pavarotti in Concert	Vocal	15.99	27
After the Rain: The Soft Sounds of Erik Satie	Instrumental	16.99	21
Out of Africa	Instrumental	16.99	29
Leonard Cohen The Best of	Vocal	15.99	12
Fundamental	Vocal	15.99	34
Blues on the Bayou	Vocal	14.99	27
Orlando	Instrumental	14.99	5

Figure 15-3 Declaring cursors on the CDInventory table

NOTE

In Module 7, when discussing the SELECT statement, I explain that, although an asterisk can be used to return all columns from a table, it is a better practice to identify each column that you want returned. This is especially important in embedded SQL because the host language relies on certain values—a specified number in a specified order—being returned from the database. If the database should change, your application may not operate properly, and the application code will have to be modified. However, for the examples in this module, I often use an asterisk to simplify the code and conserve space, but know that, in the real world, I would usually specify each column.

The ORDER BY clause is an important element because the order in which the rows are returned affects which rows are retrieved when using a FETCH statement. (I discuss the

FETCH statement later in the module, in the "Retrieve Data from a Cursor" section.) This is especially true if defining a scrollable cursor, such as the one in the following example:

```
DECLARE CD2 SCROLL CURSOR
FOR
  SELECT * FROM CDInventory
  ORDER BY CompactDisc
FOR READ ONLY ;
```

Notice that I've added two new elements to this statement: the SCROLL keyword and the FOR READ ONLY clause. The SCROLL keyword signals to the FETCH statement that the cursor is scrollable. As a result, additional options can be used within the FETCH statement that extend how your application can move through the cursor results. The FOR READ ONLY clause indicates that neither an UPDATE nor a DELETE statement can be used to modify data returned by the cursor. However, this clause is not necessary. Because the cursor declaration includes the SCROLL keyword and the SELECT statement includes an ORDER BY clause, the cursor is automatically limited to read-only operations. The use of either of these two options— or the use of the INSENSITIVE option—automatically overrides the cursor's default updatability.

The next type of read-only declaration that we'll look at also includes the INSENSITIVE keyword, as shown in the following example:

```
DECLARE CD3 SCROLL INSENSITIVE CURSOR
FOR
  SELECT * FROM CDInventory
  ORDER BY CompactDisc
FOR READ ONLY ;
```

The CD3 cursor declaration is exactly like the CD2 cursor declaration except that CD3 has also been defined as an insensitive cursor. This means that no modifications made to the data in the underlying table while the cursor is open will be reflected in the query results returned by the cursor. Of course, if you close the cursor and then reopen it, any modifications that had been made when the cursor was originally open will be reflected in the data returned by the reopened cursor.

The three preceding cursor declarations that we've looked at have all been read-only. Now let's take a look at an updatable cursor. In the following cursor declaration, the SELECT statement again returns all rows and columns from the CDInventory table:

```
DECLARE CD4 CURSOR
FOR
  SELECT * FROM CDInventory
FOR UPDATE ;
```

Notice that this DECLARE CURSOR statement does not include the SCROLL keyword, the INSENSITIVE keyword, or an ORDER BY clause, any of which would have prevented us from creating an updatable cursor. We could have specified the NO SCROLL and SENSITIVE options, but they're not necessary. Also notice, however, that the cursor declaration does include the FOR UPDATE clause. The clause is also not necessary in this particular statement because the cursor is, by default, updatable, since it contains no options to limit the updatability.

However, if you want your cursor to be updatable only for a certain column, you must include the FOR UPDATE clause, along with the column name, as shown in the following example:

```
DECLARE CD5 CURSOR
FOR
  SELECT * FROM CDInventory
FOR UPDATE OF CompactDisc ;
```

Now the FOR UPDATE clause includes the OF keyword and the column name, CompactDisc. If you were to try to modify data in the cursor results in columns other than the CompactDisc column, you would receive an error.

Once you've declared your cursor, you can open it and retrieve data from the query results. However, as you have seen in the preceding cursor declarations, the actions that you can take are limited to the restrictions defined with the DECLARE CURSOR statement.

Progress Check

1. Which statement do you use to declare a cursor?

2. Which keyword should you include in your cursor declaration if you want to extend the capabilities of your FETCH statements?

3. What clause can you include in a read-only cursor that returns query results in a specific order?

4. What option should you include in a cursor declaration to define that cursor as holdable?

1. DECLARE CURSOR statement
2. SCROLL
3. ORDER BY clause
4. WITH HOLD

15.3 Open and Close a Cursor

The process of opening a cursor is very straightforward. You need to provide only the keyword OPEN and the name of the cursor, as shown in the following syntax:

OPEN <cursor name>

For example, to open the CD1 cursor, you invoke the following SQL statement:

```
OPEN CD1 ;
```

You cannot open a cursor until you have declared it. Once you've declared it, you can open it anywhere within your program. The SELECT statement within the cursor is not invoked until you actually open the cursor. That means that any data modified between when the cursor is declared and when the cursor is opened is reflected in the query results returned by the cursor. If you close the cursor and then reopen it, data modifications that took place between when you close it and when you reopen it are reflected in the new query results.

Once you have finished using your cursor, you should close it so that you can free up system resources. To close a cursor, you can use the CLOSE statement, as shown in the following syntax:

CLOSE <cursor name>

The CLOSE statement does nothing more than close the cursor, which means that the query results from the cursor's SELECT statement are released. For example, to close the CD1 cursor, use the following SQL statement:

```
CLOSE CD1 ;
```

Once you close the cursor, you cannot retrieve any more rows from the cursor's query results. In other words, you cannot use a FETCH statement to retrieve data from that cursor. If you reopen the cursor, you can again retrieve data, but you would again have to close the cursor.

15.4 Retrieve Data from a Cursor

So far, you've learned how to declare a cursor, open it, and then close it. However, these actions alone do not allow you to retrieve any of the data that is provided by the cursor. In order to do that, you must use a FETCH statement.

Before we take a look at the syntax for the FETCH statement, let's briefly review the purpose of a cursor and its related statements. As I said earlier, one of the problems with embedding SQL statements in a programming host language is the impedance mismatch. One form of that mismatch is that SQL returns data in sets and traditional application programming languages cannot handle sets of data. In general, they can deal only with individual values. In order to address this form of impedance mismatch, you can use cursors to retrieve data one row at a time—regardless of how many rows are returned—from which you can extract individual values that can be used by the host language.

As you have seen, a cursor declaration includes a SELECT statement that returns a set of data. The OPEN statement executes the SELECT statement, and the CLOSE statement releases the query results from the SELECT statement. However, it is the FETCH statement that identifies individual rows within that set of data and extracts individual values from those rows, which are then passed to host variables. A *host variable* is a type of parameter that passes a value to the host language.

One or more FETCH statements can be executed while a cursor is open. Each statement points to a specific row in the query results, and values are then extracted from those rows. The following syntax shows the basic elements that make up the FETCH statement:

```
FETCH [ [ <fetch orientation> ] FROM ]
<cursor name> INTO <host variables>
```

As you can see by the syntax, you must specify the FETCH keyword, the name of the cursor, and an INTO clause that identifies the host variables that will receive the values returned by the FETCH statement. These values are derived from the query results that are generated by the cursor's SELECT statement when that cursor is opened. If your FETCH statement includes more than one host variable, you must separate the variables with a comma.

In addition to the mandatory components of the FETCH statement, the syntax also includes the optional <fetch orientation> placeholder and the FROM keyword. If you specify a fetch orientation option in your FETCH statement, you must include the FROM keyword, or you can specify FROM without the fetch orientation.

SQL supports six fetch orientation options that identify which row is selected from the cursor's query results. Most of these options are available only if you declare the cursor as scrollable. A scrollable cursor, as you'll recall, is one that extends the ability of the FETCH statement to move through the cursor's query results. A cursor is scrollable if the cursor declaration includes the SCROLL keyword. If you include a fetch orientation in your FETCH statement, you can choose from one of the following options:

- **NEXT**   Retrieves the next row from the query results. If you use NEXT in your first FETCH statement after you open your cursor, the first row in the query results will be returned. A second FETCH NEXT statement will return the second row.

- **PRIOR**   Retrieves the row directly preceding the one that had last been retrieved. If you use PRIOR in your first FETCH statement after you open the cursor, no row will be returned because no row precedes the first row.

- **FIRST**   Retrieves the first row from your cursor's query results, regardless of how many FETCH statements have been executed since opening the cursor.

- **LAST**   Retrieves the last row from your cursor's query results, regardless of how many FETCH statements have been executed since opening the cursor.

- **ABSOLUTE <value>**   Retrieves the row specified by the <value> placeholder. The value must be an exact numeric, although it can be derived from a host variable. The numeric identifies which row is returned by the FETCH statement. For example, ABSOLUTE 1 returns the first row, ABSOLUTE 2 returns the second row, and ABSOLUTE -1 returns the last row.

- **RELATIVE <value>**   Retrieves the row specified by the <value> placeholder, relative to the cursor's current position. If you use RELATIVE in the first FETCH statement after you open the cursor, RELATIVE 1 returns the first row from the cursor's query results, and RELATIVE -1 returns the last row. However, if the cursor is not at the beginning of the query results, as it is when you first open the cursor, RELATIVE 1 and RELATIVE -1 return rows relative to the cursor position as it was left after the last executed FETCH statement.

Whenever you open a cursor, the cursor points to the beginning of the query results. The FETCH statement moves the cursor to the row designated by the fetch orientation option. If no option is specified, NEXT is assumed, and the cursor always points to the next row in the query results.

To help illustrate how the fetch orientation options work, let's take another look at a cursor we declared earlier in the module:

```
DECLARE CD2 SCROLL CURSOR
FOR
  SELECT * FROM CDInventory
  ORDER BY CompactDisc
FOR READ ONLY ;
```

Notice that the SCROLL keyword is specified and that the SELECT statement retrieves all rows and columns from the CDInventory table. Also notice that the SELECT statement includes an ORDER BY clause that sorts the query results in ascending order according to the values in the CompactDisc column. This is important because the FETCH statements move through the rows in the query results in the order specified by the ORDER BY clause, regardless of how rows are ordered in the underlying table.

Now let's take another look at the query results returned by the SELECT statement in the CD2 cursor. The query results, in the form of a virtual table, are shown in Figure 15-4. Notice that the illustration includes pointers that represent the various types of FETCH statements (based on their fetch orientation). In each case, the pointer is based on a FETCH statement that is the first to be executed after the cursor has been opened.

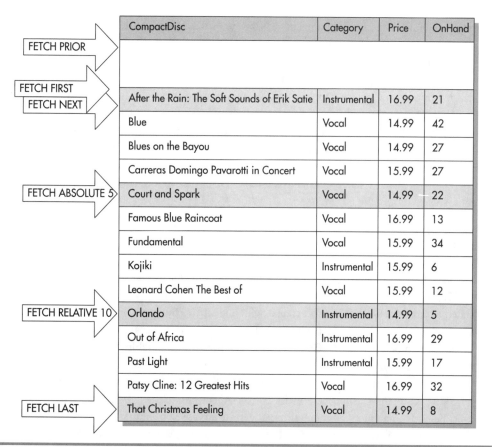

Figure 15-4 The query results (virtual table) returned by the CD2 cursor

Notice that the FETCH FIRST and FETCH NEXT pointers each point to the After the Rain row. This is the first row in the cursor's query results. FETCH FIRST will always point to this row, assuming the data in the underlying tables doesn't change. FETCH NEXT will always point to the first row whenever it is the first FETCH statement executed after the cursor is opened. In addition, the FETCH LAST pointer will always point to the That Christmas Feeling row. However, the FETCH PRIOR pointer doesn't point to any row. It points instead to a space prior to the first row of the query results. This is because PRIOR cannot retrieve a row if it is used in the first FETCH statement after the cursor is opened.

Now let's take a look at the FETCH ABSOLUTE 5 pointer. As you can see, it points to the Court and Spark row, which is the fifth row in the cursor's query results. FETCH ABSOLUTE 5 will always return this row. On the other hand, FETCH RELATIVE 10 points to the Orlando row, which is the tenth row in the cursor's query results. However, if RELATIVE were used in a FETCH statement other than the first one, FETCH RELATIVE 10 would probably be pointing to a different row.

As you can see, the six fetch orientation options provide a great deal of flexibility in moving through a cursor's query results. Keep in mind, however, that most of these options can be used in read-only cursors only, such as the CD2 cursor we've been looking at. The only option that can be used for updatable cursors is NEXT, which is the default fetch orientation. Now let's take a look at a few examples of FETCH statements so you can see how they can be used to retrieve data from your cursor's query results.

The first FETCH statement that we'll look at uses the NEXT fetch orientation option to retrieve a row from the CD2 cursor:

```
FETCH NEXT FROM CD2
  INTO :CD, :Category, :Price, :OnHand ;
```

The statement identifies the fetch orientation and the cursor name. As you'll recall, the NEXT FROM keywords are optional because NEXT is the default fetch orientation. The statement also includes the INTO clause, which identifies the host variables that will receive values returned by the FETCH statement. There are four host variables to match the number of values returned by the FETCH statement. The number of variables must be the same as the number of columns returned by the cursor's SELECT statement, and the variables must be listed in the same order as the columns returned. Notice that the host variables are separated by commas and their names begin with colons. According to the SQL standard, host variables must begin with a colon, although this can vary from one SQL implementation to the next.

Now that you've seen how a FETCH NEXT statement works, you can create any FETCH statement for whichever fetch orientation you want to specify. Simply replace one option with the other. For example, the following FETCH statement uses the ABSOLUTE fetch orientation:

```
FETCH ABSOLUTE 5 FROM CD2
  INTO :CD, :Category, :Price, :OnHand ;
```

Notice that with the ABSOLUTE option, as with the RELATIVE option, you must specify a numeric value. In this case, the cursor will retrieve the fifth row from the cursor's query results. The ABSOLUTE, FIRST, and LAST options are the only fetch orientation options that will always return the same row from the cursor's query results, assuming that the data in the underlying table has not changed. On the other hand, the NEXT, PRIOR, and RELATIVE options return rows based on the cursor's last position. As a result, you want to be certain to design your cursors and your FETCH statements with positioning in mind.

Ask the Expert

Q: You mention that a cursor's SELECT statement is not executed until the cursor is opened. How does this affect special values such as CURRENT_USER or CURRENT_TIME?

A: Because a cursor's SELECT statement is not executed until the cursor is opened, special values are not defined until the cursor is opened, not when the cursor is declared. For example, if you include the CURRENT_TIME special value in your cursor's SELECT statement and declare that cursor at the beginning of your program code, the time inserted into the CURRENT_TIME value is the time that the cursor is opened, not when the cursor is declared. In addition, if you close and then reopen the cursor, the CURRENT_TIME value is that time when you again open the cursor, not when it was first opened.

Q: You state that host variables are a type of parameter that is used in embedded SQL. How do host variables differ from other types of parameters?

A: For all practical purposes, a host variable is just like any other parameter. The main distinction is that a host variable is used in embedded SQL to pass values between the host language and SQL. The only other real distinction is that a colon must be added to the name of the variable. The reason that a colon must be included when used in an embedded SQL statement is to indicate that the name is a host variable and not a column. As a result, you can use variable names that are meaningful to your application without worrying about accidentally naming a variable the same as a column name. The colon has nothing to do with the variable itself, only in distinguishing it as a variable. A colon must also be used in SQL client modules. However, values are passed to modules through parameters, rather than host variables. Module parameters are essentially the same thing as host variables; only the names are different. If you were to refer to all of them as parameters, you would not be far off.

Progress Check

1. Which SQL statement executes the SELECT statement in a cursor?

2. What action must you take before opening a cursor?

3. What type of cursor allows you to use all the fetch orientation options in a FETCH statement?

4. Which row in a cursor's query results does a FETCH LAST statement retrieve?

CRITICAL SKILL
15.5 # Use Positioned UPDATE and DELETE Statements

Once you fetch a row from the query results of an updatable cursor, you might want your application to then update or delete that row. To do so, you must use a positioned UPDATE or DELETE statement. The positioned UPDATE and DELETE statements contain a special WHERE clause that references the opened cursor. Let's take a look at each of these two statements to show you how you can use them to modify data returned by your cursor.

Using the Positioned UPDATE Statement

The positioned UPDATE statement is, for the most part, the same as a regular UPDATE statement, except that it requires a special WHERE clause, as shown in the following syntax:

```
UPDATE <table name>
SET <set list>
WHERE CURRENT OF <cursor name>
```

A regular UPDATE statement, as you no doubt recall, contains the UPDATE clause and the SET clause, just as you see in the syntax for a positioned UPDATE statement. However, in a regular UPDATE statement, the WHERE clause is optional, but in a positioned UPDATE statement, it is required. In addition, the WHERE clause must be defined with the CURRENT OF option, which identifies the opened cursor. By using the CURRENT OF option, you're

---

1. OPEN statement
2. You must declare the cursor.
3. Scrollable cursor
4. The last row in the cursor's query results

telling your application to use the values returned by the most recent FETCH statement. For example, if your cursor is pointing to the Past Light row of the CDInventory table (the row returned by the FETCH statement), it is that row that is being referenced by the WHERE clause of the positioned UPDATE statement.

Let's take a look at an example to demonstrate how this works. In the following set of SQL statements, we declare the CD4 cursor, open that cursor, fetch a row from the cursor's query results, update that row, and close the cursor:

```
DECLARE CD4 CURSOR
FOR
  SELECT * FROM CDInventory
FOR UPDATE ;
OPEN CD4 ;
FETCH CD4 INTO :CD, :Category, :Price, :OnHand ;
UPDATE CDInventory SET OnHand = :OnHand * 2
  WHERE CURRENT OF CD4 ;
CLOSE CD4 ;
```

The first statement declares the CD4 cursor and defines a SELECT statement that returns all rows and columns from the CDInventory table. Next, we open the cursor and then fetch the next row, which in this case is the first row, Famous Blue Raincoat. After we fetch the row, we use a positioned UPDATE statement to double the amount of the OnHand value for that row. Notice that the UPDATE statement includes a WHERE clause that contains the CURRENT OF option, which identifies the CD4 cursor. After we update the row, we close the cursor.

NOTE

Keep in mind that the statements shown in the preceding example would be embedded in a host language, so they are not likely to be grouped so closely together and there may be other host language elements, such as variable declarations, looping structures, and conditional statements.

In the preceding example, we were able to update the OnHand column because it was implicitly included in the FOR UPDATE clause of the cursor's SELECT statement. When no column names are specified, all columns are updatable. However, let's look at another example that explicitly defines a column. In the following set of SQL statements, I've declared the CD5 cursor and used it to try to update a row in the CDInventory table:

```
DECLARE CD5 CURSOR
FOR
  SELECT * FROM CDInventory
FOR UPDATE OF CompactDisc ;
```

```
OPEN CD5 ;
FETCH CD5 INTO :CD, :Category, :Price, :OnHand ;
UPDATE CDInventory SET OnHand = :OnHand * 2
  WHERE CURRENT OF CD5 ;
CLOSE CD5 ;
```

As you can see, the cursor declaration specifies the CompactDisc column in the FOR UPDATE clause. If you try to execute the UPDATE statement, you will receive an error indicating that the OnHand column is not one of the columns specified in the cursor declaration.

Using the Positioned DELETE Statement

The positioned DELETE statement, like the positioned UPDATE statement, requires a WHERE clause that must include the CURRENT OF option. (A regular DELETE statement, as you'll recall, does not require the WHERE clause.) A positioned DELETE statement uses the following syntax:

DELETE <table name>
WHERE CURRENT OF <cursor name>

As you can see, you need to define a DELETE clause that identifies the table and a WHERE clause that identifies the cursor. The WHERE clause in a positioned DELETE statement works just like the WHERE clause in a positioned UPDATE statement: The row returned by the last FETCH statement is the row that is modified. In this case, the row is deleted.

Now let's look at an example of a positioned DELETE statement. The following SQL statements declare the CD4 cursor, open the cursor, return a row from the cursor, delete that row, and close the cursor:

```
DECLARE CD4 CURSOR
FOR
  SELECT * FROM CDInventory
FOR UPDATE ;
OPEN CD4 ;
FETCH CD4 INTO :CD, :Category, :Price, :OnHand ;
DELETE CDInventory WHERE CURRENT OF CD4 ;
CLOSE CD4 ;
```

You should be familiar with most of these statements. The only new one is the positioned DELETE statement. This statement deletes the row returned by the FETCH statement, which is the Famous Blue Raincoat row. Once the row is deleted, the cursor is closed.

Project 15-1 Working with SQL Cursors

`Prj15.txt`

In this module, we looked at how to declare cursors, open those cursors, retrieve data from them, and then close them. In addition, we reviewed positioned UPDATE and DELETE statements. However, as I said earlier, cursors are used primarily in embedded SQL, which makes it difficult to fully test cursor functionality if you're limited to directly invoking SQL statements (as we are in this project). Ideally, it would be best to embed the cursor-related SQL statements in a host language, but that is beyond the scope of this book. What complicates this issue even further is the fact that different SQL implementations support the use of cursors in an interactive environment in different ways, which can make it difficult to directly invoke cursor-related statements. Still, you should be able to execute most cursor-related statements interactively, but know that cursors are designed for use in embedded SQL and SQL client modules, so you might have to modify the statements a great deal in order to execute them. You can download the Prj15.txt file, which contains the SQL statements used in this project.

NOTE

Ideally, it would be good to walk you through each step of declaring and opening a cursor, retrieving data, and closing a cursor, but because of the nature of direct invocation, we will use fewer steps and larger blocks of statements.

Step by Step

1. Open the client application for your RDBMS and connect to the Inventory database.

2. The first cursor that you'll declare and access is a basic read-only cursor that retrieves data from the CompactDiscs table. The first thing you'll notice in the set of statements that you'll be creating is that you'll declare a variable named v_CDName. You'll need to create this variable in order to fully test the FETCH statement. Keep in mind that, depending on the situation, the host language, and the product, you may or may not use this method for creating your variable. Also notice that the variable name in the FETCH statement is not preceded by a colon. This is because you'll be using direct invocation to execute these statements and, for most implementations, the name of the variable in the FETCH statement will have to be the same as the name you declared at the beginning of this set of statements.

   As with any SQL statement, you will find that the exact language that you use to create statements varies from one product to the next. In addition, the fact that you're invoking the statements directly, rather than embedding the statements, can lead to other variations between SQL and the implementation (such as not using a colon in the variable name).

(continued)

For example, if you execute these statements in SQL Server, you'll have to precede your variable names with the at (@) character. Oracle deviates from the standard even more. In Oracle, you declare the cursor and variable in one block of statements. In addition, the CURSOR keyword precedes the name of the cursor, and you must use the IS keyword, rather than FOR. You must also enclose the OPEN, FETCH, and CLOSE statements in a BEGIN...END block. You will also find that not all SQL options are supported in all SQL implementations, and many products include additional features not defined in the SQL standard. Be sure to check your product's documentation before trying to declare and access any cursors.

Now let's create the cursor-related statements. Enter and execute the following SQL statements:

```
DECLARE v_CDName VARCHAR (60) ;
DECLARE CD_cursor1 CURSOR
FOR
  SELECT CDTitle FROM CompactDiscs
  ORDER BY CDTitle ASC ;
OPEN CD_cursor1 ;
FETCH CD_cursor1 INTO v_CDName ;
CLOSE CD_cursor1 ;
```

In these statements, you first declared a variable named v_CDName. Next, you declared a cursor named CD_cursor1. The cursor definition contained a SELECT statement that was qualified with an ORDER BY clause. Because you included the ORDER BY clause, your cursor was read-only. After you declared the cursor, you opened it, fetched a row from the cursor's query results, and then closed the cursor. The FETCH statement returned the value After the Rain: The Soft Sounds of Erik Satie, which could have then been used in some other operation, had you embedded these statements. After you executed the statements, you should have received a message saying that the statements were executed successfully.

3. Now you will declare and access a second cursor. This time you will specify that the cursor is insensitive and scrollable. In addition, you will specify that the cursor is read-only, although this clause is optional because you're making the cursor scrollable and insensitive. You will also fetch the last row from the cursor's query results, rather than the first. Enter and execute the following SQL statements:

```
DECLARE v_CDName VARCHAR (60) ;
DECLARE CD_cursor2 SCROLL INSENSITIVE CURSOR
FOR
  SELECT CDTitle FROM CompactDiscs
  ORDER BY CDTitle ASC
FOR READ ONLY ;
OPEN CD_cursor2 ;
FETCH LAST FROM CD_cursor2 INTO v_CDName ;
CLOSE CD_cursor2 ;
```

This time the FETCH statement retrieved the value That Christmas Feeling because LAST was specified. This value was inserted into the v_CDName variable. After you executed the statements, you should have received a message saying that the statements were executed successfully.

4. Your next cursor will be updatable, which means that it cannot include an ORDER BY clause and cannot define the cursor as insensitive or scrollable. Because the cursor is updatable, you will also create an UPDATE statement that doubles the value of the InStock column for the row returned by the FETCH statement. Enter and execute the following SQL statements:

```
DECLARE v_CDName VARCHAR (60) ;
DECLARE CD_cursor3 CURSOR
FOR
   SELECT CDTitle FROM CompactDiscs
FOR UPDATE ;
OPEN CD_cursor3 ;
FETCH CD_cursor3 INTO v_CDName ;
UPDATE CompactDiscs SET InStock = InStock * 2
   WHERE CURRENT OF CD_cursor3 ;
CLOSE CD_cursor3 ;
```

Notice that your UPDATE statement includes a WHERE clause that contains the CURRENT OF option, which specifies the CD_cursor3 cursor. This clause is mandatory. Because no ORDER BY clause was used, the first row in your cursor's query results was Famous Blue Raincoat. This is the row that was updated. After you executed the statements, you should have received a message indicating that a row had been updated.

5. Now let's take a look at the CompactDiscs table to verify that the change you made is correct. Enter and execute the following SQL statement:

```
SELECT * FROM CompactDiscs ;
```

The InStock value of the Famous Blue Raincoat row should now be 26, double its original amount.

6. Let's return the database to its original state. Enter and execute the following SQL statement:

```
UPDATE CompactDiscs SET InStock = 13
WHERE CompactDiscID = 101 ;
```

You should receive a message indicating that the row has been updated.

7. Close the client application.

(continued)

Project Summary

In this project, you declared and accessed three cursors, two that were read-only and one that was updatable. For all three cursors you declared a variable. The variable was then used in the FETCH statement to receive the value returned by that statement. For the updatable cursor, you created an UPDATE statement that modified the InStock value for the row returned by the FETCH statement. After you updated the CompactDiscs table, you updated it once more to return the database to its original state. Because no other changes were made to the database, your data should be as it was before you started this project.

✓ Module 15 Mastery Check

1. What form of impedance mismatch is addressed through the use of cursors?

2. A(n) _____ serves as a pointer that allows the application programming language to deal with query results one row at a time.

3. When using cursors in embedded SQL, what is the first step you must take before you can retrieve data through that cursor?

   A. Fetch the cursor.

   B. Declare the cursor.

   C. Close the cursor.

   D. Open the cursor.

4. What are the four cursor-related statements that you can embed in a host language?

5. Which options can be used only in read-only cursor declarations?

   A. SCROLL

   B. WITH HOLD

   C. ORDER BY

   D. INSENSITIVE

6. What are the required elements of a DECLARE CURSOR statement?

7. What type of cursors do not see changes made by statements outside the cursor?

8. Which option should you use in a cursor declaration to extend the retrieving capabilities of a FETCH statement?

A. WITHOUT HOLD

B. ASENSITIVE

C. SCROLL

D. FOR UPDATE

9. Cursor _____ refers to a characteristic in cursors that is concerned with whether a cursor is automatically closed when the transaction in which the cursor was opened is committed.

10. You're creating a cursor declaration. The SELECT statement includes an ORDER BY clause. Which clauses cannot be included in the SELECT statement?

A. SELECT

B. HAVING

C. GROUP BY

D. WHERE

11. Your cursor declaration includes a FOR UPDATE clause that does not specify any columns. Which columns in the underlying table can be updated?

12. What SQL statement should you use if you want to open the CDArtists cursor?

13. A(n) _____ statement retrieves rows from a cursor's query results once you open that cursor.

14. Which fetch orientation option should you use in a FETCH statement if you want to be sure to retrieve the first row in a cursor's query results?

A. PRIOR

B. NEXT

C. ABSOLUTE -1

D. FIRST

15. What clause is required in a positioned UPDATE statement in order to update a row returned by the most recent FETCH statement?

Module 16

Managing SQL Transactions

In Module 4, I spend a considerable amount of time discussing data integrity and the methods supported by SQL to ensure that integrity. These methods include the creation of constraints, domains, and assertions, all of which are used by your database in one way or another to ensure that your SQL data remains valid. However, these methods alone are not always enough to maintain the integrity of that data. Take, for example, the situation that can arise when more than one user tries to access and modify data in the same table at the same time or when their actions overlap and impact the same data. Actions may be taken by one user based on data that is no longer valid as a result of actions taken by the other user. Data might become inconsistent or inaccurate, without either user knowing that a problem exists. To address situations of this type, SQL supports the use of transactions to ensure that concurrent actions do not impact the validity of the data that is seen by any one user. In this module, I describe how transitions are implemented in an SQL environment and how you can control their behavior. You will learn how to set transaction properties, start transactions, terminate them, and use other options that extend their functionality.

CRITICAL SKILL
16.1 Understand SQL Transactions

Relatively few databases exist in which only one user at any one time is trying to access data within that database. For the most part, databases are used by different types of users for many different purposes, and often these users are trying to access the data at the same time. The greater the number of users, the greater the likelihood that problems could arise when they attempt to view or modify data at the same time. However, problems can arise even if only two users are accessing data at the same time, depending on the nature of their operations. For example, one user might view data in a table, take some sort of action based on that data, then return to the table to verify the data once more. However, if another user updates that table between the two times that the first user views it, the first user will see different data the second time, which can invalidate the action that was taken as a result of the viewing the table the first time.

To address these sorts of data inconsistencies, SQL uses transactions to control the actions of individual users. A *transaction* is a unit of work that is made up of one or more SQL statements that perform a related set of actions. For example, your application might use a transaction to change the number of CDs in stock. The process of updating the applicable table or tables and reporting the updated information back to you is treated as a single transaction. The transaction might include a number of SQL statements that each perform a specific task.

In order for a set of actions to qualify as a transaction, it must pass the ACID test. ACID is an acronym commonly used when referring to the four characteristics of a transaction:

● **Atomic** This characteristic refers to the all-or-nothing nature of a transaction. Either all operations in a transaction are performed or none are performed. If some statements are executed, the results of these executions are rolled back if the transaction fails at any point before it is completed. Only when all statements are executed properly and all actions are performed is a transaction complete and the results of that transaction applied to the database.

● **Consistent**   The database must be consistent at the beginning and at the end of the transaction. All rules that define the data must be applied to that data as a result of any changes that occur during the transaction. In addition, all structures within the database must be correct at the end of the transaction.

● **Isolated**   Data that might temporarily be in an inconsistent state during a transaction should not be available to other transactions until the data is once again consistent. In other words, no user should be able to access inconsistent data during a transaction implemented by another user when the data impacted by the transaction is in an inconsistent state. In addition, for a transaction to be isolated, no other transactions can affect that transaction.

● **Durable**   Once the changes made by a transaction are committed, those changes must be preserved, and the data should be in a reliable and consistent state, even if hardware or application errors occur.

If at any time during a transaction any problems arise, the entire transaction is rolled back and the database is returned to the state it was in before the transaction started. Any actions that were taken are undone and the data is restored to its original state. If the transaction is successfully completed, all changes are implemented. Throughout the entire process, regardless of whether the transaction is successfully completed or must be rolled back, the transaction always ensures the integrity of the database.

SQL supports a number of statements related to transition processing. You can use these statements to begin and end transactions, set their properties, defer constraint enforcement during the transaction, and identify places within a transaction that act as stopping points when you roll back transactions. Throughout the rest of the module, we'll examine how each of these statements are used within a transaction. However, before we go into a more detailed discussion of the statements, I want to provide you with a brief overview of each one in order to give you a better understanding of how transactions work.

The SQL:1999 standard defines seven statements related to transaction processing:

● **SET TRANSACTION**   Sets the properties of the next transaction to be executed.

● **START TRANSACTION**   Sets the properties of the transaction and starts that transaction.

● **SET CONSTRAINTS**   Sets the constraint mode within a current transaction. The constraint mode refers to whether a constraint is applied immediately to data when that data is modified or whether the application of the constraint is deferred until later in the transaction.

● **SAVEPOINT**   Creates a savepoint within a transaction. A savepoint marks a place within the transaction that acts as a stopping point when you roll back a transaction.

- **RELEASE SAVEPOINT**   Releases a savepoint.

- **ROLLBACK**   Terminates a transaction and rolls back any changes to the beginning of the transaction or to a savepoint.

- **COMMIT**   Terminates a transaction and commits all changes to the database.

Although we'll be looking at all seven statements in more detail, some of them are pivotal in understanding the nature of a transaction. Let's take a look at Figure 16-1 to help illustrate this point.

Notice that the figure includes four of the SQL transaction-related statements: SET TRANSACTION, START TRANSACTION, COMMIT, and ROLLBACK. If a SET TRANSACTION statement is used, it is executed before the transaction begins. After that, a START TRANSACTION statement begins the transaction.

NOTE

As you'll see later in this module, it would be rare in a pure SQL environment that you would want to use both the SET TRANSACTION and START TRANSACTION statements because both statements set the same properties. However, you'll find that SQL implementations vary with regard to which transaction-related statements they support and how they implement those statements.

When you start the transaction, the database is in its original state—the data is consistent and correct. Next the SQL statements within the transaction are processed. If this process is successful, a COMMIT statement is executed. The COMMIT statement causes the SQL

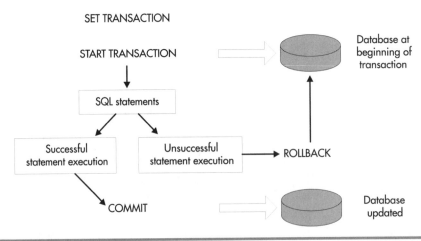

Figure 16-1 A basic SQL transaction

implementation to update the database and terminate the transaction. If the statement-execution process is not successful, a ROLLBACK statement is executed, and the implementation returns the database to its original state. An unsuccessful execution does not necessarily mean that the statements have failed. A ROLLBACK statement can be executed according to the conditions of a WHERE clause, a predefined error, or whatever other conditions are defined within the transaction. The point is, under certain circumstances, the ROLLBACK statement is executed and under other circumstances, the COMMIT statement is executed.

CRITICAL SKILL
16.2 Set Transaction Properties

The first statement that we'll look at in detail is the SET TRANSACTION statement. The SET TRANSACTION statement allows you to configure several of the properties associated with transaction processing. You can execute this statement only when no transactions are active. When you do use a SET TRANSACTION statement, the settings configured within the statement are applied only to the next transaction that is initiated. The settings do not carry over from one transaction to the next.

The SET TRANSACTION statement is not required in order to initiate a transaction. If the statement is not executed, the transaction uses the default settings. If the statement is executed, the transaction uses the settings specified in the statement. If the statement is executed but not all settings are defined, the transaction uses the defaults for the undefined settings. Regardless of which settings are configured, none of them are applicable to any transaction except the first one initiated after the SET TRANSACTION is executed.

Now let's take a look at the syntax used for a SET TRANSACTION statement. At its most basic, the syntax looks like the following:

SET [LOCAL] TRANSACTION <mode> [{ , <mode> } . . .]

The first thing that you might notice about this syntax is the optional keyword LOCAL. The LOCAL keyword applies only to transactions that encompass multiple SQL implementations. If you're working with these sorts of transactions, you can use the LOCAL option to apply settings to the local portion of the transaction. To be able to use the LOCAL option, the transaction must have been initiated on an SQL server other than the one where the local transaction settings are configured.

NOTE

The subject of encompassing transactions and local settings is beyond the scope of this book. I mention them here only to provide you with a complete picture of the SET TRANSACTION statement. As a beginning SQL programmer, you will most likely not be concerned with encompassing transactions.

Returning to the SET TRANSACTION syntax, you can see that the only other type of option that you need to specify is the one represented by the <mode> placeholder. There are three types of transaction modes that you can specify:

● Access level

● Isolation level

● Diagnostics size

You must specify one or more transaction modes. If you specify more than one, you must separate them with a comma. In addition, you cannot include more than one of any type of transaction mode. For example, you can specify an access level and an isolation level, but you cannot specify two isolation levels.

The SET TRANSACTION statement supports two access level options: READ ONLY and READ WRITE. If you select the READ ONLY option, you cannot include any statements within the transaction that modify the database. This includes statements that modify data (such as the UPDATE statement) or statements that modify the database structure (such as the CREATE TABLE statement). If you select the READ WRITE option, you can execute both types of statements in your transaction. As you will see in the next section, "Specifying an Isolation Level," the default access level depends on the isolation level. However, if no isolation level and no access level are specified, the default access level is READ WRITE.

Specifying an Isolation Level

When you create a SET TRANSACTION statement, you can specify zero or one isolation levels. An isolation level defines how isolated a transaction will be from the actions of other transactions. A SET TRANSACTION statement supports four isolation level options:

● READ UNCOMMITTED

● READ COMMITTED

● REPEATABLE READ

● SERIALIZABLE

The isolation levels are listed from least restrictive to most restrictive, with the READ UNCOMMITTED option being less effective in terms of isolating data, and the SERIALIZABLE option more effective. If no isolation level is specified, SERIALIZABLE is assumed.

Data Anomalies

The best way to understand isolation levels is to take a look at the basic types of phenomena that can occur to data, depending on how isolated one transaction is from another. In general, three types of phenomena can occur:

- Dirty reads
- Nonrepeatable reads
- Phantom reads

The type of data anomaly that you might experience during a transaction depends on which isolation level you configure for your transaction. However, before we get into any more specifications about isolation levels, let's take a look at these three types of phenomena.

Dirty Reads   The first phenomenon that we'll look at is the dirty read. A dirty read can occur when one transaction modifies data, a second transaction sees those modifications before they're actually committed to the database, and the first transaction rolls back the modifications, returning the database to its original state. However, the second transaction, having read the modified data, might have taken action based on the incorrect data. To help illustrate the concept of a dirty read, let's take a look at Figure 16-2, which shows two transactions operating concurrently.

When Transaction 1 first begins, it reads the table in its original state. The transaction then updates the table, changing the Stock value of each row. After those changes are made, Transaction 2 is initiated and reads the updated data. For example, Transaction 2 will see that the Stock value for the Past Light row is 11. Based on that information, Transaction 2 takes some sort of action, such as ordering additional *Past Light* CDs. After Transaction 2 has read the table data, Transaction 1, for one reason or another, rolls back the update, and the database is returned to its original state. As a result, the Past Light row actually has a Stock value of 22, even though Transaction 2 thinks that it has a value of 11. Transaction 2, then, is said to have experienced a dirty read.

Nonrepeatable Reads   The next phenomenon that can occur when concurrent transactions are initiated is the nonrepeatable read. The nonrepeatable read can occur when one transaction reads data from a table, another transaction then updates that data, and the first transaction

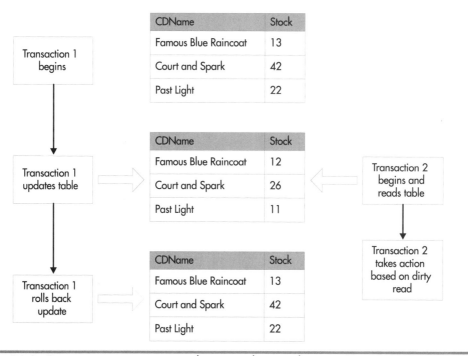

Figure 16-2 Concurrent transactions resulting in a dirty read

rereads the data, only to discover that the data has changed. As a result, the first read is not repeatable. Let's take a look at Figure 16-3 to better understand this concept.

When Transaction 1 is initiated, it reads the data in the table. At that point, the transaction might be involved in other processes or is waiting for a response from a user. For example, the user might receive a call from a manager who is trying to find out how many CDs are in stock for a particular CD. The user checks for that information. The manager then puts the user on hold for a short time, so the user must wait to complete the transaction. During that time, Transaction 2 is initiated and it updates the table. After the update, Transaction 1 again reads the data (the manager returns to the phone) and finds different information from the first read, resulting in a nonrepeatable read.

Phantom Reads   The last phenomenon that we'll look at is the phantom read. Although similar to the nonrepeatable read, the phantom read has some subtle differences, which are a factor when trying to determine an isolation level. A phantom read can occur when a transaction reads a table based on some sort of search condition, then a second transaction updates the data in the table, and then the first transaction attempts to reread the data, only this time different

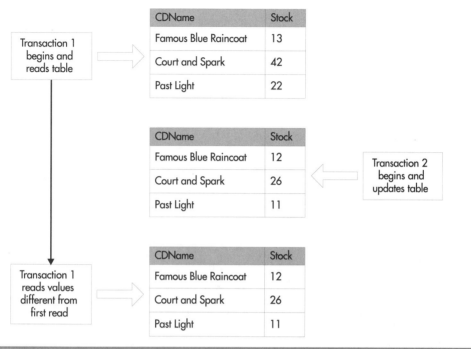

Figure 16-3 Concurrent transactions resulting in a nonrepeatable read

rows are returned because of how the search condition is defined. To clarify this, let's take a look at Figure 16-4.

When Transaction 1 is initiated, it reads the data in the table by executing a SELECT statement that queries the data. The statement includes a WHERE clause that returns only those rows with a Stock value greater than 20. That means that the Court and Spark row and the Past Light row are returned. After Transaction 1 retrieves (reads) the data, Transaction 2 begins and updates the table. Now when Transaction 1 rereads the data (using the same search criteria), only the Famous Blue Raincoat row is returned because it is now the only row with a Stock value greater than 20. As a result, the transaction has experienced a phantom read; the rows that it's reading are the not the same rows as it saw earlier.

Choosing an Isolation Level

Now that you have an overview of the type of data anomalies that you can run into when you have concurrent transactions, you should be better equipped to choose an isolation level for your transaction. The important point to remember is that the more restrictive the isolation level, the more types of phenomena you can eliminate.

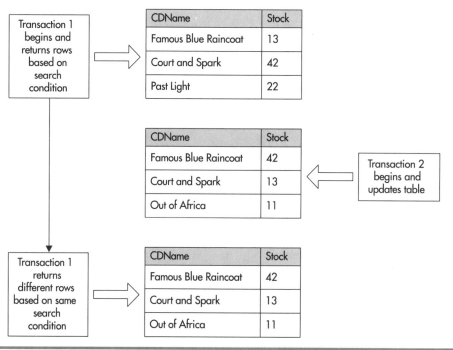

Figure 16-4 Concurrent transactions resulting in a phantom read

Let's take a look at the READ UNCOMMITTED isolation level, the least restrictive of the four levels. A transaction that's configured with this option may experience any of the data anomalies that we've looked at (dirty read, nonrepeatable read, and phantom read). As you can imagine, this is normally not a desirable state. In fact, if you define a transaction with the READ UNCOMMITTED option, the transaction cannot include statements that modify data. These transactions, by default, have a READ ONLY access level, and you cannot specify a READ WRITE level. (This is different from all other isolation levels in that the default access level is READ WRITE.) You should use the READ UNCOMMITTED isolation level only for transactions that generate approximate information, such as some types of statistical data in which the results are not critical in terms of precise accuracy.

The READ COMMITTED isolation level is only slightly more restrictive than READ UNCOMMITTED. The READ COMMITTED option prevents dirty reads, but nonrepeatable reads and phantom reads can still occur. The next option, REPEATABLE READ, is even more restrictive than READ COMMITTED. It prevents dirty reads and nonrepeatable reads, but does not prevent phantom reads. The only option that prevents all three types of data anomalies is SERIALIZABLE.

A transaction that is defined with the SERIALIZABLE isolation level fully isolates that transaction from all other transactions. As a result, the transaction is said to be *serializable,* meaning that it interacts with concurrent transactions in a way that orders transactions sequentially so that one transaction cannot impact the other. This does not mean that one transaction must close before another can open, but it does mean that the results of those transactions have to be the same as the results of operations that do operate one at a time. As long as no serializable transaction can influence another serializable transaction, the transactions are in conformance to the SERIALIZABLE isolation level.

Table 16-1 provides an overview of the phenomena that can occur for each isolation level. For example, notice that, for the READ UNCOMMITTED option, it's possible that all three data anomalies can occur.

As you can see from the table, the SERIALIZABLE isolation level provides the greatest data protection, and the READ UNCOMMITTED isolation level provides the least protection. This is why SERIALIZABLE is the default isolation level if no other level is defined.

NOTE

You may be wondering why you don't simply use the SERIALIZABLE isolation level for all transactions. However, the more restrictive the isolation level, the greater the effect on performance, so although you want to be sure to use an isolation level restrictive enough to meet your needs, you don't want to define a level that's more restrictive than necessary.

Specifying a Diagnostics Size

As you'll recall from the SET TRANSACTION syntax, one type of transaction mode that you can define is the diagnostics size. The diagnostics size refers to a diagnostics area that is used for conditions raised when an SQL statement is executed. A *condition* is a warning, exception, or other type of message generated by a statement execution. The diagnostics size actually refers to the number of conditions that will be stored for the execution of an SQL statement. For example, if the diagnostics size is 10, up to 10 conditions will be stored for the executed

Isolation Level	Dirty Read	Nonrepeatable Read	Phantom Read
READ UNCOMMITTED	Yes	Yes	Yes
READ COMMITTED	No	Yes	Yes
REPEATABLE READ	No	No	Yes
SERIALIZABLE	No	No	No

Table 16-1 Possible Data Anomalies for Isolation Levels

statement. If more than 10 conditions are raised for that statement, only 10 conditions are saved to the diagnostics area.

NOTE

You cannot assume that any specific conditions will be saved to the diagnostics area if more conditions are raised than the number defined by the diagnostics size. For example, if the diagnostics size is 15 and your statement raises 20 conditions, you cannot assume that the first 15 or last 15 conditions will be recorded. For more information on how conditions are handled for your particular SQL implementation, see the product documentation.

If you do not specify a diagnostics size in your SET TRANSACTION statement, the SQL implementation determines the size of the diagnostics area.

Creating a SET TRANSACTION Statement

Now that you've looked at the various components of the SET TRANSACTION statement, let's take a look at a couple of examples. The first example defines a transaction with an access level of READ ONLY, an isolation level of READ UNCOMMITTED, and a diagnostics size of 5:

```
SET TRANSACTION READ ONLY,
ISOLATION LEVEL READ UNCOMMITTED,
DIAGNOSTICS SIZE 5 ;
```

Notice that the transaction modes are separated by commas. Also notice that the isolation level option includes the keywords ISOLATION LEVEL, and the diagnostics size option includes the keywords DIAGNOSTICS SIZE. The transaction is configured with the least restrictive isolation level, which is why the access level must be READ ONLY. You cannot define a READ WRITE access level for this statement. Because the isolation level is READ COMMITTED, the statement does not have to specify the READ ONLY access level. It would have been assumed. However, including it causes no problems and better documents the code.

In the next example, the SET TRANSACTION statement defines a transaction with an access level of READ WRITE, an isolation level of SERIALIZABLE, and a diagnostics size of 8:

```
SET TRANSACTION READ WRITE,
ISOLATION LEVEL SERIALIZABLE,
DIAGNOSTICS SIZE 8 ;
```

Because SERIALIZABLE is the default isolation level, you do not have to specify it in your SET TRANSACTION statement. In addition, because the READ WRITE access level is the default level for serializable transactions, you do not have to specify that either. Your statement, then, might have looked like the following:

```
SET TRANSACTION DIAGNOSTICS SIZE 8 ;
```

This SET TRANSACTION statement will produce the same results as the preceding one.

As you can see, the SET TRANSACTION statement is a relatively simple statement to execute. However, be sure to check the documentation for your SQL implementation to determine the exact syntax used to set transaction properties. For example, SQL Server supports a SET TRANSACTION ISOLATION LEVEL statement that allows you to set only the isolation level. You cannot set the access level or diagnostics size. Oracle, on the other hand, supports a SET TRANSACTION statement that allows you to set a transaction's access and isolation level and assign the transaction to a rollback segment.

Progress Check

1. What is a transaction?

2. What are the four ACID characteristics of a transaction?

3. Which SQL statements can you use to set a transaction's properties?

4. Which access levels are supported in a transaction?

CRITICAL SKILL
16.3 Start a Transaction

In SQL:1999, a transaction can be started implicitly and explicitly. A transaction starts implicitly when certain types of SQL statements are executed, such as the SELECT, DELETE, UPDATE, and CREATE TABLE statements. These types of statements must be executed within the context of a transaction. If a transaction is not active, one is initiated.

Transactions can also be initiated explicitly by using the START TRANSACTION statement. The START TRANSACTION statement serves two purposes: to set the transaction's properties and to initiate the transaction. In terms of setting the properties,

1. A transaction is a unit of work that is made up of one or more SQL statements that perform a related set of actions.
2. Atomic, consistent, isolated, and durable
3. SET TRANSACTION and START TRANSACTION
4. READ ONLY and READ WRITE

the START TRANSACTION statement works just like the SET TRANSACTION statement. You can set the access level, the isolation level, and the diagnostics size. As for initiating a transaction, you simply execute the START TRANSACTION statement.

The syntax for the START TRANSACTION statement is similar to the SET TRANSACTION statement, as you can see in the following syntax:

START TRANSACTION <mode> [{ , <mode> } . . .]

After you specify the START TRANSACTION keywords, you must specify one or more transaction modes. As with the SET TRANSACTION statement, you can include only one mode for each type.

Now let's take a look at an example that defines an access level of READ ONLY, an isolation level of READ UNCOMMITTED, and a diagnostics size of 5:

```
START TRANSACTION READ ONLY,
ISOLATION LEVEL READ UNOMMITTED,
DIAGNOSTICS SIZE 5 ;
```

As you can see, this looks almost identical to a SET TRANSACTION statement. The transaction modes are applied in the same way, and if more than one transaction mode is specified, they're separated by a comma. The basic difference between a START TRANSACTION statement and a SET TRANSACTION statement is that the START TRANSACTION statement will initiate the transaction as well as set its properties.

NOTE

The START TRANSACTION statement was added to SQL with the release of SQL:1999. As a result, not all SQL implementations support a START TRANSACTION statement or any statement that explicitly initiates a transaction. Transactions in Oracle, for example, can be initiated only implicitly. However, SQL Server supports a BEGIN TRANSACTION statement, but it does not allow you to define any transaction modes.

CRITICAL SKILL
16.4 Set Constraint Deferrability

There can be times in a transaction when you want to modify data in a table that temporarily violates a constraint placed on that table. For example, you might have a table that includes a column configured with the NOT NULL constraint. It is possible that, during the course of the transaction, you want to insert a row in the table but don't yet have a value for the NOT NULL column. For this reason, the SQL standard allows you to define a constraint as deferrable.

Ask the Expert

Q: Does it matter whether your transaction includes data definition language statements or data manipulation language statements?

A: SQL allows you to include both types of statements in your transaction, but this is not the case for all SQL implementations. Some implementations do not allow you to mix the two types of statements in a single transaction. Other products allow you to mix the two types of statements, but limit which statements can be combined in one transaction. And still other implementations do not allow data definition language statements to be executed within the context of a transaction. The restrictions that various implementations place on mixing statement types can vary widely. The reason for this is that the interactions between the two types of statements can be complicated, so each implementation determines what statement mixtures it will support in its own database environment. Be sure to check the product documentation to determine what types of statements can be included in a transaction and how they can be mixed.

That means that the constraint does not have to be applied to the data immediately, when the modifying SQL statement is executed, but at a later point in a transaction, after you were able to insert a value into the NOT NULL column.

If a constraint is defined as deferrable, you can use the SET CONSTRAINTS statement within the transaction to defer the application of the constraint or to apply the constraint immediately. (Defining a constraint as deferrable doesn't automatically defer the application of that constraint. You must still explicitly defer it within the transaction.) If you explicitly defer a constraint, you can then temporarily violate the deferred constraint until the constraint is explicitly applied or the transaction ends. For a better understanding of how this works, let's take a look at Figure 16-5.

In this illustration, you'll notice that, after the transaction has been started, you can set the constraints to deferred. You don't have to defer the constraints right after the transaction starts, but you must defer them before executing any SQL statements that could violate the constraints. Once the applicable SQL statements have been executed and you're sure that no SQL data violates any of the deferred constraints, you can then apply the constraints to the applicable data. If the constraints are violated at this point, the transaction is considered unsuccessful and any updates are rolled back. Otherwise, the updates are committed to the database.

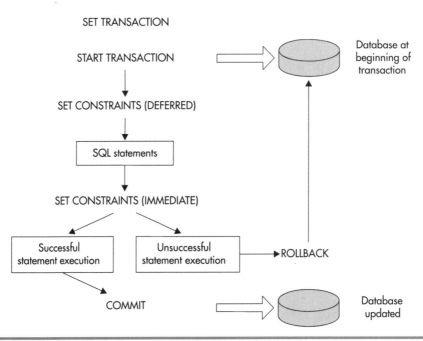

Figure 16-5 Deferring constraints in a transaction

In order to defer or apply the constraints within a transaction, you must use the SET CONSTRAINTS statement, as shown in the following syntax:

SET CONSTRAINTS { ALL | <constraint names> }
{ DEFERRED | IMMEDIATE }

As you can see from the syntax, you must choose from two sets of options. The first set of options allows you to specify the deferrable constraints that will be affected by the statement. If the statement should apply to all deferrable constraints, you can use the ALL keyword; otherwise, you must list the constraint names, separated by a column. You can specify only deferrable constraints in the SET CONSTRAINTS statement.

The next set of options you must specify is whether to defer the application of the identified constraints (DEFERRED) or to apply them immediately (IMMEDIATE). You should defer constraints before you insert or modify data, and you should apply constraints after you've modified that data.

Normally, you will use the SET CONSTRAINTS statement in sets of two: one statement to defer the constraints and the other to apply them. However, you don't actually need to use the SET CONSTRAINTS statement to apply them because all constraints are applied before the transaction commits, whether or not the constraints have been explicitly applied. However, it is generally good practice to document all actions, so be sure to explicitly apply your constraints.

Now let's take a look at an example of a SET CONSTRAINTS statement that defers Constraint1 and Constraint2:

```
SET CONSTRAINTS Constraint1, Constraint2 DEFERRED ;
```

As you can see, all you need to do is list the names of the constraints and the DEFERRED keyword. If you wanted your statement to apply to all deferrable constraints, you could have used the ALL keyword in place of the constraint names.

Once you execute all the statements you need to execute, with regard to the deferred constraints, you can then apply the constraints to the new and modified data. To apply the constraints, use the following SET CONSTRAINTS statement:

```
SET CONSTRAINTS Constraint1, Constraint2 IMMEDIATE ;
```

The only difference between this statement and the one that preceded this is that the IMMEDIATE keyword is used rather than DEFERRED.

NOTE

In order for you to use the SET CONSTRAINTS statement, your SQL implementation must support both the statement (or a similar statement) and deferrable constraints. If you cannot define deferrable constraints in your SQL database, the statement is not very useful.

Progress Check

1. What statement can you use to explicitly initiate a transaction?

2. Which transaction modes can you set in a START TRANSACTION statement?

3. What type of constraint can you specify in a SET CONSTRAINTS statement?

1. START TRANSACTION
2. Access level, isolation level, and diagnostics size
3. Deferrable constraint

CRITICAL SKILL
16.5 Create Savepoints in a Transaction

Often when you're setting up your transactions, you'll find that the set of actions that you need to perform is straightforward and easily treated as a unit. However, there might be times when some of your transactions are not as simple as others and different degrees of complexity between actions makes treating them as one unit a little more difficult, even though you still want to keep them all within the same transaction. One way to deal with this type of situation is through the use of *savepoints,* which are designated markers within your transaction that act as rollback points for portions of your transaction.

Say, for example, that the first part of your transaction contains relatively straightforward code that, although not particularly complicated, can still demand a heavy load on your system's performance. Now suppose that later in your transaction you must perform more complex actions, actions that are more likely to cause a rollback than the first set of actions. However, you don't want your rollbacks to cause you to lose the work performed by the first set of actions because of the hit on performance. If you insert a savepoint between the two sets of actions and then the second set needs to be rolled back, it will roll back only to the savepoint, rather than to the beginning of the transaction, thus making it unnecessary to perform the first set of actions over again. To help illustrate how savepoints work, let's take a look at Figure 16-6.

As you can see from the diagram, a savepoint can be inserted wherever you want to preserve a set of actions. Any changes made prior to the savepoint are preserved. In this case, two savepoints have been defined, each after a set of SQL statements have been successfully executed. If a rollback is necessary at any point after the savepoint has been defined, the database can be rolled back to that savepoint, without having to go back to the beginning of the transaction, and the actions prior to the savepoint will not have to be repeated. In addition, SQL allows you to name savepoints so that, if necessary, you can roll back the transaction to a specific savepoint, rather than to the one directly preceding the rollback. As a result, you can be more specific about which operations to preserve and which to roll back in the event that problems arise in your transaction.

NOTE

As you'll see in the "Terminate a Transaction" section later in this module, a transaction is rolled back to a savepoint only if the savepoint is identified in the ROLLBACK statement. Otherwise, the entire transaction is rolled back and the transaction is terminated, and the database is returned to its original state before the transaction was initiated.

Creating a savepoint in your transaction is very simple, as shown in the following syntax:

SAVEPOINT <savepoint name>

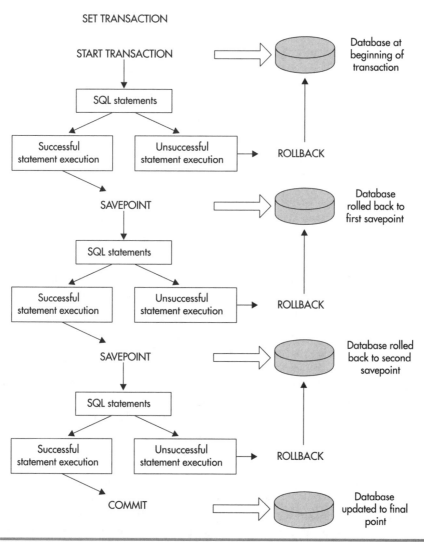

Figure 16-6 Using savepoints in your transactions

All you need to do is use the SAVEPOINT keyword, followed by a name for the savepoint. For example, to create a savepoint named Section1, you would use the following statement:

```
SAVEPOINT Section1 ;
```

Once the savepoint is created, you can use the Section1 name to identify the savepoint later in your transaction.

Releasing a Savepoint

After some operations within a transaction, you might find that you want to release a savepoint. If a savepoint is released, you can no longer roll back the transaction to that savepoint. Releasing a savepoint removes it from the transaction. In addition, all savepoints defined subsequent to the released savepoint are also released. This means that if your transaction includes three savepoints and you release the first savepoint, all three are removed from the transaction. The syntax used to release a savepoint is as follows:

RELEASE SAVEPOINT <savepoint name>

As you can see, this statement is similar to the SAVEPOINT statement. For example, to release the savepoint created in the preceding example, you would use the following statement:

```
RELEASE SAVEPOINT Section1 ;
```

When you execute this statement, the Section1 savepoint is removed from the transaction, along with any other savepoints defined subsequent to the Section1 savepoint.

CRITICAL SKILL
16.6 Terminate a Transaction

Earlier in this module, you learned that a transaction can be initiated either explicitly or implicitly. The same thing is true for ending a transaction. You can explicitly commit or roll back a transaction, which then terminates the transaction, or the transaction is terminated implicitly when circumstances force that termination.

In SQL, there are four primary circumstances that will terminate a transaction:

- A ROLLBACK statement is explicitly defined in the transaction. When the statement is executed, actions are undone, the database is returned to the state it was in when the transaction was initiated, and the transaction is terminated. If the ROLLBACK statement references a savepoint, only the actions taken after the savepoint are undone, and the transaction is not terminated.

- A COMMIT statement is explicitly defined in the transaction. When the statement is executed, all transaction-related changes are saved to the database, and the transaction is terminated.

- The program that initiated the transaction is interrupted, causing the program to abort. In the event of an abnormal interruption, which can be the result of hardware or software problems, all changes are rolled back, the database is returned to its original state, and the transaction is terminated. A transaction terminated in this way is similar to terminating a transaction by using a ROLLBACK statement.

● The program successfully completes its execution. All transaction-related changes are saved to the database, and the transaction is terminated. Once these changes are committed, they cannot be rolled back. A transaction terminated in this way is similar to terminating a transaction by using a COMMIT statement.

As you can see, the ROLLBACK and COMMIT statements allow you to explicitly terminate a transaction, whereas a transaction is terminated implicitly when the program ends or is interrupted. These methods of termination ensure that data integrity is maintained and the database is protected. No changes are made to the database unless the transaction is complete.

Now let's take a closer look at the two statements that you can use to explicitly end a transaction.

Committing a Transaction

Once all the statements have been executed in a transaction, the transaction must be terminated. The preferable type of termination is one that commits all the changes to the database. After all, why try to make changes if you don't want to commit them? To explicitly commit the changes and end the transaction, you must use the COMMIT statement, as shown in the following syntax:

COMMIT [WORK] [AND [NO] CHAIN]

At its most basic, the COMMIT statement requires only the COMMIT keyword. All other statement elements are optional. If you want, you can include the WORK keyword, which is simply a carryover from earlier versions of SQL. In other words, COMMIT and COMMIT WORK perform the same function. The only reason to use the WORK keyword is if your SQL implementation requires it.

The next optional element in the COMMIT statement is the AND CHAIN clause. The clause tells the system to start a new transaction as soon as the current transaction ends. The new transaction uses the same transaction modes as the current transaction. If you use the AND CHAIN option, you do not need to use the SET TRANSACTION or the START TRANSACTION statements for the next transaction unless you want to specify different modes.

Rather than specify AND CHAIN in your COMMIT statement, you can specify AND NO CHAIN, which tells your system not to start a new transaction based on the settings of the current transaction. If AND NO CHAIN is specified, a new transaction will not be initiated automatically when the current transaction is terminated. You must start a new transaction by using an implicit method or explicit method. If neither the AND CHAIN clause nor the AND NO CHAIN clause is specified, AND NO CHAIN is assumed.

In all likelihood, your commit statement will look like the one in the following example:

```
COMMIT ;
```

As you can see, the COMMIT keyword is the only required element. However, if you want a new transaction to be initiated after the current one, you should use the following COMMIT statement:

```
COMMIT AND CHAIN ;
```

If you don't want a new transaction to be initiated, do not include the AND CHAIN clause.

Rolling Back a Transaction

Although the goal of any transaction is to commit the changes made by the statements in that transaction, there will no doubt be times when you want to roll back those changes. To be able to control these rollbacks, you must use a ROLLBACK statement to undo changes and terminate the transaction or to undo changes back to a specified savepoint. The following syntax shows the various elements that can be included in a ROLLBACK statement:

```
ROLLBACK [ WORK ] [ AND [ NO ] CHAIN ]
[ TO SAVEPOINT <savepoint name> ]
```

The first line of syntax is very similar to the COMMIT statement. You must specify the ROLLBACK keyword. In addition, you can specify WORK, AND CHAIN, or AND NO CHAIN, all of which work the same way they did in the COMMIT statement, with AND NO CHAIN once again being the default.

However, the ROLLBACK statement, unlike the COMMIT statement, includes the optional TO SAVEPOINT clause. The TO SAVEPOINT clause specifies a savepoint that is used if changes have to be rolled back. This applies to any changes made after the specified savepoint. If you include the TO SAVEPOINT clause in your ROLLBACK statement, the transaction will be rolled back to the savepoint, but it will not be terminated. If the TO SAVEPOINT clause is not included, all changes are rolled back and the transaction is terminated.

The most basic type of ROLLBACK statement is one that includes no optional elements, as in the following example:

```
ROLLBACK ;
```

You could have included the WORK keyword and the AND NO CHAIN clause, and the statement would have performed the same function. If you want a new transaction to be initiated when the current transaction is terminated, you must specify the AND CHAIN clause. Keep in mind, however, that you cannot specify the AND CHAIN clause and the TO SAVEPOINT clause because AND CHAIN relies on the transaction being terminated in order to start a new transaction.

Ask the Expert

Q: Earlier in the module, you state that statements such as the SELECT, DELETE, UPDATE, and CREATE TABLE statements must be executed within the context of a transaction. However, we have not been using transactions in the examples and projects throughout the book. When are transactions used?

A: Throughout the book, we have been using interactive SQL (direct invocation) to communicate with the database. Most of the SQL statements that we have been executing within this environment have been done within the context of a transaction, even though you weren't aware of that happening. For most SQL implementations, each SQL statement is considered its own transaction. When you execute the statement, a transaction is initiated. If the statement is successful, any changes made are committed to the database and the transaction is terminated, in much the same way as if you had executed a COMMIT statement. If the statement is not successful, the changes are rolled back, the database is returned to the state it was in when the statement was first executed, and the transaction is terminated, as though you executed a ROLLBACK statement. Although interactive SQL tends to treat each statement as its own transaction, you can usually execute transaction-related statements in this environment. However, which statements you can execute and what options they support varies from product to product, so make sure you check the documentation. In general, it is not necessary to specifically define a transaction in interactive SQL.

Project
16-1

If you do specify the TO SAVEPOINT clause, you must include the name of the savepoint. For example, the following ROLLBACK statement specifies the Section1 savepoint:

```
ROLLBACK TO SAVEPOINT Section1 ;
```

If this statement is executed, all changes that occurred after the Section1 savepoint was created are rolled back to the state the database was in when the SAVEPOINT statement was executed. Even if other savepoints were created after the Section1 savepoint, changes are still rolled back to Section1.

Project 16-1   Working with Transactions

Prj16.txt

In this project you will create several transactions that execute statements against the Inventory database. For each transaction, you will explicitly start the transaction and execute one or more SQL statements. For this project, you will work with the

(continued)

COMMIT statement and ROLLBACK statement in separate transactions because you're working with directly invoked SQL (in your client application). However, if you were initiating transactions from within an application programming language, you would no doubt be using COMMIT and ROLLBACK together in some sort of conditional structure. In that way, certain results would cause the transaction to roll back, and other results would cause the transaction to commit, depending on how you set up the conditions in the programming language. However, for this project, we keep them separate so that you can effectively run through these steps. You can download the Prj16.txt file, which contains the SQL statements used in this project.

Step by Step

1. Open the client application for your RDBMS and connect to the Inventory database.

2. The first transaction that you'll create uses a START TRANSACTION statement to set the isolation level to READ UNCOMMITTED, retrieves information from the Artists table, and then commits the transaction. Enter and execute the following SQL transaction:

```
START TRANSACTION ISOLATION LEVEL READ UNCOMMITTED ;
SELECT * FROM Artists ;
COMMIT ;
```

The transaction should return all the rows and columns from the Artists table.

3. The next transaction that you'll create also uses a START TRANSACTION statement to set the isolation level. But this time you'll be setting the level to SERIALIZABLE. Because SERIALIZABLE is the default, you aren't required to define it; however, for the purposes of this project, we're going to include it. After you start the transaction, you'll attempt to update the CompactDiscs table by increasing the InStock value by 2 for all rows with a LabelID value equal to 832. After the UPDATE statement, you'll roll back the transaction so that no data is modified in the database. Enter and execute the following SQL transaction:

```
START TRANSACTION ISOLATION LEVEL SERIALIZABLE ;
UPDATE CompactDiscs SET InStock = InStock + 2
  WHERE LabelID = 832 ;
ROLLBACK ;
```

You should receive some sort of message acknowledging the termination of the transaction.

4. Now you'll confirm that the update you attempted in the preceding step was indeed rolled back. Enter and execute the following SQL statement:

```
SELECT CDTitle, InStock FROM CompactDiscs
WHERE LabelID = 832 ;
```

The SELECT statement should return the following query results:

```
CDTitle                     InStock
--------------------------  -------
That Christmas Feeling       8
Patsy Cline 12 Greatest Hits 32
Out of Africa                29
Blues on the Bayou           27
```

The InStock values shown in these results are what were contained in the CompactDiscs table before you executed the transaction. If the transaction had not been rolled back, each of these values would have been increased by 2.

5. Now you're going to add a savepoint to the transaction we created in the previous step. You want to be sure to reference the savepoint in the ROLLBACK statement. You will also add a SELECT statement before the savepoint. Enter and execute the following SQL transaction:

```
START TRANSACTION ISOLATION LEVEL SERIALIZABLE ;
SELECT CDTitle, InStock FROM CompactDiscs
   WHERE LabelID = 832 ;
SAVEPOINT Section1 ;
UPDATE CompactDiscs SET InStock = InStock + 2
   WHERE LabelID = 832 ;
ROLLBACK TO SAVEPOINT Section1 ;
```

Now your transaction will roll back only to the point preceding the UPDATE statement. In addition, because your transaction included a SELECT statement, you should receive the query results that you received in the previous step.

6. In the preceding transaction, the SELECT statement came before the savepoint, which means that the SELECT statement was executed before the UPDATE statement. If the transaction did not roll back the update, the query results would not reflect the correct information. As a result, you should verify that the UPDATE statement was rolled back. Enter and execute the following SQL statement:

```
SELECT CDTitle, InStock FROM CompactDiscs
WHERE LabelID = 832 ;
```

Your query results should show the same InStock values as the query results returned in the previous two steps.

7. Close the client application.

(continued)

Project Summary

In this project, you created and initiated three transactions. In the first one, you simply queried data and committed the transaction. In the next two, you updated data and then rolled back the updates. However, as you saw in the third transaction, it is possible to roll back a transaction to a specified savepoint. This allows you to protect certain portions of your transaction without having to reprocess statements that have been executed successfully. Because you rolled back the updates that you made, the Inventory database should have been left in the same state it was in when you began this project.

Module 16 Mastery Check

1. Which transaction characteristic refers to the all-or-nothing nature of a transaction?

   A. Atomic

   B. Consistent

   C. Isolated

   D. Durable

2. A(n) _____ is a unit of work that is made up of one or more SQL statements that perform a related set of actions.

3. Which SQL statements will terminate a transaction?

   A. SAVEPOINT

   B. SET TRANSACTION

   C. ROLLBACK

   D. COMMIT

4. What are the three types of transaction modes that you can specify in a SET TRANSACTION statement?

5. Which access level options can you include in a START TRANSACTION statement?

   A. READ ONLY

   B. UPDATE

   C. LOCAL

   D. READ WRITE

6. Two concurrent transactions are active in your system. The first transaction modifies data in a table. The second transaction sees those modifications before they're actually committed to the database. The first transaction then rolls back the modifications. Which type of data phenomenon has occurred?

   A. Phantom read

   B. Repeatable read

   C. Dirty read

   D. Nonrepeatable read

7. A(n) _____ read can occur when a transaction reads a table based on some sort of search condition, then a second transaction updates the data in the table, and then the first transaction attempts to reread the data, but this time different rows are returned because of how the search condition is defined.

8. Which isolation level fully isolates one transaction from another transaction?

9. You're using a SET TRANSACTION statement to configure transaction modes. You want to ensure that no nonrepeatable reads and no dirty reads can occur within that transaction. However, you're not concerned about phantom reads. Which isolation level should you use?

   A. READ UNCOMMITTED

   B. READ COMMITTED

   C. REPEATABLE READ

   D. SERIALIZABLE

10. You're setting up a transaction that defers the application of the ck_CDStock constraint until you execute several SQL statements. After you execute the statements, you want to explicitly apply the constraint to the changes you made to the database. What SQL statement should you use to apply the constraints?

11. A(n) _____ is a designated marker within your transaction that acts as a rollback point for a portion of your transaction.

12. You want to create a savepoint named svpt_Section2. What SQL statement should you use?

13. You create a transaction that includes four savepoints: Section1, Section2, Section3, and Section4. Near the end of the transaction, after all four savepoints, you define a RELEASE

SAVEPOINT that specifies the Section2 savepoint. Which savepoint or savepoints are removed from the transaction when the RELEASE SAVEPOINT statement is executed?

A. Section1

B. Section2

C. Section3

D. Section4

14. What circumstances will terminate a transaction?

15. You're creating a ROLLBACK statement in your transaction. You want the rollback to undo changes back to the svpt_Section2 savepoint. What SQL statement should you use?

16. You're creating a COMMIT statement in your transaction. After the transaction is terminated, you want a new transaction to be initiated. The new transaction should be configured with the same transaction modes as the first transaction. How should you create your COMMIT statement?

Module 17

Accessing SQL Data from Your Host Program

Throughout this book, you have been performing projects and testing examples by using a client application to work interactively with your SQL database. For example, you might have been using Query Analyzer to access a SQL Server database or SQL*Plus Worksheet to access an Oracle database. This method of data access is referred to as direct invocation, or interactive SQL. The SQL:1999 standard also provides for the use of other types of data access, including embedded SQL, SQL client modules, and the call-level interface (CLI); however, the types of data access supported by an SQL implementation can vary from product to product. Some, for example, do not support embedded SQL, and few support SQL client modules. In this module, I introduce you to the four types of data access methods and explain how they can be used to retrieve and modify data in your SQL database. Because SQL and CLI are the two methods most commonly used by programs to access SQL data, I cover these two topics in greater detail than direct invocation and SQL client modules, although I do provide a foundation in all four access types.

17.1 Invoke SQL Directly

If you've gotten this far in the book, you should already be very comfortable with interactive SQL. By using your client application, which comes with most database management products, you've been able to create ad hoc SQL statements that return immediate results to the application. These results are normally displayed in a window separate from where you executed your SQL statement. For example, let's take a look at Figure 17-1, which shows SQL Server's Query Analyzer. Notice that the top window includes a SELECT statement and the bottom window includes the query results from executing that statement. Most direct invocation client applications behave in a manner similar to this.

The types of SQL statements supported by the direct invocation method can vary from one SQL implementation to the next. Although most implementations will allow you to execute basic types of statements, such as SELECT or UPDATE, they might not allow you to execute statements specific to another method of data access. For example, some implementations might not allow you to declare a cursor within an interactive environment.

Despite the differences among SQL implementations, the SQL standard does define which types of statements should be supported in an interactive environment. These include SELECT, INSERT, UPDATE, and DELETE statements and statements related to schema definitions, transactions, connections, and sessions. You should also be able to declare temporary tables in an interactive environment. In fact, nearly any actions critical to the maintenance of data and of the underlying database structure are supported by direct invocation.

One of the main advantages to interactive SQL—in addition to the ability to execute ad hoc statements—is the elimination of any impedance mismatch. As you'll recall from earlier discussions, an impedance mismatch can occur because of differences in data types between SQL and application programming languages and in how query results (result sets) are handled

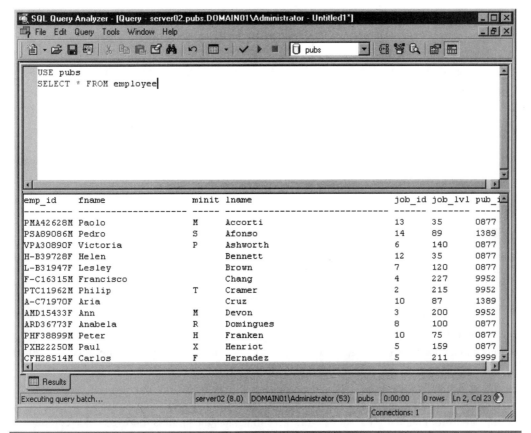

Figure 17-1 Query Analyzer in SQL Server 2000

between SQL and those languages. However, interactive SQL is a pure SQL environment, which means that only the data types supported by the implementation can be used, and result sets pose no problems to the client application because you can simply scroll through query results. Even so, direct invocation represents only a small percentage of users. You'll find that most data access is through embedded SQL and CLI-type mechanisms, and some through SQL client modules, but relatively few users rely on interactive SQL.

CRITICAL SKILL
17.2 Embed SQL Statements in Your Program

In Module 15, when I discuss SQL cursors, I introduce you to embedded SQL. As you'll recall from that discussion, embedded SQL refers to SQL statements that are interspersed in some type of application programming language. The SQL statements are blended into the host language to allow the source program to be able to access and modify SQL data and the underlying database structure.

According to the SQL:1999 standard, you can embed SQL statements in the following programming languages:

- Ada

- C

- COBOL

- Fortran

- MUMPS

- Pascal

- PL/I

Although the standard supports embedded SQL statements in these languages, SQL implementations rarely support embedding statements in all these languages. An implementation might be limited to only one or two programming languages, and some implementations might not support embedded SQL at all (although most implementations provide embedded SQL for at least one language). In addition, many implementations support embedded SQL in languages other than those specified in the SQL standard.

When a program contains embedded SQL statements, it must be compiled in a manner different from regular programs. Figure 17-2 illustrates the process followed when compiling these programs.

As you can see from the figure, we start with a program file that contains the host programming language and the embedded SQL statements. Before the program is compiled, it is submitted to a precompiler that is specific to the host programming language and the SQL implementation. The precompiler strips the SQL statements out of the host language code and replaces them with calls to the SQL statements. As a result, two files are created, one for the host language and one for the SQL statements.

Once a file is created for the host language, the source program is compiled in its normal way, as would be expected from a specific language. The output from the host language compiler is the object code, which is linked to various library routines. From this, an executable program is generated that links to the application plan. The application plan is created by a bind utility that validates and optimizes the SQL statements. The plan contains the SQL statements and information that the program needs to access the database.

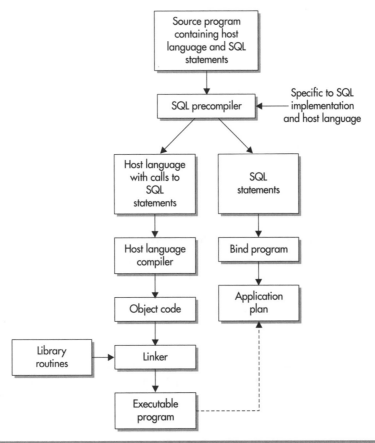

Figure 17-2 Compiling programs that contain embedded SQL

Creating an Embedded SQL Statement

When you develop a program that contains embedded SQL, you must follow specific conventions that determine how the SQL code is added to the program. These conventions are based on a combination of special SQL language elements and the requirements of the host programming language. In order to be used in a host language, an embedded SQL statement must conform to the following guidelines:

- Each SQL statement must begin with a qualified prefix.

- Each SQL statement may or may not require a qualified terminator, depending on the host language.

- Line breaks within the SQL statement must be handled according to the style of the host language.

- The placement of comments must be handled according to the style of the host language.

Most embedded SQL statements require a qualified prefix and terminator. Table 17-1 provides the prefix and terminator for each supported programming language.

As you can see from the table, the Ada, C, Pascal, and PL/I languages all handle an embedded SQL statement in the same way. For example, suppose you want to embed a SELECT statement that retrieves the CDName and InStock columns from the CDInventory table. To do so, you would use the following statement:

```
EXEC SQL SELECT CDName, InStock FROM CDInventory ;
```

Notice that the statement is preceded by the EXEC SQL prefix and ended with the semicolon terminator. If you were to create a similar statement in another language, your prefix or terminator might be different. In the case of MUMPS, they would both be different.

NOTE

Normally, it doesn't matter whether your embedded SQL statements appear in uppercase or lowercase. Programmers generally follow the conventions of the host language. However, for the purposes of this module, I'll treat embedded SQL statements as I have other SQL statements throughout the book: I'll use uppercase for SQL keywords and mixed case for SQL identifiers.

Language	Prefix	Terminator
Ada	EXEC SQL	;
C	EXEC SQL	;
COBOL	EXEC SQL	END-EXEC
Fortran	EXEC SQL	(no terminator)
MUMPS	&SQL(	)
Pascal	EXEC SQL	;
PL/I	EXEC SQL	;

Table 17-1 Beginning and Ending an SQL Statement

Using Host Variables in Your SQL Statements

In order to use embedded SQL effectively, you must be able to pass values between the host program and the SQL statements. For example, your embedded SQL statement might include a WHERE clause that requires a specific value in order to evaluate the search condition. The value might be supplied by a user or by an operation within the host program. In either case, that value must in some way be passed from the program to the SQL statement.

To pass values to and from an SQL statement, you can use host variables. A *host variable* is a type of parameter that is declared within the host language and is then referenced within the embedded SQL statement. When a host variable is used within an SQL statement, the name of the variable must be preceded by a colon. The colon signals to the precompiler that the named item is a variable and not a database object, such as a table or a column. As a result, you do not have to worry about whether the host variable shares the same name as a database object.

You can use a host variable in an embedded SQL statement in any place where you might expect to define a value. For example, the following SELECT statement can be embedded in a C program:

```
EXEC SQL SELECT CDName, InStock FROM CDInventory
  WHERE CDID = :v_CDID ;
```

Notice that the v_CDID host variable is preceded by a colon. The colon is used only within the SQL statement. When the variable is declared—earlier in the host program—no colon is used.

NOTE

The preceding example begins with EXEC SQL and ends with a semicolon. In addition, no specific continuation character is required to indicate a line break in the SQL statement. These conventions are consistent with what you would expect to find in a C program. For the examples in this module, I will be using embedded SQL statements as they would appear within a C program. Embedded SQL is well supported in C by a number of SQL implementations.

You're not limited to referencing a host variable in the WHERE clause of a SELECT statement. For example, you can reference a variable in the SET clause of an UPDATE statement, the VALUES clause of an INSERT statement, or the WHERE clause of a DELETE or UPDATE statement. However, you cannot use a host variable in place of an SQL identifier. In other words, you cannot pass an object name, such as a table name or column name, through a host variable.

Declaring Host Variables

As I mentioned earlier, you must declare your host variables within the host program. You can declare them anywhere in the program where you would normally declare variables in a particular language. In addition, you must declare the variables according to the conventions of the host language. The only difference is that you must begin the declarations with the BEGIN DECLARE SECTION statement and end the declarations with the END DECLARE SECTION statement. These two statements notify the precompiler that the variables enclosed in the statements are to be used in the other embedded SQL statements.

Let's take a look at an example of what I mean. Suppose you want to declare two variables, one to receive a value that identifies the CD and one that receives the name of the CD. Your variable declaration in C might look like the following:

```
EXEC SQL BEGIN DECLARE SECTION ;
  long v_cdid ; /* compact disc ID */
  varchar v_cdname[60] ; /* compact disc name */
EXEC SQL END DECLARE SECTION ;
```

As you can see, the variable declarations are enclosed in the two declaration-related SQL statements. Notice that these statements are treated just like any other embedded SQL statements in C. Each statement begins with EXEC SQL and ends with a semicolon.

Two host variables are being declared in this section. The first one, v_cdid, is declared with the long data type, and the second variable, v_cdname, is declared with the varchar data type. The two variable declarations follow the conventions of the host language. Notice that a comment follows each declaration. The comments also adhere to the conventions of the host language.

When host variables are used in SQL statements, an impedance mismatch can occur as a result of the differences between host language data types and SQL data types. As you can see in the preceding example, the variables are declared with C data types; however, the variables will be used in SQL statements to pass data to columns that are configured with SQL data types. If the data types are compatible, then data can be passed through the variables; otherwise, the impedance mismatch between the data types prevents values from being passed. For example, the v_cdid variable is configured with the long data type, which is compatible with the INTEGER data type in SQL, and the v_cdname variable is configured with the varchar data type, which is compatible with the CHARACTER VARYING data type in SQL. As a result, you can pass data through these variables as long as the receiving columns are configured with the compatible data types.

Retrieving SQL Data

As you have seen throughout this book, the process of querying data in an SQL database involves executing a SELECT statement that in turn retrieves data from the applicable table or tables and returns that data in a result set. A result set can be made up of one or more rows and

Ask the Expert

Q: You state that data can be passed from the variable to the SQL statement if the data types are compatible. How do you pass data if they're not compatible?

A: Most programming languages contain at least some data types that do not match up with SQL data types. If this situation arises, you can use the CAST value expression within the SQL statement to convert the variable value into a value that can be used by the SQL statement. In effect, the CAST value expression changes the data type of the value. For example, we can modify the previous embedded statement to convert the v_CDID host variable, as shown in the following example:

```
EXEC SQL SELECT CDName, InStock FROM CDInventory
  WHERE CDID = CAST(:v_CDID AS INT) ;
```

As you can see, CAST is used to convert the value in the host variable to an INTEGER data type. (For more information about CAST, see Module 10.) To determine which data types in a host language are compatible with data types in SQL, you should refer to the SQL:1999 standard, language-specific documentation, or product-specific documentation.

one or more columns. When you are querying data interactively, the multiple rows present no problems because your client application can handle more than one row. However, when querying data from an embedded SQL statement, multiple rows have to be handled through a cursor in order to allow that host language to work with one row at a time. A cursor, as you'll recall, acts as a pointer to specific rows in the result set. The cursor declaration defines the SELECT statement that retrieves data from the database, and cursor-related statements are then used to retrieve the individual rows from that result set. (For more information about cursors, see Module 15.)

Cursors, then, provide a solution to one type of impedance mismatch that can occur between SQL and the host language. Specifically, SQL returns data in sets, and most programming languages cannot handle sets. By using some sort of looping construct within the programming language and then using the SQL FETCH statement, you can cycle through each row in the result set to retrieve the data that you need.

Despite the availability of cursors to embedded SQL, there are often times when you know that your database query will return only one row. For example, you might want to retrieve data about a specific CD or performing artist, in which case, a cursor is unnecessary.

To facilitate single-row retrievals, embedded SQL supports the *singleton* SELECT statement. A singleton SELECT statement is similar to a regular SELECT statement except in two ways:

- You do not include a GROUP BY, HAVING, or ORDER BY clause.

- You include an INTO clause that specifies the host variables that will pass the data returned by the SELECT statement to the host program.

For example, suppose your SELECT statement returns the name of the CD and the number in stock, as shown in the following embedded statement:

```
EXEC SQL SELECT CDName, InStock INTO :v_CDName, :v_InStock
  FROM CDInventory WHERE CDID = :v_CDID ;
```

As you can see in this statement, the v_CDID variable is used to specify which CD should be returned. The value is entered by the user, and the variable passes that value from the host program into the SELECT statement.

Now let's take a look at the INTO clause. Notice that the clause contains two variables, the same number of variables as the number of columns retrieved from the CDInventory table. These variables are declared in the same way as the other host variables that we've looked at. Because this SELECT statement returns only one row and two columns, only two values are returned. These values are inserted into the variables. The variables must be specified in the same order as the column names are specified.

NOTE

The v_CDID variable in the WHERE clause is an input host variable, and the v_CDName and v_InStock variables in the INTO clause are output host variables.

Retrieving Null Values

In Module 4, I discuss null values and how they're used to represent unknown or unavailable data. As you'll recall from that discussion, most SQL columns, by default, permit null values, although you can override the default by defining a NOT NULL constraint on the column. However, if you don't override the default and null values are permitted, you can run into a problem with the host language because most application programming languages do not support null values.

To work around this issue, SQL allows you to declare indicator host variables. An *indicator host variable* is a type of variable that accompanies a regular host variable, also referred to as a *data host variable*. The indicator variable contains a value that specifies whether or not the value in the associated data variable is null. Indicator variables are declared in the same way as other host variables.

Let's take a look at an example of indicator host variables to illustrate how they work. In the following embedded SELECT statement, an indicator host variable has been added to each of the host variables in the INTO clause:

```
EXEC SQL SELECT CDName, InStock
   INTO :v_CDName :ind_CDName, :v_InStock :ind_InStock
   FROM CDInventory WHERE CDID = :v_CDID ;
```

The INTO clause includes two indicator host variables: ind_CDName and ind_InStock. Notice that each indicator variable follows the associated data variable. The placement of the indicator variable is the only indication the SQL implementation has that a particular host variable is an indicator variable. There is nothing in the variable declaration or naming that distinguishes indicator variables from data variables. When the implementation sees that one variable follows the other and that no comma separates the two, the implementation assigns a value of 0 to the indicator variable if the associated variable contains a real value (is not null). If the associated variable contains a null value, the implementation assigns a value of –1 to the indicator variable. The host program then takes the appropriate action based on this information.

NOTE

When you declare an indicator host variable, be sure to use a data type that supports the 0 and –1 values.

Error Handling

When you embed SQL statements into your host language, you should provide a way to take specific actions if you receive error or warning messages when you try to access data. SQL provides a relatively straightforward method that you can use to monitor errors and warnings and take actions depending on the results of that monitoring. By embedding WHENEVER statements in your host language, you can provide your program with an effective level of error handling that works alongside your other embedded statements.

The WHENEVER statement includes two sets of options, as shown in the following syntax:

```
WHENEVER
{ SQLEXCEPTION | SQLWARNING | NOT FOUND }
{ CONTINUE | GOTO <target> }
```

As you can see, you must first specify the WHENEVER keyword and then specify the necessary options. The first set of options indicates the condition that the WHENEVER statement applies to. If that condition is met, a specified action is taken. A WHENEVER statement can include one of three conditions:

- **SQLEXECPTION**   The condition is met whenever an SQL statement generates an exception. For example, an exception might be generated when you try to insert invalid data into a column.

- **SQLWARNING**   The condition is met whenever an SQL statement generates a warning. For example, a statement might generate a warning if a number has been rounded off.

- **NOT FOUND**   The condition is met whenever a SELECT statement cannot return data in its query results. This can apply to a singleton SELECT statement or to a FETCH statement at the end of the cursor's result set.

Once you specify a condition in your WHENEVER statement, you must specify an action. The WHENEVER statement supports two actions:

- **CONTINUE**   The program will continue running to the next statement.

- **GOTO <target>**   The program will jump to a section within the host language that is named in the <target> placeholder.

Now that we've looked at the options available in the WHENEVER statement, let's take a look at an example. Suppose that you want your SQL statements to go to a certain part of the program if an error occurs. In the following WHENEVER statement, an exception will cause the program to move to the Error1 section:

```
EXEC SQL WHENEVER SQLEXCEPTION GOTO Error1 ;
```

Notice that the SQLEXCEPTION option and the GOTO option are specified in this statement. The SQLEXCEPTION option tells the program to take a specified action if an SQL statement generates an exception. The GOTO option defines the action that should be taken. In this case, the option specifies that the program should move to the Error1 section of the host language.

A WHENEVER statement applies to the embedded SQL statements that follow it. You can embed as many WHENEVER statements in your host language as necessary. The last statement to appear is the one that is applied to the other statements.

Progress Check

1. What four methods can you use to access SQL data?

2. What does the precompiler do with the program file?

3. What prefix must you use for an embedded SQL statement in COBOL?

4. What statement should you use at the beginning of the declaration section for host variables?

5. What type of SELECT statement can you use in embedded SQL when retrieving only one row of data?

Project 17-1   Embedding SQL Statements

Prj17.txt

In most of the projects in this book, you used a client application to access your SQL database interactively. However, because of the subject matter of this module, particularly with regard to embedded SQL, this project will take a different approach from previous projects. For this project, you will use some type of text editing program (such as Microsoft Notepad) to complete the steps. Because programming in a host language is beyond the scope of this book, you will create only the SQL statements that are embedded in the host language. The statements will conform to C, although they might apply to other host languages. In the project, you will set up variable declarations, create an error-handling statement, and embed an SQL SELECT statement that queries data from the Inventory database. You can download the Prj17.txt file, which contains the embedded SQL statements used in this project.

Step by Step

1. Open a text editing program such as Microsoft Notepad.

2. The first step is to create one input host variable and two output host variables. The purpose of the input host variable is to be able to receive a CD identifier from the user. That identifier can then be used in the WHERE clause of the SELECT statement to determine

(continued)

---

1. Direct invocation, embedded SQL, SQL client modules, and CLI

2. The precompiler strips the SQL statements out of the host language code and replaces them with calls to the SQL statements. As a result, two files are created, one for the host language and one for the SQL statements.

3. EXEC SQL

4. BEGIN DECLARE SECTION

5. Singleton SELECT statement

which row of data will be returned from the CompactDiscs table. Along with declaring the variables, you will include comments that identify the purpose of those variables. Type the following embedded SQL statements and variable declarations into your text document:

```
EXEC SQL BEGIN DECLARE SECTION ;
  long v_cdid ; /* input variable for CD identifier */
  varchar v_cdtitle[60] ; /* output variable for CD title */
  long v_instock ; /* output variable for InStock value */
EXEC SQL END DECLARE SECTION ;
```

Notice that you were to enter in the entire variable declaration section, so you had to include the BEGIN DECLARE SECTION statement and the END DECLARE SECTION statement. These statements are necessary to notify the precompiler that the variable declarations will be used in the embedded SQL statements.

3. After you create your declaration section, you realize that you want to include indicator variables for the output data variables. As a result, you must add two declarations to your declaration section. Type the following declarations into your text document:

```
short ind_cdtitle ; /* indicator variable for v_cdtitle */
short ind_instock ; /* indicator variable for v_instock */
```

You can add the declarations anywhere into your declaration section. However, for clear coding, I suggest you add them close to each of their associated data variables, as shown in the following declaration section:

```
EXEC SQL BEGIN DECLARE SECTION ;
  long v_cdid ; /* input variable for CD identifier */
  varchar v_cdtitle[60] ; /* output variable for CD title */
  short ind_cdtitle ; /* indicator variable for v_cdtitle */
  long v_instock ; /* output variable for InStock value */
  short ind_instock ; /* indicator variable for v_instock */
EXEC SQL END DECLARE SECTION ;
```

Notice that the two new declarations have been inserted beneath their respective data variables.

4. Now let's include an error-handling statement into your test document. The statement will represent a section named Error1 in your host language. The assumption will be that if an embedded SQL statement generates an exception, the program will jump to the Error1 section and take whatever action is defined in that section. Type the following embedded SQL statement into your text document:

```
EXEC SQL WHENEVER SQLEXCEPTION GOTO Error1 ;
```

Notice that the embedded SQL code contains a WHENEVER statement that specifies the SQLEXCEPTION and GOTO options.

5. Now you're ready to create the embedded SELECT statement. The statement will contain the variables defined in your declaration section. In addition, a singleton SELECT statement will be used because the statement will retrieve only one row at a time. The WHERE clause is based on a specified CompactDiscID value, and each value is unique within the CompactDiscs table. (The CompactDiscID column is the primary key, so values must be unique within that column.) Type the following embedded SQL statement into your text document:

```
EXEC SQL SELECT CDTitle, InStock
   INTO :v_CDTitle :ind_CDTitle, :v_InStock :ind_InStock
   FROM CompactDiscs WHERE CompactDiscID = :v_CDID ;
```

Notice that an INTO clause is included in this statement. The INTO clause contains the output data variables and their associated indicator variables. Your text document should now look like the following code:

```
EXEC SQL BEGIN DECLARE SECTION ;
   long v_cdid ; /* input variable for CD identifier */
   varchar v_cdtitle[60] ; /* output variable for CD title */
   short ind_cdtitle ; /* indicator variable for v_cdtitle */
   long v_instock ; /* output variable for InStock value */
   short ind_instock ; /* indicator variable for v_instock */
EXEC SQL END DECLARE SECTION ;
EXEC SQL WHENEVER SQLEXCEPTION GOTO Error1 ;
EXEC SQL SELECT CDTitle, InStock
   INTO :v_CDTitle :ind_CDTitle, :v_InStock :ind_InStock
   FROM CompactDiscs WHERE CompactDiscID = :v_CDID ;
```

If this were an actual C program, you would also see the C code surrounding the embedded SQL statements. The C code would represent that actual program and would take actions appropriate to that program. For example, the host language would include code that would allow the program to receive the CD identifier for the user. That identifier would be passed to the v_cdid variable to be used in the embedded SELECT statement.

6. Save the file and close the application.

Project Summary

In this project, you created a host variable declaration section, declared five host variables, added an error-handling statement, and embedded a singleton SELECT statement. If this were a complete C program, the host language would have used the data in the output parameters to take any actions appropriate to the program. The C program would also include a section named Error1 that would specify a specific action to take should an exception be generated by

(continued)

17

Accessing SQL Data from Your Host Program

Project
17-1

Embedding SQL Statements

the SQL statement. You can, of course, include many more embedded SQL statements than are used in this project, and you can include other type of statements such as UPDATE or DELETE. However, the purpose of this project was to provide you with a foundation in embedded SQL. For more details on embedding SQL statements, you should refer to documentation specific to the host language and documentation for the applicable SQL implementation.

CRITICAL SKILL
17.3 Create SQL Client Modules

Now that you have a basic understanding of embedded SQL, let's take a look at SQL client modules. SQL client modules are self-contained collections of SQL statements. Unlike embedded SQL, in which the SQL statements are inserted into the host programming language, SQL client modules are separate from the host language. The host language contains calls that invoke the module, which in turn executes the SQL statements within that module.

An SQL client module is made up of the properties that define the module, temporary table and cursor declarations, and the procedures that contain the SQL statements. Each procedure can contain only one SQL statement. The following syntax provides the basic elements of an SQL client module:

```
MODULE <module name> [ NAMES ARE <character set> ]
LANGUAGE { ADA | C | COBOL | FORTRAN | MUMPS | PASCAL | PLI }
[ SCHEMA <schema name > ] [ AUTHORIZATION <authorization identifier> ]
[ <temporary table declarations> ] [ <cursor declarations> ]
PROCEDURE <procedure name> ( <parameter declarations> )
<SQL statement> ;
```

Let's take a look at each clause within the syntax so that you have a better understanding of all the elements that make up an SQL client module. The MODULE clause specifies a name for the module. This is followed by the optional NAMES ARE clause, which is used to specify a character set for the identifiers in the module. If the NAMES ARE clause is not specified, the default character set for the SQL implementation is used. The next element in the syntax is the LANGUAGE clause, which specifies the host language that will be calling the module. You must specify a language.

After you've defined the LANGUAGE clause, you must define a SCHEMA clause, an AUTHORIZATION clause, or both. The SCHEMA clause identifies the default schema to be used by SQL statements in the module. The AUTHORIZATION clause identifies the authorization identifier to be used for executing the statements within the module. If no AUTHORIZATION clause is specified, the current authorization identifier is assumed.

You can also declare temporary tables and cursors within a module. Temporary tables must be declared before any cursors or procedures. You can declare as many temporary tables as necessary. Unlike temporary table declarations, cursor declarations can be mixed in between procedures; however, a cursor declaration must always precede the procedure that references that cursor.

The final portion of the module statement is the procedure. As I mentioned earlier, your module can contain one or more procedures. However, the procedure can contain only one SQL statement and *must* contain at least one parameter declaration, which is the status parameter SQLSTATE.

NOTE

The procedure in an SQL client module is sometimes referred to as an *externally invoked procedure*.

The SQLSTATE status parameter provides a way to report errors back to your host language. Like any other host parameter, values are passed between the SQL database and the host program. In the case of SQLSTATE, the values are related to the status of SQL statement execution. By including the SQLSTATE parameter in your modules, you're allowing your host program to see the status of your statement execution. As a result, the program can monitor for errors and take appropriate actions if those errors occur.

In addition to the SQLSTATE status parameter, you must declare all other host parameters used in the procedure's SQL statement. Parameter names (except SQLSTATE) must be preceded by a colon when being declared and when used in the SQL statement. As you can see in the syntax, parameter declarations must be enclosed by parentheses. In addition, if more than one parameter is declared, those declarations must be separated by a comma.

Defining SQL Client Modules

Now that we've reviewed the syntax for an SQL client module, let's take a look at an example of how to create one. In the following statement, I create a module that contains one procedure:

```
MODULE QueryCDInventory
LANGUAGE C
SCHEMA Inventory AUTHORIZATION Sales
PROCEDURE Query1
  ( SQLSTATE, :p_CDID INT, :p_CDName VARCHAR(60) )
  SELECT CDName INTO :p_CDName
  FROM CDInventory WHERE CDID = :p_CDID ;
```

As you can see in this example, we're creating a module named QueryCDInventory. The module will be called by a C program (LANGUAGE C). The SQL statement within the module will access a table in the Inventory schema and will be executed under the context of the Sales authorization identifier. The MODULE statement includes only one procedure, which is named Query1. If more than one procedure were defined, they would each be terminated by a semicolon. Now let's take a closer look at the Query1 procedure.

The first thing you might notice is that three host parameters have been declared. The SQLSTATE parameter provides status information to the host program. The p_CDID parameter is an input parameter that will receive a value from the host program. The p_CDName parameter is an output parameter that will take the value returned by the SELECT statement and pass it to the host program. Notice that both the p_CDID and p_CDName parameters are preceded by a colon and declared with a data type. The SQLSTATE parameter does not require a semicolon or data type.

Once we declare the parameters, we can define the SELECT statement. As you can see, the input parameter is used in the WHERE clause, and the output parameter is used in the INTO clause. The use of the parameters in this way allows the module to interact with the host program. A value for the input parameter is passed to the module when the module is called within the host language, and the output parameter is returned to the host language to be used by the program as necessary.

NOTE

The process of calling a module within a host program and passing a parameter to the module is language-specific. Be sure to check the documentation for the specific programming language and for the applicable SQL implementation.

As you can see, an SQL client module can be a handy tool for developing the SQL component of an application without having to embed the SQL statements within the host language. Unfortunately, SQL client modules are not widely supported in SQL implementations, and if they are supported, they are often not well documented. However, whether or not they're widely implemented is becoming beside the point as the industry moves away from embedded SQL and SQL client modules toward CLI and CLI-like data access, which I cover in the next section.

Progress Check

1. What are SQL client modules?

2. How many SQL statements can you include in a procedure in an SQL client module?

3. Which clause in a MODULE statement do you use to specify the host programming language?

CRITICAL SKILL
17.4 Use an SQL Call-Level Interface

As you have seen so far in this module, a program can access an SQL database by using embedded SQL and SQL client modules. In embedded SQL, SQL statements are inserted directly into the host programming language. For SQL client modules, the host program calls modules that contain executable SQL statements. The statements are separate from the host language. SQL provides yet another method for accessing SQL data from within a programming language—the call-level interface, or CLI.

A CLI is an application programming interface (API) that supports a set of predefined routines that allow a programming language to communicate with an SQL database. The programming language calls the routines, which then connect to the database. The routines access data and status information from the database, as required, and return that information to the program. Figure 17-3 provides an overview of how a CLI allows a program to communicate with an SQL database.

The program invokes CLI routines through the use of functions. When calling a function, the program must specify values for the function's arguments. These values define what actions to take and what data to access. The function passes the values to the designated routine, which acts as an interface between the program and the SQL database. The CLI, in effect, hides the details of accessing the database from the program, making it possible for the program to access databases in different management systems.

---

1. SQL client modules are self-contained collections of SQL statements. Unlike embedded SQL, in which the SQL statements are inserted into the host programming language, SQL client modules are separate from the host language.
2. One
3. LANGUAGE clause

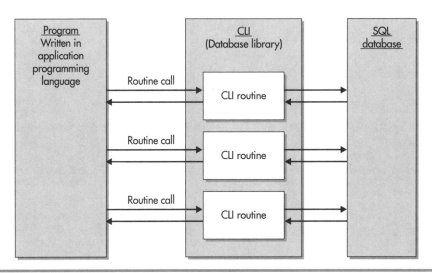

Figure 17-3 Using a CLI to access data in an SQL database

One of the most well-known implementations of the CLI model is Microsoft's Open Database Connectivity (ODBC) API, although other vendors have released CLI-like products that support similar types of database access. In addition, new generations of data access APIs are gaining popularity, such as Microsoft's OLE-DB, which is more efficient than ODBC and supports access to SQL data sources and other types of data sources. You'll also find that such products as ActiveX Data Object (ADO) provide an object-oriented interface between scripting languages or object-oriented languages and the OLE-DB API. Many development tools also make accessing an SQL data source easier than ever. For example, Visual Studio .NET allows you to build data-driven applications in such languages as Visual Basic, C++, and C#. By using the built-in ADO.NET tools, you can create applications that can access a variety of data sources, such as SQL Server and Oracle.

The key to all these products is to provide a uniform method of database access from within the programming language. The CLI specifications in SQL:1999 standardize the database access interface by providing a set of predefined CLI functions that allow your program to connect to a database, modify and retrieve data, pass information to and from the database, and obtain status information about statement execution. In this section, we'll look at several CLI functions and how they can be used in a programming language to access SQL data.

NOTE

Despite how extensively the SQL:1999 standard has defined the CLI model, applications can vary greatly in the methods they use to access a data source. As a result, you'll find that you'll want to use a data access method that is supported in your environment. For example, if you're developing a C application that connects to a data source via ODBC, the specifics of data access described in this section will be very useful to you. However, if you're developing a C# application or an Active Server Pages (ASP) application using VBScript and you're connecting to a data source via ADO, you'll want to refer to documentation related to that particular technology as well as reviewing the information in this section.

Allocating Handles

The first step that you must take when accessing a database through a CLI interface is to establish the necessary allocation handles. An *allocation handle* is an object returned by the SQL database when a resource is allocated. The handle is used by the host program to access the database. You must establish three types of allocation handles in your host program in order to access SQL data from within that program:

- **Environment handle**   Establishes the environment in which all CLI functions are called and provides a context in which to establish one or more connection handles.

- **Connection handle**   Establishes a connection context to a specific SQL database. The connection handle must be established within the context of the environment handle. A connection handle doesn't actually connect to the database. It merely provides the context to make that connection possible. Once a connection handle has been established, you must use the context of that handle to make the actual connection to the database.

- **Statement handle**   Establishes a context in which SQL statements can be executed. Any statement invoked through the CLI must be executed within the context of a statement handle, and the statement handle must be defined within the context of a connection handle.

To better understand how allocation handles operate, let's take a look at Figure 17-4. As you can see in the figure, two connection handles are allocated within an environment handle, and one statement handle is allocated within each connection handle. Each SQL statement is executed within the context of a statement handle.

Establishing an Environment Handle

To establish an environment handle in which to support database access, you can use the AllocHandle( ) function, which requires three arguments. The first argument (SQL_HANDLE_ENV) specifies the type of handle (environment) that is being allocated.

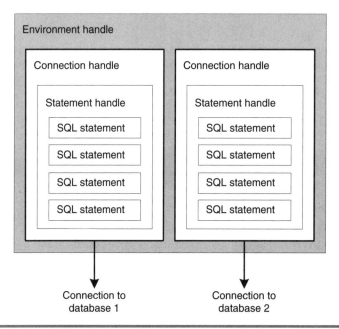

Figure 17-4 Establishing allocation handles

The second argument (SQL_NULL_HANDLE) indicates that the environment handle does not depend on any existing handle. The third argument is a host variable that identifies the environment handle. When a host variable is used in this context, it is preceded by an ampersand (&).

NOTE

Host variables are declared according to the conventions of the host language. In addition, the host program might contain other elements that support CLI functionality. For example, a C program might require special include files necessary to interact with the CLI API. In addition, the host program might contain special error-handling functions that can monitor the success or failure of a CLI routine call. For information about language-specific elements that should be included in your host program, be sure to check the documentation for the specific language, CLI API, and SQL implementation.

Now that we've reviewed the individual elements necessary to establish an environment handle, let's take a look at the AllocHandle( ) function as it would be included in your C program:

```
SQLAllocHandle ( SQL_HANDLE_ENV, SQL_NULL_HANDLE, &henv ) ;
```

The first thing you'll notice is that the AllocHandle function is preceded by the SQL prefix. In C programs, the SQL prefix is added to all CLI functions. The prefix can vary according to the host language. You'll also notice in this statement that the three arguments are enclosed in parentheses and separated by commas. In addition, the host variable that identifies the handle is preceded by an ampersand.

Establishing a Connection Handle

Once you've established your environment handle, you can establish one or more connection handles within the context of that environment. To do so, you will again use the AllocHandle( ) function, along with three arguments. The first argument (SQL_HANDLE_DBC) specifies the type of handle (connection) that is being allocated. The second argument identifies the environment in which the connection is being established. (This is the host variable identified when you established the environment handle.) The third argument is a host variable that identifies the connection handle. Again, it is preceded by an ampersand, as shown in the following function statement:

```
SQLAllocHandle ( SQL_HANDLE_DBC, henv, &hdbc ) ;
```

After you establish the connection handle, you must explicitly connect to the database within the context of the handle. To do this, you must use the SQLConnect( ) function, which takes seven arguments: the connection handle, the target SQL server, the length of the server name, the connection user, the length of the user name, the connection password, and the length of the password. For C strings, you can use SQL_NTS in place of length arguments to indicate that a length does not have to be specified for the preceding string, as shown in the following example:

```
SQLConnect ( hdbc, server01, SQL_NTS, SaleMngr, SQL_NTS, SalesPW, SQL_NTS ) ;
```

As you can see, the function specifies the hdbc connection handle and the server01 SQL server. The connection will be established using the SaleMngr user account and the SalesPW password. Instead of specifying the length of any of the strings, SQL_NTS is used.

Once you've connected to the database, you can create statement handles and execute SQL statements.

Establishing a Statement Handle

In order to execute an SQL statement from within your host program, you must create a statement handle within the context of your connection handle. As with other types of handles, you can use the AllocHandle( ) function to establish the statement handle.

As you have seen, the AllocHandle( ) function requires three arguments. In the case of a statement handle, those arguments are SQL_HANDLE_STMT, the host variable that identifies the connection handle, and the host variable that identifies the statement handle. The host variable that identifies the statement handle is preceded by an ampersand, as shown in the following example:

```
SQLAllocHandle ( SQL_HANDLE_STMT, hdbc, &hstmt ) ;
```

In this function, the connection handle referenced is hdbc, and the variable identifying the statement handle is hstmt.

Executing SQL Statements

Now that you've established your allocation handles and connected to the database, you can set up your functions that allow you to execute the SQL statements. The CLI model supports two methods that you can use to execute SQL statements. The first is direct execution and the second is preparing the statement for later execution.

Using the ExecDirect( ) Function

The first method you can use to execute an SQL statement is the ExecDirect( ) function. The function takes three arguments. The first argument is the name of the statement handle in whose context you'll be executing the statement. The second argument is the actual SQL statement, enclosed in double quotation marks. The third argument is the length of the statement. In a C program, you generally use SQL_NTS to indicate that you do not have to specify the length of the string.

Let's take a look at an example of the ExecDirect( ) function to demonstrate how you can use it to execute an SQL statement. The following function references the hstmt statement handle and defines a DELETE statement:

```
SQLExecDirect ( hstmt, "DELETE CDInventory WHERE CDID = 5731", SQL_NTS ) ;
```

As you can see, the SQL statement is passed as an argument to the CLI routine. In this case, any rows with a CDID value of 5731 will be deleted from the CDInventory table. Notice that the SQL_NTS value is used to indicate that you do not have to specify the length of the string (the actual SQL statement).

Using the Prepare( ) and Execute( ) Functions

Another method that you can use to execute a statement is to first prepare the statement and then later execute it. You would use this method if you need to execute your statement more than one time.

The first function that you use in the two-step process is the Prepare( ) function, which requires the same three arguments as the ExecDirect( ) function, as shown in the following example:

```
SQLPrepare ( hstmt, "DELETE CDInventory WHERE CDID = 5731", SQL_NTS ) ;
```

Notice that we reference the same statement handle and define the same SQL statement as in the preceding ExecDirect( ) example. The only difference is that, in the case of the Prepare( ) function, the statement isn't actually executed, but is instead prepared for execution. When a statement must be executed multiple times, this process saves on overhead because the statement has to be analyzed and optimized only once.

Once you've prepared the statement, you can then use the Execute( ) function to execute the statement. The Execute( ) function takes only one argument—the statement handle that contains the prepared statement, as shown in the following example:

```
SQLExecute ( hstmt ) ;
```

Because the statement was already prepared, you merely need to reference the statement handle to execute the statement. You can execute the statement as often as necessary simply by invoking the Execute( ) function and specifying the statement handle.

Working with Host Variables

In the preceding examples, the SQL statements that we executed were relatively straightforward because no host variables were used in the statement. However, if you plan to pass host variable values into or out of an SQL statement, you must take an extra step to bind those host variables to the SQL statement.

For example, suppose you want to set up a DELETE statement that takes an input variable identifying the row to be deleted. Your Prepare( ) function would be similar to the following:

```
SQLPrepare ( hstmt, "DELETE CDInventory WHERE CDID = ?", SQL_NTS ) ;
```

Notice that a question mark is used to indicate the position of the variable. The question mark is used in place of the host variable.

Once you've prepared your SQL statement, you must now bind the host variable to the statement. To do so in a C program, you must use a BindParameter( ) function that identifies the statement handle, the position of the host variable within the SQL statement, the name of the host variable, and a number of other arguments, as shown in the following example:

```
SQLBindParameter ( hstmt, 1, SQL_PARAMETER_MODE_IN, SQL_INT,
    SQL_INT, 4, 0, &v_CDID, 4, &ind_CDID ) ;
```

As you can see, the BindParameter( ) function takes 10 arguments. Table 17-2 lists the arguments used in the preceding example and provides a description of each of those arguments.

If more than one host variable is included in your SQL statement, a BindParameter( ) function statement should be defined for each variable, and the position (the second argument) should be incremented by one for each additional variable. Once you bind the host variables to your SQL statement, you can execute the statement by using the Execute( ) function.

Argument	Example	Description
1	hstmt	Identifies the statement handle that provides the context for the SQL statement execution
2	1	Identifies the position of the host variable in the SQL statement
3	SQL_PARAMETER_MODE_IN	Specifies whether the host variable is an in, out, or in/out variable
4	SQL_INT	Identifies the data type of the value supplied
5	SQL_INT	Identifies the data type of the host variable
6	4	Specifies the column size of the host variable
7	0	Specifies the number of digits to the right of the decimal required by the host variable
8	&v_CDID	Identifies the name of the host variable, as declared in the host program
9	4	Specifies the length in octets of the host variable
10	&ind_CDID	Identifies the name of the indicator variable, as declared by the host program

Table 17-2 Arguments Used in the BindParameter( ) Function

Retrieving SQL Data

Up to this point, the SQL statements that we've executed in the CLI environment have not returned any data. However, you'll often run into situations when your program will need to query the database and process the values that are returned by that query. As a result, you'll need some sort of mechanism to bind the output from your query to variables that you declared in the host language.

For example: suppose that you want to execute the following SELECT statement:

```
SQLExecDirect ( hstmt, "SELECT CDName, InStock FROM CDInventory", SQL_NTS ) ;
```

As you can see, the statement will return a list of CDName values and InStock values from the CDInventory table. In order to deal with those values, you must bind them to the applicable host variables. To do this in a C program, you should use the BindCol( ) function. The BindCol( ) function is a little simpler than the BindParameter( ) function and takes only six arguments, as shown in the following example:

```
SQLBindCol ( hstmt, 1, SQL_CHAR, &v_CDName, 60, &ind_CDName ) ;
SQLBindCol ( hstmt, 2, SQL_INT, &v_InStock, 5, &ind_InStock ) ;
```

Argument	Example	Description
1	hstmt	Identifies the statement handle that provides the context for the SQL statement execution
2	1	Identifies the column as it is listed in the SELECT clause of the SELECT statement
3	SQL_CHAR	Identifies the data type of the host variable
4	&v_CDName	Identifies the name of the host variable, as declared in the host program
5	60	Specifies the length in octets of the host variable
6	&ind_CDName	Identifies the name of the indicator variable, as declared by the host program

Table 17-3 Arguments Used in the BindCol( ) Function

Table 17-3 lists the arguments used in the first statement of this example and provides a description of each of those arguments.

Notice that two function statements have been defined, one for each column retrieved by the SELECT statement. You must define a function statement for each column that is listed in the SELECT clause of the SELECT statement. Once you bind the column values to the host variables, you can use those variables in the host program to process the data within the program as necessary.

Project 17-2	Using the SQL Call-Level Interface

`Prj17.txt`

In Project 17-1, you used a text editing program to create embedded SQL statements. In this project, you will perform similar actions except that you'll be defining the functions necessary to make CLI routine calls. As part of this process, you will establish the necessary allocation handles, create a connection to the database, set up SQL statement execution, bind host variables to SQL statements, and bind statement output to host variables. The CLI functions that you'll be using are those typically used in a C program. Keep in mind, however, that the CLI model supports many more functions than what we've covered in this module, so be sure to check the appropriate documentation for details on functions other than those described here. You can download the Prj17.txt file, which contains the CLI function statements used in this project.

Step by Step

1. Open a text editing program such as Microsoft Notepad.

(continued)

2. The first step that you must take is to establish an environment handle. You'll use the henv host variable to set up the handle. Type the following function statement into your text document:

```
SQLAllocHandle ( SQL_HANDLE_ENV, SQL_NULL_HANDLE, &henv ) ;
```

Notice that your functions include three arguments, enclosed in parentheses and separated by commas. Also notice that an ampersand is used for the host variable.

3. Now you can establish your connection environment. The connection environment will be established within the context of the environment handle that you created in Step 2. Type the following function statement into your text document:

```
SQLAllocHandle ( SQL_HANDLE_DBC, henv, &hdbc ) ;
```

As you can see, the henv host variable is used to indicate the environment handle, and the hdbc host variable is used to identify the connection handle.

4. Now that you've established a connection handle, you can create the actual connection. For this connection, you'll use DBServer as your SQL server, DBAdmin as the user account, and AdminPW as the password for that account. Type the following function statement into your text document:

```
SQLConnect ( hdbc, DBServer, SQL_NTS, DBAdmin, SQL_NTS, AdminPW, SQL_NTS ) ;
```

Notice that the statement includes the SQL_NTS value to indicate that a string length does not have to be specified.

5. Next you'll establish your statement handle within the context of the connection you created in Step 3. Type the following function statement into your text document:

```
SQLAllocHandle ( SQL_HANDLE_STMT, hdbc, &hstmt ) ;
```

As you can see, the hdbc host variable is used to identify the connection handle, and the hstmt variable is used to identify the statement handle.

6. Now that you've established your allocation handles and created your connection, you're ready to execute an SQL statement. You'll use the ExecDirect( ) function to specify a DELETE statement. Type the following function statement into your text document:

```
SQLExecDirect ( hstmt, "DELETE CompactDiscs
   WHERE CompactDiscID = 122", SQL_NTS ) ;
```

The DELETE statement is included as one of the function's arguments. Notice that it is enclosed in double quotation marks. Also notice that the statement is being prepared within the context of the hstmt host variable, which is assigned to the statement environment.

7. In the last step, you executed your SQL statement in one step by using the ExecDirect( ) function. In this step, you will prepare an SQL statement for execution, but you will

actually execute it in a later step. Type the following function statement into your text document:

```
SQLPrepare ( hstmt, "SELECT CDTitle, InStock FROM CompactDiscs
   WHERE CompactDiscID = ?", SQL_NTS ) ;
```

Notice that the WHERE clause of the SELECT statement includes a question mark to indicate that a value will be passed into the statement through a host variable.

8. In order to execute the statement in the previous step, you'll need to bind the host variable to the statement. Type the following function statement into your text document:

```
SQLBindParameter ( hstmt, 1, SQL_PARAMETER_MODE_IN, SQL_INT,
    SQL_INT, 3, 0, &v_CDID, 4, &ind_CDID ) ;
```

As you can see, the v_CDID host variable is being bound to the SQL statement in the context of the statement environment created earlier. Because only one host variable is referenced in the SQL statement, only one BindParameter( ) function statement is required.

9. Now you can execute the statement prepared in Step 7. Type the following function statement into your text document:

```
SQLExecute ( hstmt ) ;
```

The statement will be executed in the context of the hstmt statement environment.

10. Next you must bind the query results to the host variables. Because two columns are identified in the SELECT clause of the SELECT statement, you must include two BindCol( ) function statements. Type the following function statements into your text document:

```
SQLBindCol ( hstmt, 1, SQL_CHAR, &v_CDTitle, 60, &ind_CDTitle ) ;
SQLBindCol ( hstmt, 2, SQL_INT, &v_InStock, 5, &ind_InStock ) ;
```

Your C program should now be able to use the values returned by your SELECT statement. If you review the document that you created, it should contain the following code:

```
SQLAllocHandle ( SQL_HANDLE_ENV, SQL_NULL_HANDLE, &henv ) ;
SQLAllocHandle ( SQL_HANDLE_DBC, henv, &hdbc ) ;
SQLConnect ( hdbc, DBServer, SQL_NTS, DBAdmin, SQL_NTS, AdminPW, SQL_NTS ) ;
SQLAllocHandle ( SQL_HANDLE_STMT, hdbc, &hstmt ) ;
SQLExecDirect ( hstmt, "DELETE CompactDiscs
   WHERE CompactDiscID = 122", SQL_NTS ) ;
SQLPrepare ( hstmt, "SELECT CDTitle, InStock FROM CompactDiscs
   WHERE CompactDiscID = ?", SQL_NTS ) ;
SQLBindParameter ( hstmt, 1, SQL_PARAMETER_MODE_IN, SQL_INT,
    SQL_INT, 3, 0, &v_CDID, 4, &ind_CDID ) ;
SQLExecute ( hstmt ) ;
SQLBindCol ( hstmt, 1, SQL_CHAR, &v_CDTitle, 60, &ind_CDTitle ) ;
SQLBindCol ( hstmt, 2, SQL_INT, &v_InStock, 5, &ind_InStock ) ;
```

11. Save the file and close the application.

(continued)

Project Summary

This project introduced you to the basic functions necessary to use CLI to access an SQL database from a host program. What the project did not cover is the actual C code that would provide the foundation for your program. For example, a C program would usually include variable declarations, include files, error-handling capabilities, user-related operations, and conditional language that allowed you to use the values returned by the SQL database. The CLI functions that we covered in this project would usually be interspersed into and work in conjunction with the host language. Still, this project should have helped you understand the basic concepts involved in using CLI and better prepared you for working in the host language environment when trying to access SQL data.

Module 17 Mastery Check

1. Which data access method should you use if you want to create and execute ad hoc SQL statements?

    A. CLI

    B. SQL client modules

    C. Direct invocation

    D. Embedded SQL

2. What is embedded SQL?

3. Which files are created by an SQL precompiler?

    A. A file for the CLI functions

    B. A file for the host language

    C. A file for the CLI calls

    D. A file for the embedded SQL statements

4. Which prefix should embedded SQL statements use when those statements are embedded in the MUMPS programming language?

    A. &SQL(

    B. EXEC SQL

    C. START-EXEC

    D. Statements embedded in MUMPS do not require a prefix.

5. A(n) _____ is a type of parameter that is declared within the host language and is then referenced within the embedded SQL statement.

6. Which prefix must you provide for a host variable when it is included in an SQL statement?

  A. Question mark

  B. Ampersand

  C. Semicolon

  D. Colon

7. You plan to embed SQL statements in your host program. You want to declare several host variables to be used in the SQL statements. Which SQL statement should you use to terminate the declaration section of your program?

  A. TERMINATE DECLARE SECTION

  B. END DECLARE SECTION

  C. TERMINATE DECLARATIONS

  D. END DECLARATIONS

8. What can cause an impedance mismatch to occur when passing a variable from a host program to an SQL statement?

9. When can you use a singleton SELECT statement to retrieve data?

10. A(n) _____ is a type of variable that specifies whether an associated data variable contains a null value.

11. Which statement can you use in embedded SQL to provide your host program with exception and warning information?

  A. WHENEVER

  B. INTO

  C. CAST

  D. PROCEDURE

12. A(n) _____ is a self-contained collection of SQL statements that are separate from a host programming language but that can be called from within that language.

13. What allocation handles must you establish in order to execute an SQL statement through a CLI API?

14. Which function should you use to establish a CLI connection handle?

   A. ExecDirect( )

   B. Connect( )

   C. Prepare( )

   D. AllocHandle( )

15. You're allocating an environment handle within a C program and associating the handle with the henv host variable. What function statement should you use?

16. You're creating the following Prepare( ) function statement in your host program:

    ```
    SQLPrepare ( hstmt, "SELECT CDID, CDTitle, InStock FROM CompactDiscs
       WHERE CompactDiscID = ?", SQL_NTS ) ;
    ```

    How many BindCol( ) function statements should you create?

    A. One

    B. Two

    C. Three

    D. Four

17. What CLI function should you use if you want to execute an SQL statement in one step?

Part IV

Appendixes

Appendix A

Answers to Mastery Checks

Module 1: Introduction to Relational Databases and SQL

1. What is a database?

A database is a collection of data organized in a structured format defined by metadata that describes the structure.

2. Which of the following objects make up a relation?

A. Data types

B. Tuples

C. Attributes

D. Forms

    B and **C** are the correct answers.

3. A(n) _____ is a set of data whose values make up an instance of each attribute defined for that relation.

Tuple

4. What are the differences between the first normal form and the second normal form?

According to the first normal form, each attribute of a tuple must contain only one value, each tuple in a relation must contain the same number of values, and each tuple in a relation must be different. According to the second normal form, a relation must be in first normal form and all attributes in a relation must be dependent on the entire candidate key.

5. A relation is in third normal form if it is in second normal form and if it complies with the other guidelines of that form. What are those guidelines?

All nonkey attributes must be independent of each other and dependent on the key.

6. What are the three primary types of relationships supported by a relational database?

One-to-one, one-to-many, many-to-many

7. In your data model, you have two relations associated with each other by a many-to-many relationship. How will this relationship be physically implemented in a relational database?

The relationship will be implemented by adding a third relation between the original two relations in order to create two one-to-many relationships.

8. How does SQL differ from programming languages such as C, COBOL, and Java?

Programming languages such as C, COBOL, and Java are procedural languages that define how an application's operations should be performed and the order in which they are performed. However, SQL is a nonprocedural language and is more concerned with the results of an operation; the underlying software environment determines how the operations will be processed. Even so, SQL does support some procedural functionality.

9. What factors have contributed to the SQL:1999 standard incorporating object-oriented capabilities?

The advent of object-oriented programming, advancements in hardware and software technologies, and the growing complexities of applications.

10. Which level of conformance must an RDBMS support in order to comply with SQL:1999?

A. Entry

B. Core

C. Full

D. Intermediate

B is the correct answer.

11. What are the differences between a DDL statement and a DML statement?

DDL statements are used to create, modify, and delete database objects such as tables, views, schemas, domains, triggers, and stored procedures. DML statements are used to view, add, modify, or delete data stored in the database objects.

12. What method of executing SQL statements would you use if you want to communicate directly with an SQL database from a front-end application?

Direct invocation

13. What four methods does the SQL:1999 standard support for the execution of SQL statements?

Direct invocation, embedded SQL, module binding, and CLI

14. What is a relational database management system?

An RDBMS is a program or set of programs that store, manage, retrieve, modify, and manipulate data in one or more relational databases.

15. What is an example of an RDBMS?

Any of the following are examples of RDBMSs: DB2, MySQL, Oracle, SQL Server, PostgreSQL, Sybase, Informix, Ocelot, or any other RDBMS on the market.

Module 2: Working with the SQL Environment

1. What are the differences between an SQL agent and an SQL implementation?

An SQL agent is any structure that causes SQL statements to be executed. The SQL agent is bound to the SQL client within the SQL implementation. An SQL implementation is a processor that executes

SQL statements according to the requirements of the SQL agent. The SQL implementation includes one SQL client and one or more SQL servers. The SQL client establishes SQL connections with the SQL servers and maintains data related to interactions with the SQL agent and the SQL servers. An SQL server manages the SQL session that takes place over the SQL connection and executes SQL statements received from the SQL client.

2. **Which component of an SQL environment represents a user or role that is granted specific access privileges to objects and data?**

A. Catalog

B. Authorization identifier

C. SQL client module

D. SQL agent

  B is the correct answer.

3. **A(n) _____ is a collection of schemas that form a namespace within the SQL environment.**

Catalog

4. **What is a schema?**

A *schema* is a set of related objects that are collected under a common namespace. The schema acts as a container for those objects, which in turn store the SQL data or perform other data-related functions.

5. **Which statement do you use to add a schema to an SQL environment?**

A. ADD SCHEMA

B. INSERT SCHEMA

C. CREATE SCHEMA

  C is the correct answer.

6. **What is the name of the schema that contains definitions for schema objects in a catalog?**

INFORMATION_SCHEMA

7. **What are the 11 types of schema objects that can be contained in a schema?**

Base tables, views, domains, UDTs, constraints, SQL server modules, triggers, SQL-invoked routines, character sets, collations, and translations

8. **What is a view?**

A view is a virtual table that is created when the view is invoked (by calling its name). The table doesn't actually exist, only the SQL statement that defines the table.

9. **Which schema objects provide the basic unit of data management in the SQL environment?**

A. Views

B. Domains

C. Base tables

D. Character sets

    C is the correct answer.

10. **How does the SQL:1999 standard define a database?**

The SQL:1999 standard doesn't define a database.

11. **A(n) _____ is a name given to an SQL object.**

Identifier

12. **How is a regular identifier distinguished from a delimited identifier in an SQL statement?**

A delimited identifier is enclosed in double quotation marks. A regular identifier is not.

13. **Which type of identifier permits spaces to be used as part of the name of an object?**

A delimited identifier

14. **Your SQL environment includes a catalog named Inventory. In that catalog is a schema named CompactDiscs, and in that schema is a table named Artists. What is the qualified name of that table?**

Inventory.CompactDiscs.Artists

15. **What three forms can the <name clause> component of a CREATE SCHEMA statement take?**

A <name clause> in a CREATE SCHEMA statement can take any of the following three forms:

<schema name>
AUTHORIZATION <authorization identifier>
<schema name> AUTHORIZATION <authorization identifier>

16. **What are the differences between the CASCADE option and the RESTRICT option in a DROP SCHEMA statement?**

If the CASCADE option is specified, all schema objects and SQL data within those objects are deleted from the system. If the RESTRICT option is used, the schema is deleted only if no schema objects exist.

Module 3: Creating and Altering Tables

1. **Which kinds of base tables can you create by using a CREATE TABLE statement?**

A. Persistent base tables

B. Global temporary base tables

C. Created local temporary tables

D. Declared local temporary tables

    A, **B**, and **C** are the correct answers.

2. What is the primary difference between a global temporary table and a created local temporary table?

A global temporary table can be accessed from anywhere within the associated SQL session, whereas a created local temporary table can be accessed only within the associated module.

3. You're creating a table named Agents. The table includes the AgentID column, which has an INT data type, and the AgentName column, which has a CHAR (60) data type. What SQL statement should you use?

You should use the following SQL statement:

```
CREATE TABLE Agents
( AgentID INT, AgentName CHAR (60) ) ;
```

4. What are the three types of data types that SQL supports?

Predefined, constructed, and user-defined

5. What are the four types of string data types?

Character strings, national character strings, bit strings, and binary strings

6. A(n) _____ data type permits values that are based on data bits, rather than character sets or collations. This type of data type allows only values of 0 and 1.

Bit string

7. What are the precision and the scale of the number 5293.472?

The precision is 7 and the scale is 3.

8. What are the differences between exact numeric data types and approximate numeric data types?

With exact numeric data types, permitted values have a precision and scale. With approximate numeric data types, permitted values have a precision but no scale.

9. Which data types are exact numeric data types?

A. DOUBLE PRECISION

B. DECIMAL

C. REAL

D. SMALLINT

B and **D** are the correct answers.

10. A(n) _____ data type specifies the year, month, and day values of a date.

DATE

11. **What are the two types of interval data types that SQL supports?**

Year-month intervals and day-time intervals

12. **Which data type should you use to support a true/false construct that can be used for comparing values?**

BOOLEAN

13. **You are creating a distinct user-defined type named City. The user type is based on the CHAR (40) data type. Which SQL statement should you use?**

You should use the following SQL statement:

```
CREATE TYPE City AS CHAR (40)
FINAL ;
```

14. **You're creating a table named Customers. The table includes the CustomerName column and the CustomerCity column. Both columns have a VARCHAR (60) data type. The CustomerCity column also has a default value of *Seattle*. Which SQL statement should you use?**

You should use the following SQL statement:

```
CREATE TABLE Customers
( CustomerName VARCHAR (60),
CustomerCity VARCHAR (60) DEFAULT 'Seattle' ) ;
```

15. **Which SQL statement should you use to delete a column from an existing table?**

ALTER TABLE

16. **Which SQL statement should you use to delete a table definition and all its SQL data from a database?**

DROP TABLE

17. **Your database includes a table named OperaSingers. You want to add a column named Nationality to the table. The column should have a VARCHAR (40) data type. What SQL statement should you use?**

You should use the following SQL statement:

```
ALTER TABLE OperaSingers
ADD COLUMN Nationality VARCHAR (40) ;
```

18. **You want to delete the table definition for the OperaSingers table from your database. You also want to delete all the data and any dependencies on the table. What SQL statement should you use?**

You should use the following SQL statement:

```
DROP TABLE OperaSingers CASCADE ;
```

Module 4: Enforcing Data Integrity

1. **What is the difference between a table constraint and an assertion?**

   A table constraint is defined within a table definition and applies only to that table. An assertion is a type of constraint that is defined within an assertion definition (separate from the table definition). An assertion can be associated with one or more tables.

2. **What does a null value signify?**

   A null signifies that a value is undefined or not known. This is not the same as a zero, a blank, or a default value. Instead, it indicates that a data value is absent.

3. **Which of the following types of constraints support NOT NULL constraints?**

   A. Table constraints

   B. Column constraints

   C. Domain constraints

   D. Assertions

   B is the correct answer.

4. **You are creating a table that includes a column that allows null values but whose non-null values should be unique. Which type of constraint should you use?**

   UNIQUE

5. **You're creating a table that includes the TypeName column. The column is defined with the CHAR (10) data type and requires a UNIQUE constraint, which you'll define as a column constraint. What SQL code should you use for the column definition?**

   You should use the following code:

   ```
   TypeName CHAR (10) UNIQUE
   ```

6. **What two restrictions apply to PRIMARY KEY constraints but not to UNIQUE constraints?**

   A column that is defined with a PRIMARY KEY constraint cannot contain null values, and only one PRIMARY KEY constraint can be defined for each column.

7. **You're creating a PRIMARY KEY constraint named pk_ArtistMusicTypes on the ArtistMusicTypes table. The primary key includes the ArtistName and ArtistDOB columns. What SQL code should you use for a table constraint?**

   You should use the following code:

   ```
   CONSTRAINT pk_ArtistMusicTypes PRIMARY KEY
   ( ArtistName, ArtistDOB )
   ```

8. **How does a referential constraint differ from a unique constraint?**

   Referential constraints are concerned with how data in one table relates to data in another table. Unique constraints ensure the integrity within a table.

9. **A(n) _____ constraint enforces referential integrity between two tables by ensuring that no action is taken to either table that affects the data protected by the constraint.**

   FOREIGN KEY

10. **You're creating a table that includes a column named BusinessTypeID, with a data type of INT. The column will be defined with a FOREIGN KEY constraint that references the primary key in a table named BusinessTypes. The foreign key will be added as a column constraint. What SQL code should you use for the column definition?**

    You should use the following code:

    ```
    BusinessTypeID INT REFERENCES BusinessTypes ;
    ```

11. **What three options can you use in the MATCH clause of a FOREIGN KEY constraint?**

    FULL, PARTIAL, and SIMPLE

12. **What are the two types of referential triggered actions that can be defined in a FOREIGN KEY constraint?**

    ON UPDATE and ON DELETE

13. **You're creating a FOREIGN KEY constraint and want the values in the referencing column to be updated if values in the referenced column are updated. Which <referential triggered action> clause should you use?**

    A. ON UPDATE RESTRICT

    B. ON UPDATE NO ACTION

    C. ON UPDATE CASCADE

    D. ON UPDATE SET DEFAULT

       C is the correct answer.

14. **What syntax should you use for a CHECK constraint that you're defining as a table constraint?**

    [CONSTRAINT <constraint name>] CHECK (<search condition>)

15. **What types of constraints can you define within an assertion?**

    CHECK constraints

16. **You're creating a CHECK constraint on the NumberInStock column. You want to limit the values that can be entered into the column to the range of 11 through 29. What should you use for the <search condition> clause of the constraint?**

    (NumberInStock BETWEEN 10 AND 30)

Module 5: Creating SQL Views

1. What are the three types of stored tables supported by SQL?

Base tables, derived tables, and viewed tables (views)

2. How do you assign data types to view columns?

You don't assign data types to view columns. The view columns inherit their data types from their respective table columns.

3. In what circumstances must you provide the view column names in a view definition?

You must provide names if any columns are arrived at through some sort of operation that calculates the value to be inserted in the column, rather than the value coming directly from the table. You must also provide names if table column names are duplicated, which can happen when joining tables together.

4. You're creating a view named EmpBDays. The view is based on the EmpName column and the BDay column of the Employees table. The view column names will be the same as the table column names. What SQL code should you use to create the view?

You should use the following code:

```
CREATE VIEW EmpBDays AS SELECT EmpName, BDay FROM Employees ;
```

5. You're creating a view based on the CompactDiscs table in the Inventory database. You want the view to include only those rows whose value in the LabelID column is 546. What clause—in addition to the SELECT clause and the FROM clause—should be included in the SELECT statement for the view?

You should use the following WHERE clause:

```
WHERE LabelID = 546
```

6. You're creating a view that references the Employee table and the JobTitle table. The data in the two tables is matched together by the JobTitleID column in each table. How should you write the WHERE clause in the view's SELECT statement?

You should write the following WHERE clause:

```
WHERE Employee.JobTitleID = JobTitle.JobTitleID
```

7. You're creating a view that references the Employee table and the JobTitle table. The data in the two tables is matched together by the JobTitleID column in each table. You want the view to display only those rows whose value in the JobTitleID column of the JobTitle table is 109. How should you write the WHERE clause in the view's SELECT statement?

You should write the following WHERE clause:

```
WHERE Employee.JobTitleID = JobTitle.JobTitleID
AND JobTitle.JobTitleID = 109
```

8. What is a query specification?

A query specification is an SQL expression that begins with the SELECT keyword and includes a number of elements that form that expression.

9. Which guidelines should you follow if you want to create an updatable view?

A. Data within the view cannot be summarized, grouped together, or automatically eliminated.

B. At least one column in the source table must be updatable.

C. Each column in the view must be traceable to exactly one source column in one table.

D. Each row in the view must be traceable to exactly one source row in one table.

A, **B**, **C**, and **D** are correct. A view must adhere to all four guidelines to be updatable.

10. You create the following view based on the CompactDiscs table in the Inventory database:

```
CREATE VIEW InStock(Average)
AS SELECT AVG(InStock) FROM CompactDiscs ;
```

How do you insert data through this view?

You can't insert data through this view because the data is being summarized (by using the AVG function), which means that the row in the view isn't traceable to exactly one source row in one table.

11. What type of view does the WITH CHECK OPTION clause apply to?

The WITH CHECK OPTION clause applies to updatable views that include a WHERE clause in the SELECT statement.

12. You create the following view definition:

```
CREATE VIEW EmpComm
AS SELECT EmployeeID, Year1999, Year2000 FROM EmployeeCommissions
WHERE Year1999 > 100 ;
```

You want to use the view to update data. What happens if you change the Year1999 value to an amount less than 100?

The row is changed but you will no longer be able to use the view to display the row or update it. To avoid having this occur, you can use the WITH CHECK OPTION clause in the CREATE VIEW statement.

13. You want to alter the EmpComm view definition in your database. How do you alter that definition?

You must drop the view and then re-create the view.

14. You want to drop the EmpBDays view definition from your database. What SQL statement should you use?

You should use the following SQL statement:

```
DROP VIEW EmpBDays ;
```

15. What happens to the SQL data when you drop a view from the database?

None of the underlying data (which is stored in the base tables) is affected when you drop a view. Only the view definition is removed.

Module 6: Managing Database Security

1. What is the difference between a user identifier and a role name?

A user identifier is an individual security account that can represent an individual, an application, or a system service. A role name is a defined set of privileges that can be assigned to a user or to another role.

2. What is the name of the special authorization identifier that grants access to all database users?

PUBLIC

3. Each _____ is associated with a user identifier and role name.

SQL session

4. An SQL session is associated with which of the following?

A. Privilege

B. User identifier

C. PUBLIC

D. Role name

   B and **D** are the correct answers.

5. When an SQL session is first established, the user identifier is always the _____.

SQL session user identifier

6. What is the value of the current role name when an SQL session is first established?

A null value

7. What is an authorization identifier?

An authorization identifier is an object in the SQL environment that represents a user or group of users that are granted specific access privileges to objects and data within the SQL environment.

8. You establish an SQL session with your database. The current user identifier is EthanW. The current role name is null. What is the current authorization identifier?

EthanW

9. **On which schema objects can you define access privileges?**

Base tables, views, columns, domains, character sets, collations, translations, user-defined types, triggers, and SQL-invoked routines

10. **On which types of database objects can you assign the DELETE privilege?**

A. Tables

B. Views

C. Columns

D. Domains

A and **B** are the correct answers.

11. **On which types of database objects can you assign the TRIGGER privilege?**

A. Tables

B. Views

C. Columns

D. Domains

A is the correct answer.

12. **You're creating a role named Accounting. Which SQL statement should you use?**

You should use the following SQL statement:

```
CREATE ROLE Accounting ;
```

13. **You're granting all privileges on the CDNames view to everyone who uses the database. Which SQL statement should you use?**

You should use the following SQL statement:

```
GRANT ALL PRIVILEGES ON TABLE CDNames TO PUBLIC ;
```

14. **You're granting the SELECT privilege to the SalesClerk role on a table in your database. You want the SalesClerk role to be able to assign the SELECT privilege to other users. What clause should you include in your GRANT statement?**

WITH GRANT OPTION

15. **You want to grant the Acct role to the MaxN user authorization. You do not want the user to be able to grant the role to other users. What SQL statement should you use to grant the role?**

You should use the following SQL statement:

```
GRANT Acct TO MaxN ;
```

Module 7: Querying SQL Data

1. **Which clauses in a SELECT statement are part of the table expression?**

A. SELECT

B. FROM

C. WHERE

D. ORDER BY

> **B** and **C** are the correct answers.

2. **In what order are the clauses of a SELECT statement applied?**

The clauses are applied in the following order: FROM, WHERE, GROUP BY, HAVING, SELECT, and ORDER BY.

3. **You are writing a SELECT statement that retrieves the CDTitle column and all rows from the Inventory table. Which SELECT statement should you use?**

You should use the following SQL statement:

```
SELECT CDTitle FROM Inventory;
```

4. **You are writing a SELECT statement that retrieves the CDTitle column and all rows from the Inventory table. You want the column in the query results to be named CompactDisc. Which SELECT statement should you use?**

You should use the following SQL statement:

```
SELECT CDTitle AS CompactDisc FROM Inventory;
```

5. **Which clauses in a SELECT statement are required?**

A. SELECT

B. FROM

C. WHERE

D. GROUP BY

> **A** and **B** are the correct answers.

6. **Which keyword should you add to the SELECT clause to ensure that each row of the query result is unique?**

A. ALL

B. ROLLUP

C. DISTINCT

D. CUBE

    C is the correct answer.

7. You're creating a SELECT statement for the Inventory table and you want to ensure that only rows with a RetailPrice value of less than $16.00 are included in the query results. What WHERE clause should you use?

You should use the following WHERE clause:

```
WHERE RetailPrice < 16.00
```

8. You're creating a SELECT statement that includes a WHERE clause. The WHERE clause contains two predicates. You want the condition of either one of the predicates to be met, but it's not necessary for both conditions to be met. What keyword should you use to connect the two predicates?

OR

9. Each predicate in a WHERE clause is evaluated to which of the following?

A. True

B. Not

C. False

D. Unknown

    A, C, and **D** are the correct answers.

10. Which clause allows you to group together values in a specified column?

A. ROLLUP

B. HAVING

C. ORDER BY

D. GROUP BY

    D is the correct answer.

11. Which two operators can you use in a GROUP BY clause to return additional summary data in a query result?

A. ROLLUP

B. HAVING

C. CUBE

D. DISTINCT

    A and **C** are the correct answers.

12. **You're writing a SELECT statement that retrieves the Category and Price columns from the CompactDiscStock table. You want to group data together first by the Category column and then by the Price column. Which SELECT statement should you use?**

    You should use the following SQL statement:

    ```
    SELECT Category, Price FROM CompactDiscStock
    GROUP BY Category, Price ;
    ```

13. **You're writing a SELECT statement that retrieves the Category and Price columns from the CompactDiscStock table. You want to group together data first by the Category column and then by the Price column. You then want to filter out any groups that have a Price value over 15.99. Which SELECT statement should you use?**

    You should use the following SQL statement:

    ```
    SELECT Category, Price FROM CompactDiscStock
    GROUP BY Category, Price
    HAVING Price < 16.00 ;
    ```

14. **You're creating a SELECT statement that includes a SELECT clause, FROM clause, WHERE clause, GROUP BY clause, and HAVING clause. From which clause will the HAVING clause receive output?**

    A. SELECT

    B. FROM

    C. WHERE

    D. GROUP BY

    D is the correct answer.

15. **How does the HAVING clause differ from the WHERE clause?**

    The HAVING clause is similar to the WHERE clause in that it defines a search condition. However, unlike the WHERE clause, the HAVING clause is concerned with groups, not individual rows.

16. **From which clause does the ORDER BY clause receive output?**

    The SELECT clause

17. **Which keyword should you add to an ORDER BY clause to sort data in descending order?**

    DESC

Module 8: Modifying SQL Data

1. **Which SQL statement should you use to add data to a table?**

   A. SELECT

   B. INSERT

C. UPDATE

D. DELETE

B is the correct answer.

2. **In which clause in the INSERT statement do you identify the table that will receive the new data?**

INSERT INTO

3. **You create the following INSERT statement to add data to the PerformingArtists table:**

```
INSERT INTO PerformingArtists VALUES ( 12, 'Frank Sinatra' ) ;
```

The PerformingArtists table includes three columns. What will happen when you try to execute this statement?

You'll receive an error because there are not enough values defined for the table and no columns have been specified to distinguish where the two values should be inserted.

4. **What information must you specify in the VALUES clause of an INSERT statement?**

You must specify one or more values to be inserted into the table.

5. **What requirements must be met by the values in a VALUES clause?**

The values must be enclosed in parentheses and, if more than one is specified, must be separated by a comma. If the column names are not specified in the INSERT INTO clause, then there must be one value for each column in the table and the values must be in the same order as they are defined in the table. If the column names are specified in the INSERT INTO clause, then there must be exactly one value per specified column and those values must be in the same order as they are defined in the INSERT INTO clause. Each value with a character string data type must be enclosed in single quotes.

6. **You're creating an INSERT statement to insert data into the ArtistTypes table. The table includes only two columns: ArtID and TypeName. You want to insert one row that includes the ArtID value of 27 and the TypeName value of Gospel. Which SQL statement should you use?**

You should use the following SQL statement:

```
INSERT INTO ArtistTypes VALUES ( 27, 'Gospel' ) ;
```

7. **You're creating an INSERT statement that inserts values taken from another table. Which type of statement or clause can you use in place of the VALUES clause to pull data from that other table?**

A. UPDATE

B. SET

C. SELECT

D. WHERE

C is the correct answer.

8. **Which statement should you use to modify existing data in one or more rows in a table?**

A. SELECT

B. INSERT

C. UPDATE

D. DELETE

   C is the correct answer.

9. **What is the purpose of the WHERE clause in an UPDATE statement?**

The WHERE clause specifies a condition or set of conditions that act as a filter for the rows that are updated. Only the rows that meet these conditions are updated.

10. **You're creating an UPDATE statement to update data in the PerformingArtists table. You want to update the ArtID value in the row that contains the PerfArtID value of 139. The new ArtID value is 27. Which SQL statement should you use?**

You should use the following SQL statement:

```
UPDATE PerformingArtists SET ArtID = 27
WHERE PerfArtID = 139 ;
```

11. **You're creating an UPDATE statement to update data in the PerformingArtists table. You want to update the ArtID value of every row to 27. Which SQL statement should you use?**

You should use the following SQL statement:

```
UPDATE PerformingArtists SET ArtID = 27 ;
```

12. **You're updating two columns in the CDInventory table. You want to change the Publisher value to MCA Records and you want to double the InStock value. Which SET clause should you use?**

You should use the following SET clause:

```
SET Publisher = 'MCA Records', InStock = (InStock * 2) ;
```

13. **You're creating an UPDATE statement that includes a SET clause with one value expression. You want the value expression to pull a value from another table in the database. Which statement or clause can you use as a value expression to choose data from another table?**

A. SELECT

B. WHERE

C. UPDATE

D. INSERT

   A is the correct answer.

14. **Which clause in a DELETE statement is required?**

DELETE FROM

15. Which statement or clause do you use in a DELETE statement to specify which rows are deleted from a table?

A. SELECT

B. WHERE

C. UPDATE

D. INSERT

B is the correct answer.

Module 9: Using Predicates

1. In which SELECT statement clause do you include predicates?

WHERE clause

2. Which comparison operator symbol should you use to express a not equal condition?

A. <=

B. >=

C. <>

D. =<

C is the correct answer.

3. Which keywords can you use to combine predicates in a WHERE clause?

The AND keyword and the OR keyword

4. You want to query a table that includes the Price column. You want to ensure that all rows returned have a Price value of 13.99. What predicate should you use?

Price = 13.99

5. You create the following SQL statement:

```
SELECT CDTitle, RetailPrice FROM CDsOnHand
WHERE RetailPrice >= 14 AND RetailPrice <= 16 ;
```

What predicate can you use in place of the two predicates shown in this statement?

RetailPrice BETWEEN 14 AND 16

6. What keyword can you add to a BETWEEN predicate to find the inverse of the condition specified by the predicate?

NOT

7. **You want to query a table to determine which values are null. What type of predicate should you use?**

NULL predicate

8. **You're creating a SELECT statement that queries the ArtistsBio table. You want to return all columns in the table, but you want to return only those rows that do not contain null values in the PlaceOfBirth column. Which SELECT statement should you use?**

You should use the following SQL statement:

```
SELECT * FROM ArtistsBio
WHERE PlaceOfBirth IS NOT NULL ;
```

9. **You're querying the CDInventory table. You want to view all columns, but you want to view only rows that contain the word Christmas in the name of the CD. The names are stored in the CDTitle column. Which SELECT statement should you use?**

You should use the following SQL statement:

```
SELECT * FROM CDInventory
WHERE CDTitle LIKE ('%Christmas%') ;
```

10. **What is the difference between a percentage sign and an underscore when used in a LIKE predicate?**

The percentage sign represents zero or more unknown characters, and the underscore represents exactly one unknown character.

11. **What two types of data sources can you use in an IN predicate?**

A defined list or a subquery

12. **Which type of predicate is concerned only with determining whether or not a subquery returns any rows?**

EXISTS predicate

13. **What column names must be specified in an EXISTS predicate?**

It does not matter what columns or how many columns you specify in the SELECT clause of the subquery in an EXISTS predicate. This type of predicate is concerned only with whether rows are being returned, not with the content of those rows. You can specify any column names or just an asterisk.

14. **You're creating a SELECT statement that includes a predicate in the WHERE clause. You want to use a comparison operator to compare the values in one of the columns to the results of a subquery. You want the predicate to evaluate to true for any of the subquery results. Which type of predicate should you use?**

A. EXISTS

B. ANY

C. ALL

D. IN

B is the correct answer.

15. **What is the difference between a SOME predicate and an ANY predicate?**

There is no difference. The two predicates return identical results.

16. **How does the ALL predicate differ from the SOME predicate?**

In many respects, the ALL predicate works the same way as the SOME predicate. The ALL predicate compares column values to the subquery results. However, rather than the column values having to evaluate to true for any of the result values, the column values must evaluate to true for all the result values; otherwise, the row is not returned.

Module 10: Working with Functions and Value Expressions

1. **What is a set function?**

A set function is a type of function that processes or calculates data and returns the appropriate values.

2. **You're creating a SELECT statement that queries the ArtistCDs table. The table includes the ArtistName and CDName columns. You want your statement to return the total number of rows in the table. Which COUNT function should you include in your SELECT clause?**

A. COUNT(*)

B. COUNT(ArtistName)

C. COUNT(CDName)

D. COUNT(ArtistName, CDName)

A is the correct answer.

3. **Which set function should you use to add together the values in a column?**

A. MAX

B. COUNT

C. SUM

D. AVG

C is the correct answer.

4. **Set functions require that the data be _____ in some way.**

Grouped

5. What are value functions?

Value functions are a type of function that allow you to return a value that in some way calculates or derives information from the data stored within your tables or from the SQL implementation itself.

6. You're using the SUBSTRING function to extract characters from the CompactDisc column of the SalesDates table. You want to start with the third character and extract eight characters. What parameters should you use in the SUBSTRING function?

(CompactDisc FROM 3 FOR 8)

7. You're using the LOWER function on the Past Light value of the CDName column. What value will be returned?

The following value will be returned: past light

8. Which function returns a value that represents the current date and time as well as information related to UCT?

A. LOCALTIMESTAMP

B. CURRENT_DATE

C. LOCALTIME

D. CURRENT_TIMESTAMP

   D is the correct answer.

9. What are four types of operators that you use in a numeric value expression?

Addition, subtraction, multiplication, and division

10. You are querying data from the CDTracking table. You want to add values in the InStock column to values in the OnOrder column. You then want to double the column totals. How do you set up the numeric value expression?

(InStock + OnOrder) * 2

11. Which value expression do you use to set up a series of conditions that modify values?

CASE

12. You're creating a SELECT statement that includes a CASE value expression. You want one of the conditions to specify that any OnOrder values greater than 10 should be increased by 5. How should you set up the WHEN/THEN clause?

WHEN OnOrder > 10 THEN OnOrder + 5

13. What is a CAST value expression?

A CAST value expression is a type of expression that allows you to change a value's data type when retrieving that value from your database.

14. You're querying the DateSold column in the SalesDates table. You want to convert the values to a CHAR (25) data type, and you want the data displayed in the CharDate column in the query results. How do you define the CAST value expression?

CAST(DateSold AS CHAR (25)) AS CharDate

15. Which special value can you use to identify the current SQL session user identifier?

SESSION_USER

Module 11: Accessing Multiple Tables

1. You are using a comma-separated join operation to join two tables. The first table contains five rows and the second table contains three rows. How many rows will the Cartesian product table contain?

15

2. Which clause contains the equi-join condition in a comma-separated join?

WHERE clause

3. What basic guidelines should you follow when creating a comma-separated join?

Your FROM clause should include all table names, your WHERE clause should define an equi-join condition, and your column references should be qualified when column names are shared among tables.

4. You're creating a join on two tables. You assign correlation names to each of these tables. Which names should you use in the SELECT clause: the correlation names or the actual table names?

The correlation names

5. Which type of join is nearly identical to the comma-separated join?

A. Condition join

B. Natural join

C. Cross join

D. Named column join

C is the correct answer.

6. How many tables are contained in a self-join?

One

7. What guidelines must you follow when creating natural joins or named column joins?

The joined columns must share the same name and have compatible data types, and the names of the joined columns cannot be qualified with table names.

8. **What is the difference between a natural join and a named column join?**

   The natural join automatically matches rows for those columns with the same name. You do not have to specify any sort of equi-join condition for natural joins. The SQL implementation determines which columns have the same names and then tries to form a match. In a named column join, you must specify the matching column. The matching columns are not determined automatically.

9. **Which type of join contains a USING clause to specify the equi-join condition?**

   A named column join

10. **What are the two types of condition joins?**

    Inner and outer

11. **What are the three types of outer joins?**

    Left, right, and full

12. **Which type of condition join should you use if you want to return only matched rows?**

    A. Inner join

    B. Left outer join

    C. Right outer join

    D. Full outer join

    A is the correct answer.

13. **Which type of join contains an ON clause?**

    A. Cross join

    B. Comma-separated join

    C. Natural join

    D. Condition join

    D is the correct answer.

14. **A(n) _____ operator allows you to combine separate SELECT statements into one statement in order to join data in a query result.**

    UNION

15. **What keyword can you use with a UNION operator to return all rows in the query results, regardless of whether there are duplicate values?**

    ALL keyword

Module 12: Using Subqueries to Access and Modify Data

1. **In which types of statements can you include subqueries?**

   A. SELECT

   B. INSERT

   C. UPDATE

   D. DELETE

   A, **B**, **C**, and **D** are the correct answers.

2. **What is a subquery?**

   A subquery is an embedded SELECT statement that acts as a gateway to data in a second table. The data returned by the subquery is used by the primary statement to meet whatever conditions have been defined for that statement.

3. **In which clauses of a SELECT statement can you include a subquery?**

   A. SELECT

   B. WHERE

   C. GROUP BY

   D. HAVING

   A, **B**, and **D** are the correct answers.

4. **Into what two general categories can you divide subqueries in a WHERE clause?**

   Subqueries that can return multiple rows and those that can return only one value

5. **Which types of predicates are you prevented from using with subqueries that return multiple rows?**

   A. IN and EXISTS predicates

   B. SOME, ANY, and ALL predicates

   C. Comparison predicates

   D. Quantified comparison predicates

   C is the correct answer.

6. **When does an EXISTS condition evaluate to true?**

   An EXISTS condition evaluates to true if one or more rows are returned by the subquery; otherwise, it evaluates to false.

7. **In addition to numbers, _____ data can be compared in comparison predicates.**

   Character string

8. **Which types of predicates allow you to use subqueries that return multiple rows?**

   A. IN and EXISTS predicates

   B. SOME, ANY, and ALL predicates

   C. Comparison predicates

   D. Quantified comparison predicates

   A, **B**, and **D** are the correct answers.

9. **What is a correlated subquery?**

   A correlated subquery is one that is dependent on the outer statement in some way.

10. **How often is a correlated subquery evaluated when a SELECT statement is processed?**

    The correlated subquery must be evaluated for each row returned by the outer SELECT statement.

11. **A(n) _____ is a subquery that is a component of another subquery.**

    Nested subquery

12. **How many subqueries can be included in a SELECT statement, as specified by the SQL standard?**

    The SQL:1999 standard does not limit the number of subqueries that can be included in a statement.

13. **Which clause in an INSERT statement can contain a subquery?**

    VALUES clause

14. **How many values can a subquery return if it is used in an INSERT statement?**

    One

15. **Which clauses in an UPDATE statement can contain a subquery?**

    WHERE and SET

Module 13: Creating SQL-Invoked Routines

1. **Which statement do you use to invoke an SQL-invoked procedure?**

   A. RETURN

   B. CALL

C. SET

D. DECLARE

B is the correct answer.

2. A(n) _____ **is a value passed to a statement in a procedure when you invoke that procedure.**

Parameter

3. Which types of parameters can you use in an SQL-invoked function?

A. Input

B. Output

C. Input/output

D. Variable

A is the correct answer.

4. What is another name for an SQL-invoked procedure?

Stored procedure

5. What are the two primary differences between procedures and functions?

Procedures are invoked by using a CALL statement, and they support input and out parameters. Functions are invoked as a value in an expression, and they support input parameters only.

6. What information must you include in a CALL statement when invoking a procedure?

The name of the procedure and the values that are passed to the parameters

7. Which types of statements can you include in a procedure?

A. SELECT

B. INSERT

C. UPDATE

D. DELETE

A, B, C, and **D** are the correct answers.

8. Which statement do you use to assign an initial value to a variable?

A. DECLARE

B. RETURN

C. SET

D. CALL

C is the correct answer.

9. A(n) _____ statement allows you to group SQL statements into blocks.

Control

10. Which keyword do you use to begin a conditional statement?

A. IF

B. BEGIN

C. THEN

D. ELSE

    A is the correct answer.

11. What keyword do you use in a LOOP statement to end that loop?

LEAVE

12. What is the difference between a conditional statement and a compound statement?

A conditional statement determines whether a statement is executed based on whether a specified condition evaluates to true. A compound statement groups statements into a block.

13. What are two types of looping statements?

A. BEGIN...END

B. IF...END IF

C. LOOP...END LOOP

D. WHILE...END WHILE

    C and **D** are the correct answers.

14. Which type of parameter can return a value when you invoke a procedure?

Output

15. What step must you take when calling a procedure that includes an output parameter?

You must declare a variable that is then used in the CALL statement as a parameter value.

16. How does a CREATE FUNCTION statement differ from a CREATE PROCEDURE statement?

In a CREATE FUNCTION statement, the input parameter definitions cannot include the IN keyword. In addition, a RETURNS clause must follow the parameter definitions, and the routine body must include a RETURN statement.

Module 14: Creating SQL Triggers

1. What type of actions can be performed by the triggered SQL statements?

The triggered SQL statements can take such actions as updating tables, deleting data, invoking procedures, or performing most tasks that you can perform with SQL statements.

2. **Which actions can invoke a trigger?**

A. Updating data

B. Querying data

C. Deleting data

D. Inserting data

　　A, **C**, and **D** are the correct answers.

3. **When is an insert trigger invoked?**

When data is inserted into the table on which the trigger is defined

4. **A trigger can be defined on how many tables?**

A. Only one

B. One or more

C. One to three

D. Any number of tables

　　A is the correct answer.

5. **A(n) _____ is a space created in memory that holds a trigger process during the execution of that trigger.**

Trigger execution context

6. **You insert data into Table 1, which invokes an insert trigger defined on that table. The trigger updates information in Table 2, which invokes an update trigger defined on that table. The update trigger deletes information in Table 3, which invokes a delete trigger defined on that table. Which trigger execution context is active at this point?**

A. The trigger execution context for the insert trigger

B. The trigger execution context for the update trigger

C. The trigger execution context for the delete trigger

　　C is the correct answer.

7. **If three triggers are invoked during a session, how many trigger execution contexts are created in that session?**

Three

8. **What information is included in a trigger execution context?**

A trigger execution context contains the information necessary for the trigger to be executed correctly. This information includes details about the trigger itself and about the subject table. In addition, the execution context includes one or two transition tables.

9. In which clause of the CREATE TRIGGER statement do you assign correlation names to old and new data?

A. FOR EACH

B. ON

C. REFERENCING

D. WHEN

C is the correct answer.

10. In which clause of the CREATE TRIGGER statement do you specify whether the triggered SQL statements are executed once for each row or once for each statement?

A. FOR EACH

B. ON

C. REFERENCING

D. WHEN

A is the correct answer.

11. You're creating a trigger definition for an insert trigger. Which REFERENCING clauses can you include in your CREATE TRIGGER statement?

A. REFERENCING OLD ROW AS Old

B. REFERENCING NEW ROW AS New

C. REFERENCING OLD TABLE AS Old

D. REFERENCING NEW TABLE AS New

B and **D** are the correct answers.

12. A(n) _____ trigger allows you to specify the column names of a subject table.

Update

13. You're creating an update trigger on the CDInventory table. The table includes a column named InStock. You want the triggered SQL statements to be executed only when the InStock value of the updated row exceeds 20. Which clause should you include in your CREATE TRIGGER statement to restrict when the statements are executed?

A. WHERE

B. HAVING

C. FOR EACH

D. WHEN

D is the correct answer.

14. What statement must you include in your CREATE TRIGGER statement if the trigger definition includes more than one triggered SQL statement?

BEGIN...END statement

15. What SQL statement do you use to alter a trigger definition?

SQL does not support a statement that allows you to alter a trigger definition. You must first use the DROP TRIGGER statement to delete the trigger from the database, and then use the CREATE TRIGGER statement to re-create the trigger.

Module 15: Using SQL Cursors

1. What form of impedance mismatch is addressed through the use of cursors?

The fact that SQL returns data in sets but other programming languages can process only a few pieces of data at the same time

2. A(n) _____ serves as a pointer that allows the application programming language to deal with query results one row at a time.

Cursor

3. When using cursors in embedded SQL, what is the first step you must take before you can retrieve data through that cursor?

A. Fetch the cursor.

B. Declare the cursor.

C. Close the cursor.

D. Open the cursor.

B is the correct answer.

4. What are the four cursor-related statements that you can embed in a host language?

DECLARE CURSOR, OPEN, FETCH, and CLOSE

5. Which options can be used only in read-only cursor declarations?

A. SCROLL

B. WITH HOLD

C. ORDER BY

D. INSENSITIVE

A, **C**, and **D** are the correct answers.

6. **What are the required elements of a DECLARE CURSOR statement?**

DECLARE <cursor name> CURSOR FOR <query expression>

7. **What type of cursors do not see changes made by statements outside the cursor?**

Insensitive cursors

8. **Which option should you use in a cursor declaration to extend the retrieving capabilities of a FETCH statement?**

A. WITHOUT HOLD

B. ASENSITIVE

C. SCROLL

D. FOR UPDATE

    C is the correct answer.

9. **Cursor _____ refers to a characteristic in cursors that is concerned with whether a cursor is automatically closed when the transaction in which the cursor was opened is committed.**

Holdability

10. **You're creating a cursor declaration. The SELECT statement includes an ORDER BY clause. Which clauses cannot be included in the SELECT statement?**

A. SELECT

B. HAVING

C. GROUP BY

D. WHERE

    B and **C** are the correct answers.

11. **Your cursor declaration includes a FOR UPDATE clause that does not specify any columns. Which columns in the underlying table can be updated?**

All columns

12. **What SQL statement should you use if you want to open the CDArtists cursor?**

You should use the following statement:

```
OPEN CDArtists ;
```

13. **A(n) _____ statement retrieves rows from a cursor's query results once you open that cursor.**

FETCH

14. Which fetch orientation option should you use in a FETCH statement if you want to be sure to retrieve the first row in a cursor's query results?

A. PRIOR

B. NEXT

C. ABSOLUTE -1

D. FIRST

   D is the correct answer.

15. What clause is required in a positioned UPDATE statement in order to update a row returned by the most recent FETCH statement?

WHERE CURRENT OF <cursor name>

Module 16: Managing SQL Transactions

1. Which transaction characteristic refers to the all-or-nothing nature of a transaction?

A. Atomic

B. Consistent

C. Isolated

D. Durable

   A is the correct answer.

2. A(n) _____ is a unit of work that is made up of one or more SQL statements that perform a related set of actions.

Transaction

3. Which SQL statements will terminate a transaction?

A. SAVEPOINT

B. SET TRANSACTION

C. ROLLBACK

D. COMMIT

   C and **D** are the correct answers.

4. What are the three types of transaction modes that you can specify in a SET TRANSACTION statement?

Access level, isolation level, and diagnostics size

5. Which access level options can you include in a START TRANSACTION statement?

A. READ ONLY

B. UPDATE

C. LOCAL

D. READ WRITE

  A and **D** are the correct answers.

6. Two concurrent transactions are active in your system. The first transaction modifies data in a table. The second transaction sees those modifications before they're actually committed to the database. The first transaction then rolls back the modifications. Which type of data phenomenon has occurred?

A. Phantom read

B. Repeatable read

C. Dirty read

D. Nonrepeatable read

  C is the correct answer.

7. A(n) _____ read can occur when a transaction reads a table based on some sort of search condition, then a second transaction updates the data in the table, and then the first transaction attempts to reread the data, but this time different rows are returned because of how the search condition is defined.

Phantom

8. Which isolation level fully isolates one transaction from another transaction?

SERIALIZABLE

9. You're using a SET TRANSACTION statement to configure transaction modes. You want to ensure that no nonrepeatable reads and no dirty reads can occur within that transaction. However, you're not concerned about phantom reads. Which isolation level should you use?

A. READ UNCOMMITTED

B. READ COMMITTED

C. REPEATABLE READ

D. SERIALIZABLE

  C is the correct answer.

10. You're setting up a transaction that defers the application of the ck_CDStock constraint until you execute several SQL statements. After you execute the statements, you want to explicitly apply the constraint to the changes you made to the database. What SQL statement should you use to apply the constraints?

You should use the following statement:

```
SET CONSTRAINTS ck_CDStock IMMEDIATE ;
```

11. A(n) _____ is a designated marker within your transaction that acts as a rollback point for a portion of your transaction.

Savepoint

12. You want to create a savepoint named svpt_Section2. What SQL statement should you use?

You should use the following statement:

```
SAVEPOINT svpt_Section2 ;
```

13. You create a transaction that includes four savepoints: Section1, Section2, Section3, and Section4. Near the end of the transaction, after all four savepoints, you define a RELEASE SAVEPOINT that specifies the Section2 savepoint. Which savepoint or savepoints are removed from the transaction when the RELEASE SAVEPOINT statement is executed?

A. Section1

B. Section2

C. Section3

D. Section4

B, **C**, and **D** are the correct answers.

14. What circumstances will terminate a transaction?

A ROLLBACK statement is explicitly defined in the transaction; a COMMIT statement is explicitly defined in the transaction; the program that initiated the transaction is interrupted, causing the program to abort; or the program successfully completes its execution.

15. You're creating a ROLLBACK statement in your transaction. You want the rollback to undo changes back to the svpt_Section2 savepoint. What SQL statement should you use?

You should use the following statement:

```
ROLLBACK TO SAVEPOINT svpt_Section2 ;
```

16. You're creating a COMMIT statement in your transaction. After the transaction is terminated, you want a new transaction to be initiated. The new transaction should be configured with the same transaction modes as the first transaction. How should you create your COMMIT statement?

You should use the following statement:

```
COMMIT AND CHAIN ;
```

Module 17: Accessing SQL Data from Your Host Program

1. Which data access method should you use if you want to create and execute ad hoc SQL statements?

A. CLI

B. SQL client modules

C. Direct invocation

D. Embedded SQL

C is the correct answer.

2. What is embedded SQL?

Embedded SQL refers to SQL statements that are interspersed in some type of application programming language. The SQL statements are blended into the host language to allow the source program to be able to access and modify SQL data and the underlying database structure.

3. Which files are created by an SQL precompiler?

A. A file for the CLI functions

B. A file for the host language

C. A file for the CLI calls

D. A file for the embedded SQL statements

B and **D** are the correct answers.

4. Which prefix should embedded SQL statements use when those statements are embedded in the MUMPS programming language?

A. &SQL(

B. EXEC SQL

C. START-EXEC

D. Statements embedded in MUMPS do not require a prefix.

A is the correct answer.

5. A(n) _____ is a type of parameter that is declared within the host language and is then referenced within the embedded SQL statement.

Host variable

6. Which prefix must you provide for a host variable when it is included in an SQL statement?

A. Question mark

B. Ampersand

C. Semicolon

D. Colon

    D is the correct answer.

7. **You plan to embed SQL statements in your host program. You want to declare several host variables to be used in the SQL statements. Which SQL statement should you use to terminate the declaration section of your program?**

A. TERMINATE DECLARE SECTION

B. END DECLARE SECTION

C. TERMINATE DECLARATIONS

D. END DECLARATIONS

    B is the correct answer.

8. **What can cause an impedance mismatch to occur when passing a variable from a host program to an SQL statement?**

The differences between the host language data type and SQL data type

9. **When can you use a singleton SELECT statement to retrieve data?**

When your query results will return only one row

10. **A(n) _____ is a type of variable that specifies whether an associated data variable contains a null value.**

Indicator host variable

11. **Which statement can you use in embedded SQL to provide your host program with exception and warning information?**

A. WHENEVER

B. INTO

C. CAST

D. PROCEDURE

    A is the correct answer.

12. **A(n) _____ is a self-contained collection of SQL statements that are separate from a host programming language but that can be called from within that language.**

SQL client module

13. **What allocation handles must you establish in order to execute an SQL statement through a CLI API?**

Environment, connection, and statement

14. **Which function should you use to establish a CLI connection handle?**

A. ExecDirect( )

B. Connect( )

C. Prepare( )

D. AllocHandle( )

    D is the correct answer.

15. **You're allocating an environment handle within a C program and associating the handle with the henv host variable. What function statement should you use?**

You should use the following function statement:

```
SQLAllocHandle ( SQL_HANDLE_ENV, SQL_NULL_HANDLE, &henv ) ;
```

16. **You're creating the following Prepare( ) function statement in your host program:**

```
SQLPrepare ( hstmt, "SELECT CDID, CDTitle, InStock FROM CompactDiscs
   WHERE CompactDiscID = ?", SQL_NTS ) ;
```

How many BindCol( ) function statements should you create?

A. One

B. Two

C. Three

D. Four

    C is the correct answer.

17. **What CLI function should you use if you want to execute an SQL statement in one step?**

ExecDirect( )

Appendix B

SQL:1999 Keywords

The SQL:1999 standard defines a set of reserved keywords and nonreserved keywords that are used within your SQL statements. You cannot use reserved keywords as identifiers. In addition, it is generally a good idea to avoid using unreserved keywords. Note that the SQL standard warns that it makes no guarantees about what keywords might be added to the standard in the future. As a result, an identifier you use in a current database might not be usable in future releases of SQL. You can avoid conflicts with future reserved keywords by adding a digit or an underscore to your identifier and by not beginning an identifier with current_, session_, system_, or timezone_, or ending an identifier with _length. You should also note that various SQL implementations might include additional keywords that cannot be used as identifiers. Be sure to check the product documentation.

SQL Reserved Keywords

Table B-1 lists SQL reserved keywords.

ABSOLUTE	ACTION	ADD	ADMIN
AFTER	AGGREGATE	ALIAS	ALL
ALLOCATE	ALTER	AND	ANY
ARE	ARRAY	AS	ASC
ASSERTION	AT	AUTHORIZATION	BEFORE
BEGIN	BINARY	BIT	BLOB
BOOLEAN	BOTH	BREADTH	BY
CALL	CASCADE	CASCADED	CASE
CAST	CATALOG	CHAR	CHARACTER
CHECK	CLASS	CLOB	CLOSE
COLLATE	COLLATION	COLUMN	COMMIT
COMPLETION	CONNECT	CONNECTION	CONSTRAINT
CONSTRAINTS	CONSTRUCTOR	CONTINUE	CORRESPONDING
CREATE	CROSS	CUBE	CURRENT
CURRENT_DATE	CURRENT_PATH	CURRENT_ROLE	CURRENT_TIME
CURRENT_TIMESTAMP	CURRENT_USER	CURSOR	CYCLE
DATA	DATE	DAY	DEALLOCATE
DEC	DECIMAL	DECLARE	DEFAULT

Table B-1 SQL Reserved Keywords

DEFERRABLE	DEFERRED	DELETE	DEPTH
DEREF	DESC	DESCRIBE	DESCRIPTOR
DESTROY	DESTRUCTOR	DETERMINISTIC	DICTIONARY
DIAGNOSTICS	DISCONNECT	DISTINCT	DOMAIN
DOUBLE	DROP	DYNAMIC	EACH
ELSE	END	END-EXEC	EQUALS
ESCAPE	EVERY	EXCEPT	EXCEPTION
EXEC	EXECUTE	EXTERNAL	FALSE
FETCH	FIRST	FLOAT	FOR
FOREIGN	FOUND	FROM	FREE
FULL	FUNCTION	GENERAL	GET
GLOBAL	GO	GOTO	GRANT
GROUP	GROUPING	HAVING	HOST
HOUR	IDENTITY	IGNORE	IMMEDIATE
IN	INDICATOR	INITIALIZE	INITIALLY
INNER	INOUT	INPUT	INSERT
INT	INTEGER	INTERSECT	INTERVAL
INTO	IS	ISOLATION	ITERATE
JOIN	KEY	LANGUAGE	LARGE
LAST	LATERAL	LEADING	LEFT
LESS	LEVEL	LIKE	LIMIT
LOCAL	LOCALTIME	LOCALTIMESTAMP	LOCATOR
MAP	MATCH	MINUTE	MODIFIES
MODIFY	MODULE	MONTH	NAMES
NATIONAL	NATURAL	NCHAR	NCLOB
NEW	NEXT	NO	NONE
NOT	NULL	NUMERIC	OBJECT
OF	OFF	OLD	ON
ONLY	OPEN	OPERATION	OPTION
OR	ORDER	ORDINALITY	OUT

Table B-1   SQL Reserved Keywords *(continued)*

OUTER	OUTPUT	PAD	PARAMETER
PARAMETERS	PARTIAL	PATH	POSTFIX
PRECISION	PREFIX	PREORDER	PREPARE
PRESERVE	PRIMARY	PRIOR	PRIVILEGES
PROCEDURE	PUBLIC	READ	READS
REAL	RECURSIVE	REF	REFERENCES
REFERENCING	RELATIVE	RESTRICT	RESULT
RETURN	RETURNS	REVOKE	RIGHT
ROLE	ROLLBACK	ROLLUP	ROUTINE
ROW	ROWS	SAVEPOINT	SCHEMA
SCROLL	SCOPE	SEARCH	SECOND
SECTION	SELECT	SEQUENCE	SESSION
SESSION_USER	SET	SETS	SIZE
SMALLINT	SOMESPACE	SPECIFIC	SPECIFICTYPE
SQL	SQLEXCEPTION	SQLSTATE	SQLWARNING
START	STATE	STATEMENT	STATIC
STRUCTURE	SYSTEM_USER	TABLE	TEMPORARY
TERMINATE	THAN	THEN	TIME
TIMESTAMP	TIMEZONE_HOUR	TIMEZONE_MINUTE	TO
TRAILING	TRANSACTION	TRANSLATION	TREAT
TRIGGER	TRUE	UNDER	UNION
UNIQUE	UNKNOWN	UNNEST	UPDATE
USAGE	USER	USING	VALUE
VALUES	VARCHAR	VARIABLE	VARYING
VIEW	WHEN	WHENEVER	WHERE
WITH	WITHOUT	WORK	WRITE
YEAR	ZONE		

Table B-1 SQL Reserved Keywords (continued)

SQL Nonreserved Keywords

Table B-2 lists SQL nonreserved keywords.

ABS	ADA	ASENSITIVE
ASSIGNMENT	ASYMMETRIC	ATOMIC
AVG	BETWEEN	BIT_LENGTH
BITVAR	C	CALLED
CARDINALITY	CATALOG_NAME	CHAIN
CHAR_LENGTH	CHARACTER_LENGTH	CHARACTER_SET_CATALOG
CHARACTER_SET_NAME	CHARACTER_SET_SCHEMA	CHECKED
CLASS_ORIGIN	COALESCE	COBOL
COLLATION_CATALOG	COLLATION_NAME	COLLATION_SCHEMA
COLUMN_NAME	COMMAND_FUNCTION	COMMAND_FUNCTION_CODE
COMMITTED	CONDITION_NUMBER	CONNECTION_NAME
CONSTRAINT_CATALOG	CONSTRAINT_NAME	CONSTRAINT_SCHEMA
CONTAINS	CONVERT	COUNT
CURSOR_NAME	DATETIME_INTERVAL_CODE	DATETIME_INTERVAL_PRECISION
DEFINED	DEFINER	DISPATCH
DYNAMIC_FUNCTION	DYNAMIC_FUNCTION_CODE	EXISTING
EXISTS	EXTRACT	FINAL
FORTRAN	G	GENERATED
GRANTED	HIERARCHY	HOLD
IMPLEMENTATION	INFIX	INSENSITIVE
INSTANCE	INSTANTIABLE	INVOKER
K	KEY_MEMBER	KEY_TYPE
LENGTH	LOWER	M
MAX	MIN	MESSAGE_LENGTH
MESSAGE_OCTET_LENGTH	MESSAGE_TEXT	METHOD
MOD	MORE	MUMPS
NAME	NULLABLE	NUMBER

Table B-2 SQL Nonreserved Keywords

NULLIF	OCTET_LENGTH	OPTIONS
OVERLAPS	OVERLAY	OVERRIDING
PASCAL	PARAMETER_MODE	PARAMETER_NAME
PARAMETER_ORDINAL_POSITION	PARAMETER_SPECIFIC_CATALOG	PARAMETER_SPECIFIC_NAME
PARAMETER_SPECIFIC_SCHEMA	PLI	POSITION
REPEATABLE	RETURNED_LENGTH	RETURNED_OCTET_LENGTH
RETURNED_SQLSTATE	ROUTINE_CATALOG	ROUTINE_NAME
ROUTINE_SCHEMA	ROW_COUNT	SCALE
SCHEMA_NAME	SECURITY	SELF
SENSITIVE	SERIALIZABLE	SERVER_NAME
SIMPLE	SOURCE	SPECIFIC_NAME
SIMILAR	SUBLIST	SUBSTRING
SUM	STYLE	SUBCLASS_ORIGIN
SYMMETRIC	SYSTEM	TABLE_NAME
TRANSACTIONS_COMMITTED	TRANSACTIONS_ROLLED_BACK	TRANSACTION_ACTIVE
TRANSFORM	TRANSFORMS	TRANSLATE
TRIGGER_CATALOG	TRIGGER_SCHEMA	TRIGGER_NAME
TRIM	TYPE	UNCOMMITTED
UNNAMED	UPPER	USER_DEFINED_TYPE_CATALOG
USER_DEFINED_TYPE_NAME	USER_DEFINED_TYPE_SCHEMA	

Table B-1   SQL Nonreserved Keywords *(continued)*

Appendix C

SQL Code Used in the Book's Projects

n the projects throughout this book, you created a number of SQL statements that allowed you to define database objects in the Inventory database, modify those objects, insert data into the tables that you created, retrieve that data, and update and delete the data. The statements are included here so that you can see the progression of the statements as you move through the projects and also so that you can reference them as necessary in case you need to redo certain elements of a project. In addition, I've provided the SQL statements (in a consolidated form) used to create the Inventory database and populate the tables with data. You might find that, as you work your way through this book, you'll want to be able to re-create the database and bring it into a consistent state. By using the consolidated code, you can simply create the database objects and populate the tables as often as necessary, without having to pick the statements out of different projects.

NOTE

The SQL statements are written in pure SQL. However, some SQL implementations might require that you modify the statements to conform to the standards of that particular implementation. Be sure to check the product documentation.

SQL Code By Project

The SQL statements are presented here according to the order in which the projects were presented in the book. You can reference these statements as necessary to use them to re-create projects or to use them as a foundation for other projects. If you're re-creating the Inventory database and want to ensure that you're including all the necessary elements, see the "The Inventory Database" section later in this appendix.

Project 1-2: Connecting to a Database

```
SELECT * FROM <table>

SELECT * FROM scott.emp ;

USE pubs

SELECT * FROM ocelot.emps ;
```

Project 2-1: Creating a Database and a Schema

```
CREATE DATABASE Inventory ;

USE Inventory

CREATE SCHEMA CDInventory ;
```

Project 3-1: Creating SQL Tables

```
CREATE TABLE CompactDiscs
( CompactDiscID INT, CDTitle VARCHAR (60), LabelID INT ) ;

CREATE TABLE CDLabels
( LabelID INT, CompanyName VARCHAR (60) ) ;

CREATE TABLE MusicTypes
( TypeID INT, TypeName VARCHAR (20) ) ;
```

Project 3-2: Altering and Deleting SQL Tables

```
CREATE TABLE CompactDiscTypes
( CompactDiscID INT, TypeID INT ) ;

DROP TABLE CompactDiscTypes CASCADE ;

CREATE TABLE CompactDiscTypes
( CompactDiscID INT, CDTitle VARCHAR (60), TypeID INT ) ;

ALTER TABLE CompactDiscTypes
DROP COLUMN CDTitle CASCADE ;
```

Project 4-1: Adding NOT NULL, Unique, and Referential Constraints

```
DROP TABLE CompactDiscs CASCADE ;
DROP TABLE CompactDiscTypes CASCADE ;
DROP TABLE MusicTypes CASCADE ;
DROP TABLE CDLabels CASCADE ;

CREATE TABLE MusicTypes
( TypeID INT, TypeName VARCHAR (20) NOT NULL,
CONSTRAINT un_TypeName UNIQUE (TypeName),
CONSTRAINT pk_MusicTypes PRIMARY KEY (TypeID) ) ;

CREATE TABLE CDLabels
( LabelID INT, CompanyName VARCHAR (60) DEFAULT 'Independent' NOT NULL,
CONSTRAINT pk_CDLabels PRIMARY KEY (LabelID) ) ;

CREATE TABLE CompactDiscs
( CompactDiscID INT, CDTitle VARCHAR (60) NOT NULL, LabelID INT NOT NULL,
CONSTRAINT pk_CompactDiscs PRIMARY KEY (CompactDiscID),
CONSTRAINT fk_LabelID FOREIGN KEY (LabelID) REFERENCES CDLabels ) ;

CREATE TABLE CompactDiscTypes
( CompactDiscID INT, MusicTypeID INT,
```

```
CONSTRAINT pk_CompactDiscTypes PRIMARY KEY ( CompactDiscID, MusicTypeID ),
CONSTRAINT fk_CompactDiscID_01 FOREIGN KEY (CompactDiscID)
   REFERENCES CompactDiscs,
CONSTRAINT fk_MusicTypeID FOREIGN KEY (MusicTypeID)
   REFERENCES MusicTypes ) ;

CREATE TABLE Artists
( ArtistID INT, ArtistName VARCHAR (60) NOT NULL,
PlaceOfBirth VARCHAR (60) DEFAULT 'Unknown' NOT NULL,
CONSTRAINT pk_Artists PRIMARY KEY (ArtistID) ) ;

CREATE TABLE ArtistCDs
( ArtistID INT, CompactDiscID INT,
CONSTRAINT pk_ArtistCDs PRIMARY KEY ( ArtistID, CompactDiscID ),
CONSTRAINT fk_ArtistID FOREIGN KEY (ArtistID) REFERENCES Artists,
CONSTRAINT fk_CompactDiscID_02 FOREIGN KEY (CompactDiscID)
   REFERENCES CompactDiscs ) ;
```

Project 4-2: Adding a CHECK Constraint

```
ALTER TABLE CompactDiscs
ADD COLUMN InStock INT NOT NULL ;

ALTER TABLE CompactDiscs
ADD CONSTRAINT ck_InStock CHECK ( InStock > 0 AND InStock < 50 ) ;
```

Project 5-1: Adding Views to Your Database

```
CREATE VIEW CDsInStock
AS SELECT CDTitle, InStock FROM CompactDiscs
WHERE InStock > 10 WITH CHECK OPTION ;

CREATE VIEW CDPublishers ( CDTitle, Publisher )
AS SELECT CompactDiscs.CDTitle, CDLabels.CompanyName
FROM CompactDiscs, CDLabels
WHERE CompactDiscs.LabelID = CDLabels.LabelID
AND CDLabels.LabelID = 5403 OR CDLabels.LabelID = 5402 ;

DROP VIEW CDPublishers ;

CREATE VIEW CDPublishers ( CDTitle, Publisher )
AS SELECT CompactDiscs.CDTitle, CDLabels.CompanyName
FROM CompactDiscs, CDLabels
WHERE CompactDiscs.LabelID = CDLabels.LabelID ;
```

Project 6-1: Managing Roles and Privileges

```
CREATE ROLE Mrkt ;

CREATE ROLE SalesStaff ;

GRANT SELECT ON TABLE CDsInStock TO PUBLIC ;

GRANT SELECT, INSERT, UPDATE (CDTitle) ON TABLE CompactDiscs
TO SalesStaff WITH GRANT OPTION ;

GRANT SalesStaff TO Mrkt ;

REVOKE SELECT ON TABLE CDsInStock FROM PUBLIC CASCADE ;

REVOKE ALL PRIVILEGES ON TABLE CompactDiscs FROM SalesStaff CASCADE ;

REVOKE SalesStaff FROM Mrkt CASCADE ;

DROP ROLE Mrkt ;

DROP ROLE SalesStaff ;
```

Project 7-1: Querying the Inventory Database

NOTE

The INSERT statements used for this project are listed at the bottom of the "The Inventory Database" section later in this appendix.

```
SELECT * FROM Artists ;

SELECT CDTitle, InStock FROM CompactDiscs ;

SELECT * FROM CDsInStock ;

SELECT CDTitle, InStock FROM CompactDiscs
WHERE InStock > 10 AND InStock < 30 ;

SELECT LabelID, SUM(InStock) AS TotalInStock
FROM CompactDiscs
GROUP BY LabelID ;
```

```
SELECT LabelID, SUM(InStock) AS TotalInStock
FROM CompactDiscs
GROUP BY LabelID
HAVING SUM(InStock) > 10 ;

SELECT * FROM CompactDiscs
WHERE InStock > 10
ORDER BY CDTitle DESC ;
```

Project 8-1: Modifying SQL Data

```
INSERT INTO CDLabels VALUES ( 837, 'DRG Records' ) ;

INSERT INTO CompactDiscs
VALUES ( 116, 'Ann Hampton Callaway', 836, 14 ) ;

INSERT INTO CompactDiscs
VALUES ( 117, 'Rhythm Country and Blues', 832, 21 ) ;

UPDATE CompactDiscs SET InStock = 25
WHERE CompactDiscID = 117 ;

UPDATE CompactDiscs
SET LabelID =
   ( SELECT LabelID FROM CDLabels WHERE CompanyName = 'DRG Records' )
WHERE CompactDiscID = 116 ;

SELECT * FROM CompactDiscs
WHERE CompactDiscID = 116 OR CompactDiscID = 117 ;
DELETE FROM CompactDiscs
WHERE CompactDiscID = 116 OR CompactDiscID = 117 ;

DELETE FROM CDLabels WHERE LabelID = 837 ;
```

Project 9-1: Using Predicates in SQL Statements

```
SELECT TypeID, TypeName FROM MusicTypes
WHERE TypeID = 11 OR TypeID = 12 ;

SELECT ArtistName, PlaceOfBirth FROM Artists
WHERE ArtistName <> 'Patsy Cline' AND ArtistName <> 'Bing Crosby' ;

SELECT ArtistID, ArtistName FROM Artists
WHERE ArtistID > 2004 AND ArtistID < 2014 ;
```

```
SELECT ArtistID, ArtistName FROM Artists
WHERE ArtistID BETWEEN 2004 AND 2014 ;

SELECT * FROM Artists
WHERE PlaceOfBirth IS NULL ;

SELECT * FROM Artists
WHERE PlaceOfBirth IS NOT NULL ;

SELECT CDTitle, InStock FROM CompactDiscs
WHERE CDTitle LIKE ('%Greatest%') OR CDTitle LIKE ('%Best%') ;

SELECT CDTitle, InStock FROM CompactDiscs
WHERE CDTitle NOT LIKE ('%Greatest%')
  AND CDTitle NOT LIKE ('%Best%') ;
```

Project 9-2: Using Subqueries in Predicates

```
SELECT CDTitle, InStock FROM CompactDiscs
WHERE LabelID IN
( SELECT LabelID FROM CDLabels
WHERE CompanyName = 'Decca Record Company' ) ;

SELECT CDTitle, InStock FROM CompactDiscs
WHERE EXISTS
( SELECT LabelID FROM CDLabels
WHERE CompactDiscs.LabelID = CDLabels.LabelID AND LabelID > 830 ) ;

SELECT LabelID, CompanyName FROM CDLabels
WHERE LabelID = ANY
( SELECT LabelID FROM CompactDiscs WHERE InStock > 20 ) ;

SELECT LabelID, CompanyName FROM CDLabels
WHERE LabelID = ALL
( SELECT LabelID FROM CompactDiscs WHERE InStock > 20 ) ;

SELECT LabelID, CompanyName FROM CDLabels
WHERE LabelID = ALL
( SELECT LabelID FROM CompactDiscs WHERE InStock > 40 ) ;
```

Project 10-1: Using Functions and Value Expressions

```
SELECT COUNT(DISTINCT ArtistName) AS Artists FROM Artists ;

SELECT MIN(InStock) AS MinStock FROM CompactDiscs ;
```

```
SELECT LabelID, SUM(InStock) AS Total
FROM CompactDiscs GROUP BY LabelID ;

SELECT ArtistName, SUBSTRING(PlaceOfBirth FROM 1 FOR 8) AS Birthplace
FROM Artists ;

SELECT UPPER(CDTitle) AS CDName FROM CompactDiscs ;

SELECT CDTitle, InStock,
(InStock * 2) AS Doubled, (InStock * 3) AS Tripled
FROM CompactDiscs WHERE InStock < 25 ;

SELECT CDTitle, InStock, ToOrder =
CASE
  WHEN InStock < 10 THEN InStock * 2
  WHEN InStock BETWEEN 10 AND 15 THEN InStock + 3
  ELSE InStock
END
FROM CompactDiscs WHERE InStock < 20 ;

SELECT TypeID, CAST(TypeName AS CHAR (20)) AS CharType
FROM MusicTypes ;
```

Project 11-1: Querying Multiple Tables

```
SELECT * FROM Artists a, ArtistCDs c
WHERE a.ArtistID = c.ArtistID ;

SELECT d.CDTitle, a.ArtistName, a.PlaceOfBirth
FROM Artists a, ArtistCDs c, CompactDiscs d
WHERE a.ArtistID = c.ArtistID AND d.CompactDiscID = c.CompactDiscID ;

SELECT d.CDTitle, a.ArtistName, a.PlaceOfBirth
FROM Artists a CROSS JOIN ArtistCDs c CROSS JOIN CompactDiscs d
WHERE a.ArtistID = c.ArtistID AND d.CompactDiscID = c.CompactDiscID ;

SELECT d.CDTitle, t.TypeName
FROM CompactDiscs d JOIN CompactDiscTypes dt
  ON d.CompactDiscID = dt.CompactDiscID
JOIN MusicTypes t
  ON dt.MusicTypeID = t.TypeID ;

SELECT d.CDTitle, t.TypeName
FROM CompactDiscs d FULL JOIN CompactDiscTypes dt
  ON d.CompactDiscID = dt.CompactDiscID
FULL JOIN MusicTypes t
  ON dt.MusicTypeID = t.TypeID ;
```

Project 12-1: Working with Subqueries

```
SELECT CDTitle, InStock FROM CompactDiscs
WHERE LabelID IN
( SELECT LabelID FROM CDLabels WHERE CompanyName = 'MCA Records' ) ;

SELECT CompanyName FROM CDLabels l
WHERE EXISTS
( SELECT * FROM CompactDiscs d
  WHERE l.LabelID = d.LabelID AND CDTitle = 'Out of Africa' ) ;

SELECT CompanyName FROM CDLabels
WHERE LabelID = ANY
( SELECT LabelID FROM CompactDiscs WHERE InStock > 30 ) ;

SELECT CDTitle, InStock FROM CompactDiscs
WHERE LabelID =
( SELECT LabelID FROM CDLabels WHERE CompanyName = 'Capitol Records' ) ;

SELECT CDTitle, InStock FROM CompactDiscs d, CDLabels l
WHERE d.LabelID = l.LabelID AND CompanyName = 'Capitol Records' ;

SELECT ArtistName FROM Artists
WHERE ArtistID IN
( SELECT ArtistID FROM ArtistCDs WHERE CompactDiscID IN
  ( SELECT CompactDiscID FROM CompactDiscs WHERE CDTitle = 'Past Light' ) ) ;

SELECT CDTitle, TypeName
FROM CompactDiscs d, CompactDiscTypes t, MusicTypes m
WHERE d.CompactDiscID = t.CompactDiscID AND t.MusicTypeID = m.TypeID
  AND CDTitle = 'Kojiki' ;

UPDATE CompactDiscTypes
SET MusicTypeID =
  ( SELECT TypeID FROM MusicTypes WHERE TypeName = 'Classical' )
WHERE CompactDiscID =
  ( SELECT CompactDiscID FROM CompactDiscs WHERE CDTitle = 'Kojiki' )
AND MusicTypeID =
  ( SELECT TypeID FROM MusicTypes WHERE TypeName = 'New Age' ) ;

UPDATE CompactDiscTypes
SET MusicTypeID =
  ( SELECT TypeID FROM MusicTypes WHERE TypeName = 'New Age' )
WHERE CompactDiscID =
  ( SELECT CompactDiscID FROM CompactDiscs WHERE CDTitle = 'Kojiki' )
AND MusicTypeID =
  ( SELECT TypeID FROM MusicTypes WHERE TypeName = 'Classical' ) ;
```

Project 13-1: Creating SQL-Invoked Procedures

```
CREATE PROCEDURE GetCDArtists ( )
SELECT cd.CDTitle, a.ArtistName
```

```
FROM CompactDiscs cd, ArtistCDs ac, Artists a
WHERE cd.CompactDiscID = ac.CompactDiscID AND ac.ArtistID = a.ArtistID ;

CALL GetCDArtists ( ) ;

DROP PROCEDURE GetCDArtists CASCADE ;

CREATE PROCEDURE GetCDArtists ( IN p_CD VARCHAR (60) )
SELECT cd.CDTitle, a.ArtistName
FROM CompactDiscs cd, ArtistCDs ac, Artists a
WHERE cd.CompactDiscID = ac.CompactDiscID
  AND ac.ArtistID = a.ArtistID AND cd.CDTitle = p_CD ;

CALL GetCDArtists ('Fundamental') ;

CREATE PROCEDURE GetCDAmount ( )
BEGIN
  DECLARE v_InStock INT ;
  SET v_InStock = ( SELECT AVG(InStock) FROM CompactDiscs ) ;
  SELECT CDTitle, InStock FROM CompactDiscs WHERE InStock < v_InStock ;
END ;

CALL GetCDAmount ( ) ;
```

Project 13-2: Creating SQL-Invoked Functions

```
CREATE FUNCTION CDLabel ( p_CD VARCHAR (60) )
RETURNS VARCHAR (60)
BEGIN
  RETURN
  ( SELECT CompanyName FROM CompactDiscs d, CDLabels l
  WHERE d.LabelID = l.LabelID AND CDTitle = p_CD ) ;
END ;

SELECT CDTitle, CompanyName FROM CompactDiscs d, CDLabels l
WHERE d.LabelID = l.LabelID
  AND CompanyName = CDLabel ('Blues on the Bayou') ;

DROP FUNCTION CDLabel CASCADE ;
```

Project 14-1: Creating SQL Triggers

```
CREATE TABLE ArtistLog
( ActionType CHAR (6), ArtistID INT,
    ModDate TIMESTAMP DEFAULT CURRENT_TIMESTAMP ) ;
```

```
CREATE TRIGGER InsertLog
AFTER INSERT ON Artists
REFERENCING NEW ROW AS New
FOR EACH ROW
BEGIN ATOMIC
  INSERT INTO ArtistLog ( ActionType, ArtistID )
  VALUES ( 'INSERT', New.ArtistID ) ;
END ;

CREATE TRIGGER UpdateLog
AFTER UPDATE ON Artists
REFERENCING NEW ROW AS New
FOR EACH ROW
BEGIN ATOMIC
  INSERT INTO ArtistLog ( ActionType, ArtistID )
  VALUES ( 'UPDATE', New.ArtistID ) ;
END ;

CREATE TRIGGER DeleteLog
AFTER DELETE ON Artists
REFERENCING OLD ROW AS Old
FOR EACH ROW
BEGIN ATOMIC
  INSERT INTO ArtistLog ( ActionType, ArtistID )
  VALUES ( 'DELETE', Old.ArtistID ) ;
END ;

INSERT INTO Artists ( ArtistID, ArtistName )
VALUES ( 2019, 'John Lee Hooker' ) ;

UPDATE Artists
SET PlaceOfBirth = 'Clarksdale, Mississippi, USA'
WHERE ArtistID = 2019 ;

DELETE Artists
WHERE ArtistID = 2019 ;

SELECT * FROM ArtistLog ;

DROP TRIGGER InsertLog ;

DROP TRIGGER UpdateLog ;

DROP TRIGGER DeleteLog ;

DROP TABLE ArtistLog ;
```

Project 15-1: Working with SQL Cursors

```
DECLARE v_CDName VARCHAR (60) ;
DECLARE CD_cursor1 CURSOR
FOR
  SELECT CDTitle FROM CompactDiscs
  ORDER BY CDTitle ASC ;
OPEN CD_cursor1 ;
FETCH CD_cursor1 INTO v_CDName ;
CLOSE CD_cursor1 ;

DECLARE v_CDName VARCHAR (60) ;
DECLARE CD_cursor2 SCROLL INSENSITIVE CURSOR
FOR
  SELECT CDTitle FROM CompactDiscs
  ORDER BY CDTitle ASC
FOR READ ONLY ;
OPEN CD_cursor2 ;
FETCH LAST FROM CD_cursor2 INTO v_CDName ;
CLOSE CD_cursor2 ;

DECLARE v_CDName VARCHAR (60) ;
DECLARE CD_cursor3 CURSOR
FOR
  SELECT CDTitle FROM CompactDiscs
FOR UPDATE ;
OPEN CD_cursor3 ;
FETCH CD_cursor3 INTO v_CDName ;
UPDATE CompactDiscs SET InStock = InStock * 2
  WHERE CURRENT OF CD_cursor3 ;
CLOSE CD_cursor3 ;

SELECT * FROM CompactDiscs ;

UPDATE CompactDiscs SET InStock = 13
WHERE CompactDiscID = 101 ;
```

Project 16-1: Working with Transactions

```
START TRANSACTION ISOLATION LEVEL READ UNCOMMITTED ;
SELECT * FROM Artists ;
COMMIT ;

START TRANSACTION ISOLATION LEVEL SERIALIZABLE ;
UPDATE CompactDiscs SET InStock = InStock + 2
  WHERE LabelID = 832 ;
ROLLBACK ;
```

```
SELECT CDTitle, InStock FROM CompactDiscs
WHERE LabelID = 832 ;

START TRANSACTION ISOLATION LEVEL SERIALIZABLE ;
SELECT CDTitle, InStock FROM CompactDiscs
   WHERE LabelID = 832 ;
SAVEPOINT Section1 ;
UPDATE CompactDiscs SET InStock = InStock + 2
   WHERE LabelID = 832 ;
ROLLBACK TO SAVEPOINT
```

```
                                                    scs



                                              CD identifier */
                                              riable for CD title */
                                              for InStock value */


                                              lable for v_cdtitle */
                                              lable for v_instock */


                                              CD identifier */
                                              riable for CD title */
                                              lable for v_cdtitle */
                                              for InStock value */
                                              lable for v_instock */


                                              or1 ;


                                              ock :ind_InStock
                                              = :v_CDID ;


                                              D identifier */
                                              iable for CD title */
                                              able for v_cdtitle */
```

```
      long v_instock ; /* output variable for InStock value */
      short ind_instock ; /* indicator variable for v_instock */
EXEC SQL END DECLARE SECTION ;
EXEC SQL WHENEVER SQLEXCEPTION GOTO Error1 ;
EXEC SQL SELECT CDTitle, InStock
   INTO :v_CDTitle :ind_CDTitle, :v_InStock :ind_InStock
   FROM CompactDiscs WHERE CompactDiscID = :v_CDID ;
```

Project 17-2: Using the SQL Call-Level Interface

```
SQLAllocHandle ( SQL_HANDLE_ENV, SQL_NULL_HANDLE, &henv ) ;

SQLAllocHandle ( SQL_HANDLE_DBC, henv, &hdbc ) ;

SQLConnect ( hdbc, DBServer, SQL_NTS, DBAdmin, SQL_NTS, AdminPW, SQL_NTS ) ;

SQLAllocHandle ( SQL_HANDLE_STMT, hdbc, &hstmt ) ;

SQLExecDirect ( hstmt, "DELETE CompactDiscs
  WHERE CompactDiscID = 122", SQL_NTS ) ;

SQLPrepare ( hstmt, "SELECT CDTitle, InStock FROM CompactDiscs
  WHERE CompactDiscID = ?", SQL_NTS ) ;

SQLBindParameter ( hstmt, 1, SQL_PARAMETER_MODE_IN, SQL_INT,
   SQL_INT, 3, 0, &v_CDID, 4, &ind_CDID ) ;

SQLExecute ( hstmt ) ;

SQLBindCol ( hstmt, 1, SQL_CHAR, &v_CDTitle, 60, &ind_CDTitle ) ;
SQLBindCol ( hstmt, 2, SQL_INT, &v_InStock, 5, &ind_InStock ) ;

SQLAllocHandle ( SQL_HANDLE_ENV, SQL_NULL_HANDLE, &henv ) ;
SQLAllocHandle ( SQL_HANDLE_DBC, henv, &hdbc ) ;
SQLConnect ( hdbc, DBServer, SQL_NTS, DBAdmin, SQL_NTS, AdminPW, SQL_NTS ) ;
SQLAllocHandle ( SQL_HANDLE_STMT, hdbc, &hstmt ) ;
SQLExecDirect ( hstmt, "DELETE CompactDiscs
  WHERE CompactDiscID = 122", SQL_NTS ) ;
SQLPrepare ( hstmt, "SELECT CDTitle, InStock FROM CompactDiscs
  WHERE CompactDiscID = ?", SQL_NTS ) ;
SQLBindParameter ( hstmt, 1, SQL_PARAMETER_MODE_IN, SQL_INT,
   SQL_INT, 3, 0, &v_CDID, 4, &ind_CDID ) ;
SQLExecute ( hstmt ) ;
SQLBindCol ( hstmt, 1, SQL_CHAR, &v_CDTitle, 60, &ind_CDTitle ) ;
SQLBindCol ( hstmt, 2, SQL_INT, &v_InStock, 5, &ind_InStock ) ;
```

The Inventory Database

AppC.txt

You might find that, as you work through the projects in this book, you need to re-create the Inventory database. This might be as a result of switching to a different SQL implementation, reinstalling your SQL implementation, or wanting to start with a fresh database and data. The following SQL statements will allow you to re-create the Inventory database objects (tables and views) in their entirety. Once you create the necessary tables, you can use the INSERT statements to add data to them. If you want to be able to copy the SQL statements directly from a file, you can download the AppC.txt file, which contains the data definition statements and the INSERT statements.

```
CREATE TABLE MusicTypes
( TypeID INT, TypeName VARCHAR (20) NOT NULL,
CONSTRAINT un_TypeName UNIQUE (TypeName),
CONSTRAINT pk_MusicTypes PRIMARY KEY (TypeID) ) ;

CREATE TABLE CDLabels
( LabelID INT, CompanyName VARCHAR (60) DEFAULT 'Independent' NOT NULL,
CONSTRAINT pk_CDLabels PRIMARY KEY (LabelID) ) ;

CREATE TABLE CompactDiscs
( CompactDiscID INT, CDTitle VARCHAR (60) NOT NULL,
LabelID INT NOT NULL, InStock INT NOT NULL,
CONSTRAINT pk_CompactDiscs PRIMARY KEY (CompactDiscID),
CONSTRAINT fk_LabelID FOREIGN KEY (LabelID) REFERENCES CDLabels,
CONSTRAINT ck_InStock CHECK ( InStock > 0 AND InStock < 50 ) ) ;

CREATE TABLE CompactDiscTypes
( CompactDiscID INT, MusicTypeID INT,
CONSTRAINT pk_CompactDiscTypes PRIMARY KEY ( CompactDiscID, MusicTypeID ),
CONSTRAINT fk_CompactDiscID_01 FOREIGN KEY (CompactDiscID)
   REFERENCES CompactDiscs,
CONSTRAINT fk_MusicTypeID FOREIGN KEY (MusicTypeID)
   REFERENCES MusicTypes ) ;

CREATE TABLE Artists
( ArtistID INT, ArtistName VARCHAR (60) NOT NULL,
PlaceOfBirth VARCHAR (60) DEFAULT 'Unknown' NOT NULL,
CONSTRAINT pk_Artists PRIMARY KEY (ArtistID) ) ;
```

```
CREATE TABLE ArtistCDs
( ArtistID INT, CompactDiscID INT,
CONSTRAINT pk_ArtistCDs PRIMARY KEY ( ArtistID, CompactDiscID ),
CONSTRAINT fk_ArtistID FOREIGN KEY (ArtistID) REFERENCES Artists,
CONSTRAINT fk_CompactDiscID_02 FOREIGN KEY (CompactDiscID)
   REFERENCES CompactDiscs ) ;

CREATE VIEW CDsInStock
AS SELECT CDTitle, InStock FROM CompactDiscs
WHERE InStock > 10 WITH CHECK OPTION ;

CREATE VIEW CDPublishers ( CDTitle, Publisher )
AS SELECT CompactDiscs.CDTitle, CDLabels.CompanyName
FROM CompactDiscs, CDLabels
WHERE CompactDiscs.LabelID = CDLabels.LabelID ;

--Insert data into the CDLabels table
INSERT INTO CDLabels VALUES ( 827, 'Private Music' ) ;
INSERT INTO CDLabels VALUES ( 828, 'Reprise Records' ) ;
INSERT INTO CDLabels VALUES ( 829, 'Asylum Records' ) ;
INSERT INTO CDLabels VALUES ( 830, 'Windham Hill Records' ) ;
INSERT INTO CDLabels VALUES ( 831, 'Geffen' ) ;
INSERT INTO CDLabels VALUES ( 832, 'MCA Records' ) ;
INSERT INTO CDLabels VALUES ( 833, 'Decca Record Company' ) ;
INSERT INTO CDLabels VALUES ( 834, 'CBS Records' ) ;
INSERT INTO CDLabels VALUES ( 835, 'Capitol Records' ) ;
INSERT INTO CDLabels VALUES ( 836, 'Sarabande Records' ) ;
--End inserts for the CDLabels table

--Insert data into the CompactDiscs table
INSERT INTO CompactDiscs VALUES ( 101, 'Famous Blue Raincoat', 827, 13 ) ;
INSERT INTO CompactDiscs VALUES ( 102, 'Blue', 828, 42 ) ;
INSERT INTO CompactDiscs VALUES ( 103, 'Court and Spark', 829, 22 ) ;
INSERT INTO CompactDiscs VALUES ( 104, 'Past Light', 830, 17 ) ;
INSERT INTO CompactDiscs VALUES ( 105, 'Kojiki', 831, 6 ) ;
INSERT INTO CompactDiscs VALUES
  ( 106, 'That Christmas Feeling', 832, 8 ) ;
INSERT INTO CompactDiscs VALUES
  ( 107, 'Patsy Cline: 12 Greatest Hits', 832, 32 ) ;
INSERT INTO CompactDiscs VALUES
  ( 108, 'Carreras Domingo Pavarotti in Concert', 833, 27 ) ;
INSERT INTO CompactDiscs VALUES
  ( 109, 'After the Rain: The Soft Sounds of Erik Satie', 833, 21 ) ;
INSERT INTO CompactDiscs VALUES
  ( 110, 'Out of Africa', 832, 29 ) ;
```

```
INSERT INTO CompactDiscs VALUES
  ( 111, 'Leonard Cohen The Best Of', 834, 12 ) ;
INSERT INTO CompactDiscs VALUES
  ( 112, 'Fundamental', 835, 34 ) ;
INSERT INTO CompactDiscs VALUES
  ( 113, 'Bob Seger and the Silver Bullet Band Greatest Hits', 835, 16 ) ;
INSERT INTO CompactDiscs VALUES
  ( 114, 'Blues on the Bayou', 832, 27 ) ;
INSERT INTO CompactDiscs VALUES
  ( 115, 'Orlando', 836, 5 ) ;
--End inserts for the CompactDiscs table

--Insert data into the MusicTypes table
INSERT INTO MusicTypes VALUES ( 11, 'Blues' ) ;
INSERT INTO MusicTypes VALUES ( 12, 'Jazz' ) ;
INSERT INTO MusicTypes VALUES ( 13, 'Pop' ) ;
INSERT INTO MusicTypes VALUES ( 14, 'Rock' ) ;
INSERT INTO MusicTypes VALUES ( 15, 'Classical' ) ;
INSERT INTO MusicTypes VALUES ( 16, 'New Age' ) ;
INSERT INTO MusicTypes VALUES ( 17, 'Country' ) ;
INSERT INTO MusicTypes VALUES ( 18, 'Folk' ) ;
INSERT INTO MusicTypes VALUES ( 19, 'International' ) ;
INSERT INTO MusicTypes VALUES ( 20, 'Soundtracks' ) ;
INSERT INTO MusicTypes VALUES ( 21, 'Christmas' ) ;
--End inserts for the MusicTypes table

--Insert data into the CompactDiscTypes table
INSERT INTO CompactDiscTypes VALUES ( 101, 18 ) ;
INSERT INTO CompactDiscTypes VALUES ( 101, 13 ) ;
INSERT INTO CompactDiscTypes VALUES ( 102, 11 ) ;
INSERT INTO CompactDiscTypes VALUES ( 102, 18 ) ;
INSERT INTO CompactDiscTypes VALUES ( 102, 13 ) ;
INSERT INTO CompactDiscTypes VALUES ( 103, 18 ) ;
INSERT INTO CompactDiscTypes VALUES ( 103, 13 ) ;
INSERT INTO CompactDiscTypes VALUES ( 104, 16 ) ;
INSERT INTO CompactDiscTypes VALUES ( 105, 16 ) ;
INSERT INTO CompactDiscTypes VALUES ( 106, 21 ) ;
INSERT INTO CompactDiscTypes VALUES ( 107, 13 ) ;
INSERT INTO CompactDiscTypes VALUES ( 107, 17 ) ;
INSERT INTO CompactDiscTypes VALUES ( 108, 13 ) ;
INSERT INTO CompactDiscTypes VALUES ( 108, 15 ) ;
INSERT INTO CompactDiscTypes VALUES ( 109, 15 ) ;
INSERT INTO CompactDiscTypes VALUES ( 110, 20 ) ;
INSERT INTO CompactDiscTypes VALUES ( 111, 13 ) ;
INSERT INTO CompactDiscTypes VALUES ( 111, 18 ) ;
```

```
INSERT INTO CompactDiscTypes VALUES ( 112, 11 ) ;
INSERT INTO CompactDiscTypes VALUES ( 112, 13 ) ;
INSERT INTO CompactDiscTypes VALUES ( 113, 13 ) ;
INSERT INTO CompactDiscTypes VALUES ( 113, 14 ) ;
INSERT INTO CompactDiscTypes VALUES ( 114, 11 ) ;
INSERT INTO CompactDiscTypes VALUES ( 115, 20 ) ;
--End inserts for the CompactDiscTypes table

--Insert data into the Artists table
INSERT INTO Artists VALUES
  ( 2001, 'Jennifer Warnes', 'Seattle, Washington, USA' ) ;
INSERT INTO Artists VALUES
  ( 2002, 'Joni Mitchell', 'Fort MacLeod, Alberta, Canada' ) ;
INSERT INTO Artists VALUES
  ( 2003, 'William Ackerman', 'Germany' ) ;
INSERT INTO Artists VALUES
  ( 2004, 'Kitaro', 'Toyohashi, Japan' ) ;
INSERT INTO Artists VALUES
  ( 2005, 'Bing Crosby', 'Tacoma, Washington, USA' ) ;
INSERT INTO Artists VALUES
  ( 2006, 'Patsy Cline', 'Winchester, Virginia, USA' ) ;
INSERT INTO Artists VALUES
  ( 2007, 'Jose Carreras', 'Barcelona, Spain' ) ;
INSERT INTO Artists VALUES
  ( 2008, 'Luciano Pavarotti', 'Modena, Italy' ) ;
INSERT INTO Artists VALUES
  ( 2009, 'Placido Domingo', 'Madrid, Spain' ) ;
INSERT INTO Artists VALUES
  ( 2010, 'Pascal Roge', 'Unknown' ) ;
INSERT INTO Artists VALUES
  ( 2011, 'John Barry', 'Unknown' ) ;
INSERT INTO Artists VALUES
  ( 2012, 'Leonard Cohen', 'Montreal, Quebec, Canada' ) ;
INSERT INTO Artists VALUES
  ( 2013, 'Bonnie Raitt', 'Burbank, California, USA' ) ;
INSERT INTO Artists VALUES
  ( 2014, 'Bob Seger', 'Dearborn, Michigan, USA' ) ;
INSERT INTO Artists VALUES
  ( 2015, 'Silver Bullet Band', 'Does not apply' ) ;
INSERT INTO Artists VALUES
  ( 2016, 'B.B. King', 'Indianola, Mississippi, USA' ) ;
INSERT INTO Artists VALUES
  ( 2017, 'David Motion', 'Unknown' ) ;
INSERT INTO Artists VALUES
  ( 2018, 'Sally Potter', 'Unknown' ) ;
--End inserts for the Artists table
```

```
--Insert data into the ArtistCDs table
INSERT INTO ArtistCDs VALUES ( 2001, 101 ) ;
INSERT INTO ArtistCDs VALUES ( 2002, 102 ) ;
INSERT INTO ArtistCDs VALUES ( 2002, 103 ) ;
INSERT INTO ArtistCDs VALUES ( 2003, 104 ) ;
INSERT INTO ArtistCDs VALUES ( 2004, 105 ) ;
INSERT INTO ArtistCDs VALUES ( 2005, 106 ) ;
INSERT INTO ArtistCDs VALUES ( 2006, 107 ) ;
INSERT INTO ArtistCDs VALUES ( 2007, 108 ) ;
INSERT INTO ArtistCDs VALUES ( 2008, 108 ) ;
INSERT INTO ArtistCDs VALUES ( 2009, 108 ) ;
INSERT INTO ArtistCDs VALUES ( 2010, 109 ) ;
INSERT INTO ArtistCDs VALUES ( 2011, 110 ) ;
INSERT INTO ArtistCDs VALUES ( 2012, 111 ) ;
INSERT INTO ArtistCDs VALUES ( 2013, 112 ) ;
INSERT INTO ArtistCDs VALUES ( 2014, 113 ) ;
INSERT INTO ArtistCDs VALUES ( 2015, 113 ) ;
INSERT INTO ArtistCDs VALUES ( 2016, 114 ) ;
INSERT INTO ArtistCDs VALUES ( 2017, 115 ) ;
INSERT INTO ArtistCDs VALUES ( 2018, 115 ) ;
--End inserts for the ArtistCDs table
```

Index

E

U

V

INTERNATIONAL CONTACT INFORMATION

AUSTRALIA
McGraw-Hill Book Company Australia Pty. Ltd.
TEL +61-2-9900-1800
FAX +61-2-9878-8881
http://www.mcgraw-hill.com.au
books-it_sydney@mcgraw-hill.com

CANADA
McGraw-Hill Ryerson Ltd.
TEL +905-430-5000
FAX +905-430-5020
http://www.mcgraw-hill.ca

GREECE, MIDDLE EAST, & AFRICA
(Excluding South Africa)
McGraw-Hill Hellas
TEL +30-210-6560-990
TEL +30-210-6560-993
TEL +30-210-6560-994
FAX +30-210-6545-525

MEXICO (Also serving Latin America)
McGraw-Hill Interamericana Editores S.A. de C.V.
TEL +525-117-1583
FAX +525-117-1589
http://www.mcgraw-hill.com.mx
fernando_castellanos@mcgraw-hill.com

SINGAPORE (Serving Asia)
McGraw-Hill Book Company
TEL +65-6863-1580
FAX +65-6862-3354
http://www.mcgraw-hill.com.sg
mghasia@mcgraw-hill.com

SOUTH AFRICA
McGraw-Hill South Africa
TEL +27-11-622-7512
FAX +27-11-622-9045
robyn_swanepoel@mcgraw-hill.com

SPAIN
McGraw-Hill/Interamericana de España, S.A.U.
TEL +34-91-180-3000
FAX +34-91-372-8513
http://www.mcgraw-hill.es
professional@mcgraw-hill.es

UNITED KINGDOM, NORTHERN,
EASTERN, & CENTRAL EUROPE
McGraw-Hill Education Europe
TEL +44-1-628-502500
FAX +44-1-628-770224
http://www.mcgraw-hill.co.uk
computing_europe@mcgraw-hill.com

ALL OTHER INQUIRIES Contact:
McGraw-Hill/Osborne
TEL +1-510-596-6600
FAX +1-510-596-7600
http://www.osborne.com
omg_international@mcgraw-hill.com